AQA
AS Geography

HIGHGATE SCHOOL

Department _____

Ref_____

Date	Name	House	Condition

Philip Allan Updates, an imprint of Hodder Education, part of Hachette Livre UK, Market Place, Deddington, Oxfordshire OX15 0SE

Orders
Bookpoint Ltd, 130 Milton Park, Abingdon, Oxfordshire OX14 4SB
tel: 01235 827720
fax: 01235 400454
e-mail: uk.orders@bookpoint.co.uk

Lines are open 9.00 a.m.–5.00 p.m., Monday to Saturday, with a 24-hour message answering service. You can also order through the Philip Allan Updates website: www.philipallan.co.uk

© Philip Allan Updates 2008

ISBN 978-0-340-94611-4

Impression number   5 4 3 2
Year   2012 2011 2010 2009 2008

The front cover photographs are reproduced by permission of Corel, Jean-Léo Dugast/Still Pictures, John Walmsley Education Photos.

All Office for National Statistics material is Crown copyright, reproduced under the terms of PSI Licence Number C2007001 85

Printed in Italy.

Hachette Livre UK's policy is to use papers that are natural, renewable and recyclable products and made from wood grown in sustainable forests. The logging and manufacturing processes are expected to conform to the environmental regulations of the country of origin.

Contents

Unit 1 Physical and human geography

Core physical topic

Optional physical topics

Core human topic

Optional human topics

Introduction

This textbook provides a resource specifically for the AQA specification in AS geography. It covers the subject content of the specification, unit by unit and option by option, as it is laid out in the specification document, and forms a backbone for studies of AQA geography. However, it should be supplemented by reference to topical sources of information including newspapers, television, periodicals aimed at post-16 geography students and the internet.

The following are key features of the content:

➤ concepts are clearly and concisely explained, and related issues are explored and analysed
➤ relevant, up-to-date and detailed case studies are provided
➤ a variety of stimulus material is provided, including full-colour maps, graphs, diagrams and photographs
➤ sample examination questions are included at the end of each chapter
➤ the skills required for the units that assess practical abilities are covered in depth

The sample questions included can be used for formal or informal assessment. Further advice and guidance can be found in the *AQA AS Geography Student Unit Guide*, also published by Philip Allan Updates.

An overview of AQA geography

This specification enables students to follow a thematic people–environment approach to geography throughout the course. It has a developmental structure designed to facilitate progression.

All students study a range of themes, places and environments at different scales and in different contexts, including **the UK and countries that are in various states of development**. It is important that students exemplify the concepts and themes by reference to relevant contemporary examples and case studies.

The trend towards **global interdependence** is highlighted and it is important that students appreciate that this has economic, social and environmental dimensions, as well as political.

At appropriate points during the course, students have to consider different roles, **values and attitudes** (including their own) regarding a range of issues.

Assessment objectives

Like other geography specifications, AQA has three assessment objectives. Candidates should:

➤ demonstrate knowledge and understanding of the content, concepts and processes

➤ analyse, interpret and evaluate geographical information, issues and viewpoints and apply understanding to unfamiliar contexts

➤ select and use a variety of methods, skills and techniques (including new technologies) to investigate questions and issues, reach conclusions and communicate findings

Quality of written communication (QWC)

Candidates must:

➤ ensure that text is legible and that spelling, punctuation and grammar are accurate so that meaning is clear

➤ select and use a form and style of writing appropriate to purpose and to complex subject matter

➤ organise information clearly and coherently, using specialist vocabulary when appropriate

AQA assesses QWC in all units where extended writing is required. Each mark scheme includes an overall assessment of the quality of written communication by embedding the three strands above within the levels marking criteria.

Scheme of assessment

The scheme of assessment is modular. The AS examination consists of two units that make up 70% and 30% respectively of the total award.

➤ **Unit 1** is focused on **physical and human geography**. The exam lasts 2 hours, and consists of structured short and extended questions. These are based on each of the physical and human core sections, together with a choice of one from three physical options (cold environments, coastal environments, hot desert environments) and one from three human options (food supply issues, energy issues, health issues).

➤ **Unit 2** is based on **geographical skills**. The exam lasts 1 hour and consists of structured skills and generic fieldwork questions.

Command words used in the examinations

One of the major challenges in any examination is interpreting the demands of the questions. Thorough revision is essential, but an awareness of what is expected in the examination itself is also required. Too often candidates attempt to answer the question they think is there rather than the one that is actually set. Answering an examination question is challenging enough, without the self-inflicted handicap of misreading the question.

Correct interpretation of the **command words** of a question is therefore important. In AQA geography examination papers, a variety of command words are used. Some demand more of the candidate than others; some require a simple task to be performed; others require greater thought and a longer response.

The notes below offer advice on the main command words that are used in AS examinations.

Identify…, What…? Name…, State…, Give…

These words ask for brief answers to a simple task, such as:
- identifying a landform from a photograph
- giving a named example of a feature

Do not answer using a single word. It is always better to write a short sentence.

Define…, Explain the meaning of…, What is meant by…? Outline…

These words require a relatively short answer, usually two or three sentences, giving the precise meaning of a term. Use of an example is often helpful. The size of the mark allocation indicates the length of answer required.

Describe…

This is one of the most widely used command words. A factual description is required, with no attempt to explain. Usually the question will give some clue about exactly what is to be described. Some examples are given below.

Describe the characteristics of…

In the case of a landform, for example, the following sub-questions can be useful in writing the answer:
- What does it look like?
- What is it made of?
- How big is it?
- Where is it in relation to other features?

Describe the changes in…

This command often relates to a graph or a table. Good use of accurate adverbs is required here — words such as rapidly, steeply, gently, slightly, greatly.

Describe the differences between…

Here only differences between two sets of data will be credited. It is better if these are presented as a series of separate sentences, each identifying one difference. Writing a paragraph on one data set, followed by a paragraph on the other, forces the examiner to complete the task on your behalf.

Describe the relationship between…

Here only the links between two sets of data will be credited. It is important, therefore, that you establish the relationship and state the link clearly. In most cases the relationship will either be positive (direct) or negative (inverse).

Describe the distribution of…

This is usually used in conjunction with a map or set of maps. A description of the location of high concentrations of a variable is required, together with a similar description of those areas with a lower concentration. Better answers will also tend to identify anomalous areas or areas which go against an overall trend in the distribution, for example a spot of high concentration in an area of predominantly low concentration.

Compare...

This requires a point by point account of the similarities and differences between two sets of information or two areas. Two separate accounts do not make up a comparison, and candidates will be penalised if they present two such accounts and expect the examiner to do the comparison on their behalf. A good technique is to use comparative adjectives, for example larger than, smaller than, steeper than, less gentle than. Note that 'compare' refers to similarities and differences, whereas the command word 'contrast' just asks for differences.

Explain..., Suggest reasons for..., How might...? Why...?

These commands ask for a statement about why something occurs. The command word tests your ability to know or understand why or how something happens. Such questions tend to carry a large number of marks, and expect candidates to write a relatively long piece of extended prose. It is important that this presents a logical account which is both relevant and well organised.

Using only an annotated diagram..., With the aid of a diagram...

Here the candidate must draw a diagram, and in the first case provide only a diagram. Annotations are labels which provide additional description or explanation of the main features of the diagram. For example, in the case of a hydrograph, the identification of 'a rising limb' would constitute a label, whereas 'a steep rising limb caused by an impermeable ground surface' would be an annotation.

Analyse...

This requires a candidate to break down the content of a topic into its constituent parts, and to give an in-depth account. As stated above, such questions tend to carry a large number of marks, and candidates will be expected to write a relatively long piece of prose. It is important that candidates present a logical account that is both relevant and well-organised.

Discuss...

This is one of the most common higher-level command words, and is used most often in questions which carry a large number of marks and require a lengthy piece of prose. Candidates are expected to build up an argument about an issue, presenting more than one side of the argument. They should present arguments for and against, making good use of evidence and appropriate examples, and express an opinion about the merits of each side. In other words, they should construct a verbal debate.

In any discussion there are likely to be both positive and negative aspects — some people are likely to benefit (the winners), and others are likely not to benefit (the losers). Candidates are invited to weigh up the evidence from both points of view, and may be asked to indicate where their sympathies lie.

Sometimes, additional help is provided in the wording of the question, as shown below.

Discuss the extent to which…

Here a judgement about the validity of the evidence or the outcome of an issue is clearly requested.

Discuss the varying/various attitudes to…

Here the question states that a variety of views exists, and candidates are required to debate them. There is often a range of people involved in an issue, including those responsible for the decision to go ahead with an idea or policy (the decision makers), and those who will be affected, directly or indirectly, by the decision. Each of these individuals or groups will have a different set of priorities, and a different viewpoint on the outcome.

Evaluate…, Assess…

These command words require more than the discussion described above. In both cases an indication of the candidate's viewpoint, having considered all the evidence, is required. 'Assess' asks for a statement of the overall quality or value of the feature or issue being considered, and 'evaluate' asks the candidate to give an overall statement of value. The candidate's own judgement is requested, together with a justification for that judgement.

The use of 'critically' often occurs in such questions, for example 'Critically evaluate…'. In this case the candidate is being asked to look at an issue or problem from the point of view of a critic. There may be weaknesses in the argument and the evidence should not be taken at face value. The candidate should question not only the evidence itself but also where it came from, and how it was collected. The answer should comment on the strengths of the evidence as well as its weaknesses.

Justify…

This is one of the most demanding command words. At its most simplistic, a response to this command must include a strong piece of writing in favour of the chosen option(s) in a decision-making exercise, and an explanation of why the other options were rejected.

However, decision making is not straightforward. All the options in a decision-making scenario have positive and negative aspects. The options that are rejected will have some good elements, and equally, the chosen option will not be perfect in all respects. The key to good decision making is to balance the pros and cons of each option and to opt for the most appropriate based on the evidence available.

A good answer to the command 'justify' should therefore provide the following:
➤ for each of the options that are rejected: an outline of their positive and negative points, but with an overall statement of why the negatives outweigh the positives
➤ for the chosen option: an outline of the negative and the positive points, but with an overall statement of why the positives outweigh the negatives

Developing extended prose and essay-writing skills

For many students essay writing is one of the most difficult parts of the exam, but it is also an opportunity to demonstrate your strengths. Before starting to write a piece of extended prose or an essay you must have a plan of what you are going to write, either in your head or on paper. All such pieces of writing must have a beginning (introduction), a middle (argument) and an end (conclusion).

The introduction
This does not have to be too long — a few sentences should suffice. It may define the terms in the question, set the scene for the argument to follow, or provide a brief statement of the idea, concept or viewpoint you are going to develop in the main body of your answer.

The argument
This is the main body of the answer. It should consist of a series of paragraphs, each developing one point only and following on logically from the previous one. Try to avoid paragraphs that list information without any depth, but do not write down all you know about a particular topic without any link to the question set. Make good use of examples, naming real places (which could be local to you). Make your examples count by giving accurate detail specific to those locations.

The conclusion
In an extended prose answer the conclusion should not be too long. Make sure it reiterates the main points stated in the introduction, but now supported by the evidence and facts given in the argument.

Should you produce plans in the examination?
If you produce an essay plan at all, it must be brief, taking only 2 or 3 minutes to write on a piece of scrap paper. The plan must reflect the above formula — make sure you stick to it. Be logical, and only give an outline — retain the examples in your head, and include them at the most appropriate point in your answer.

Other important points
Always keep an eye on the time. Make sure you write clearly and concisely. Do not provide confused answers, endlessly long sentences, or pages of prose with no paragraphs. Above all: *read the question and answer the question set.*

How are questions marked?
Most examination questions for AQA are marked according to levels based on certain criteria. The following general criteria relate to knowledge, understanding and critical analysis, and to the quality of written communication:

Level 1
A Level 1 answer is likely to:
- display a basic understanding of the topic
- make one or two points without the support of appropriate exemplification or application of principle
- demonstrate a simplistic style of writing, perhaps lacking close relation to the terms of the question and unlikely to communicate complexity of subject matter
- lack organisation, relevance and specialist vocabulary
- demonstrate deficiencies in legibility, spelling, grammar and punctuation, which detract from the clarity of meaning

Level 2

A Level 2 answer is likely to:

- ➤ display a clear understanding of the topic
- ➤ make one or two points with the support of appropriate exemplification and/or application of principle
- ➤ give a number of characteristics, reasons and attitudes where the question requires it
- ➤ provide detailed case studies
- ➤ give responses to more than one command word, e.g. 'describe and explain'
- ➤ demonstrate a style of writing which matches the requirements of the question and acknowledges the potential complexity of subject matter
- ➤ demonstrate relevance and coherence with appropriate use of specialist vocabulary
- ➤ demonstrate legibility of text, and qualities of spelling, grammar and punctuation, which do not detract from the clarity of meaning

Level 3

A Level 3 (the highest level) answer is likely to:

- ➤ display a detailed understanding of the topic
- ➤ make several points with the support of appropriate exemplification and/or application of principle
- ➤ give a wide range of characteristics, reasons and attitudes
- ➤ provide highly detailed accounts of a range of case studies
- ➤ respond well to more than one command word
- ➤ demonstrate evidence of evaluation and synthesis
- ➤ demonstrate a sophisticated style of writing, incorporating measured and qualified explanation and comment as required by the question and reflecting awareness of the complexity of subject matter and incompleteness/ tentativeness of explanation
- ➤ demonstrate a clear sense of purpose so that the responses are seen to closely relate to the requirements of the question, with confident use of specialist vocabulary
- ➤ demonstrate legibility of text, and qualities of spelling, grammar and punctuation, which contribute to complete clarity of meaning

For more details on the assessment process, see the CD-ROM that accompanies this book.

Unit 1

Physical and human geography

Core physical topic

Rivers, floods and management

The drainage basin hydrological cycle

The drainage basin is the catchment area from which a river system obtains its water. An imaginary line called the **watershed** delimits one drainage basin from another. The watershed generally follows a ridge of high land; any rain falling on the other side of the ridge will eventually flow into another river in the adjacent drainage basin.

The drainage basin hydrological cycle is an open system with inputs and outputs — water and energy from the sun are introduced into the drainage basin from outside and water can be lost from the drainage basin in a number of ways (Figures 1.1 and 1.2).

The drainage basin hydrological cycle can be studied using a systems approach:
➤ **Inputs** into the drainage basin include:
  – energy from the sun for evaporation
  – precipitation (rain, snow)

Figure 1.1
The drainage basin
hydrological cycle

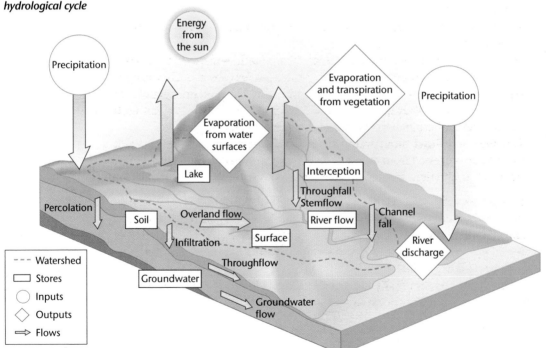

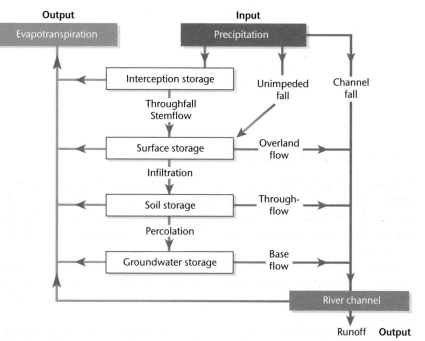

Figure 1.2
A flow diagram
of drainage basin
hydrology

➤ **Outputs** move moisture out of the drainage basin and include:
  – evaporation and transpiration from plants (collectively called evapo-transpiration)
  – runoff into the sea
  – water percolating deep into underground stores where it can be effectively lost from the system
➤ Many **stores of water** within the drainage basin (such as glaciers, rivers, lakes and puddles) occur on the surface. Other stores are less obvious. For example, vegetation stores water by interception and plants also contain a significant amount of water taken up from the soil through their roots. The soil itself holds water and groundwater is stored in permeable rocks.
➤ **Transfers** and **flows** move water through the system and enable inputs of water to be processed from one store to another. Transfers include throughfall, stemflow, infiltration, throughflow and groundwater flow.

Within the drainage basin, the balance between inputs (precipitation) and outputs (runoff, evapotranspiration, soil and groundwater storage) is known as the **water balance** or **budget**. Rivers are present on the surface only if the stores are capable of releasing water and if there is direct surface runoff. This is a dynamic relationship; river levels rise and fall over the short term following heavy rainfall and often show an annual pattern (called the river's **regime**) in terms of their discharge. The water balance can be shown using the formula:

precipitation (P) = streamflow (Q) + evapotranspiration (E) ± changes in storage (S)
$$P = Q + E \pm S$$

Key terms

Evaporation The process by which liquid water is transformed into water vapour, which is a gas. A large amount of energy is required for this to occur. The energy is usually provided by heat from the sun or by the movement of air (wind).

Evapotranspiration The total amount of moisture removed by evaporation and transpiration from a vegetated land surface. Transpiration is the process by which water is lost from a plant through stomata (very small pores) in its leaves.

Groundwater flow The slowest transfer of water within the drainage basin. It provides the main input of water into a river during drought or dry seasons. Groundwater flows at a slow but steady rate through bands of sedimentary rock. It can take thousands of years for moisture that seeps into permeable rocks deep under the surface to be returned to the drainage basin hydrological cycle as groundwater flow.

Infiltration The passage of water into the soil. Infiltration takes place relatively quickly at the beginning of a storm, but as the soil becomes saturated the infiltration rate falls rapidly. Infiltration rates are affected by the nature of the soil itself. Sandy soils let more water pass through than clay soils.

Interception The process by which raindrops are prevented from directly reaching the soil surface. Leaves, stems and branches on trees, and herbaceous plants and grasses growing close to the surface, intercept water. Evaporation removes some of this moisture from the system and it does not reach the river as runoff.

Percolation The downward movement of water within the rock under the soil surface. The rate of percolation depends on the nature of the rock. Some rocks, particularly those of an igneous or metamorphic nature, are impermeable so there is no percolation or groundwater flow.

Precipitation Water in any form that falls from the atmosphere to the surface of the Earth. It includes rain, snow, sleet and hail.

Runoff All the water that enters a river and eventually flows out of the drainage basin. It can be quantified by measuring the discharge of a river.

Stemflow The water that runs down the stems and branches of plants and trees during and after rain to reach the ground. It takes place after interception has occurred.

Throughfall The water that drips off leaves during a rainstorm. It occurs when more water falls onto the interception layer of the tree canopy than can remain on the leaves.

Throughflow The water that moves down-slope through the subsoil, pulled by gravity. It is particularly effective when underlying impermeable rock prevents percolation.

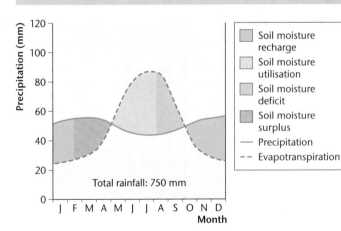

Total rainfall: 750 mm

Figure 1.3 Water budget graph for eastern England

When precipitation is greater than evapotranspiration, at first the pores of the soil are refilled with water. When the soil becomes saturated, excess water has difficulty infiltrating into the ground and may then flow over the surface.

The water balance of a particular location can be studied using a water budget graph (Figure 1.3). This shows the relationship between temperature, precipitation and evaporation rates over the year. During the months of the year when precipitation exceeds evapotranspiration, once the soil has been recharged there will be a water surplus available to supply rivers and streams.

Factors affecting river discharge

River discharge is defined as the volume of water passing a measuring point or gauging station in a river in a given time. It is measured in cubic metres per second (cumecs). The overall discharge from the drainage basin depends on the relationship between precipitation, evapotranspiration and storage factors and can be summarised as follows:

drainage basin discharge = precipitation − evapotranspiration ± changes in storage

Discharge can be illustrated using **hydrographs**. These can show annual patterns of flow (the river regime) in response to climate. Short-term variations in discharge are shown using a flood or storm hydrograph.

The storm hydrograph

The storm hydrograph (Figure 1.4) shows variations in a river's discharge over a short period of time, usually during a rainstorm. The starting and finishing level show the **base flow** of the river. As storm water enters the drainage basin the discharge rises, shown by the **rising limb**, to reach the **peak discharge**, which indicates the highest flow in the channel. The **receding limb** shows the fall in the discharge back to the base level. The time delay between maximum rainfall amount and peak discharge is the **lag time**.

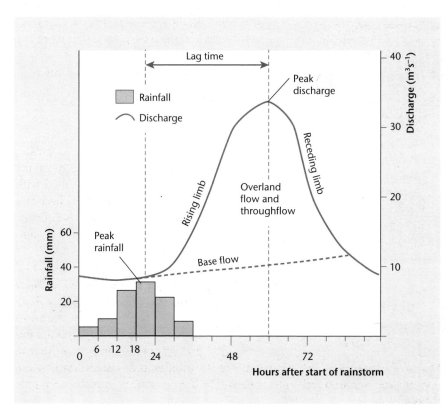

Figure 1.4
A storm hydrograph

The shape of the hydrograph is influenced by a number of factors:

➤ The **intensity and duration of the storm** — if both are high they produce a steep rising limb as the infiltration capacity of the soil is exceeded.

➤ The **antecedent rainfall** — heavy rain falling on a soil which is saturated from a previous period of wet weather will produce a steep rising limb.

➤ **Snow** — heavy snowfall may not initially show on a hydrograph since the water is being 'stored' in snow on the ground. Indeed, water levels in a river may fall during a prolonged period of snowfall and cold weather. When temperatures rise and melting occurs, massive amounts of water are released, greatly increasing discharge. This water may reach the river channel even quicker if the ground remains frozen and restricts infiltration.

➤ **Porous soil types** and/or **permeable rock types**, such as limestone — these produce less steep (or less flashy) hydrographs because water is regulated more slowly through the natural systems.

➤ **Impermeable rock types** such as granite and clay — these tend to have higher densities of surface streams (higher drainage densities). The higher the density the faster the water reaches the main river channel, causing rapid increases in discharge.

➤ **Size of drainage basin** — a small drainage basin tends to respond more rapidly to a storm than a larger one, so the lag time is shorter.

➤ **Shape of drainage basin** — rainfall reaches the river more quickly from a round basin than from an elongated basin.

➤ **Slope angle** — in steep-sided upland river basins the water reaches the channels much more quickly than in gently sloping lowland river basins, producing a steeper rising limb and shorter lag times.

➤ **Temperature** — high temperatures increase the rate of evapotranspiration, thereby reducing discharge. Cold temperatures may freeze the ground, restrict infiltration, increase overland flow and increase river discharge.

➤ **Vegetation** — this varies with the season. In summer there are more leaves on deciduous trees, so interception is higher and peak discharge lower. Plantations of conifers have a less variable effect.

➤ **Land use** — water runs more quickly over impermeable surfaces such as caravan parks or agricultural land which has been trampled by cattle. Lag time is reduced and peak discharge increased.

➤ **Urbanisation** — this is the main human impact on a storm hydrograph. The following processes combine to alter the shape of the hydrograph by reducing the lag time and increasing peak discharge (Figure 1.5):

Figure 1.5
The shape of the storm hydrograph before and after urbanisation

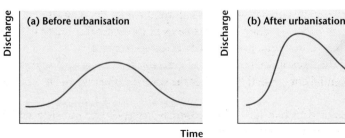

- removal of topsoil and compaction of the ground with earth-moving machinery during building work
- building of roads which increases the impermeable surface area
- building of drains and sewers that transport water rapidly to river channels, reducing the lag time
- straightening of river channels and lining with concrete (Photograph 1.1). This also leads to the faster delivery of water downstream of the urban area and increases the risk of flooding in downstream areas

Photograph 1.1 The River Thames in Oxford. River channels in urban areas are often straightened and reinforced

Less water reaches the channel by throughflow and base flow, and more gets there by overland flow. Local authorities and water companies may need to respond to these changes to prevent damaging flooding in their areas.

Channel processes

The work of a river involves three main processes: **erosion**, **transportation** and **deposition**. At any one time the dominant process operating within the river depends on the amount of energy available. This is governed by the velocity of the flow and the amount of water flowing within the channel (discharge).

Erosion

Rivers erode because they possess energy. Their total energy depends on:
➤ the weight of the water — the greater the mass of the water the more energy it will possess due to the influence of gravity on its movement
➤ the height of the river above its base level (usually sea level) — this gives it a source of potential energy, and the higher the source of the river the more such energy it has
➤ the steepness of the channel — this controls the speed of the river which determines how much kinetic energy it has

Much of this energy is lost through friction, either internally through turbulence within the flow of the river, or externally through contact with the bed and banks of the river channel. Energy loss through friction can be great in all parts of a river, but it is perhaps easier to understand in the context of an upland river channel. Here, the channel often has a rocky bed with many large boulders. The rough shape of the channel means that the **wetted perimeter** — the overall length of the bed and banks that the river is in contact with — is large. More energy is thus lost through friction, and the river's velocity, and therefore its energy level, is reduced. Hence, in normal conditions, the river is unable to perform much erosion. However, when the river contains large quantities of water following heavy rain or snowmelt, it does possess the energy to perform great amounts of erosion.

There are four main processes of river erosion:

➤ **Abrasion** (corrasion) is the scraping, scouring and rubbing action of materials carried along by a river (the **load**). Rivers carry rock fragments in the flow of the water or drag them along the bed, and in doing so wear away the banks and bed of the river channel. Abrasion is most effective in short turbulent periods when the river is at bankfull or in flood. During times when river levels are low, the load consists of small particles, such as sand grains, and these tend to smooth the surface of the river channel.

➤ **Hydraulic action** is caused by the sheer power of moving water. It is the movement of loose unconsolidated material due to the frictional drag of the moving water on sediment lying on the channel bed. As velocity increases, turbulent flow lifts a larger number of grains, particularly sand-sized particles, from the floor of the channel. Hydraulic action is particularly effective at removing loose material in the banks of meanders, which can lead to under-cutting and collapse. It can be locally strong within rapids or below waterfalls where it may cause the rocks to fragment along joints and bedding planes or other lines of weakness.

➤ **Corrosion** is most active on rocks that contain carbonates, such as limestone and chalk. The minerals in the rock are dissolved by weak acids in the river water and carried away in solution.

➤ **Attrition** is the reduction in the size of fragments and particles within a river due to the processes described above. The fragments strike one another as well as the river bed. They therefore become smoother, smaller and more rounded as they move along the river channel. Consequently larger, more angular fragments tend to be found upstream while smaller, more rounded fragments are found downstream.

In the upper reaches of a river, where the land lies high above sea level, river erosion is predominantly vertical. **Vertical erosion** dominates because the river is attempting to cut down to its base level, which is usually sea level. In times of spate, when the river level and velocity are high, the river cuts down into its valley

Key terms

Deposition The laying down of solid material, in the form of sediment, on the bed of a river or on the sea floor.

Erosion The break up of rocks by the action of rock particles being moved over the Earth's surface by water, wind and ice.

Transportation The movement of particles from the place they were eroded to the place where they are deposited.

mainly by abrasion and hydraulic action. Such rivers often produce steep-sided valleys.

Lateral erosion occurs more frequently in the middle and lower stretches of the river, where the valley floor lies closer to sea level. Here the river possesses a great deal of energy, particularly when close to bankfull. However, this energy is used laterally to widen the valley as the river meanders. The strongest current is found on the outside of the bend and hydraulic action causes the bank to be undermined and to collapse.

Transport

River energy not used for erosion or not lost through friction can be used to transport the river's load. A river obtains its load from two main sources:
➤ material that has been washed, or has fallen, into the river from the valley sides
➤ material that has been eroded by the river itself from the bed or banks

A river transports its load in four main ways:
➤ **Traction** — large stones and boulders are rolled along the river bed by water moving downstream. This process operates only at times of high discharge (and consequently high energy levels). During the Boscastle flood of August 2004, when the River Valency burst its banks, large boulders transported from further upstream contributed significantly to the damage to the town.
➤ **Saltation** — small stones bounce or leap-frog along the channel bed. This process is associated with relatively high energy conditions. Small particles may be thrust up from the bed of the river only to fall back to the bottom again further downstream. As these particles land they in turn dislodge other particles upwards, causing more such bouncing movements to take place.
➤ **Suspension** — very small particles of sand and silt are carried along by the flow of the river. Such material is not only carried but is also picked up, mainly through the turbulence that exists within the water. Suspension normally contributes the largest proportion of sediment to the load of the river. The suspended load is the main cause of the brown appearance of many rivers and streams.
➤ **Solution** — dissolved minerals are transported within the mass of the moving water.

Two other terms are often used in the context of river transport — capacity and competence. Both of these are influenced by the velocity, and therefore the discharge, of the river.

The **capacity** of a river is a measure of the amount of material it can carry, that is, the total volume of the load. Research has found that a river's capacity increases according to the third power of its velocity. For example, if a river's velocity doubles, then its capacity increases by eight times (2^3).

The **competence** of a river is the diameter of the largest particle that it can carry for a given velocity. Again, research has shown that a river's competence increases according to the sixth power of its velocity. For example, if a river's velocity doubles, then its competence increases by 64 times (2^6). This is because fast-flowing rivers have greater turbulence and are therefore better able to lift particles from the river bed.

Deposition

A river **deposits** when, owing to a decrease in its level of energy, it is no longer competent to transport its load. Deposition usually occurs when:

➤ there is a reduction in the gradient of the river, for example when it enters a lake
➤ the discharge is reduced, such as during and after a dry spell of weather
➤ there is shallow water, for example on the inside of a meander
➤ there is an increase in the calibre (size) of the load. This may be due to a tributary bringing in larger particles, increased erosion along the river's course, or a landslide into the river
➤ the river floods and overtops its banks, resulting in a reduced velocity on the floodplain outside the main channel

In general, the largest fragments are the first to be deposited, followed by successively smaller particles, although the finest particles may never be deposited (Photograph 1.2 and Figure 1.6). This pattern of deposition is reflected in the sediments found along the course of a river. The channels of upland rivers are often filled with large boulders. Gravels, sands and silts can be carried further and are often deposited further downstream. Sands and silts are deposited on the flat floodplains either side of the river in its lower course.

Photograph 1.2
The River Eea in
Cumbria. (a) Upper
course, and (b)
middle course

Amanda Barker

How are erosion, transport and deposition related to changes in discharge?

The Hjulström graph (Figure 1.6) shows the relationship between the velocity of a river and the size of particles that can be eroded, transported or deposited. Velocity increases as discharge rises and generally this enables a river to pick up larger particles from the bed or banks of the channel. Similarly, as velocity and

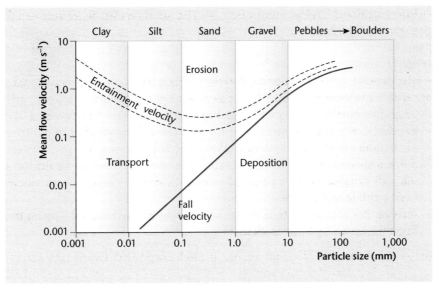

Figure 1.6
Hjulström's curve

discharge reduce, then particles are generally deposited according to their size, largest first. However, Hjulström's research showed three interesting relationships:

➤ Sand particles are moved by lower pick up or critical erosion velocities than *smaller* silts and clays or *larger* gravels. The small clay and silt particles are difficult to pick up (entrain) because they tend to stick together. They lie on the river bed and offer less resistance to water flow than larger particles. Much more powerful flows of water are required to lift them into the water.

➤ Once entrained (picked up), particles can be carried at lower velocities than those required to pick them up. However, for larger particles there is only a small difference between the critical erosion velocity and the settling velocity. Such particles will be deposited soon after they have been entrained.

➤ The smallest particles — clays and silts — are only deposited at very low velocities. Indeed, some clay particles may never be deposited on the river bed and can be carried almost indefinitely. This explains why such deposits occur in river estuaries. Here the fresh water of the river meets the salt water of the sea, causing chemical settling of the clays and silts to occur and creating extensive areas of mudflats. This process is called **flocculation**. This coagulation (clustering) of the clay and silt particles causes them to sink more rapidly.

River load

The type, source and character of the load of the river depend upon the nature of the drainage basin, its location and, increasingly, on human activity. The Hjulström graph (Figure 1.6) categorises the type of river load by size. These data are also given in Table 1.1. **Dissolved load** consists of soluble materials carried as chemical ions, so there are no measurable particles.

Table 1.1 River load categorised by size

Type of load	Particle diameter (mm)
Boulders and cobbles	> 100.0
Pebbles	10.0–99.99
Gravel	1.0–9.99
Sand	0.1–0.99
Silt	0.01–0.099
Clay	< 0.01

Large particles only form part of the load of a river during and immediately after extreme events that lead to significant increases in stream discharge. Such temporal changes occur following prolonged heavy rainfall (particularly if the ground is also saturated), after flash floods or after significant snowmelt. In these circumstances, the competence of the river increases and allows larger particles to be carried. Boulders and cobbles form part of the load in the upper course because rivers seldom have the capacity to transport these particles great distances.

In general, the further downstream the river travels, the smaller the particles making up the load. This is partly the result of attrition — when particles are rounded and smoothed by this process they are also broken down into smaller pieces.

Total sediment yields tend to increase with distance downstream, due mainly to increases in both average discharge and velocity in the lower reaches of the river. Here, the river possesses a greater capacity, so it is able to transport more material.

Spatial variations in load can be seen when comparing rivers located in different parts of the world. The Mississippi River has a vast drainage basin, roughly one-third the size of the entire USA. On average every year, it transports some 136 million tonnes of load in solution, 340 million tonnes in suspension and 40 million tonnes by saltation. Other major sediment-bearing rivers are located in Asia and South America, for example the Yangtze in China and the Amazon in Brazil. In other parts of the world, for example in Australia, sediment yields are much smaller.

Spatial variations in load are influenced by the following factors:

➤ **Size of the drainage basin** — large drainage basins with many tributaries have a greater potential for transporting sediment, particularly in their lower courses, than do small drainage basins. In the UK, a relatively small country, the largest drainage basin — that of the River Severn — covers a much smaller area than the largest continental drainage basins.

➤ **Rock type** — in drainage basins where the underlying geology consists of relatively soft (and easily eroded) sandstones and clays, the sediment transported consists mainly of sand or clay particles. Where the rock is limestone, more material will be transported as dissolved load because this rock type is soluble. Moving water does not easily erode resistant igneous rocks, such as granite and basalt. Therefore, the total sediment yield in river basins of igneous rock may be low whereas in drainage basins where the underlying rock is softer, sediment yield may be high.

➤ **Relief** — in drainage basins with low relief, where there is a small difference in altitude between the source and base level, the energy available for erosion and transport is limited. Such rivers have low loads compared with rivers that have upper reaches in areas of high relief.

➤ **Precipitation** — low loads are generally found in drainage basins with low rates of precipitation. In such areas, less water is available as runoff compared with drainage basins with high precipitation. Seasonal differences in sediment yield occur in some drainage basins, particularly those in areas where the climate has wet and dry seasons and where snowmelt in the spring adds to normal runoff from precipitation.

➤ **Human activity** — this can both increase and decrease sediment yield. In areas of the world where deforestation is occurring rapidly, there have been marked increases in the load carried by rivers. This is mainly caused by increased soil erosion, which occurs because the vegetation that protected the soil from the actions of moving water on its surface has been removed. There is also reduced water uptake by trees and other plants in deforested areas. The result is that soil is washed into the river and adds to the suspended load.

Many farmers use nitrates and phosphates as chemical fertilisers. These substances can enter rivers by throughflow and overland flow and are then transported in solution.

Major dams have been constructed on some rivers, for example the Aswan dam on the River Nile and the Hoover dam on the Colorado River. Such dams trap sediment, significantly lowering downstream sediment yields.

The effects of channel load on landforms

A fast-flowing river, at bankfull, has the competence to carry a large load. The particles erode the river bed and banks by abrasion, creating distinctive features such as potholes, waterfalls and gorges.

If the volume of water in the river falls quickly, the load is deposited because of a fall in competence. When this occurs, depositional features such as levées, floodplains and deltas are created.

In some sections of the river, both erosion and deposition occur. This is particularly noticeable on a meander bend, where suspended load carried by the river erodes the outside edge of the bend by abrasion and load is deposited on the inside of the bend to form a point bar (Photograph 1.3).

Photograph 1.3 Both deposition and erosion occur on meanders

Ingram

Valley profiles

Long profile

The long profile of a river illustrates the changes in the altitude of the course of the river from its source, along the entire length of its channel, to the river mouth. In general, the long profile is smoothly concave, with the gradient being steeper in the upper course and becoming progressively gentler towards the mouth. Irregularities in the gradient frequently occur and may be represented by rapids, waterfalls or lakes. There may also be marked breaks or changes in slope, known as

knick points, which are generally the product of rejuvenation. Rejuvenation occurs either when the sea level (in relation to the land) falls or when the land surface rises. Either situation allows the river to revive its erosion activity in a vertical direction. The river adjusts to the new base level, at first in its lowest reaches, and then progressively inland. The processes of erosion, transportation and deposition along the long profile of a typical river are summarised in Figure 1.7.

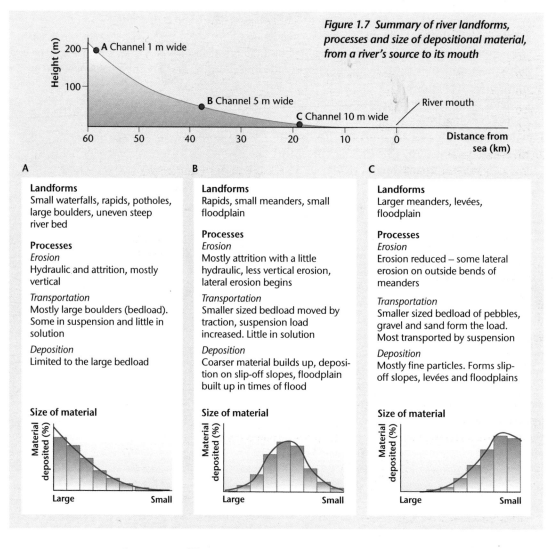

Figure 1.7 Summary of river landforms, processes and size of depositional material, from a river's source to its mouth

A

Landforms
Small waterfalls, rapids, potholes, large boulders, uneven steep river bed

Processes
Erosion
Hydraulic and attrition, mostly vertical

Transportation
Mostly large boulders (bedload). Some in suspension and little in solution

Deposition
Limited to the large bedload

Size of material

B

Landforms
Rapids, small meanders, small floodplain

Processes
Erosion
Mostly attrition with a little hydraulic, less vertical erosion, lateral erosion begins

Transportation
Smaller sized bedload moved by traction, suspension load increased. Little in solution

Deposition
Coarser material builds up, deposition on slip-off slopes, floodplain built up in times of flood

Size of material

C

Landforms
Larger meanders, levées, floodplain

Processes
Erosion
Erosion reduced – some lateral erosion on outside bends of meanders

Transportation
Smaller sized bedload of pebbles, gravel and sand form the load. Most transported by suspension

Deposition
Mostly fine particles. Forms slip-off slopes, levées and floodplains

Size of material

Cross profile

The valley cross profile is the view of the valley from one side to another. For example, the valley cross profile of a river in an upland area typically has a V-shape, with steep sides and a narrow bottom.

Variations in the cross profile can be described and explained as follows (and as illustrated in Figure 1.8).

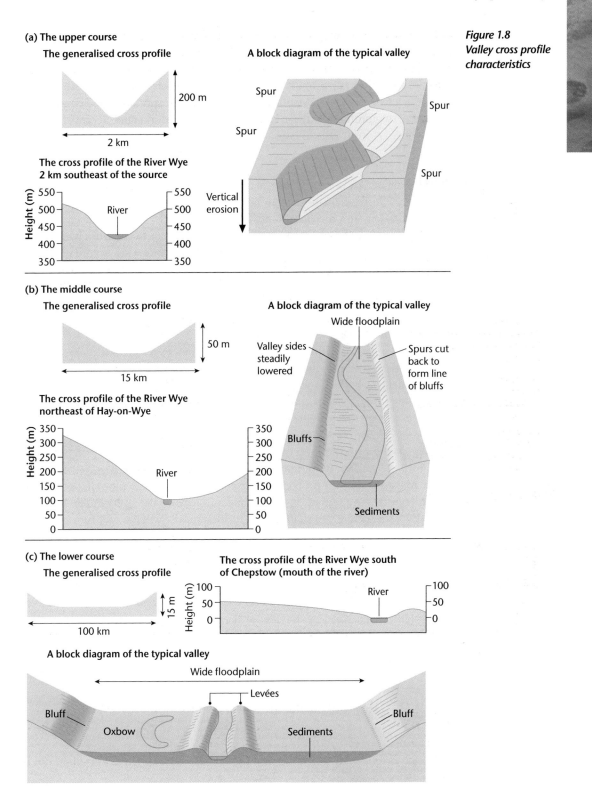

Figure 1.8
Valley cross profile characteristics

(a) The upper course

The generalised cross profile

A block diagram of the typical valley

200 m

2 km

The cross profile of the River Wye 2 km southeast of the source

Height (m)

550
500 — River
450
400
350

550
500
450
400
350

Vertical erosion

Spur

Spur

Spur

Spur

(b) The middle course

The generalised cross profile

A block diagram of the typical valley

50 m

15 km

The cross profile of the River Wye northeast of Hay-on-Wye

Height (m)

350
300
250
200
150 — River
100
50
0

350
300
250
200
150
100
50
0

Wide floodplain

Valley sides steadily lowered

Spurs cut back to form line of bluffs

Bluffs

Sediments

(c) The lower course

The generalised cross profile

The cross profile of the River Wye south of Chepstow (mouth of the river)

15 m

100 km

Height (m)

100
50
0

River

100
50
0

A block diagram of the typical valley

Wide floodplain

Levées

Bluff

Oxbow

Sediments

Bluff

- in the upper course — a narrow steep-sided valley where the river occupies all of the valley floor. This is the result of dominant vertical erosion by the river
- in the middle course — a wider valley with distinct valley bluffs, and a flat floodplain. This is the result of lateral erosion, which widens the valley floor
- in the lower course — a very wide, flat floodplain in which the valley sides are difficult to locate. Here there is a lack of erosion, and reduced competence of the river, which results in large-scale deposition

Graded profile

Over a long period of time a river may display an even and progressive decrease in gradient down the valley, creating the typical smooth concave shape which has adjusted to the discharge and load of the river. The idea of grade was originally put forward by W. M. Davies, who argued that irregularities in the long profile which would reflect changes in underlying geology are eventually worn away by river erosion to give a smooth graded profile. This may also be referred to as the **profile of dynamic equilibrium**, where a balance has been achieved between the processes of erosion and deposition. More recently, it has been accepted that the channel may still be graded if it exhibits some irregularities in its long profile.

Some geographers define the graded river as that which has been attained when the river uses up all of its energy in the movement of water and sediment so that no free energy is left to undertake further erosion. In this situation the gradient at each point along the river is sufficient to discharge the water and load but there is little excess energy available for further erosion. Such a balance between energy and work cannot occur at a particular moment in time but is suggested as an average position over a long time. Theoretically, river systems should reach an equilibrium when the inputs and outputs are balanced, but changes in the system bring adjustments to the profile as the river attempts to counter the change. In this way it regulates the system. If the volume and load of the river change over the long term, then the river's channel and its long profile will also adjust to the new conditions.

Potential and kinetic energy

In relation to rivers, **potential** or (stored) energy is fixed by the altitude of the source of the stream in relation to base level. **Kinetic** energy, or energy due to movement, is generated by the flow of the river which converts potential energy into moving energy. The amount of kinetic energy is determined by the volume of flowing water (discharge), the slope or channel gradient down which it is flowing and its average velocity. An increase in velocity and/or discharge results in an increase in kinetic energy.

All channel processes are dependent on the amount of energy available. This is a delicate balance. If there is excess energy after transportation of load the river will erode, but if energy is insufficient to move the load deposition will occur. The river channel adjusts in shape and size to accommodate changes in the volume of water and sediment.

Changing channel characteristics

Channel cross profiles

The channel cross profile (or section) is a view of the river bed and banks from one side to the other at any one point on its course. As a river flows from its source to its mouth, a number of typical changes take place in the channel morphology. In the upper course, the channel is narrow and uneven, because of the presence of deposited boulders. Where both banks are being eroded channels tend to be broadly rectangular in shape. As the river enters its middle course and starts to meander, the channel becomes asymmetrical on the river bends but mainly smooth and symmetrical on the straight stretches. In the lower course, the river widens and deepens further, but banks of deposition and **eyots** (islands of deposition) can disrupt the shape of the channel cross-section, leading to a braided channel. Sometimes embankments called **levées** can be seen on either side of the channel. Levées can also be man-made.

The shape of the channel influences the velocity of the river. In the upper course, where the channel is narrow and uneven due to the presence of large boulders, there is a large **wetted perimeter**. The wetted perimeter is the total length of the river bed and banks in cross section that are in contact with the water in the channel.

River levels only rise after heavy rain or snowmelt and in the upper course the river is relatively shallow. When there is a large wetted perimeter in relation to the amount of water in the river, there is more friction. Friction results in energy loss and, consequently, the velocity of the river is slowed. As channels become larger and smoother, in the middle and lower courses of the river, they tend to be more efficient. The wetted perimeter is proportionately smaller than the volume of water flowing in the channel. Therefore, there is less friction to reduce velocity. Although the turbulent flow of mountain streams might appear faster than that of the gently meandering downstream channel, average velocity is actually slower. This is because so much energy is expended overcoming friction on the uneven channel bed in the upper course, whereas in the lower course there is little to disrupt water flow.

Channel shape is described by the **hydraulic radius**. This is calculated using the formula:

$$\text{hydraulic radius} = \frac{\text{cross-sectional area of the channel}}{\text{wetted perimeter}}$$

A high hydraulic radius means that the river is efficient. This is because the moving water loses proportionately less energy in overcoming friction than when the ratio between the cross-sectional area and the wetted perimeter is low (Figure 1.9). Larger channels tend to be more efficient; area increases to a greater degree than wetted perimeter. For example, at bankfull, a channel that is 10 m wide and 2 m deep has a hydraulic radius of 20/14 = 1.43. A channel that is 20 m wide and 4 m deep has a hydraulic radius of 80/28 = 2.86.

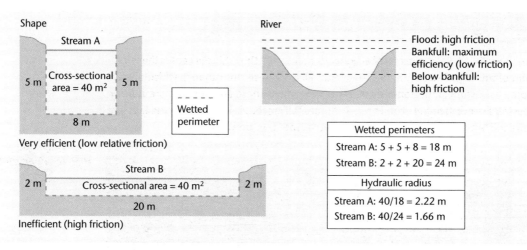

*Figure 1.9
Channel shape
efficiency*

Landforms of fluvial erosion and deposition

As a river flows from its source to its mouth a number of changes take place in its morphology. These changes affect the shape and size of the channel and result in distinctive landforms along its course. Some of these landforms are the result of erosion, some are the result of deposition and some are a consequence of both.

*Figure 1.10
A waterfall*

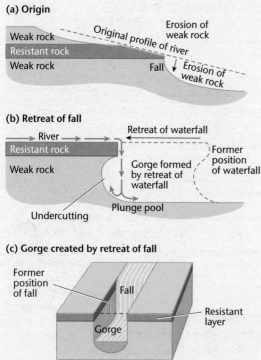

Waterfalls and rapids

Waterfalls and rapids occur when there is a sudden change in the gradient of the river as it flows downstream. Waterfalls are more dramatic features than rapids and may be the result of:

➤ a resistant band of rock occurring across the course of the river
➤ the edge of a plateau
➤ the rejuvenation of the area, giving the river renewed erosional power as sea level falls

The river falls over a rock edge into a deep plunge pool at the foot of the fall, where the layers of weak rock are excavated more quickly than the overlying resistant rock. The force of the swirling water around the rocks and boulders enlarges and deepens the plunge pool by hydraulic action and abrasion. This undercuts the resistant (cap) rock above. Eventually the overhanging cap rock collapses and the waterfall retreats upstream, leaving a gorge ahead of it (Figure 1.10).

Case study | **High Force in upper Teesdale**

In upper Teesdale an outcrop of an igneous rock called the Whin Sill causes the formation of the High Force waterfall. The Whin Sill is the resistant cap rock which overlies
softer sandstone, limestone, shales and coal seams. These are eroded more quickly,
leaving the overhang of High Force. The waterfall created is 22 m high — the tallest in
England. Ahead of it lies a gorge stretching over 500 m downstream.

John Pallister

*Photograph 1.4
High Force waterfall*

Potholes

Potholes are cylindrical holes drilled into the
rocky bed of a river by turbulent high-velocity
water loaded with pebbles (Figure 1.11). The
pebbles become trapped in slight hollows and
vertical eddies in the water are strong enough to
allow the sediment to grind a hole into the rock
by abrasion (corrasion). Attrition rounds and
smooths the pebbles caught in the hole and
helps to reduce the size of the bedload.

River bed

Pothole

*Figure 1.11
Potholes are created
in a rocky river bed
when swirling water
in a slight
depression turns it
into a cylindrical
hole*

Potholes can vary in width from a few centimetres to several metres. They are
generally found in the upper or early-middle course of a river. This is where the
valley lies well above base level, giving more potential for downcutting, and where
the river bed is more likely to be rocky in nature.

Braided channels

Braiding occurs when the river is forced to split into several channels separated
by islands. It is a feature of rivers that are supplied with large loads of sand and
gravel. It is most likely to occur when a river has variable discharges. The banks
formed from sand and gravel are generally unstable and easily eroded. As a

consequence, the channel becomes very wide in relation to its depth. The river can become choked, with several sandbars and channels that are constantly changing their locations.

Braiding also occurs in environments in which there are rapidly fluctuating discharges:

➤ semi-arid areas of low relief that receive rivers from mountainous areas
➤ glacial streams with variable annual discharge. In spring, meltwater causes river discharge and competence to increase, therefore the river can transport more particles. As the temperature drops and the river level falls, the load is deposited as islands of deposition in the channel

Photograph 1.5
A meander on the River Hodder

Meanders and oxbow lakes

Meanders

Meanders are sinuous bends in a river. Explaining the formation of meanders in a river has caused some problems for geographers. In low flow conditions straight channels are seen to have alternating bars of sediment on their beds and the moving water is forced to weave around these bars. This creates alternating shallow sections (riffles) and deeper sections (pools). The swing of the flow that has been induced by the riffles directs the maximum velocity towards one of the banks, and results in erosion by undercutting on that side. An outer concave bank is therefore created. Deposition takes place on the inside of the bend, the convex bank (Photograph 1.5). Consequently, although the river does not get any wider, its sinuosity increases.

The cross-section of a meander is asymmetrical (Figure 1.12). The outer bank forms a river cliff or bluff with a deep pool close to the bank. This bank is undercut by erosion, particularly abrasion and hydraulic action. The inner bank is a gently sloping deposit of sand and gravel, called a **point bar**.

Figure 1.12
A meander

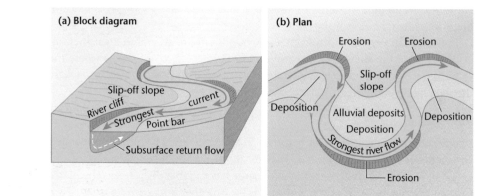

Once they have been created, meanders are perpetuated by a surface flow of water across to the concave outer bank with a compensatory subsurface return flow back to the convex inner bank. This corkscrew-like movement of water is called **helicoidal flow**. In this way, eroded material from the outer bank is transported away and deposited on the inner bank. Modern research suggests that the flow is rarely strong enough for the river to transport material across to the point bar on the opposite bank. Point bars are most likely to be maintained by sediment from erosion at the bluff of the meander upstream on the same side of the channel.

The zone of greatest erosion is downstream of the midpoint in the meander bend, because the flow of the strongest current does not exactly match the shape of the meander. As erosion continues on the outer bank, the whole feature begins to migrate slowly, both laterally and downstream. Imprints of former channels can be seen on the floodplain. These are particularly clear on aerial photographs.

Oxbow lakes

Oxbow lakes are features of both erosion and deposition. An oxbow lake is a horseshoe-shaped lake separated from an adjacent river. The water is stagnant, and in time the lake gradually silts up, becoming a crescent-shaped stretch of marsh called a **meander scar**. An oxbow lake is formed by the increasing sinuosity of a river meander. Erosion is greatest on the outer bank, and with deposition on the inner bank, the neck of the meander becomes progressively narrower. During

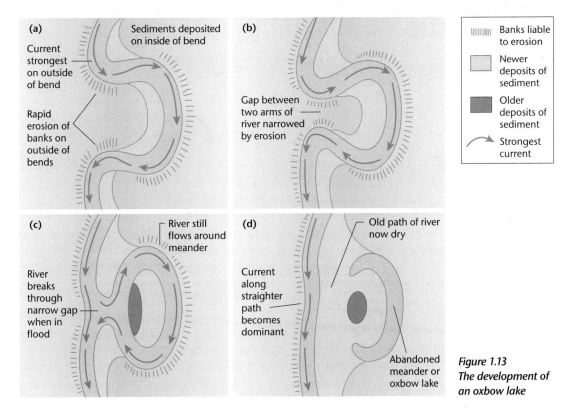

Figure 1.13
The development of an oxbow lake

times of high discharge, such as floods, the river cuts through this neck, and the new cut eventually becomes the main channel. The former channel is sealed off by deposition (Figure 1.13).

Levées

In its middle and lower courses, a river is at risk from flooding during times of high discharge. If it floods, the velocity of the water falls as it overflows the banks. This results in deposition, because the competence of the river is suddenly reduced. It is usual for the coarsest material to be deposited first, forming small raised banks (**levées**) along the sides of the channel. Subsequent floods increase the size of these banks and further deposition on the bed of the river also occurs. This means that the river, with channel sediment build-up, now flows at a higher level than the floodplain. For this reason, the authorities sometimes strengthen levées and increase their heights. On the Mississippi River (USA), for example, levée strengthening began in 1699. By the 1990s, the length of engineered levées was 3,200 km.

Floodplains

Floodplains are created as a result of both erosion and deposition, although the accumulation of river deposits suggests that they are predominantly depositional features. They are the relatively flat areas of land either side of the river, which form the valley floor in the middle and lower courses of the river. They are composed of alluvium — river-deposited silts and clays. Over time, a floodplain becomes wider and the depth of sediment accretions increases. The width of the floodplain is determined by the amount of meander migration and lateral erosion that has taken place. Lateral erosion is most powerful just downstream of the apex of the meander bend. Over time, this results in the migration of meanders, leaving their scars clearly visible on the floodplain. Interlocking spurs are eventually removed by lateral erosion in the middle course, leaving behind a bluff line and widening the valley. The depth of the alluvial deposits depends partly on the amount of flooding in the past, so floodplain creation is linked to extreme events. Over time, point bars and old meander scars become incorporated into the floodplain, adding to the alluvial deposits. These become stabilised by vegetation as the meanders migrate and abandon their former courses.

Studies in the USA suggest that point-bar deposits account for around 80% of the volume of sediment contained within a floodplain. In Britain, a large proportion of the accumulated sediment in floodplain deposits was laid down by post-glacial streams following the last ice age, when the volume of water in rivers was higher and frequency of flooding much increased.

Deltas

A **delta** is a feature of deposition, located at the mouth of a river as it enters a sea or lake. Deposition occurs as the velocity and sediment-carrying capacity of the river decrease on entering the lake or sea, and bedload and suspended material are dumped. Flocculation occurs as fresh water mixes with seawater and clay particles coagulate due to chemical reaction. The clay settles on the river bed.

Deltas form only when the rate of deposition exceeds the rate of sediment removal. In order for a delta to form the following conditions are likely to be met:

➤ The sediment load of the river is very large, as in the Mississippi and Nile rivers.
➤ The coastal area into which the river empties its load has a small tidal range and weak currents. This means that there is limited wave action and, therefore, little transportation of sediment after deposition has taken place. This is a feature of the Gulf of Mexico and the Mediterranean Sea.

Deltas are usually composed of three types of deposit (Figure 1.14):

➤ The larger and heavier particles are the first to be deposited as the river loses its energy. These form the **topset beds**.
➤ Medium graded particles travel a little further before they are deposited as steep-angled wedges of sediment, forming the **foreset beds**.
➤ The very finest particles travel furthest into the lake before deposition and form the **bottomset beds**.

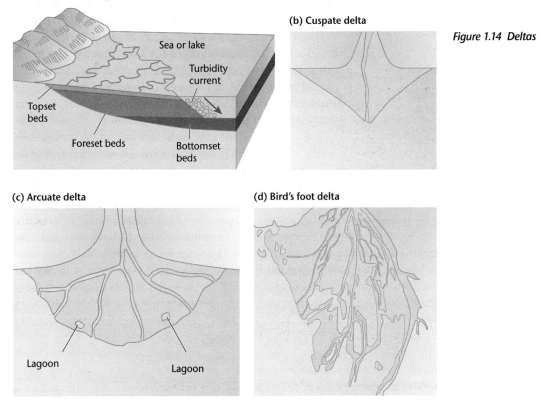

(a) Structure of a simple delta

Sea or lake

Turbidity current

Topset beds

Foreset beds

Bottomset beds

(b) Cuspate delta

Figure 1.14 Deltas

(c) Arcuate delta

Lagoon

Lagoon

(d) Bird's foot delta

Deltas can be described according to their shape. The most commonly recognised is the characteristic **arcuate delta**, for example the Nile delta, which has a curving shoreline and a dendritic pattern of drainage. Many distributaries break away from the main channel as deposition within the channel itself occurs, causing the river to braid. Longshore drift keeps the seaward edge of the delta relatively smooth in shape. The Mississippi has a **bird's foot delta**. Fingers of deposition build out into the sea along the distributaries' channels, giving the appearance, from the air, of a bird's claw. A **cuspate** delta is pointed like a cup or tooth and is shaped by gentle, regular, but opposing, sea currents or longshore drift.

Rejuvenation

Rejuvenation occurs when there is either a fall in sea level relative to the level of the land or a rise of the land relative to the sea. This enables a river to renew its capacity to erode as its potential energy is increased. The river adjusts to its new base level, at first in its lower reaches and then progressively inland. In doing so, a number of landforms may be created: knick points, waterfalls and rapids, river terraces and incised meanders.

Knick points

A **knick point** is a sudden break or irregularity in the gradient along the long profile of a river. Some knick points are sharply defined, for example waterfalls, whereas others are barely noticeable. Although a number of factors can cause such features to occur, they are most commonly attributed to rejuvenation.

When a river is rejuvenated, adjustment to the new base level starts at the sea and gradually works its way up the river's course. The river gains renewed cutting power (in the form of vertical erosion), which encourages it to adjust its long profile. In this sense the knick point is where the old long profile joins the new. The knick point recedes upstream at a rate which is dependent on the resistance of the rocks, and may linger at a relatively hard outcrop. It can be difficult to determine whether a waterfall occurs due to variability in rock type or to rejuvenation. Headward erosion upstream may mean that a waterfall cuts back through the valley towards its source until the long profile eventually adjusts to its new energy equilibrium.

River terraces

A **river terrace** is a remnant of a former floodplain, which has been left at a higher level after **rejuvenation** of the river. Where a river renews its downcutting, it sinks its new channel into the former floodplain, leaving the old floodplain above the level of the present river. The terraces are cut back as the new valley is widened by lateral erosion. If renewed rejuvenation takes place, the process is repeated and a new pair of terraces is formed beneath the original ones. The River Thames has created terraces in its lower course by several stages of rejuvenation. Terraces provide useful shelter from floods in a lower-course river valley, and natural routeways for roads and railways. The built-up areas of Oxford and London are mainly located along the terraces of the River Thames.

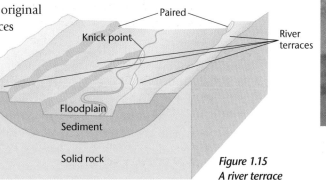

Figure 1.15
A river terrace

Incised meanders

If a rejuvenated river occupies a valley with well-developed meanders, renewed energy results in them becoming **incised** or deepened. Incised streams and rivers have cut deeply into the landscape in many parts of the British Isles. The nature of the landforms created is largely a result of the rate at which vertical erosion has taken place. When incision is slow and lateral erosion is occurring, an **ingrown** meander may be produced. The valley becomes asymmetrical, with steep cliffs on the outer bends and more gentle slip-off slopes on the inner bends. With rapid incision, where downcutting or vertical erosion dominates, the valley is more symmetrical, with steep sides and a gorge-like appearance. These are described as **entrenched meanders** (Photograph 1.6).

Photograph 1.6
The city of Durham is built inside an entrenched meander

Causes of flooding

Physical causes of flooding

Flooding occurs when a river's discharge exceeds the capacity of its channel to carry that discharge. The river overflows its banks. Flooding may be caused by a number of natural causes or physical factors:

➤ Excessive levels of precipitation occurring over a prolonged period of time. This eventually leads to saturation of the soil. When the water table reaches the ground surface, there is increased overland flow or runoff.
➤ Intensive precipitation over a short period of time, particularly when the ground surface is baked hard after a long period without rainfall. In such circumstances the infiltration capacity is such that the ground cannot soak up the rainfall quickly enough, so more water reaches the river than would normally be the case.
➤ The melting of snow, particularly when the subsoil is still frozen, so that infiltration capacity is reduced.
➤ Climatic hazards such as cyclones in Bangladesh, hurricanes in the Gulf of Mexico or deep low-pressure weather systems in mid-latitudes bring abnormally large amounts of precipitation.

The nature of the drainage basin has an influence on the likelihood of flooding. Some drainage basins are more likely to flood than others. Relief, vegetation, soil type and geology all have a part to play. In areas of the world vegetated by dense forest, interception and uptake by plants reduce the risk of flooding during times of heavy rainfall.

Key terms

Hazard A natural event that threatens life and property. A disaster is the realisation of the hazard. Flooding is an example of a natural hazard.

River management River basins are subject to strategies designed to prevent flooding and to ensure that there is an adequate supply of water.

Case study — Boscastle floods, Cornwall, August 2004

By midday on 16 August 2004, heavy, thundery downpours had developed across southwest England as a result of an intensive low-pressure weather system that encouraged the uplift of warm, moist air. Some 200 mm of rain fell in 24 hours, most of it between midday and 5.00 p.m. The rainfall was particularly intensive between 3 p.m. and 4 p.m., when it exceeded 100 mm h^{-1} for short periods of time.

This rainfall was, however, very localised. The weather system appeared to stall over the hills above Boscastle. Rainfall was heaviest to the east of Boscastle on high ground. Indeed, the high land encouraged precipitation in the form of orographic rainfall. The ground was already saturated, due to previous wet weather, so infiltration of water into the ground was limited. The topography of the area also contributed to the scale of the flooding. The village of Boscastle lies in a deep valley just downstream of the confluence of the rivers Valency and Jordan.

Runoff into the river was rapid on that day and flooding in the town was first reported at 4.00 p.m. The situation developed swiftly from this point onwards and 60 or so properties were submerged under floodwater. Not all of these were in the town itself; some were in the catchment of the tributary River Jordan and were flooded as surface water cascaded down the hillsides. Around 70–80 cars were swept away in Boscastle and 100 people were airlifted to safety by the emergency services. There was significant damage to property, roads, bridges and services but, mercifully, no loss of life.

The impact of human activities on flooding

Urbanisation

Flooding is a natural event. However, in recent times its effects have been exacerbated by human activity. Over the last two centuries urbanisation has resulted in an ever-increasing proportion of the world's population living in towns and cities. This first occurred in Europe and developed countries elsewhere, such as the USA. Since the middle of the twentieth century, urbanisation has been an important feature in many less developed countries.

Coupled with natural population growth, urbanisation has led to an increasing demand for space to build housing and for other urban land uses. Floodplains were an obvious choice — their flat land is suitable to build on and good communications are relatively easy to establish. However, floodplains, by their very nature, are susceptible to flooding.

Human activity on the flat land surrounding the river has added to the risk of flooding. Concrete and tarmac are used in urban areas for roads and pavement. Such surfaces are impermeable, so precipitation is unable to infiltrate slowly into the soil, as it would in a vegetated area. In addition to this, there is less interception from trees and uptake from plants is reduced. Overall, a higher proportion of the original rainfall makes its way into a river in a town or city.

To add to the flood risk, surface water is channelled directly into drains and sewers in an urban area, so precipitation reaches the river quickly. This leads to a reduced lag time between peak rainfall and peak discharge.

Natural river channels may become constricted by bridges, which can slow down discharge and reduce the carrying capacity of the river. In times of spate, debris can be deposited directly behind the supports holding up a bridge and exaggerate the effects of a flood. During the Boscastle floods in August 2004, huge amounts of debris blocked culverts upstream of the town, which had been constructed to allow water to drain quickly through the town.

Deforestation

In some (mainly less developed) countries rapid deforestation has taken place over recent decades. The rainforests of South America, Africa and Asia have been at particular risk as new land has been opened up for farming, settlement and other uses. Other countries, for example Nepal in the Himalayas, have also suffered from deforestation — timber is a valuable resource, used for building and firewood.

Once trees have been removed there is a greater risk of soil erosion and sediment finds its way into rivers, obstructing them and adding to the flood risk. Trees intercept water and take it up through their roots, so in deforested areas more water reaches the channel as runoff.

Flood damage is greatest near the mouth of a river because wide, flat floodplains are most susceptible to damage. Here, the volume of water is at its greatest because many tributaries have joined the river.

Bangladesh lies downstream from Nepal and most of the land is low-lying floodplain that is less than 1 m above sea level, forming the delta of the rivers

Brahmaputra, Meghna and Ganges. During the spring snowmelt occurs and once the heavy monsoon rains start in early summer there is a natural rise in the volume of water in the rivers. In recent years, it has been claimed that flooding in Bangladesh has been more severe, partly as a consequence of deforestation in Nepal.

River management

The main aim of river management is to reduce the likelihood of flooding. However, in some circumstances it can actually increase the risk:

➤ In Bangladesh, embankments have been built along the river channels in some places. These are designed to increase river capacity, but at times have prevented flood water draining back into the rivers.

➤ The Farakka dam lies on the upper reaches of the River Ganges in northern India. In 1988, the Indian government allowed the floodgates of the dam to be opened during the rainy season, because the reservoir behind the dam was at risk of flooding. This saved the land surrounding the dam but downstream in Bangladesh it was a different matter. The extra discharge in the river coincided with the normal floods expected at that time of year and greatly increased their severity.

➤ The Mississippi River in the southern states of the USA is one of the most managed rivers in the world. Artificial embankments (levées) have been built along the lower reaches of the channel to protect the heavily settled floodplain. The city of New Orleans lies below sea level on the banks of the Mississippi and is at particular risk of flooding but is protected by levées and diversion channels, built by the government. In August 2005, devastating floods occurred, submerging the city as the levées were breached (Photograph 1.7). A storm surge, brought about by Hurricane Katrina, gushed up the river from the coast. This, coupled with the heavy rainfall brought by the storm, caused the river to rise dramatically. Major damage to the embankments resulted as they were breached in several places.

Photograph 1.7 Much of New Orleans had to be evacuated as levées on the Mississippi were breached following Hurricane Katrina in 2005

➤ Some rivers in urban areas have been channelised. This involves lining the river channel with concrete and straightening it. Channelisation enables water to be directed through the urban area more rapidly. It may protect the immediate surrounding area, but there is a greater flood risk downstream. This is because water is delivered to downstream areas more rapidly than usual and the unmanaged river channel in these stretches is unable to cope with the rapid increase in discharge.

Climate change

In recent years, global warming has been blamed for what some claim is an increasing frequency of flooding. There is evidence that average sea temperatures have risen and this rise has been blamed for the increasing frequency and severity of tropical revolving storms in the Caribbean. Such storms bring heavy rainfall and storm surges along the coastlines of countries lying in their path. In spring 2005, scientists reported that average sea temperatures were 3°C above normal and predicted that the 2005 hurricane season in the Caribbean and southern states of the USA would be particularly savage. This proved to be the case. Notable hurricanes included Katrina, which led to the flooding of New Orleans.

It is predicted that global warming will result in reduced rainfall in some areas, but in others, such as western Europe, rainfall totals might increase. Higher temperatures will result in increased evaporation over the seas and oceans, leading to greater precipitation. Such an increase will inevitably cause more rivers to flood, particularly since most floodplains have become heavily urbanised over the last two centuries.

Global warming has also been linked to an increased frequency of El Niño events. El Niño is caused by a reversal in ocean currents in the Pacific Ocean. Normally, a cold current flows up the coast of Peru, encouraging high-pressure weather conditions. In an El Niño year, low-pressure weather dominates, bringing increased rainfall and flooding to the west coast of South America.

Global warming could lead to the melting of the polar ice caps. One major consequence of this would be a rise in sea level, so floodplains lying close to present sea levels would be at risk from flooding. The major deltas of the world, such as those of the Nile, the Mississippi and the Ganges–Brahmaputra, would be at particular risk.

The impact of flooding

Areas of high flood risk in the UK

Figure 1.16 shows the areas of England and Wales considered by the Environment Agency to be most at risk from flooding. It highlights the extent to which those areas are likely

*Figure 1.16
Areas at high risk
of flooding in
England and Wales*

Newcastle
Redcar
Whitby
Leeds
Hull
Manchester
Hunstanton
Heacham
Snettisham
Birmingham
King's Lynn
Cardiff
London
Ramsgate
Bristol
Folkestone
Southampton
Hastings
Portsmouth
Plymouth

Potential extent of flooding in areas predicted to be at risk

Most at risk from tidal flooding/history of flooding

At risk of serious flooding

Source: Environment Agency/Science Media Centre

to flood from overflowing rivers and exceptionally high seas if there are no flood defences in place. Flooding is a natural occurrence, which cannot always be prevented or predicted in advance. If our climate changes as many experts predict, bringing fiercer storms and wetter winters, along with a rise in sea levels, the likelihood of floods will increase.

Flood prediction

Hydrologists try to forecast the likelihood of future flood events using past records. The data they use include river discharge records in relation to precipitation, and flood recurrence interval graphs. These graphs calculate statistically the probability of flooding in the future based on past records. The further back flood records go, the more accurate the prediction.

Records of a river's discharge are ranked over the longest period available, from highest peak discharge to the lowest recorded. The following formula is used to calculate the recurrence interval:

$$\text{recurrence interval (years)} = \frac{\text{number of years on record} + 1}{\substack{\text{ranking of flood being considered} \\ \text{(in terms of flood size in } m^3 s^{-1})}}$$

Figure 1.17
Flood frequency graph for the Licking River, Ohio

When the recurrence interval is plotted against discharge as a scatter graph on semi-logarithmic graph paper, it is possible to use the line of best fit to predict when the next flood of a particular magnitude might occur. This is called the **flood return period**. So using Figure 1.17, it may be predicted that the next flood where discharge is recorded at 10,000 m³ s⁻¹ would occur approximately 90 years after the last one. The Department for Environment Food and Rural Affairs (DEFRA) and the Environment Agency are the main organisations responsible for flood management of major rivers like the Thames and the Severn in the British Isles and they use flood recurrence interval graphs to plan flood defence strategies. They recommend that densely populated urban areas are sufficiently protected against 1 in 100 year flood events but that grassland and low productivity agricultural land should not be protected at all.

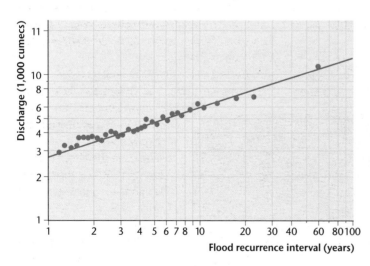

In addition to studying the likelihood of flooding on an annual basis, hydrologists use past data records showing the regime or yearly pattern of discharge in relation to annual precipitation patterns. In this way the likelihood of seasonal flooding can be assessed.

Comparing a major flood in an MEDC and an LEDC

Case study **MEDC: southern Britain, July 2007**

Weather conditions throughout the summer of 2007 were exceptional. The jet stream, which influences the path taken by low-pressure weather systems in the north Atlantic, had followed an abnormally southerly track. This meant that the usual anticyclonic weather conditions influenced by the high-pressure cell in the Azores did not materialise.

Rainfall totals for May to July 2007 were the highest on record for England and Wales since 1766, with many areas registering more than twice the long-term average. On 20 July there was exceptional rainfall. Outstanding storm totals were reported across much of southern Britain, including 145 mm of rain in Pershore (Worcestershire), 111 mm at Chieveley (Berkshire) and 120 mm at Brize Norton (Oxfordshire). On the basis of historical data such a storm would be expected to occur only once in several hundred years.

Flood risk during the summer is normally reduced by dry soil conditions. However, in this case the record early summer rainfall meant that soils were already close to saturation. Groundwater levels were also much higher than normal, so there was little infiltration or percolation capacity.

The intense storms on 20 July resulted in a number of localised but severe flash floods in urban areas of southern England, including Stratford-upon-Avon and Leamington Spa in Warwickshire, Ludlow in Shropshire, and Buckingham in Buckinghamshire. The rainfall quickly overwhelmed urban drainage systems and the emergency services were widely deployed to rescue stranded people and to organise evacuations. Transport networks were severely disrupted, and as this was the last day of the school year for many students, the volume of holiday traffic was high. Thousands of motorists were stranded in their vehicles for hours on the M5 motorway. As the water began to move downstream many floodplains were inundated, causing catastrophic flooding and extensive crop damage.

Over the following week the worst-affected areas were the lower parts of the Severn and Warwickshire Avon basins, including Gloucester, Cheltenham and Tewkesbury (Photograph 1.8), and some upper reaches of the Thames catchment, including Oxford. Three people died as a direct result of the floods in Gloucestershire and at one point 45,000 households were without power. Some 350,000 homes in the county had no running water after a water treatment works was flooded, and 140,000 were still affected more than a week later.

The economic costs of the floods included:
- £25 million damage to Gloucestershire's roads, the equivalent of the local authority's entire annual budget for highway works
- farmers in the affected areas lost up to 50% of their crops, leading to shortages and price rises in the following autumn
- £3 billion flood damage covered by insurance — uninsured losses were estimated to be of an equivalent amount
- £1 billion cost to the water industry

Photograph 1.8 The floods surrounding Tewkesbury Abbey

TopFoto

Case study

LEDC: Bangladesh, 2004

Bangladesh is a low-lying country most of which lies on the delta land of three major rivers, the Ganges, Brahmaputra and Meghna (Figure 1.18). The sources of these rivers are in the Himalayas, so snowmelt adds to their discharge during spring.

This part of south Asia has a monsoon climate and experiences a wet season between May and September, when low pressure and winds blowing from the southwest bring heavy rain to coastal regions.

At times during the rainy season, Bangladesh suffers from tropical revolving storms (cyclones) that bring exceptional winds, intense precipitation and storm surges. Such conditions severely affect the discharge of the three rivers and their distributaries, and cause regular floods.

Human factors have played an increasing role in the severity of the floods in recent decades. As in more developed countries, urbanisation has occurred and the capital city Dhaka now has a population of more than 1 million. In addition to this, rapid deforestation in the Himalayas has had a negative effect on the rates of interception and evapotranspiration, resulting in more water reaching the rivers.

River management is difficult to implement in less developed countries like Bangladesh. The country is one of the poorest in the world, with the average gross domestic product per capita standing at around $300. Most of the population rely on subsistence agriculture to survive, growing rice on rented plots of land. This means taxation revenue is limited and

Bangladesh relies heavily on foreign aid to finance large-scale development projects which might help prevent floods. In 2004, the monsoon season brought more rainfall than usual. From late June through to September the three main rivers burst their banks, resulting in widespread flooding.

Impacts

■ During July and August 2004, approximately 38% of the total land area of the country was flooded, including 800,000 hectares of agricultural land and the capital city, Dhaka.

■ Nationwide, 36 million people (from a total population of 125 million) were made homeless.

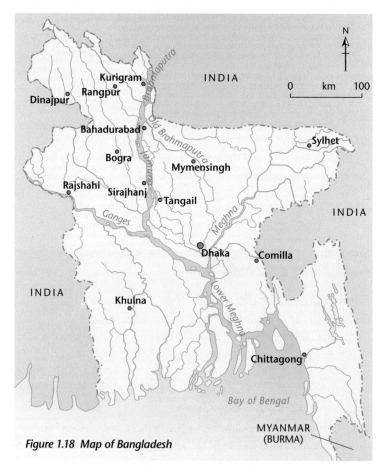

Figure 1.18 Map of Bangladesh

- By mid-September, the death toll had risen to 800. Many people died as a result of disease because they had no access to clean water.
- The flood also caused serious damage to the country's infrastructure, including roads, bridges and embankments, railway lines and irrigation systems. Boats were afloat on the main runway at Sylhet airport and all domestic and internal flights had to be suspended during July. Road and rail links into Dhaka were also severely affected.
- The value of the damage was assessed as being in the region of $2.2 billion or 4% of the total GDP for 2004.
- Although the flood affected both poor and wealthy households, the poor were generally less able to withstand its impacts. Landless labourers and small farmers were the most severely affected in rural areas. In the urban areas, it was typically the slum dwellers, squatting on poorly drained land, who suffered the most.

The floods caused four environmental impacts: river-bank erosion, especially on embankment areas close to the main channels; soil erosion; water-logging, particularly in urban areas; and water-contamination, with its associated health risks.

Short-term responses

The government, working with non-governmental organisations (NGOs) provided emergency relief in the form of rice, clothing, medicines, blankets and towels. In July, the UN activated a disaster management team to coordinate the activities of the various UN agencies. They supplied critical emergency supplies and conducted a 'damage and needs assessment' in the affected areas. Bilateral aid from individual countries was directed to the UN team. People in Bangladesh are resilient, and self-help schemes, in which local people work together to rebuild their properties and lives, are common.

Long-term responses

For a developing country such as Bangladesh, long-term responses to major floods are largely dependent on foreign aid from both official and unofficial sources. In the past, river management schemes implemented by foreigners and funded by aid have proved to be inadequate. Such schemes paid little attention to local knowledge of rivers and many attempts at river management failed. More recently, small-scale community-based projects have resulted in lives being saved. Flood shelters and early-warning systems have been successfully put in place.

Following the 2004 floods, additional financial aid was granted for a period of 5 years. This was mainly in the form of a loan from the World Bank, to pay for, in the first instance, repairs to infrastructure, water resource management and education.

Disaster-preparedness is a key priority for the future. This includes flood management and improved water resources. It is also planned that, in future, flood-resistant designs should be used in all social and economic infrastructure projects.

Responses to flooding

How well a flood hazard is dealt with depends on:
➤ the level of preparedness at the location of the expected hazard
➤ the amount of warning there has been
➤ the level of economic development, which influences such factors as emergency service provision, infrastructure and the ability to repair and rebuild

Flood management strategies

Flood management seeks to reduce the frequency and magnitude of flooding and, therefore, to limit the damage that floods cause. Flood protection can be achieved by the following hard-engineering methods:

➤ The banks and/or channel can be modified to enable the river to carry a larger volume of water. Artificially raised and strengthened banks form a significant part of this strategy. In some cases, parallel lines of flood banks act as a double form of protection — if the river overtops the first barrier, then it has difficulty rising over the second bank some distance behind. The removal of large boulders from the bed of the river reduces roughness, therefore increasing the velocity of flow.

➤ Dams and weirs can be built to regulate the rate at which water passes down a river.

➤ Diversion channels can be constructed to divert rivers away from areas vulnerable to flooding.

➤ Dredging can be used to create a deeper channel so that greater volumes of water can pass through.

➤ The height of the floodplain can be increased by dumping material on it.

➤ Retention basins and balancing lakes can be constructed into which water is diverted at times of high discharge.

Case study — Hard engineering: Three Gorges dam, China

The Three Gorges dam in China is the largest hard-engineering project ever undertaken on a river. The project, due for completion in 2009, is located on the Yangtze River in China. This river has a long history of flooding. The dam will be used to generate electricity from hydroelectric power for central and eastern China. This includes the city of Shanghai, which has a population of more than 13 million people. The dam will also reduce the flood risk for 15 million people and improve navigation along the river. A huge reservoir, some 660 km long and 1 km wide, has been created behind the dam. The dam itself, completed in 2006, is 2.3 km long and more than 100 m high. According to official figures, it has cost somewhere in the region of £25 billion to build.

Impacts

The creation of the reservoir has forced the resettlement of 1.2 million people from several cities, 11 district centres and over 100 villages to newly built settlements (Photograph 1.9). The area of resettlement runs along the Yangtze River and most people have been located as near as possible to their former homes.

Many cultural monuments have been lost as a result of the flooding, including the Zhang Fei temple.

Photograph 1.9 Schoolchildren in the new city of Wushan, rebuilt on higher ground to make way for the Three Gorges dam

Pierre Montavon/Strales/Panos

Between 1998 and 2004 the amount of sediment transported by the river below the dam fell by over 50%, resulting in increased rates of erosion downstream. Sediment will accumulate behind the dam and this will require dredging.

Afforestation is needed on the slopes in the drainage basin to reduce the amount of sediment washed into the river and the reservoir behind the dam.

The dam will have negative environmental and ecological effects. There is an increased likelihood of landslides in the immediate area around the reservoir and many species, such as white flag dolphin, will have their habitats disrupted.

Softer approaches to flood management are mainly concerned with flood abatement — changing land use upstream. In recent years conservation and sustainability of management schemes have been taken seriously and water managers now balance the needs of flood protection with those of the environment. Soft engineering is generally more sustainable and can be achieved by:

➤ Afforestation in the drainage basin. Increased interception slows down the rate at which water reaches a river and greater evapotranspiration by trees reduces the amount that reaches the channel. Although this method can be effective in the long term, it takes time for trees to mature after they have been planted and large areas must be planted in order to reduce discharge downstream.

➤ Contour ploughing and strip farming in semi-arid areas, which reduce the amount of surface runoff and, therefore, reduce the liability to flooding.

➤ Floodplain zoning, which allows certain areas of the floodplain to flood naturally — land uses are limited to grazing and recreation in such areas. This method protects other, more economically valuable, areas.

➤ River restoration schemes (see case study on page 36), which return rivers to their original state before they were managed. This involves compromise between sustainable environmental gain and social and economic considerations. Such schemes aim to improve the quality of river water as well as implementing more sustainable, soft flood management schemes, and they aim to work with nature. Many rivers in lowland England have been channelised and dredged, which may mean they are disconnected from their former floodplains. In many cases artificial embankments, constructed on both sides of the channel, create a sharp break between the river and its floodplain. These are unsightly and support little wildlife but once they are removed the flood water can spill onto the floodplain once again. Functional floodplains upstream can act as a buffer against catastrophic flooding downstream. Occasional flooding can be beneficial in improving soil fertility.

➤ Wetland and riverbank conservation schemes, which involve protecting existing natural river channels and their valleys so that habitats and species diversity can be maintained. In some cases arable land is returned to its former use as natural meadowland.

➤ Forecasting floods and warnings, in areas where flooding is regular and unavoidable. In Bangladesh the yearly floods which engulf most of the countryside cannot be prevented, but if people are given enough warning they can take refuge in flood shelters.

Case study **Soft engineering: River Quaggy restoration scheme, UK**

Photograph 1.10 *Sutcliffe Park, Greenwich, after the restoration scheme*

Photograph 1.11 *River restoration in Chinbrook Meadows*

The River Quaggy runs through southeast London. Since the 1960s it has been heavily managed and artificial channels and culverts were built to divert it beneath the ground surface as it passed through Greenwich. As a result of increased flood risk due to continued urban development in Lewisham and Greenwich, more needed to be done to protect the area from flooding. Hard engineering methods, such as further widening and deepening of the existing channel, were considered, but instead the Environment Agency chose a more sustainable soft approach.

This solution was proposed by local residents, who formed the Quaggy Waterways Action Group (QWAG) to campaign for a sustainable approach which would improve the local environment.

The plan was to bring the river back above ground once again, cutting a new channel for it through Sutcliffe Park, and creating a multi-functional open space. In this way flood management and the quality of the park would be improved. Although a culvert remained to take some water underground during flood conditions, a new lake was created to take over when this became full. The park itself was lowered and shaped to create a floodplain where water could collect naturally instead of rushing downstream through artificial channels to flood Lewisham town centre. The park's flood storage capacity of 85,000 m³ of water, equivalent to 35 Olympic swimming pools, has reduced the risk of flooding for 600 homes and businesses in Greenwich and Lewisham, and has created a diverse environment for wildlife.

By redirecting the river to a more natural course and including a flood storage area, the scheme has created a wetland environment with reedbeds, wild flower meadows and trees. The scheme won the Natural Environment category in the 2007 Waterways Renaissance Awards and the Living Wetlands Award, run jointly by the RSPB and the Chartered Institution of Water and Environmental Management.

Assessment exercises

1 Figures A and B show changes in the River Omo Delta on the northern shore of Lake Turkana that took place between 1975 and 1995.

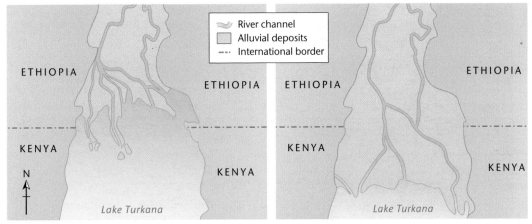

Figure A 1975   Figure B 1995

a (i) Identify two changes to the delta that took place between 1975 and 1995.   (2 marks)
  (ii) Suggest a reason for the changes identified in (i).   (2 marks)
b Why do features of deposition exist throughout the long profile of most rivers?   (5 marks)
c Assess the costs and benefits of one river management scheme you have studied.   (15 marks)
d Examine the reasons why soft engineering is considered to be a sustainable form of river management.   (6 marks)

          (30 marks)

2 Figure C is a simplified systems diagram of the drainage basin component of the hydrological cycle.

a (i) Distinguish between the inputs and outputs of the drainage basin hydrological cycle.   (2 marks)
  (ii) Name the transfers labelled x, y and z on the diagram.   (3 marks)
  (iii) How is the water balance within the drainage basin determined?   (4 marks)
  (iv) How might human activity modify the drainage basin hydrological cycle?   (6 marks)

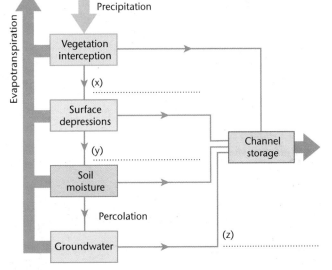

Figure C

b Compare the physical and human causes of flooding for two contrasting case studies you have studied.

(15 marks)

(30 marks)

3 Photograph A shows Torver Beck, near Coniston in Cumbria, in its upper course.

Photograph A

Amanda Barker

a (i) Describe Torver Beck's channel. (2 marks)

(ii) Outline how the channel shape at this point might affect the efficiency of the river. (2 marks)

(iii) Examine the physical factors that might affect the discharge of rivers such as the one in Photograph A. (6 marks)

(iv) What changes are likely to occur in the shape of the channel along the river's long profile? (5 marks)

b Describe and explain the formation of channel features that can be created by the process of river rejuvenation.

(15 marks)

(30 marks)

Unit 1

Physical and human geography

Optional physical topics

Cold environments

Global distribution

Cold environments are the icy landscapes that occur in high latitudes (around the poles) and high mountain areas (often referred to as Alpine regions). Such regions have severely cold temperatures, an abundance of snow and ice with little vegetation and, as they are difficult to exploit, they remain sparsely populated (Figure 2.1). The term includes maritime areas such as the Arctic and Southern Oceans. Much of the Arctic Ocean is covered by floating ice, although many scientists believe that this coverage will reduce substantially in the next century as a result of global warming. The Southern Ocean (which borders Antarctica), is rich in animal life and has a high level of biological productivity despite being so cold.

Glacial environments are the areas covered by ice sheets and glaciers. The largest of these is the continent of Antarctica and its surrounding ice shelves, which covers around 13 million km². The other major glacial area is Greenland.

Figure 2.1
Cold environments

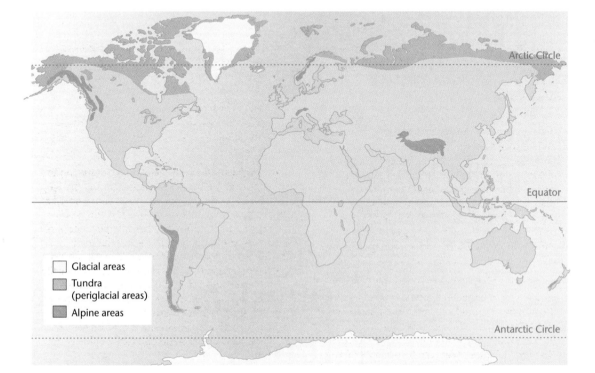

Glacial areas
Tundra (periglacial areas)
Alpine areas

Periglacial (and **tundra**) **regions** exist in dry high-latitude areas not permanently covered by snow and ice. Such areas include northern Alaska and Canada, northern Scandinavia, Siberia and the islands of the Arctic Ocean such as Spitsbergen. The cold conditions create permanently frozen ground known as permafrost. Vegetation is sparse in such areas.

Alpine regions occur in Asia (Himalayas, Karakoram, Tibet plateau), Europe (Alps, Norwegian mountains), Australasia (Southern Alps in New Zealand) and the Americas (Rockies, Cascades, Andes). Such areas may contain small ice caps, mountain glaciers and tundra environments.

Ice formation and movement

When a climate starts to become colder, more precipitation in winter falls as snow. Summers also begin to shorten, so there is less time for the winter snow to melt. At first, this leads to permanent snow cover in upland areas, the lower edge of which is known as the **snow line**. As the climate continues to deteriorate, the snow line moves down the slope.

At present, the snow line is at sea level in Greenland but at 6,000 m on the equator. There is no permanent snow cover in the British Isles, so there is no snow line, but scientists estimate that if the Scottish mountains were 200–250 m higher, there would be. In the northern hemisphere, the snow line is found at a higher

Table 2.1 The area of the Earth covered by ice at the present time

Region	Estimated area (million km^2)
Antarctica	13.50
Greenland	1.80
Arctic Basin	0.24
Asia	0.12
Alaska	0.05
Rest of North America	0.03
Andes	0.03
Scandinavia	0.004
Alps	0.004
Australasia	0.001
Africa	0.0001
Total	15.8

Key terms

Fluvioglacial (glacifluvial) Processes and landforms associated with the action of glacial meltwater.

Glacier A tongue-shaped mass of ice moving slowly down a valley.

Ice ages The common term for the period when there were major cold phases known as glacials, and ice sheets covered large areas of the world. The last ice age lasted from about 2 million years ago to about 10,000 BP (before present). It was also known as the Quaternary glaciation. During the Quaternary there were many episodes of glaciation, the last major period beginning around 120,000 BP and reaching its maximum in 18,000 BP. At that time about 30% of the Earth's surface was covered by ice, compared with 10% today.

Ice sheet A body of ice covering an area of at least 50,000 km^2. Ice sheets are dome-shaped and the ice flows outward from the centre. Today, ice sheets cover Antarctica and Greenland, with smaller sheets (ice caps) covering areas of Iceland, Spitsbergen and Norway. Major ice sheets can be up to 2,000 m

thick today; those that occurred at the maximum extent of the Quaternary glaciation could have been up to twice that thickness. The Quaternary ice sheets covered substantial areas of northern North America and Europe.

Periglacial Processes and landforms associated with the fringe of, or the area near to, an ice sheet or glacier.

Tundra A climatic and vegetation type found in the most northerly parts of Eurasia and North America. Tundra-like environments also occur above the tree line in mountainous areas such as the Alps, Rockies, Andes and Himalayas. The main differences between mountain and Arctic tundra are that the sun is higher in the sky in mountain tundra areas, giving warmer conditions, and that permafrost is generally absent from these areas. During the Quaternary glaciation, when the ice sheets were more extensive, tundra climate affected large areas of central North America and Europe, including the British Isles. At present, tundra occupies around 25% of the Earth's surface.

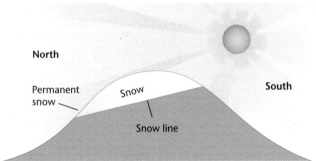

Figure 2.2
The snow line in
the northern
hemisphere

altitude on south-facing slopes than on those that face north, as the south-facing slopes receive more insolation (Figure 2.2).

Snow initially falls as flakes, which have an open, feathery structure that traps air. As the snow accumulates, compression by the upper layers gradually turns the lower snow into a more compact form known as **firn** or **névé**. Meltwater seeps into the gaps and then freezes, further compacting the mass. As more snow falls, air is progressively squeezed out of the lower snow by the weight of the upper layers and after a period of some years (most experts put it between 20 and 40) a mass of solid ice develops. Where there is no summer melting, this process takes longer. During this period, the mass changes colour from white, indicating the presence of air, to a bluish colour, indicating that the air has been largely expelled. This is the ice that begins to flow downhill as a **glacier**.

There are two types of glacier — temperate and polar. The characteristics of each affect ice movement and glacial processes.

Temperate (alpine) glaciers (Photograph 2.1) melt in summer, releasing huge amounts of meltwater. This acts as a lubricant, reducing friction. Temperate glaciers move by basal flow, extending/compressing flow, creep and surges. This type of glacier is more likely to erode, transport and deposit material.

Photograph 2.1
Franz-Joseph glacier
in New Zealand

Polar glaciers occur in areas where the temperature is permanently below 0°C, and therefore no melting occurs. Movement is slower than in temperate glaciers as they are frozen to their beds and thus move mainly by internal flow. Much less erosion, transportation and deposition occurs.

As ice moves downhill it does not always behave in the same way. It has great rigidity and strength, but under steady pressure it behaves as a plastic (mouldable) body. In contrast, when put under sudden compression or tension, it will break or shear apart. This gives two zones within the glacier (Figure 2.3):

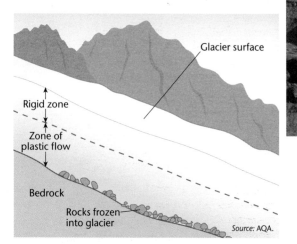

Source: AQA.

Figure 2.3
Zones within a glacier

➤ the upper zone where the ice is brittle, breaking apart to form crevasses
➤ the lower zone which has steady pressure. Here meltwater resulting from that pressure and from friction with the bedrock allows a more rapid, plastic flow. At depth in the glacier the melting point of the ice is raised slightly by the increased pressure. Basal ice is therefore more likely to melt at temperatures close to 0°C (pressure melting point)

Ice movement is complex, and several types of movement can be identified. The main types are:

➤ **Compressing flow** which occurs where there is a reduction in the gradient of the valley floor leading to ice deceleration and a thickening of the ice mass. At such points ice erosion is at its maximum (Figure 2.4).
➤ **Extending flow** which occurs when the valley gradient becomes steeper. The ice accelerates and becomes thinner, leading to reduced erosion (Figure 2.4).
➤ **Basal flow (sliding/slippage)** — as the glacier moves over the bedrock, there is friction. The lower ice is also under a great deal of pressure and this, combined with the friction, results in some melting. The resulting meltwater acts as a lubricant, enabling the ice to flow more rapidly.
➤ **Surges** occur from time to time when an excessive build-up of meltwater under the glacier leads to the ice moving rapidly forward, perhaps by as much as 250–300 m in one day. Such surges represent a hazard to people living in the glacial valley below the **snout**.
➤ **Internal flow** occurs when ice crystals orientate themselves in the direction of the glacier's movement and slide past each other. As surface ice moves faster, crevasses develop. Internal flow is the main feature of the flow of polar glaciers as, without the presence of meltwater, they tend to be frozen to their beds.
➤ **Creep** occurs when stress builds up within a glacier, allowing the ice to behave with plasticity and flow. It occurs particularly when obstacles are met.
➤ **Rotational flow** occurs within the corrie (cirque), the birthplace of many glaciers. Here ice moving downhill can pivot about a point, producing a rotational movement. This, combined with increased pressure within the rock hollow, leads to greater erosion and an over-deepening of the corrie floor.

*Figure 2.4
Extending and
compressing flow*

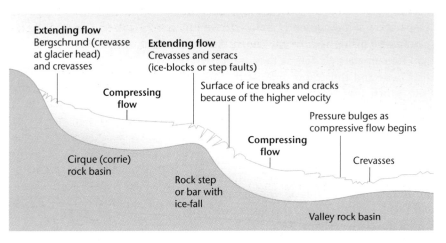

Within a glacier there are different rates of movement. The sides and base of the glacier move at a slower rate than the centre surface ice (Figure 2.5). As a result, the ice cracks, producing crevasses on the surface. These also occur where extending flow speeds up the flow of ice and where the valley widens or the glacier flows from a valley on to a plain (**piedmont glacier**).

*Figure 2.5
Differential rates
of flow within a
glacier*

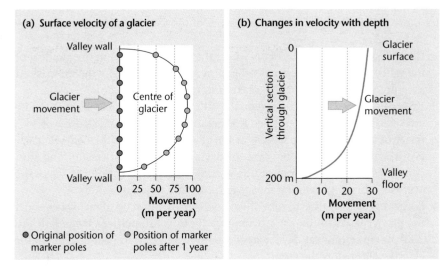

Glacial budgets

A glacier can be viewed as a system with inputs, stores, transfers and outputs:
- **inputs** are precipitation in the form of snow and ice, and avalanches which add snow, ice and debris from the valley side
- **storage** is represented by the glacier itself
- **transfer (throughput)** is the way that the ice moves (the various types of flow are described above)
- **outputs** are water vapour (from evaporation of water on the ice surface and

sublimation — the direct change of state from ice to water vapour), calving (the formation of icebergs), and water in liquid form from **ablation** (melting). The debris deposited at the snout (moraine) can also be considered an output

The upper part of the glacier, where inputs exceed outputs and therefore where more mass is gained than lost over a year, is known as the **zone of accumulation**; the lower part, where outputs exceed inputs, and where mass is lost rather than gained, is known as the **zone of ablation**. Between the two zones is the line of **equilibrium** which separates net loss from net gain and represents the snow line on the glacier (Figure 2.6). A glacier that is characterised by large volumes of gains and losses will discharge a large volume of ice through its equilibrium line to replace mass lost at the snout and will therefore have a high erosive capacity.

The **net balance** is the difference between the total accumulation and the total ablation during 1 year (Figure 2.7). In temperate glaciers, there is a negative balance in summer when ablation exceeds accumulation, and the reverse in winter. If the summer and winter budgets cancel each other out, the glacier appears to be stationary. In other words, the snout of the glacier remains in the same position, although ice is still advancing down the valley from the zone of accumulation into the zone of ablation.

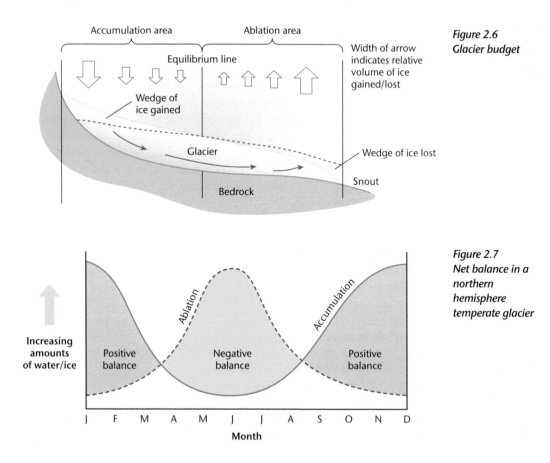

Figure 2.6
Glacier budget

Figure 2.7
Net balance in a northern hemisphere temperate glacier

If the 'supply' begins to exceed the losses, then the snout moves down the valley. This is known as **glacial advance**. When the reverse is true, the glacier begins to shrink in size and the snout moves its position up the valley. This is called **glacial retreat**. Even though the *position* of the snout is moving backwards (retreating), ice continues to move down from the upper parts of the system.

Glacial erosion

Glacial erosion tends to occur in upland regions and is carried out by two main processes:

➤ **Abrasion** occurs where the material the glacier is carrying rubs away at the valley floor and sides. It can be likened to the effect of sandpaper or a giant file. The coarser material may leave scratches on the rock known as **striations**; the finer debris smoothes and polishes rock surfaces. The debris involved in abrasion is often worn down by the process into a very fine material known as **rock flour**.

➤ **Plucking** involves the glacier freezing onto and into rock outcrops. As the ice moves forward, it pulls away masses of rock. Plucking is mainly found at the base of the glacier where pressure and friction often result in the melting of the ice. It is also marked in well-jointed rocks and in those where the surface has been weakened by freeze–thaw action (frost shattering). Plucking leaves a very jagged landscape.

There are two other processes associated with glacial action that produce the debris glaciers use in their erosive action. Both of these are weathering processes:

➤ **Freeze–thaw action/frost shattering** occurs in areas where temperatures rise during the day but drop below freezing at night for a substantial part of the winter. Water which enters cracks in the rocks freezes overnight. Ice occupies more space than water (just under 10% more) and therefore exerts pressure on the crack. As the process continues, the crack widens, and eventually pieces of rock break off (Photograph 2.2). On steep slopes this leads to the collection of material at the base, known as **scree**. In a glacial valley, much of this material falls from the valley side onto the edges of the glacier and some finds its way to the base of the ice via the numerous crevasses which cross the glacier's surface.

➤ **Nivation** is a series of processes that operate underneath a patch of snow, leading to the disintegration of the rock surface (see page 57).

There are a number of major landforms which are mainly produced by glacial erosion. These include corries (cirques), arêtes, pyramidal peaks, glacial troughs, hanging valleys and truncated spurs.

Corries and associated landforms

A **corrie** is an armchair-shaped rock hollow, with a steep back wall and an over-deepened basin with a rock lip. It often contains a small lake (**tarn**). In the British Isles, corries are mainly found on north, northeast and east-facing slopes where reduced insolation allows more accumulation of snow.

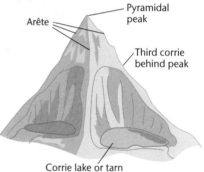

*Photograph 2.2
A frost-shattered
peak in Snowdonia*

Helen Morton

If several corries develop in a highland region, they will jointly produce other erosional features. When two corries lie back to back or alongside each other, enlargement will often leave a narrow, steep-sided ridge between the two hollows, called an **arête**. An example is Striding Edge on Helvellyn in the Lake District. If more than two corries develop on a mountain, the central mass will survive as a **pyramidal peak**, which often takes on a very sharp appearance due to frost shattering (Figure 2.8). An example is the Matterhorn in the Alps.

Corrie formation is the result of several interacting processes (Figure 2.9). The original process is believed to be **nivation**, which acts upon a shallow, preglacial hollow and enlarges it into an embryo corrie (this may take a long time and be spread

Figure 2.8 Arêtes and pyramidal peaks

Figure 2.9 The formation of a corrie

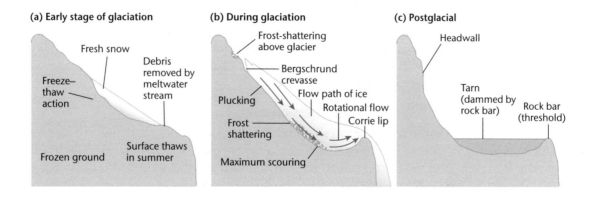

(a) Early stage of glaciation

Fresh snow

Debris removed by meltwater stream

Freeze–thaw action

Frozen ground

Surface thaws in summer

(b) During glaciation

Frost-shattering above glacier

Bergschrund crevasse

Flow path of ice

Rotational flow

Plucking

Corrie lip

Frost shattering

Maximum scouring

(c) Postglacial

Headwall

Tarn (dammed by rock bar)

Rock bar (threshold)

across several glacial periods within an ice age). As the hollow grows, the snow becomes thicker and is increasingly compressed to form firn and then ice. The back wall becomes steeper through the action of **plucking**. The **rotational movement** of the ice, together with the debris supplied by plucking and frost shattering on the back wall, abrades the floor of the hollow which over-deepens the corrie.

As the hollow deepens, the thinner ice at its edge does not produce the same amount of downcutting and a rock lip develops on the threshold of the feature. Some thresholds have their height increased by morainic deposits formed when the glacier's snout was in that position. After the last ice has melted, the corrie fills with meltwater and rainwater to form a small lake (tarn).

Glacial troughs and associated landforms

Glaciers flow down pre-existing river valleys as they move from upland areas. They straighten, widen and deepen these valleys, changing the original V-shaped river feature into the U-shape typical of glacial erosion. The action of ice, combined with huge amounts of meltwater and subglacial debris, has a far greater erosive power than that of water.

As both extending and compressing flow are present, the amount of erosion varies down the valley. Where compressing flow is present, the glacier will over-deepen parts of the valley floor, leading to the formation of **rock basins**. It is also suggested that over-deepening is caused by increased erosion at the confluence of glaciers, areas of weaker rocks or zones of well-jointed rocks.

The major features of glacial troughs are:
➤ usually fairly straight with a wide base and steep sides — a U-shape
➤ stepped long profile with alternating steps and rock basins
➤ some glacial valleys end abruptly at their heads in a steep wall, known as a **trough end**, above which lie a number of corries (Figures 2.10 and 2.11)
➤ rock basins filled with **ribbon lakes**, e.g. Wast Water in the Lake District
➤ over-deepening below the present sea level — this led to the formation of **fjords** when sea levels rose after the ice ages and submerged the lower parts of glacial valleys, for example on the coasts of Norway and southwest New Zealand (Milford Sound)

Figure 2.10
The long profile of a glacial valley: Easedale, Lake District

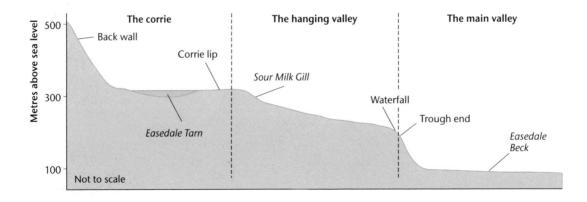

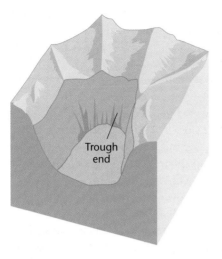

Figure 2.11 A trough end

Jane Buekett

➤ **hanging valleys** on the side of the main valley (e.g. the valley of Church Beck which flows down into Coniston Water in the Lake District). These are either pre-existing tributary river valleys which were not glaciated, or tributary glacial valleys (Figure 2.12 and Photograph 2.3). In tributary glacial valleys there would have been less ice and therefore less erosion than in the main valley. The tributary valley floor was therefore left higher than that of the main valley when the ice retreated

➤ areas of land projecting from the river-valley side (spurs) have been removed by the glacier, producing **truncated spurs**

Photograph 2.3 Lady Bowen waterfall in Milford Sound, New Zealand, is a hanging valley

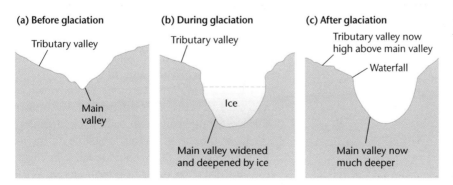

(a) Before glaciation
Tributary valley
Main valley

(b) During glaciation
Tributary valley
Ice
Main valley widened and deepened by ice

(c) After glaciation
Tributary valley now high above main valley
Waterfall
Main valley now much deeper

Figure 2.12 The formation of a hanging valley

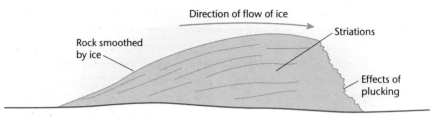

Figure 2.13
The formation of a
roche moutonnée

> small areas of rock on the valley floor are not always completely removed and this leaves **roches moutonnées**. These have an upstream side polished by abrasion and a downstream side made jagged by plucking (Figure 2.13)
> after ice retreat, many glacial troughs were filled with **shallow lakes** which were later infilled, and their sides were modified by frost shattering and the development of screes which altered the glacial U-shape (e.g. Great Langdale, Lake District) (Figure 2.14)

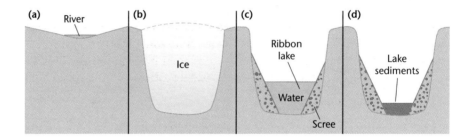

Figure 2.14
The formation of
a glacial valley

Glacial transportation and deposition

Figure 2.15
Transport of debris
within a glacier

As well as eroding the rock over which it is flowing, a valley glacier is also capable of transporting large amounts of debris. Some of this may be derived from rockfalls on the valley side. It is then transported on the surface of the glacier (**supraglacial debris**) or buried within the ice (**englacial**). Material found at the base of the glacier is known as **subglacial** and may include rock fragments that have fallen down crevasses and material eroded at the base. Another way of describing the material carried by the glacier is shown in Figure 2.15. Strictly speaking, **moraine** applies to a type of landform, but many textbooks now use the term in this way.

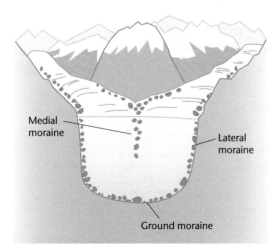

The huge amounts of material carried down by a glacier will eventually be deposited. The bulk of this will be the debris released by the melting of the ice at the snout. It is also possible for the ice to become overloaded with material, reducing its capacity. This may occur near to the snout, as the glacier melts, or in areas where the glacier changes between compressing and extending flow. Material that is deposited directly by the ice is known as **till** or **boulder clay**, although the latter term tends not to be used today.

Till is used to describe an unsorted mixture of rocks, clay and sand that was mainly transported as supraglacial or englacial debris and deposited when the ice melted. Individual stones tend to be angular to sub-angular, unlike river and beach material which is rounded. Till reflects the character of the rocks over which the ice has passed. In the till of south Lancashire, for example, it is possible to find rocks from the Lake District (e.g. Shap granite) and southern Scotland (e.g. riebeckite from Ailsa Craig in the Firth of Clyde). In the till of East Anglia, there are pieces of granite from southern Norway. This indicates not only the passage of the ice but the fact that the sea level must have been considerably lower to allow ice to move over the area that later became the North Sea.

Sometimes it is possible to find a large block of rock that has been moved from one area and deposited in another which has a very different geology. Such a feature is known as an **erratic**.

Two types of glacial deposit are recognised:

➤ **lodgement till** — subglacial material that was deposited by the actively moving glacier. A **drumlin** is a typical feature formed from this material
➤ **ablation till** — produced at the snout when the ice melts. **Terminal (end)**, **push** and **recessional moraines** are typical features produced from ablation till

Drumlins

The term drumlin is derived from the Gaelic word *druim*, meaning a rounded hill (Figure 2.16). The main features of drumlins are:

➤ they are smooth, oval-shaped small hills, often resembling the top half of an egg
➤ they can be as long as 1.5 km (although most are much smaller) and up to 50–60 m in height
➤ they have a steep end known as the **stoss** and a gently sloping end, the **lee**
➤ they are elongated in the direction of ice advance with the stoss at the upstream end and the lee at the downstream end
➤ they are often found in groups known as **swarms** and, given their shape, this is sometimes referred to as a 'basket of eggs topography' (Photograph 2.4)

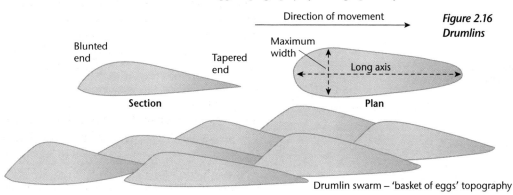

Figure 2.16
Drumlins

Direction of movement

Blunted end

Tapered end

Maximum width

Long axis

Section

Plan

Drumlin swarm – 'basket of eggs' topography

Alan Young

➤ they are formed from unsorted till

➤ they are found on low-land plains such as the central lowlands of Scotland. A well-known swarm is at Hellifield in the Ribble Valley. Many are found at the lower end of glacial valleys

There is some controversy over the origin of drumlins, which are formed underneath the ice. The most widely held view is that they are the result of the ice being overloaded with debris. This reduces its capacity to carry and deposition occurs at the base of the ice. Once this material has been deposited it is streamlined by further ice advance. There could also be pre-existing sediment (older till from a previous glacial advance, for example) that is caught up in the streamlining process.

Photograph 2.4 Risebrigg Hill in North Yorkshire is a drumlin, lying within a swarm of drumlins known as the Hills of Alslack

Moraines

Moraines are lines, or a series of mounds of material, mainly running across glacial valleys. The main type is the terminal or end moraine which is found at the snout of the glacier. **Terminal moraines** show the following features:

➤ they consist of a ridge of material (or several mounds) stretching across a glacial valley

➤ they are elongated at right angles to the direction of ice advance

➤ they are often steep-sided, particularly the ice-contact side, and reach heights of 50–60 m

➤ they are often crescent-shaped, moulded to the form of the snout

➤ they are formed from unsorted ablation material

Terminal moraines are formed when the ice melts during a period of snout standstill and the material it has been carrying is deposited. This is why they contain a range of unsorted material, from clay to boulders.

Figure 2.17 Moraines

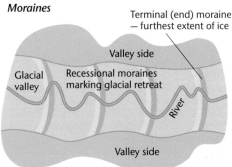

Terminal (end) moraine — furthest extent of ice

Valley side

Glacial valley

Recessional moraines marking glacial retreat

River

Valley side

As the glacier retreats, it is possible for a series of moraines to be formed along the valley, marking points where the retreat halted for some time. These are known as **recessional moraines** (Figure 2.17).

If the climate cools for some time, leading to a glacial advance, a previously deposited moraine may be shunted up into a mound known as a **push moraine**. Such features are recognised by the orientation of individual pieces of rock which may have been pushed upwards from their original horizontal position.

Fluvioglacial processes

Deposition

The melting of ice produces a great deal of water which has the capacity to carry much debris. As the water often flows under considerable pressure, it has a high velocity and is very turbulent. It can therefore pick up and transport a larger amount of material than a normal river of similar size. It is now believed that this water, with its load, is responsible for the creation of subglacial valleys that are often deep and riddled with potholes.

When the meltwater discharge decreases, the resultant loss of energy causes the material being carried by the meltwater to be deposited. As with all water deposition, the heavier particles will be dropped first, resulting in sorting of the material. Deposits may also be found in layers (**stratified**) as a result of seasonal variations in the meltwater flow. The main features produced by fluvioglacial deposition are eskers, kames and the outwash plain (Figure 2.18). Lakes on the outwash plain may have layered deposits in them called varves.

*Figure 2.18
Features of lowland glaciation*

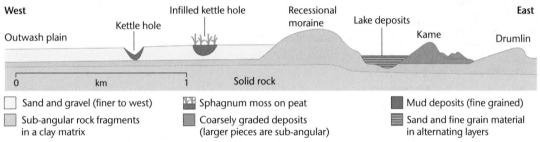

Eskers

Eskers have the following main features:
➤ they are long ridges of material running in the direction of ice advance
➤ they have a sinuous (winding) form, 5–20 m high
➤ they consist of sorted coarse material, usually coarse sands and gravel
➤ they are often stratified (layered)

Eskers are believed to be deposits made by subglacial streams. The channel of the stream will be restricted by ice walls, so there is considerable hydrostatic pressure which enables a large load to be carried and also allows the stream to flow uphill for short distances. This accounts for the fact that some eskers run up gentle gradients. The bed of the channel builds up above the surrounding land, and a ridge is left when the glacier retreats during deglaciation. In some areas, the ridge of an esker is combined with mounds of material, possibly kames (see below). Such a feature is known as a **beaded esker**.

Kames

Kames are mounds of fluvioglacial material (sorted, and often stratified, coarse sands and gravel). They are deltaic deposits left when meltwater flows into a lake dammed up in front of the glacial snout by recessional moraine deposits. When the ice retreats further, the delta kame often collapses. Kame terraces are frequently found along the side of a glacial valley and are the deposits of meltwater streams flowing between the ice and the valley side.

Outwash plains (sandur)

Outwash plains are found in front of the glacier's snout and are deposited by the meltwater streams issuing from the ice. They consist of material that was brought down by the glacier and then picked up, sorted and dropped by running water beyond the position of the ice front. The coarsest material travels the shortest distance and is therefore found near to the glacier; the fine material, such as clay, is carried some distance across the plain before being deposited. The deposits are also layered vertically, which reflects the seasonal flow of meltwater streams.

Meltwater streams that cross the outwash plain are **braided**. This happens as the channels become choked with coarse material because of marked seasonal variations in discharge. On the outwash plain there is often a series of small depressions filled with lakes or marshes. These are known as **kettle holes**. It is believed that they are formed when blocks of ice, washed onto the plain, melt and leave a gap in the sediments. Such holes then fill with water to form small lakes. Aquatic plants become established in the lakes and this leads over time to the development of a marshy area and then peat.

Lakes on the fringe of the ice are filled with deposits that show a distinct layering. A layer of silt lying on top of a layer of sand represents 1 year's deposition in the lake and is known as a **varve** (Figure 2.19). The coarser, lighter-coloured layer is the spring and summer deposition when meltwater is at its peak and the meltwater streams are carrying maximum load. The thinner, darker-coloured and finer silt settles during autumn and through the winter as stream discharge decreases and the very fine sediment in the lake settles to the bottom. Varves are a good indicator of the age of lake sediments and of past climates as the thickness of each varve indicates warmer and colder periods.

Figure 2.19
Varves

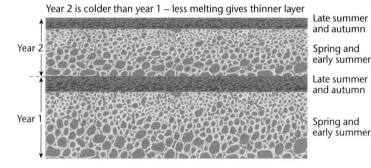

Year 2 is colder than year 1 – less melting gives thinner layer

Year 2

Late summer and autumn

Spring and early summer

Late summer and autumn

Year 1

Spring and early summer

Erosion

Proglacial lakes and overflow channels

Glacial meltwater has great erosive power because of its volume and the large amounts of debris it contains. During deglaciation, lakes develop on the edges of the ice, some occupying large areas. Overflows from these lakes which cross the lowest points of watersheds will create new valleys. When the ice damming these meltwater lakes totally melts, many of the new valleys are left dry, as drainage patterns revert to the preglacial stage. In certain cases, however, the postglacial drainage adopts them, giving rise to new drainage patterns.

Large meltwater lakes of this kind occurred in the English Midlands (Lake Harrison), the Vale of Pickering in North Yorkshire (Lake Pickering) and the Welsh borders (Lake Lapworth, Figure 2.20) at the end of the last glaciation. The River Thames is thought to have followed a much more northerly course before the Quaternary glaciation — its modern course was formed when ice filled the northern part of its basin and forced it to take a different route.

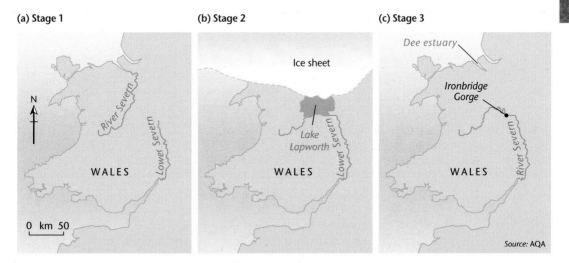

(a) Stage 1　　**(b) Stage 2**　　**(c) Stage 3**

Source: AQA

Figure 2.20
Theoretical stages in the diversion of the River Severn

The River Severn is also believed to have been diverted during the last glaciation. Figure 2.20 shows the stages of this process.

➤ **Stage 1 Preglacial** The River Severn flowed northwards to enter the Irish Sea in what is now the estuary of the River Dee. The present Lower Severn was a shorter river flowing from the Welsh borderlands to the Bristol Channel.

➤ **Stage 2 The last ice age** Ice coming down from the north blocked the River Severn valley to the north. The water from the blocked river formed a huge proglacial lake known as Lake Lapworth. The lake eventually overflowed the watershed to the south to join the original Lower Severn. In the process it cut through a solid rock area, creating the gorge at Ironbridge.

➤ **Stage 3 Deglaciation and the postglacial period** As the ice retreated to the north, the way should have been left open for the two rivers to return to the preglacial situation. The route north, however, was blocked with glacial deposits, and as the Ironbridge Gorge had been cut very deep (lower than the exit to the north), the new drainage adopted this rather than its former route. The River Severn now flows from central Wales to the Bristol Channel.

Periglacial processes

Periglacial areas are those which, although not actually glaciated, are exposed to very cold conditions with intense frost action and the development of permanently frozen ground or permafrost. At present, areas such as the tundra of northern Russia, Alaska and northern Canada, together with high mountainous areas such as the Alps, experience a periglacial climate. In the past, however, as ice sheets and glaciers spread, many areas which are now temperate were subject to such conditions.

The climate of periglacial regions is marked by persistently low temperatures. Summers are short but temperatures can sometimes reach above 15°C. In winter, the temperature remains well below zero and in some areas may fall below −50°C at times.

Permafrost

Where subsoil temperatures remain below zero for at least 2 consecutive years, permafrost will occur. Today, it is estimated that permafrost covers around a quarter of the Earth's surface. When summer temperatures rise above freezing, the surface layer thaws from the surface downwards to form an **active layer**. The thickness of this layer depends upon local conditions, but may extend to 4 m. As the ice in this layer melts, large volumes of water are released. This water is unable to drain through the permafrost layer and, as low temperatures do not encourage much evaporation, the surface becomes very wet. On slopes as gentle as 2°, saturation of this upper layer encourages soil movement downslope, a periglacial process known as **solifluction** (see below).

There are three kinds of permafrost (Figure 2.21):

➤ **Continuous permafrost** is found in the coldest regions, reaching deep into the surface layers. In Siberia today, it is estimated that the permafrost can reach down over 1,500 m. In the very coldest areas, there is hardly any melting of the uppermost layer.

➤ **Discontinuous permafrost** occurs in regions that are slightly warmer, where the ground is not frozen to such great depths. On average the frozen area will extend 20–30 m below the ground surface, although it can reach 45 m. There are also gaps in the permafrost under rivers, lakes and near the sea.

➤ **Sporadic permafrost** is found where mean annual temperatures are around or just below freezing point. In these places, permafrost occurs only in isolated spots where the local climate is cold enough to prevent complete thawing of the soil during the summer.

Figure 2.21
Variations in the
depth of permafrost

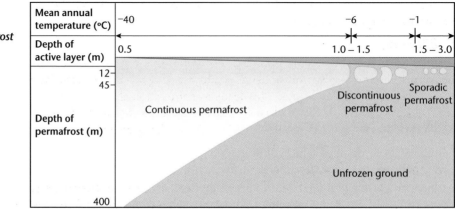

Mean annual temperature (°C)	−40		−6	−1
Depth of active layer (m)	0.5		1.0 – 1.5	1.5 – 3.0

AQA AS Geography

Periglacial processes

There is a clear link between the landforms of periglacial regions and the processes that form them. The main processes are described below.

Freeze–thaw action (frost shattering)

This process has already been described on page 46 because it provides a great deal of the erosive material in glaciers. In periglacial areas, **screes** develop at the foot of slopes as a result of frost shattering. On relatively flat areas, extensive spreads of angular boulders are left, which are known as **blockfield** or **felsenmeer** (sea of rocks) (Figure 2.22).

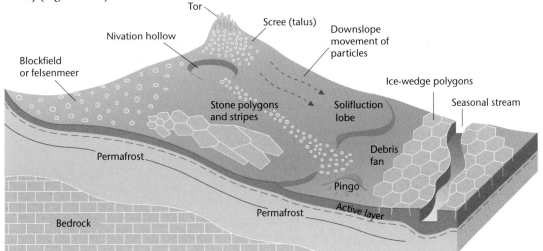

Figure 2.22
A periglacial landscape

Nivation

Nivation takes place beneath patches of snow in hollows, particularly on north- and east-facing slopes. Freeze–thaw action and possibly chemical weathering, operating under the snow, cause the underlying rock to disintegrate. As some of the snow melts in spring, the weathered particles are moved downslope by the meltwater and by solifluction (see below). Over some period of time, this leads to the formation of **nivation hollows** which, when enlarged, can be the beginnings of a corrie (cirque).

Solifluction

When the active layer thaws in summer, excessive lubrication reduces the friction between soil particles. Even on slopes as shallow as 2°, parts of the active layer then begin to move downslope. This leads to solifluction sheets or lobes — rounded, tongue-like features often forming terraces on the sides of valleys. Solifluction was widespread in southern Britain during the Quaternary ice age, and such deposits are often known here as head.

Frost heave

As the active layer starts to refreeze, ice crystals begin to develop. They increase the volume of the soil and cause an upward expansion of the soil surface. Frost heave is most significant in fine-grained material and, as it is uneven, it forms small domes on the surface.

Within the fine-grained material there are stones which, because of their lower specific heat capacity, heat up and cool faster than the surrounding finer material.

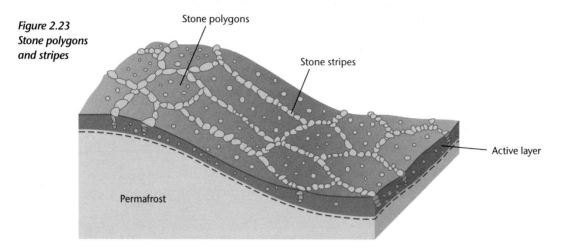

**Figure 2.23
Stone polygons
and stripes**

Stone polygons

Stone stripes

Active layer

Permafrost

Cold penetrating from the surface passes through the stones faster than through the surrounding material. This means that the soil immediately beneath a stone is likely to freeze and expand before the other material, pushing the stone upwards until it reaches the surface. On small domes, the larger stones move outwards, effectively sorting the material which, when viewed from above, takes on a pattern. This **patterned ground** on gentler slopes takes the form of **stone polygons**, but where the ground is steeper (slopes exceeding 6°), the stones move downhill to form **stone stripes** (Figure 2.23).

Groundwater freezing

Where the permafrost is thin or discontinuous, water is able to seep into the upper layers of the ground and then freeze. The expansion of this ice causes the overlying sediments to heave upwards into a dome-shaped feature known as a **pingo** which may rise as high as 50 m. This type of pingo is referred to as an open-system or East Greenland type.

In low-lying areas with continuous permafrost on the site of small lakes, groundwater can be trapped by freezing from above and the permafrost beneath. As this water freezes it will expand, pushing up the overlying sediments into a closed-system pingo or Mackenzie type. It is named after the Mackenzie delta in northern Canada where over 1,000 pingos have been recorded. Sometimes the surface of a pingo will collapse, leaving a hollow that is filled with meltwater.

Ground contraction

The refreezing of the active layer during winter causes the soil to contract. Cracks open up on the surface in a similar way to cracks on the beds of dried-up lakes. During melting the following summer, the cracks open again and fill with meltwater. As the meltwater contains fine sediment, this also begins to fill the crack. The process occurs repeatedly through the cycle of winter and summer, widening and deepening the crack to form an **ice wedge** which eventually, over a period of hundreds of years, can become at least 1 m wide and 2–3 m deep (Figure 2.24). The cracking produces a pattern on the surface which, when viewed from above, is similar to the polygons produced by frost heaving. These are therefore known as **ice-wedge polygons**.

*Figure 2.24
The formation of
ice wedges*

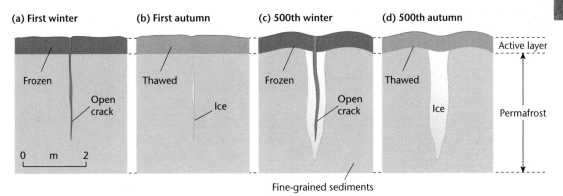

Water and wind action

Owing to the open and sparsely vegetated periglacial landscape, rates of erosion caused by water and wind can be high.

Water erosion is highly seasonal, occurring mainly in spring and summer when the active layer melts. This can cause short periods of very high discharge in rivers, bringing about far more fluvial erosion than would be expected given the relatively low mean precipitation. Drainage is typically **braided** because of the high amount of debris being carried by meltwater streams.

Unobstructed **winds** blowing across periglacial landscapes can reach high velocities. They cause erosion through abrasion and dislodge the fine unconsolidated materials that cover the area. The effects of erosion can be seen in grooved and polished rock surfaces and in stones shaped by the wind, known as **ventifacts**. The fine material of the outwash plain is picked up by the wind and carried long distances to be deposited elsewhere as extensive areas of **loess**. Loess is found in many parts of North America and Eurasia, south of the boundary of the Pleistocene ice sheets. In England, loess deposits, rarely more than 2 m in depth, cover parts of East Anglia and the London Basin where they are known as brickearth deposits. In China, loess deposits are widespread and in places reach depths of over 300 m.

Human activity in cold environments

Local economies of the indigenous population

The traditional economic activity of the indigenous population of the tundra was hunting and fishing. In the north of North America, the main activity of the **Inuit** was hunting seals, which provided them with meat, oil and skins. Fishing

Bryan and Cherry Alexander

*Photograph 2.5
A Sami woman
reindeer herder at
a round-up in
northern Norway*

(including whales) was also a major activity. Some groups occasionally hunted polar bears and smaller mammals. Mobility was a key to their continued existence. Sledges were pulled by teams of dogs over the icy areas; kayaks, and sometimes larger boats, were used on water. The number of Inuit was always small in terms of the vast area in which they lived, so very little pressure was put on the environment, which remained relatively undisturbed.

In the north of Europe, the **Sami** (Photograph 2.5) followed the seasonal movements of the herds of wild reindeer that provided them with most of the food and materials that they needed. Fishing was used to supplement their diet. Reindeer spend the winter period in the boreal forests living on tree mosses and bark. They move back into the tundra during the summer. Like the Inuit, the Lapps lived in an environment that provided all that they needed but which could only support a low-density population.

Both Inuit and Lapps developed strategies to survive in a difficult natural environment. The ways of life that they adopted were totally **sustainable**.

Resource exploitation by newcomers

From the seventeenth century onwards, the resources of tundra areas began to be exploited by outsiders. The major forms of economic activity that occurred included sealing, whaling, trapping for fur, and mining, particularly for gold. Mining led to the establishment of permanent settlements whereas the other activities tended to be temporary or seasonal.

In the last 100 years or so, exploitation of the tundra has been on a much larger scale and has had a dramatic impact on the lifestyle of the indigenous populations. Activities include mining (particularly for oil), production of hydro-electric power (HEP), fishing, and, latterly, tourism. Military, strategic and geo-political concerns have given these areas increasing importance, particularly in

Alaska and northern Russia. Strategic interest in the northern areas of North America dates back to the Second World War. With the threat of Japanese invasion, the USA constructed the Alaska Highway, which runs northwest from Dawson Creek in Canada to Fairbanks in Alaska. The purpose was to carry heavy weapons to the north. The rise of the USSR after the Second World War, and the beginning of the Cold War, increased the strategic significance of Alaska and northern Canada. Such is the involvement of the armed forces that military personnel have, at times, made up at least 25% of the population of Alaska. Numerous roads, air-force bases, radar and early-warning stations have been built. However, the military presence has led to little permanent settlement beyond the main bases, which are maintained from outside and are not dependent on local resources.

Human activities and the physical environment

The physical environment has an undoubted impact on human activities. In turn, human activities in such cold regions can have a great impact on the physical environment. The harsh conditions of cold environments present a challenge for human occupation and development. These conditions include:

➤ very low temperatures
➤ short summers and therefore short growing seasons
➤ low precipitation
➤ thin, stony, poorly developed soils
➤ permafrost
➤ surface thaw in summer leading to waterlogging
➤ snow lying for long periods
➤ blizzards

Indigenous peoples have adapted their ways of life to cope with the climate and to make the most of the limited resources. Establishing permanent settlements and developing activities such as mining has required major technical advances, primarily because the permafrost creates a unique set of problems for construction work and engineering.

Problems are caused when vegetation is cleared from the ground surface. This reduces insulation and results, in summer, in the deepening of the active layer. Even minor disturbances, such as vehicle tracks, can greatly increase melting, because the vegetation is very slow to re-establish itself.

Buildings speed up this process by spreading heat into the ground. The thawing of ground ice leads to the development of **thermokarst**, a landscape of topographic depressions characterised by extensive areas of irregular, hummocky ground interspersed with waterlogged hollows. The damage caused by this form of ground subsidence can be seen in tilted and fractured older buildings and in damage to roads, railways and airfield runways.

In recent years, many new methods of construction have been employed to protect the permafrost and prevent subsidence. Although they are successful, these methods are more expensive than conventional construction, adding to the costs of living in the region, and continual maintenance is often necessary. Some of the methods include the following:

Photograph 2.6 Buildings on stilts and insulated ducting for water and power in Prudhoe Bay, Alaska

Bryan and Cherry Alexander

➤ Smaller buildings, such as houses, can be elevated above the ground on piles driven into the permafrost. The gap below the building allows air to circulate and remove heat that would otherwise be conducted into the ground.

➤ Larger structures can be built upon aggregate pads, which are layers of coarse sand and gravel, 1–2 m thick. This substitutes the insulating effect of vegetation and reduces the transfer of heat from building to ground. These pads can also be placed beneath roads, railways and landing strips.

➤ In large settlements **utilidors** (Figure 2.25) have been built. A utilidor is an insulated box, elevated above the ground, that carries water supplies, heating pipes and sewers between buildings. Pipes cannot be buried underground because of the damage that would be caused by freezing and thawing in the upper soil layers.

Figure 2.25 A utilidor

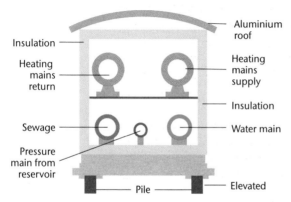

Insulation

Heating mains return

Sewage

Pressure main from reservoir

Pile

Aluminium roof

Heating mains supply

Insulation

Water main

Elevated

Apart from the production of thermokarst, human impacts on the physical environment include:

➤ hunting — over-exploitation

➤ transport — risks of spillages, road vehicles damaging the ground

➤ tourism — vegetation removal, litter and waste not easily degraded

➤ general air pollution

These factors add to the effects of global warming, melting the snow and ice of the region.

Wilderness areas

Much of the Arctic tundra and Antarctica typify the common perception of wild and natural places. Their remoteness and the extremes of physical processes keep them inaccessible to mass tourism and the excesses of economic development. Conservationists believe wilderness areas have intrinsic value and possess outstanding qualities that are worth conserving for the future. Areas such as these have an aesthetic value for people seeking spiritual refreshment and contemplation. Scientifically, they are important because:

➤ there is a need to maintain the gene pool of wild organisms to ensure that genetic variety is maintained
➤ animal communities can be studied in their natural environment in such regions
➤ wilderness is a natural laboratory for the scientific study of ecosystems
➤ there is a need for pure natural systems to be used as a yardstick against which managed or mismanaged systems can be compared

There are good reasons for conserving wilderness regions, but they also often contain a range of exploitable resources. Pressure for the development of these resources comes from national and transnational groups that require both energy sources and raw materials to support industrial growth. Balancing developmental pressures against the need to conserve the essential values of wilderness is the increasingly difficult task of management. Sustainable development has an important role to play here but there is disagreement about how it may be successfully applied in many wilderness environments.

In 1964, the Wilderness Act in the USA designated a number of wilderness areas. The largest number of designated areas in any state is in Alaska, which instituted its own wilderness legislation, the National Interest Lands Conservation Act, in 1980.

A fragile environment

The tundra, because of its climate and limited productivity, is considered to be a fragile environment. There are a number of reasons for this.

The slow rate of plant growth means that any disruption to the ecosystem takes a long time to be corrected. Some scientists estimate that it could take over 50 years to return an area of tundra to its former state after interference. (It can take this length of time before tyre tracks are completely revegetated.) The low productivity and limited species diversity mean that the plants are very specialised and any disruption causes difficulty when it comes to regeneration. In such circumstances, species have great difficulty in adapting to a changed environment.

Wide fluctuations occur in the amount of energy held in each trophic level of food chains because population numbers change rapidly. For example, variations in the numbers of lemmings and arctic hares, both of which are liable to short-term and long-term fluctuations, have consequences for the populations of their predators, such as arctic foxes and snowy owls.

Disruption to the functioning of the biome has long-term implications. This is why there has been so much concern over the proposed exploitation of resources such as the oil reserves of north Alaska that fall within the Arctic National Wildlife Refuge.

Case study **The trans-Alaskan oil pipeline**

In 1968, vast deposits of oil were discovered on the North Slope of Alaska in the area of Prudhoe Bay. The removal of the oil after extraction from the ground was a major problem, because the presence of pack ice in the seas to the north meant that the oil could not be removed by tanker (two failed supertanker attempts were made). The alternative was to transport the oil by pipeline to the southern shores of Alaska, in particular to the ice-free port of Valdez. Lobbying by environmentalists at first prevented construction of the pipeline. They argued that the tundra environment should be protected. There were real concerns and uncertainties about the pipeline's design, route and ecological impact. It could not be buried in the ground because the warm oil would melt the permafrost. There were also concerns about earthquakes, avalanche hazards and animals crossing the pipeline.

However, oil demand in the USA was increasing and exploitation of this, the biggest oil field in the country, was seen as essential, particularly as it would reduce dependence upon supplies from the politically unstable Middle East.

The trans-Alaskan pipeline took over 5 years to design and 3 years to build. The environmental lobby ensured that the oil companies were not allowed to use the cheapest option. It has been estimated that the total cost of the operation

was around $8 billion. The pipeline has a maximum daily throughput of 1.4 million barrels and the oil is pumped through at a temperature of 65°C. For some of its length it crosses permafrost-free areas or regions where the permafrost sediment is coarse grained. Such surface deposits are free draining and less susceptible to subsidence on thawing and so the pipeline can be buried in the conventional way. For most of its length, though, the pipeline incorporates features designed to cope with the permafrost conditions:

■ Where the pipeline crosses areas of fine-grained permafrost sediment (for over half of its length), it

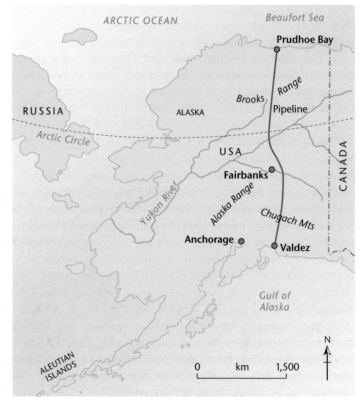

Figure 2.26 The route of the trans-Alaskan oil pipeline

is **elevated above the ground** so that heat from the line is not conducted into the ground surface. If this happened thawing of the permafrost would cause subsidence.

■ The elevated structure also allows the pipeline to **shift sideways** on its supports as an extra protection against damage caused by ground movement.

■ The pilings are specially designed to **resist being jacked up** by successive years of frost heave.

■ The line itself is built in a **zigzag pattern** so that it able to adjust to ground movements caused by either temperature changes or earthquakes.

■ The pipe is buried where it passes under roads, through avalanche-sensitive areas and where it could block major caribou migration routes. Here, the pipe is covered by **thick insulation**. In a few areas (only 6.5 km of its length) **refrigeration units** have been installed to keep the ground frozen.

Case study | **Antarctica and the Southern Ocean**

The discovery of the islands of the Southern Ocean in the eighteenth century led to the start of exploitation of the area. A number of economic activities have taken place in the region.

Sealing began in the eighteenth century on and around the island of South Georgia. By 1800, the fur seals of South Georgia were wiped out and interest then centred on the South Shetland Islands. Within 3 years, over 300,000 seals had been killed and the population had been virtually eradicated. This was exploitation at its worst, with no thought given to future development.

Whaling began in the nineteenth century. The main targets were blue and right whales; the main products, oil and whalebone (baleen). As the whale population of the North Atlantic became reduced by massive exploitation, the whalers turned their attention to the Southern Ocean. Whalers sailed from several countries in the northern hemisphere, particularly Norway, the USA and the UK.

Whaling was a highly profitable business and whaling stations were established on South Georgia and the South Shetlands. In 1904, the Norwegians developed Grytviken on South Georgia, which at its height employed over 300 people. The range of products increased to include meat meal, bonemeal, meat extract and, in later years, frozen whale meat. Grytviken was abandoned in 1965 because whale stocks were becoming seriously depleted and whaling was no longer commercially viable. The

establishment of the International Whaling Convention in 1946 eventually led to an end to most whaling in 1985. Most, but not all, whaling nations agreed to halt the slaughter, as stocks of many species were running dangerously low.

Fishing has now replaced whaling in the area. In the 1960s, Russian ships began to exploit the Southern Ocean for a number of fish species, including the Antarctic rock cod. Concerns have been expressed recently over the number of fish being taken, particularly fishing for krill by the Russians and Japanese. Krill underpins the whole of the Southern Ocean food web and scientists do not know how many krill can be taken before the ecosystem is harmed.

Antarctic Treaty

The issue of **sovereignty** was resolved in December 1959, when 12 nations signed up to the Antarctic Treaty. This formalised and guaranteed free access and research rights so that all countries could work together for the common causes of scientific research and exchange of ideas.

The treaty further stated that Antarctica should be used for peaceful purposes only, prohibiting activities of a military nature and subjecting all areas and stations to onsite inspection. The treaty prohibits nuclear explosions and the dumping of nuclear waste. In addition, the 1991 Protocol on Environmental Protection requires that comprehensive assessment and monitoring should be carried out to minimise human impacts on the fragile ecosystems of the region. This protocol also bans all mineral resource activity in Antarctica, including exploration of the continental shelf. The treaty now has 45 signatories representing around two-thirds of the world's population.

Tourism

Antarctica is an unusual **tourist destination** in that it is not populated, except by scientists at a small number of permanent research stations. Polar scientists have always been concerned about tourism to the continent because they fear it will interfere with their scientific work and destroy the near-perfect environment. On the other hand, committed tourists can be supportive of such scientific work, publicising it and helping to raise funds.

Antarctic tourism is of three types:

- camping trips for naturalists, photographers and journalists
- ship-board visits, largely by cruise ships but also by converted Russian ice breakers. Most start either in Ushuaia (Argentina), which is the nearest port, or in Port Stanley (the Falkland Islands)

- over-flights — these have restarted after an interval of nearly 20 years following the crash of an Air New Zealand DC10 on Mount Erebus, in which all passengers died

Tourists go to Antarctica to see the glacial landscapes and the wildlife, particularly seals, whales and penguins. They also go for the remoteness and isolation and the chance to test themselves in adverse weather conditions. Tourists may be interested in historic sites, such as McMurdo Sound with its huts dating from the Scott and Shackleton expeditions. Tourism is concentrated in the short southern summer period, from mid-November to March.

Ship-borne tourism in Antarctica takes the form of 'expeditions'. This concept is reinforced by the issue of polar-style clothing. Most of the ships are comparatively small, with an average capacity of between 50 and 100 people. Therefore, the ship-based programme of educational lectures by Antarctic specialists creates a cohesive and motivated group. Tourists are carefully briefed on the require-

Photograph 2.7 Emperor penguins and chicks inspect a tourist, Antarctica

Bryan and Cherry Alexander

ments of the Antarctic Treaty and the environmental protocol. They are informed of the code of conduct in terms of behaviour ashore, adherence to health and safety requirements and rules about wildlife observation. When visiting any one of around 200 possible sites (tourists are free to land anywhere except at designated preservation areas or near active scientific research sites), the overall group is divided into boatloads of around 20, each led by an expert guide. Each site may be visited only every 2 or 3 days.

Research on the impacts of tourism is being undertaken by the Scott Polar Research Institute in Cambridge, particularly at the high-pressure sites of King George Island and Elephant Island, and at all 200 approved landing places. Some findings have already been published and they show that the Antarctic environment has been little affected:

■ Antarctic tourism is a well-run industry, living up to its sound record for environmental concern.
■ Guidelines are widely accepted by operators and tourists alike, but they need updating to include the environmental protocol of the UN.
■ Damage to vegetation (especially the fragile moss mat) is due to natural causes, such as breeding seals. Tourists are usually scrupulous in not walking on areas of fragile vegetation.
■ No litter is attributed to tourists; they tend to be concerned about the waste they see around the scientific research stations.

■ Virtually no stress is caused to penguins by tourists visiting their breeding colonies. However, tern colonies seem to suffer from disturbance.
■ Seals are largely indifferent to the presence of humans. Tourists who follow wildlife guidelines cause no impact.
■ Out of 200 landing sites surveyed, only 5% showed any wear and tear. These need to be rested, but at present there is no mechanism to implement this type of management.

Despite these encouraging signs, there are some concerns:

■ The Antarctic ecosystem is extremely fragile — disturbances leave their imprint for a long time (footprints on moss can remain for decades).
■ The summer tourist season coincides with peak wildlife breeding periods.
■ The land-based installations and wildlife are clustered in the few ice-free locations on the continent.
■ The demand for fresh water is difficult to meet.
■ Visitor pressure is felt on cultural heritage sites such as old whaling and sealing stations and early exploration bases.
■ There is some evidence that over-flying by light planes and helicopters is causing some stress to breeding colonies of penguins and other birds.
■ The unique legal status of Antarctica makes enforcement of any code of behaviour difficult.

Assessment exercises

1 a Photograph A shows an upland area in the British Isles.
   (i) Using the grid provided, identify and locate three landforms in the photograph that have been produced mainly by glacial erosion. (3 marks)
   (ii) Choose one of the landforms you have identified in (i) and explain how glacial processes produced that landform. (6 marks)

Photograph A

b In the uplands of the British Isles, corrie basins tend to have a dominant orientation (direction faced).
   (i) What is that direction?
   (ii) How may their orientation have helped their formation? (6 marks)
c Explain why Antarctica needs protection from development. (15 marks)
(30 marks)

2 a Figure A shows the typical features left behind on a lowland area after the retreat of a glacier or ice sheet.

  (i) In which direction did the ice advance?

  (ii) Which major feature of glacial/fluvioglacial deposition is not included in Figure A?

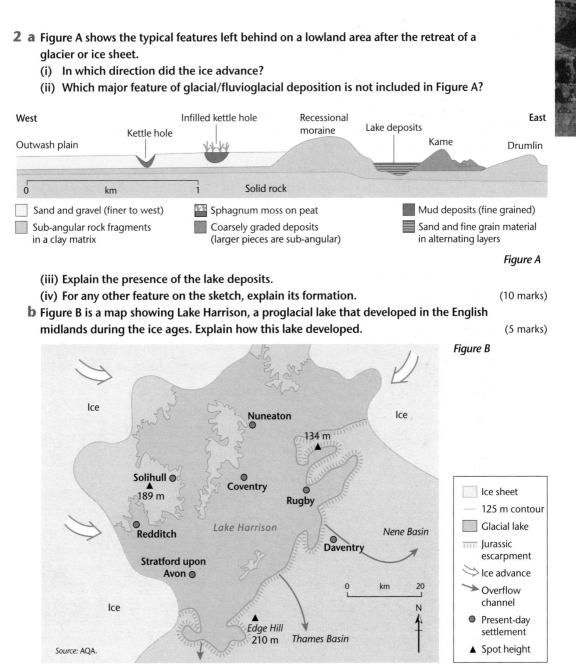

Figure A

  (iii) Explain the presence of the lake deposits.

  (iv) For any other feature on the sketch, explain its formation. (10 marks)

b Figure B is a map showing Lake Harrison, a proglacial lake that developed in the English midlands during the ice ages. Explain how this lake developed. (5 marks)

Figure B

c To what extent should cold environments be considered as fragile? How far does this affect their development? (15 marks)

(30 marks)

Coastal environments

Coastlines are important to the human race. Fifty per cent of the world's population live on coastal plains and in other locations with easy access to the sea. The coastline itself consists of a series of different zones in which specific conditions prevail that depend on factors such as tides, wave action and the depth of the sea. Figure 3.1 illustrates how these zones relate to each other:

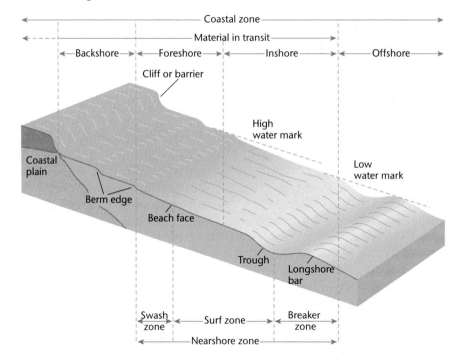

Figure 3.1
Coastal zones

➤ **Backshore** is the area between the high water mark (HWM) and the landward limit of marine activity. Changes normally take place here only during storm activity.
➤ **Foreshore** is the area lying between the HWM and the low water mark (LWM). It is the most important zone for marine processes in times that are not influenced by storm activity.
➤ **Inshore** is the area between the LWM and the point where waves cease to have any influence on the land beneath them.
➤ **Offshore** is the area beyond the point where waves cease to impact upon the sea bed and in which activity is limited to deposition of sediments.

There are a number of factors that determine the shape, form and appearance of a coastline:

➤ **wave** size, frequency, type, energy produced and direction
➤ **local sea currents**
➤ **longshore drift**
➤ **tides**
➤ **depth of water offshore**
➤ type and amount of **sediments offshore**
➤ **rock type and structure**
➤ **sub-aerial processes** — runoff, weathering and mass movement
➤ **land-based agents of erosion** — rivers and glaciers
➤ **climate and weather**
➤ **fetch** — the distance over open sea that a wind blows to generate waves; the longer the fetch, the greater the potential for large waves
➤ **long-term sea-level change** — eustatic (worldwide) and isostatic (local)
➤ **coastal ecosystems** — sand dunes, salt marshes and mangroves
➤ the presence of **coral**
➤ **human activity**

Coastlines are **dynamic** environments that are undergoing continual change. In the short term, tides, waves and longshore drift change the shape, form and appearance of elements of a coastline. Changes in sea level bring about long-term change. The shape of the British Isles has altered continually over the last few thousand years. At the end of the Pleistocene glaciation, Britain was joined to the rest of the European continent. Rising sea levels from around 9,000 years ago eventually formed the Straits of Dover, much of the English Channel and the North Sea (Figure 3.2).

The position of the coastline is continually changing. In some places, such as Christchurch Bay (Photograph 3.1 and the case study of Barton-on-Sea, later in this chapter) land is being lost to wave erosion and sub-aerial processes. In other parts, land is being gained by deposition. In Roman times, the Holderness coastline of Yorkshire was several kilometres further east of its present position. However, erosion of the mainly boulder-clay cliffs has resulted in the loss of 29 villages with many modern settlements surviving only because of extensive coastal protection schemes. At the present time, the small village of Mappleton is the most threatened by this action.

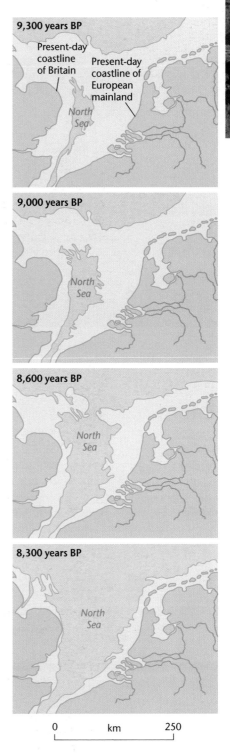

Figure 3.2 The growth of the North Sea

Photograph 3.1 *Cliff collapse in Christchurch Bay, just to the east of Highcliffe, in Dorset*

There have been repeated warnings that other parts of the east coast of England could be threatened if the sea breaks through coastal defences. In East Anglia in the winter of 2004, there was a real threat that this would happen in the Aldeburgh area and that the line of the coast would be completely redrawn. Even though the sea did not break through, inhabitants of the area remain pessimistic about the future. The attitude of the Department for Environment Food and Rural Affairs (DEFRA) is that there is not enough money to meet every flood and coastal defence need and, as the Aldeburgh area is sparsely populated, the value of property defended is not high enough to justify the cost. The newspaper extract from October 2004 (Figure 3.3) shows the extent to which the coastline would be redrawn in this area if the sea were to break through the coastal defences.

Figure 3.3
Extract from the
Daily Telegraph,
October 2004

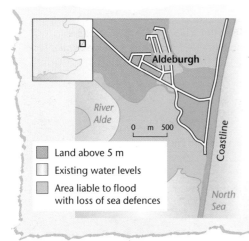

A ldeburgh could become an island and the Suffolk coastline could alter as far south as Felixstowe if the sea breaks through obsolete sea defences this winter, experts have told local residents.

Among the features under threat if the sea wall is breached at Bawdsey is a line of four Martello towers, built to fend off invasion by Napoleon, including one that is now at 'imminent risk' of sliding into the sea.

The Environment Agency accepts the need for repairs but says the area is too thinly populated for funding.

The coastal system

A coastline is regarded as an **open** system because inputs are received, and outputs are transferred, across the boundary of the system.

   Inputs consist of:

➤ **Energy** to drive the system. This is provided by waves, winds, tides and currents. The input is irregularly boosted by storm surges and tidal waves. **Spatial variations** in energy result from variations in the strength of the wind, the fetch, and the number and intensity of storms. Storms are most frequent in mid-latitudes where low-pressure systems often dominate and in the tropics where low-pressure systems (tropical storms/hurricanes) occur. There are also **temporal variations** on a seasonal and even a daily scale. For example, in the mid-latitudes depressions are more frequent in winter whereas in the part of the tropics that is in the northern hemisphere, the hurricane season is in late summer and autumn.

➤ **Sediment**, provided within the system from the erosion of coastlines by waves. However, most sediment comes from outside the system. It is brought mainly by rivers, which transport a whole range of different sediments from land to sea. Weathering and mass-wasting also contribute material from cliff-faces.

➤ **Changes in sea level**.

➤ **Human activities**.

Coastline **processes** are mainly those associated with erosion, constructive wave action, longshore drift and the wind. Longshore drift is the main agent that relocates materials from coastlines dominated by erosion processes to areas where depositional landforms are constructed, such as beaches, spits and bars. Wind can also carry material, in this case from the shoreline inland.

   The **outputs** of the system are:

➤ coastal **landforms**, both erosive and depositional

➤ accumulations of **sediment** above the tidal limit

➤ loss of **wave energy**

Waves

Waves (Figure 3.4) are created by transfer of energy from the wind blowing over the sea surface. The energy acquired by waves depends upon the strength of the wind, the length of time it is blowing and the distance over which it blows (**fetch**). As waves approach shallow water, friction with the sea bed increases and the base of the wave begins to slow down. This has the effect of increasing the height and steepness of the wave until the upper part plunges forward and the wave 'breaks' onto the beach (Figure 3.5). The rush of water up the beach is known as **swash** and any water running back down the beach into the sea is the **backwash**. Waves can be described as constructive or destructive.

Figure 3.4
Wave terminology

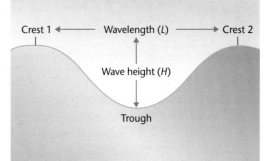

Figure 3.5
Wave movement

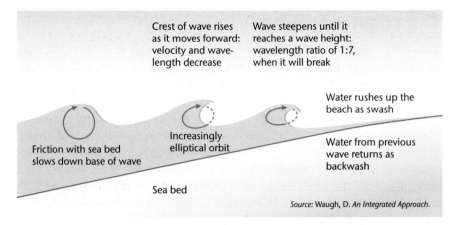

Crest of wave rises as it moves forward: velocity and wave-length decrease

Wave steepens until it reaches a wave height: wavelength ratio of 1:7, when it will break

Water rushes up the beach as swash

Increasingly elliptical orbit

Friction with sea bed slows down base of wave

Water from previous wave returns as backwash

Sea bed

Source: Waugh, D. An Integrated Approach.

Constructive waves

Constructive waves (Figure 3.6) tend to be low waves, but with a long wavelength, often up to 100 m. They have a low frequency of around six to eight per minute. As they approach the beach, the wave front steepens only slowly, giving a gentle spill onto the beach surface. Swash rapidly loses volume and energy as water percolates through the beach material. This tends to give a very weak backwash which has insufficient force to pull sediment off the beach or to impede swash from the next wave. As a consequence, material is slowly, but constantly, moved up the beach, leading to the formation of ridges (**berms**).

Figure 3.6
A constructive wave

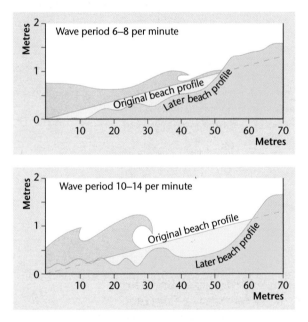

Wave period 6–8 per minute

Original beach profile

Later beach profile

Metres

Wave period 10–14 per minute

Original beach profile

Later beach profile

Metres

Figure 3.7
A destructive wave

Destructive waves

Destructive waves (Figure 3.7) are high waves with a steep form and a high frequency (10–14 per minute). As they approach the beach, they rapidly steepen and, when breaking, they plunge down. This creates a powerful backwash as there is little forward movement of water. It also inhibits the swash from the next wave. Very little material is moved up the beach, leaving the backwash to pull material away. Destructive waves are commonly associated with steeper beach profiles. The force of each wave may project some shingle well towards the rear of the beach where it forms a large ridge known as the **storm beach**.

Effects of waves

Most beaches are subject to the alternating action of constructive and destructive waves. Constructive waves build up the beach and result in a steeper beach profile. This encourages waves to become more destructive (as destructive waves are associated with steeper profiles). With time, though, destructive waves move material back towards the sea, reducing the beach angle and encouraging more constructive waves. So the pattern repeats itself. This type of **negative feedback** should encourage a state of **equilibrium**, but this is impossible as other factors, such as wind strength and direction, are not constant.

When waves approach a coastline that is not of a regular shape, they are **refracted** and become increasingly parallel to the coastline. Figure 3.8 shows a headland separating two bays. As each wave nears the coast, it tends to drag in the shallow water which meets the headland. This causes the wave to become higher and steeper with a shorter wavelength. That part of the wave in deeper water moves forward faster, causing the wave to bend. The overall effect is that wave energy becomes concentrated on the headland, causing greater erosion. The low-energy waves spill into the bay, resulting in beach deposition. As the waves pile against the headland, there may be a slight local rise in sea level that results in a longshore current from the headland, moving some of the eroded material towards the bays and contributing to the build-up of the beaches.

Figure 3.8
Wave refraction

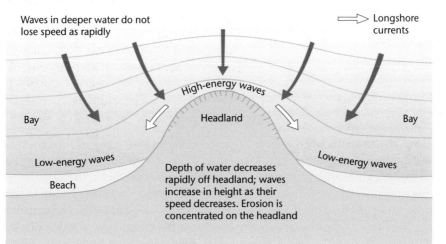

Tides

Tides are the periodic rise and fall in the level of the sea. They are caused by the gravitational pull of the sun and moon, although the moon has much the greatest influence because it is nearer. The moon pulls water towards it, creating a high tide, and there is a compensatory bulge on the opposite side of the Earth (Figure 3.9). In the areas of the world between the two bulges, the tide is at its lowest.

As the moon orbits the Earth, the high tides follow it. Twice in a lunar month, when the moon, sun and Earth are in a straight line, the tide-raising force is strongest. This produces the highest monthly tidal range or **spring tide**. Also twice a month, the moon and sun are positioned at 90° to each other in relation to the Earth. This alignment gives the lowest monthly tidal range, or **neap tide**.

Figure 3.9
The causes of tides

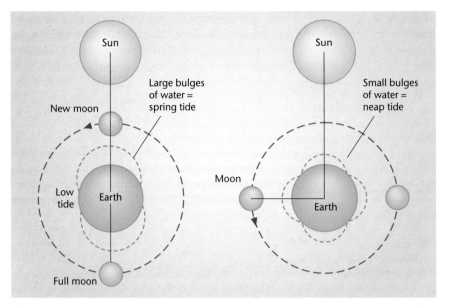

Tidal range can be a significant factor in the development of a coastline. Along the coasts of the Mediterranean Sea, tidal ranges are low. This restricts wave action to a narrow width in the coastal zone. In parts of the British Isles, however, tidal ranges are high. This gives a wide zone of wave attack, resulting in the formation of wide wave-cut platforms in many places.

Storm surges

There are occasions when meteorological conditions giving rise to strong winds can produce much higher water levels than those at high tide. One area affected by this phenomenon is the North Sea. Depressions over the North Sea produce low-pressure conditions that have the effect of raising sea levels. Strong winds drive waves ahead of the storm, and this also builds up water levels. The shape of the area means that water is increasingly concentrated into a space that is decreasing in size. High tides intensify the effect. The North Sea storm surge of 1953 claimed many lives in southeast England and the Netherlands (see case study).

Case study   The North Sea storm surge, 1953

The 1953 event was the most serious storm surge in the twentieth century to hit the coasts of countries bordering the North Sea. The reasons for the build-up of water in the southern part of the sea were:

- a deep Atlantic depression moved across Scotland, deepening all the time, and by the time

it had reached the coast of Denmark, the central pressure had fallen to around 970 mb
- such a rapid fall of pressure could have been responsible for a rise in the surface of the sea of about 0.5 m
- with an anticyclone lying to the west of the British Isles, a steep pressure gradient developed which

Figure 3.10
The meteorological conditions of the North Sea storm surge, 1 February 1953

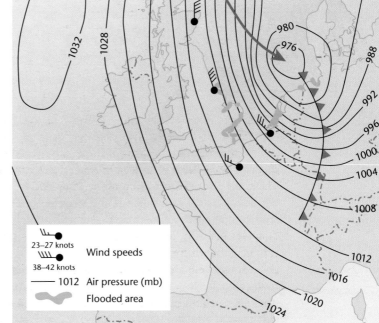

- resulted in strong winds moving south across the North Sea
- with the large fetch from the north, combined with the strong winds, storm waves were produced that were over 6 m high
- all this coincided with high spring tides and rivers discharging into the sea at flood levels

With so much water pushing through the North Sea, it is not surprising that the consequences for southeast England were severe. Sea defences were breached in several places, particularly in those areas that depended upon sand dunes for protection, and thousands of hectares of low-lying land were flooded. There was a great deal of damage to property. Communication systems and agriculture were disrupted — there were huge livestock losses. Over 250 people were drowned.

In the Netherlands the damage was even greater. The dyke system, which protects huge areas of land, was breached. Over 1,800 people lost their lives and about 10% of the country's agricultural land was flooded. The Dutch government resolved that this should not happen again. Its response was to plan the Delta Scheme. The fear of a repeat in the Thames estuary led to the construction of the Thames Barrier.

Sediment sources and cells

Coastal sediment comes from a variety of sources, including the sea bed, beaches, river channels and estuaries, and cliff erosion. The source of sediment which leads to the build-up of certain depositional features around the British coast is in dispute. Research has suggested that sediment movements occur in distinct areas or **cells**, within which inputs and outputs are balanced. Along the coastline of

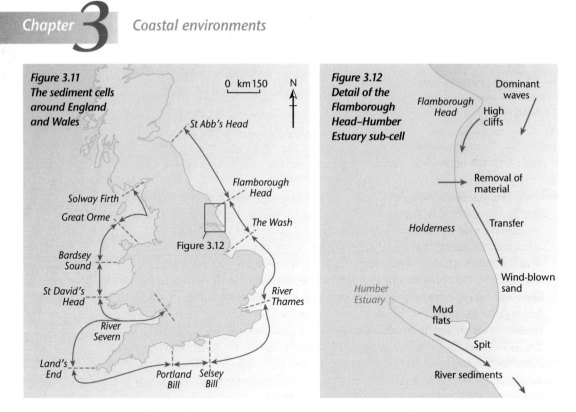

Figure 3.11 The sediment cells around England and Wales

0 km 150 N

St Abb's Head

Flamborough Head

Solway Firth
Great Orme

The Wash

Figure 3.12

Bardsey Sound

St David's Head

River Thames

River Severn

Land's End

Portland Bill Selsey Bill

Figure 3.12 Detail of the Flamborough Head–Humber Estuary sub-cell

Flamborough Head

Dominant waves

High cliffs

Removal of material

Holderness

Transfer

Wind-blown sand

Humber Estuary

Mud flats

Spit

River sediments

England and Wales, 11 of these sediment cells have been identified (Figure 3.11). These are distinct areas of coastline separated from other areas by well-defined boundaries, such as headlands and stretches of deep water. In theory, sediment cells can be regarded as closed systems from which nothing is gained or lost. However, in reality, it is easy for fine sediments to find their way around headlands into neighbouring cells.

Sediment cells vary in size. The larger ones are divided into smaller sections (**sub-cells**), to allow closer study and management. An example of a sub-cell is the one that operates between Flamborough Head and the Humber Estuary on the east coast of England (Figure 3.12).

High-energy and low-energy coastlines

High-energy coastlines are those in which wave power is strong for a greater part of the year, for example the western coast of the British Isles. The prevailing and dominant wind direction on these coasts is westerly and they face the direction of the longest fetch. The maximum recorded wave height on western coasts is therefore greater than that on eastern coasts. For example, waves of up to 30 m have been recorded on the west coast of Ireland.

Many estuaries, inlets and sheltered bays are **low-energy** environments where wave heights are considerably lower. Here, waves spread outwards and energy is dissipated, leading to the deposition of transported material. Enclosed seas also contain low-energy environments. The Baltic Sea, for example, contains some of the longest depositional landforms in the world, mainly because of its sheltered waters and low tidal range.

Coastal processes

Processes of marine erosion

When waves break on a coastline they often do so with considerable energy. It has been estimated that waves breaking against the foot of a cliff can generate energy of 25–30 tonnes m^{-2}. There are several ways in which waves are able to erode coastlines:

➤ **Hydraulic action (wave quarrying)** — a breaking wave traps air as it hits a cliff face. The force of water compresses this air into any gap in the rock face, creating enormous pressure within the fissure or joint. As the water pulls back, there is an explosive effect of the air under pressure being released. The overall effect of this over time is to weaken the cliff face. Storms may then remove large chunks of it. This process can also lead to extensive damage to sea defences. Some coastal experts also point out that the sheer force of water itself (without debris) can exert an enormous pressure upon a rock surface, causing it to weaken. Such an activity is sometimes referred to as **pounding**.

➤ **Abrasion/corrasion** — the material the sea has picked up also wears away rock faces. Sand, shingle and boulders hurled against a cliff line will do enormous damage. This is also apparent on intertidal rock platforms, where sediment is drawn back and forth, grinding away at the platform.

➤ **Attrition** — the rocks in the sea which carry out abrasion are slowly worn down into smaller and more rounded pieces.

➤ **Solution (corrosion)** — although this is a form of weathering rather than erosion, it is included here as it contributes to coastal erosion. It includes the dissolving of calcium-based rocks (e.g. limestone) by the chemicals in sea water and the evaporation of salts from water in the rocks to produce crystals. These expand when they form and put stress upon rocks. Salt from sea-water spray is capable of corroding several types of rock.

There are many factors that affect the rate of erosion:

➤ **Wave steepness and breaking point** — steeper waves are higher-energy waves and have a greater erosive power than low-energy waves. The point at which waves break is also important; waves that break at the foot of a cliff release more energy and cause more damage than those that break some distance away.

➤ **Fetch** — how far a wave has travelled determines the amount of energy it has collected.

➤ **Sea depth** — a steeply-shelving sea bed at the coast will create higher and steeper waves.

➤ **Coastal configuration** — headlands attract wave energy through refraction.

➤ **Beach presence** — beaches absorb wave energy and can therefore provide protection against marine erosion. Steep, narrow beaches easily dissipate the energy from flatter waves, while flattish, wide beaches spread out the incoming wave

> ### Key terms
>
> **Marine processes** Processes operating upon a coastline that are connected with the sea, such as waves, tides and longshore drift.
>
> **Sub-aerial processes** Processes operating on the land but affecting the shape of the coastline, such as weathering, mass movement and runoff.

energy and are best at dissipating high and rapid energy inputs. Shingle beaches also deal with steep waves as energy is rapidly dissipated through friction and percolation.

➤ **Human activity** — people may remove protective materials from beaches (sand), which may lead to more erosion, or they may reduce erosion by the construction of sea defences (discussed later in this chapter). Sea defences in one place, however, may lead to increased rates of erosion elsewhere on the same coastline.

Geology

Several geological factors affect the rate of erosion.

Lithology refers to the characteristics of rocks, especially resistance to erosion and permeability. Very resistant rocks such as granite, and to a lesser extent chalk, tend to be eroded less than weaker materials such as clay. Some rocks are well-jointed (e.g. limestone), which means that the sea can penetrate along lines of weakness, making them more vulnerable to erosion. Variation in the rates at which rocks wear away is known as **differential erosion**.

The **structure** and variation of the rocks also affects erosion. When rocks lie parallel to the coast, they produce a very different type of coastline than when they lie at right angles. Figure 3.13 shows two contrasting types of coastline that can be found close to one another in Purbeck (southern England). The southern part of the coast has the rocks running parallel to it — known as a **concordant** coastline. Here the resistant Portland limestone forms cliffs, and these have protected the coast from erosion, only allowing the sea to break through in a few places (the large area of Worbarrow Bay and the small area of Lulworth Cove) to the clay behind.

To the east, the rocks run at right angles to the coast (known as **discordant**), allowing the sea to penetrate along the weaker clays and gravels and produce large bays (e.g. Swanage Bay) flanked by outstanding headlands (The Foreland and Peveril Point).

Figure 3.13
The Purbeck coast

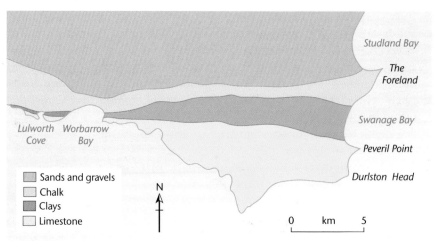

The **dip** of the rocks is also a major factor. The steepest cliffs tend to form in rocks that have horizontal strata or which dip gently inland, whereas rocks that dip towards the coast tend to produce much more gently sloping features (Figure 3.14).

Processes of marine transportation and deposition

Longshore drift

When waves approach the shore at an angle, material is pushed up the beach by the swash in the same direction as the wave approach. As the water runs back down the beach, the backwash drags material down the steepest gradient, which is generally at right angles to the beach line. Over a period of time, sediment moves in this zig-zag fashion down the coast (Figure 3.15). If the material is carried some distance it will become smaller, more rounded and better sorted.

Obstacles such as groynes (wooden breakwaters) and piers interfere with this drift, and accumulation of sediment occurs on the windward side of the groynes, leading to entrapment of beach material. Deposition of this material also takes place in sheltered locations, such as at the head of a bay, and where the coastline changes direction abruptly — here spits tend to develop.

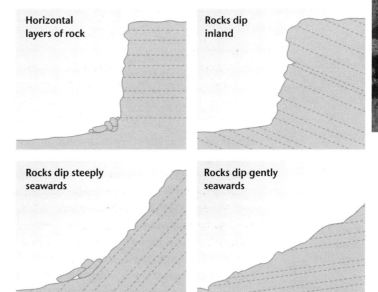

*Figure 3.14
The influence of rock strata on coastlines*

*Figure 3.15
Longshore drift*

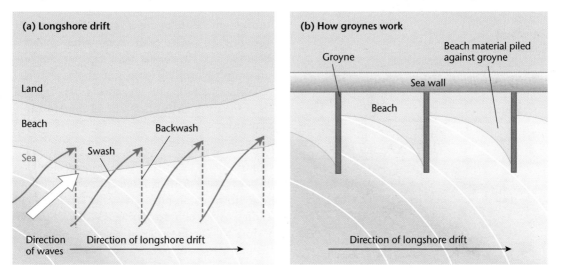

Sub-aerial processes

In addition to marine processes, there are also sub-aerial (land-based) processes which shape the coastline. These processes come under the general headings of **weathering** and **mass movement**. Solution was included in the marine processes listed above because it is a major process that combines with erosion to produce coastlines. Other weathering processes that can be effective include frost shattering, exfoliation (thermal expansion), biological weathering and forms of chemical weathering other than solution.

Biological weathering is quite active on coastlines. Some marine organisms, such as the piddock (a shellfish), have specially adapted shells that enable them to drill into solid rock. They are particularly active in chalk areas where they can produce a sponge-like rock pitted with holes. Seaweed attaches itself to rocks and the action of the sea can be enough to cause swaying seaweed to prise away loose rocks from the sea floor. Some organisms, algae for example, secrete chemicals capable of promoting solution.

Figure 3.16 Rotational slumping

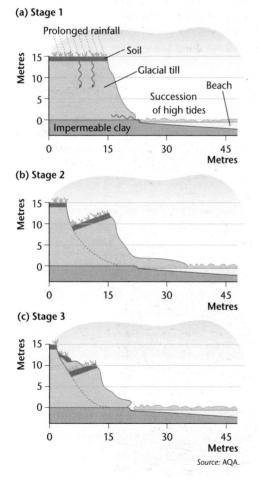

(a) Stage 1

Prolonged rainfall
Soil
Glacial till
Beach
Succession of high tides
Impermeable clay

(b) Stage 2

(c) Stage 3

Source: AQA.

Mass movement is common on coastlines, particularly those that are steep, and includes the following:

➤ **rock falls** from cliffs undercut by the sea
➤ **landslides** on cliffs made from softer rocks or deposited material, which slip down when lubricated
➤ **mudflows** — heavy rain can cause large quantities of fine material to flow downhill
➤ where softer material overlies much more resistant materials, cliffs are subject to **slumping**. With excessive lubrication, whole sections of the cliff face may move downwards with a slide plane that is concave, producing a rotational movement. Slumps are a common feature of the British coast, particularly where glacial deposits form the coastal areas, e.g. east Yorkshire and north Norfolk. Figure 3.16 shows a typical rotational slump in an area where glacial deposits form cliffs on top of an impermeable clay layer

Runoff is another process that operates on coastlines. It may take the form of a stream emerging in a bay, taking with it large quantities of load during times of flood, or it may be a stream cascading over a cliff excavating a V-shaped groove as it does so. The presence of water will also assist many of the mass movement processes mentioned above.

Landforms produced by coastal erosion

Headlands and bays

Figure 3.13 shows the impact of geology on a coastline. There are many similar parts of the British coastline where there are areas of alternating resistant and less resistant rocks. The less resistant rocks experience most erosion and develop into bays, while the more resistant rocks become headlands. Because of refraction, the headlands receive the highest-energy waves and are more vulnerable to the forces of erosion than are the bays. The bays experience low-energy waves that allow sediment to accumulate and form beaches. These act to protect that part of the coastline.

Where the rocks run parallel with the coast, as in Purbeck (Figure 3.13), it is possible for continued erosion to break through the more resistant rocks on the coast and begin to attack the weaker strata behind. If that happens, a cove will form which will be enlarged by erosion into a bay. In Purbeck, the sea has broken through the more resistant Portland stone to form Lulworth Cove in the clay behind (Photograph 3.2), although there is some evidence that this could have been a former river mouth. Just along from Lulworth Cove is Stair Hole. Here the sea enters through two arches and has begun to work its way along the weaker clays (Figure 3.17).

Kitchenham

*Photograph 3.2
Aerial view of
Lulworth Cove,
Dorset. Worbarrow
Bay is visible
beyond*

Figure 3.17
The geology of
south Purbeck

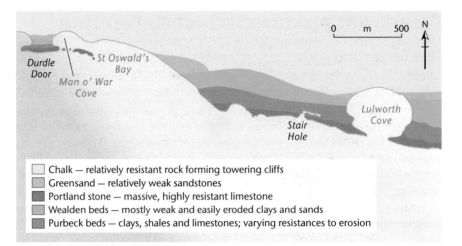

☐ Chalk — relatively resistant rock forming towering cliffs
☐ Greensand — relatively weak sandstones
■ Portland stone — massive, highly resistant limestone
☐ Wealden beds — mostly weak and easily eroded clays and sands
☐ Purbeck beds — clays, shales and limestones; varying resistances to erosion

Cliffs and wave-cut platforms

When high and steep waves break at the foot of a cliff they concentrate their erosive capabilities into only a small area of the rock face. This concentration eventually leads to the cliff being undercut, forming a feature known as a **wave-cut notch**. Continued activity at this point increases the stress on the cliff and in time it collapses.

The cliff begins to retreat, leaving at its base a gently sloping (less than 5°) wave-cut platform (Figure 3.18). When viewed from a distance, the platform looks remarkably even as it cuts across the rocks, regardless of their hardness. On closer inspection, the platform is often deeply cut into by abrasion from the huge amount of material that is daily carried across it, and by the effects of chemical action.

Figure 3.18
Formation of a
wave-cut platform

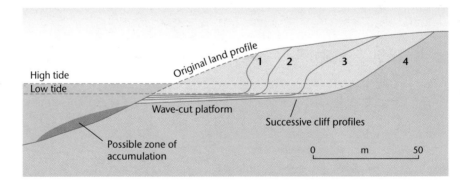

The platform continues to grow and, as it does, the waves break further out to sea and have to travel across more platform before reaching the cliff line. This leads to a greater dissipation of wave energy, reducing the rate of erosion on the headland and slowing down the growth rate of the platform. There tends, therefore, to be a limit to how big the feature can grow and some experts have suggested that growth beyond 0.5 km is unusual.

Geos, caves, blowholes, arches, stacks and stumps

These features are all independently observable on British coastlines, but they also represent a sequence of events in the erosion of a cliff or headland. On any cliff line the sea will attack the weakest parts such as cracks, joints or along bedding planes. Along a joint the sea will cut inland, widening the crack to form a narrow, steep-sided inlet known as a **geo**.

In other circumstances the cliff is undercut and a **cave** is formed, usually from a combination of marine processes. If erosion continues upwards, it is possible for the cave to be extended to the top of the cliff, where a **blowhole** will form. Much more likely is that the cave will extend backwards to meet another, eventually creating a hole all the way through the headland, known as an **arch**.

As the cliff recedes and the wave-cut platform develops, the arch will eventually collapse, leaving its isolated portion as a **stack** standing above the platform. In time, the sea will exploit the wave-cut notch at the base of the stack, leading eventually to its collapse. A small raised portion of the wave-cut platform may be left marking the former position of the stack. This is known as a **stump**.

There are several well-known areas of Britain where these features stand out. Flamborough Head in Yorkshire has a well-developed wave-cut platform in chalk, along with sea caves, arches and a large blowhole. In the old red sandstone rocks of the Orkney Islands there is a well-known stack, the Old Man of Hoy, and the Needles on the Isle of Wight are another example of the same feature, although they look different because they are formed from chalk.

On Purbeck, in the Portland stone (a highly resistant limestone), the sea has cut the well-known arch of Durdle Door. Also on Purbeck the chalk escarpment culminates in The Foreland and its detached pieces that are known as Old Harry Rocks. Figure 3.19 is a sketch of this area, where the sequence from headland to stack can be seen. Marine erosion and sub-aerial processes will eventually reduce the upstanding parts of this area to a wave-cut platform.

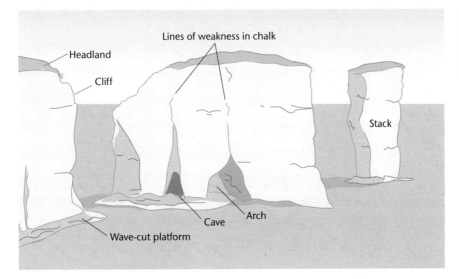

Figure 3.19
Coastal erosion features seen at Old Harry Rocks, Purbeck

Holbeck Hall, one of Yorkshire's premier coastal hotels, was built on top of the cliffs behind South Bay in Scarborough at the end of the nineteenth century. Although the cliffs here consist largely of clay, the hotel was not considered to be in any danger, because it was at least 60–70 m away from the edge.

All this changed in the early summer of 1993 when a period of dry weather cracked much of the clay on the cliff top. This dry period was followed by heavy rainfall that penetrated the cracks and began to lubricate the clay along certain lines of slippage. The first warning came on 3 June when cracks began to appear in the hotel lawns and rose garden towards the edge of the cliff. The following morning, more cracks appeared and sections of the garden began to slide towards the beach. By late afternoon, the area of slides had reached the hotel buildings, resulting in the collapse of the terraces and the conservatory. In the early evening the collapse had affected the main part of the hotel, a large section of which fell into the slide and began to move towards the beach. As a result of this, the remainder of the hotel had to be demolished by contractors.

The owners of the hotel sued the local authority for being 'in breach of its duty of care to maintain the supporting land and the undercliff it owned between the hotel grounds and the sea'.

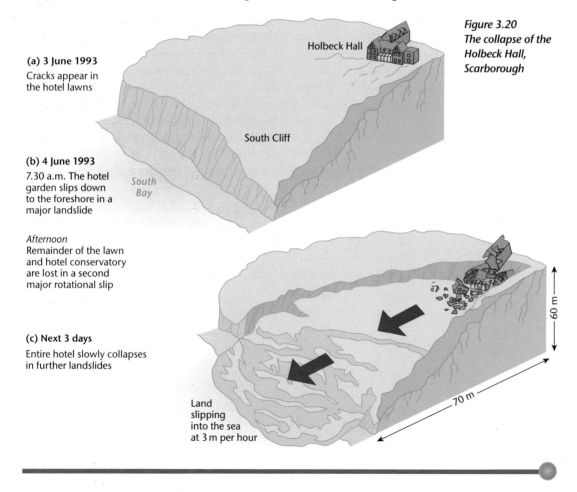

(a) 3 June 1993
Cracks appear in the hotel lawns

Holbeck Hall

South Cliff

(b) 4 June 1993
7.30 a.m. The hotel garden slips down to the foreshore in a major landslide

South Bay

Afternoon
Remainder of the lawn and hotel conservatory are lost in a second major rotational slip

(c) Next 3 days
Entire hotel slowly collapses in further landslides

Land slipping into the sea at 3 m per hour

60 m

70 m

Figure 3.20
The collapse of the Holbeck Hall, Scarborough

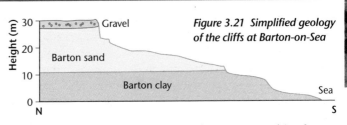

Case study   Barton-on-Sea, Hampshire

The cliffs of Barton and Highcliffe in Christchurch Bay are most famous for their remarkable fossil content. The fossils are exposed because the sea attacks the cliffs and erodes them at a maximum rate of about 1 m a year.

Figure 3.21 Simplified geology of the cliffs at Barton-on-Sea

The coast of Barton and Highcliffe is well known as a site of rapid coastal erosion where there have been major engineering activities to try to stop or slow down this action. In parts of the cliffs there is a relatively soft clay (Barton clay) with a water-bearing sand (Barton sand or Becton sand) above. In addition, most this stretch of coast has cliffs capped by porous and permeable gravel. Water from precipitation and runoff drains into this gravel. The cliffs therefore have a structure that is particularly vulnerable to landslides. This part of the English Channel is also subject to large waves with a long fetch.

Pressures for coastal defence schemes result from the fact that Barton and Highcliffe are popular residential areas and there has been much housing development on this coast. It is between the beautiful New Forest and the sea, yet with easy access to Bournemouth and Southampton, and is little more than an hour from London by train. Not surprisingly, many retired people live here and enjoy the sea views and cliff walks.

Fortunately, most of the houses are set back from the cliff and there is a greensward (a stretch of grass that has not generally been built on) separating them from the edge. This greensward is of great value because it is potentially sacrificial land between most of the houses and the cliff edge. On the north (landward) side of Marine Drive, there are large houses and some flats. It will probably take many decades for the sea to destroy the greensward, but the rate is difficult to estimate. Further inland there is an extensive estate of bungalows and other fairly modern buildings. These are generally out of reach of coastal problems likely to occur in the near future.

However, there is a small number of older houses in the Barton Court area that are now quite close to the cliff. The local authority's view is that these buildings will probably be lost in the next 10–20 years. A number of them are already within 20 m of the cliff edge, some as close as 3 m. An area at risk from erosion has been identified in the District Local Plan and is defined by the line to which the cliff could recede in the next 60 years.

One property in Barton Court has already been demolished. There has been much debate about the building of sea defences to protect the more vulnerable houses here because of the geological importance of the cliffs.

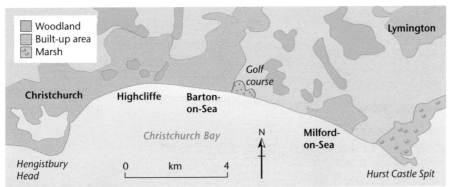

Figure 3.22 Location of Barton-on-Sea

Figure 3.23 Map of Barton and Highcliffe coast

Landslides and undercutting by the action of the sea are the main causes of erosion here. Some of the events in recent years have been as follows.

December 1993

Major cliff slip at the western end of the frontage. The cliff toe revetment was displaced by up to 8 m. Extensive emergency works followed. Analysis indicated a complex multi-plane failure with substantial movement. It was proposed that more rock armour should be placed seaward of that already there and

a new area of fill created to regrade the cliffs to a lower gradient.

September 2001

There was collapse of an area of sea defences at the western end, near Cliff House (west of Barton Court) and on a smaller scale between the Cliff House and Barton Court areas. The main feature was a rotational landslide which had developed in the Barton clay, probably facilitated by water from the Becton sand or Barton sand (upper part of the

Photograph 3.3
View of sea defences looking west towards Highcliffe at Barton-on-Sea

cliff). The rotation produced an up-bulge in the lower cliff. This broke and lifted a drainage system. In addition, sheet piling in the area was moved by the landslide and rotated from the vertical to various angles.

November 2003

After heavy rain it was noticed that there were some small signs of movement in the middle cliff in the landslide at the western end of the Barton sea defences (near Cliff House). There have been some recent small falls of gravel in the uppermost cliff edge here. No major movement of landslides was observed, but there is much water on the cliff.

January 2007

There were several winter storms, including a particularly fierce one on 18 January. Beach erosion took place at Highcliffe in the area of rock armour groynes between Highcliffe Castle and Chewton Bunny (particularly just east of the castle).

The BBC news website reported:

> Work has begun to replace a Dorset beach which was lost to the sea in storms over the winter. Up to 60% of the sand and shingle from Highcliffe Beach, near Christchurch, Dorset, was eroded and an access road crumbled away in the damaging winds. The council is erecting a stone wall around the beach, with 600 tonnes of boulders, to act as a sea defence. The main beach work is expected to take 8 weeks, with some areas not due to be repaired until late spring.

Steve Woolard, coast protection officer, said: 'Highcliffe Beach is particularly susceptible when there are storms of this ferocity as it takes the full brunt of long-wave action coming from the southwest. The backwash from the waves causes a rapid reduction in sand and shingle from the beach. When the beach levels are eroded the secondary defences, such as the timber retaining wall built during the 1960s, are exposed. If they start to wear away, there could be a catastrophic knock-on effect to the Highcliffe cliffs above. Most of the damage is thought to have occurred earlier this month when gales hit the south coast.'

April 2007

A new phase of collapse commenced in dry weather after a very wet winter. In recent years there have been signs of small movement in the upper cliffs between the Cliff House location and the Barton Court shopping area of Barton-on-Sea (about 300 m along the cliff). The indications have been small but laterally extensive cracks, particularly in the gravel near the top of the cliff.

Landforms produced by coastal deposition

Deposition occurs on coastlines where sand and shingle accumulate faster than they are removed. It often takes place where the waves are low energy or where rapid coastal erosion provides an abundant supply of material.

Beaches

Beaches represent the accumulation of material deposited between low spring tides and the highest point reached by storm waves. They are mainly constructed from sand and shingle. Sand produces beaches with a gentle gradient (usually under 5°) because its small particle size means the sand becomes compact when wet, and allows very little percolation. Most of the swash therefore returns as backwash, little energy is lost to friction, and material is carried down the beach. This leads to the development of **ridges** and **runnels** in the sand at the low-water mark. These run parallel to the shoreline and are broken by channels that drain the water off the beach (Figure 3.24).

Figure 3.24
Beach features

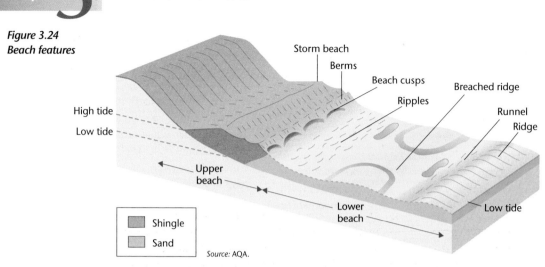

Source: AQA.

Shingle may make up the whole or just the upper parts of the beach. The larger the size of the material, generally the steeper is the gradient of the beach (usually 10–20°). This is because water rapidly percolates through shingle, so the backwash is somewhat limited. This, together with the uneven surface, means that very little material is moved down the beach.

At the back of the beach, strong swash at spring high-tide level will create a **storm beach** — a ridge composed of the biggest boulders thrown by the largest waves. Below this will be a series of ridges marking the successively lower high tides as the cycle goes from spring to neap. These beach ridges are known as **berms** and are built up by constructive waves. **Cusps** are semicircular-shaped depressions which form when waves break directly on to the beach and swash and backwash are strong. They usually occur at the junction of the shingle and sand beaches. The sides of the cusps channel incoming swash into the centre of the embayment and this produces a stronger backwash in the central area which drags material down the beach, deepening the cusp.

Below this, **ripples** are developed on the sand by wave action or tidal currents.

Spits and bars

A spit is a long, narrow piece of land that has one end joined to the mainland and projects out into the sea or across an estuary. Like other depositional features, it is composed of sand and/or shingle and the mixture very much depends upon the availability of material and the wave energy required to move it.

Figure 3.25 shows the formation of a spit. On the diagram, the prevailing winds and maximum fetch are from the southwest, so material will be carried from west to east along the coast by the process of longshore drift. Where the coastline changes to a more north–south orientation, there is a build-up of sand and shingle in the more sheltered water in the lee of the headland. As this material begins to project eastwards, storms build up more material above the high-water mark, giving a greater degree of permanence to the feature. Finer material is then carried further eastward, extending the feature into the deeper water of the estuary.

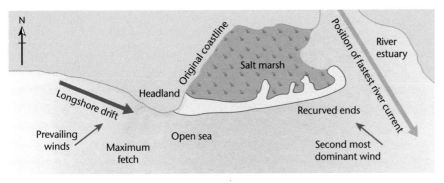

Figure 3.25
The formation
of a spit

Increasingly, though, the end of the spit begins to curve round as wave refraction carries material round into the more sheltered water. The second most dominant wind direction and fetch may contribute to this, pushing the spit material back towards the mainland. Several curved ends may develop during a period of southeast weather until the dominant southwest movement reasserts itself. The spit cannot grow all the way across the estuary as the material is carried seaward by the river and the deeper water at the centre inhibits growth.

Spits are often associated with two other features:

➤ **Sand dunes** form as dried-out sand is blown to the back of the spit where it increasingly accumulates. Stability is achieved if vegetation such as marram grass begins to colonise the area and hold the dunes together.

➤ **Salt marshes** form as low-energy, gentle waves enter the sheltered area behind the spit and deposit the finer material such as silt and mud. This builds up to form a feature which is then colonised by vegetation.

Figure 3.26
The spit at Orford
Ness

Around the British coasts, well-known spits are found at Borth (west Wales), Dawlish Warren (Devon), Hurst Castle (Solent, Photograph 3.4), Orford Ness (East Anglia, Figure 3.26) and Spurn Head (Humber estuary). A spit that joins an island to the mainland is known as a **tombolo**. The best example in Britain is Chesil Beach on the south coast of England. This links the Isle of Portland to the mainland and is about 30 km long.

If a spit develops across a bay where there is no strong flow of water from the landward side, it is possible for the sediment to reach across to the other side. In this case, the feature is known as a **bar**. Some bars, however, may simply be the result of the onshore migration of material from offshore as sea levels rose following the last ice age. Slapton Ley, a bar formed in Devon, is believed to have come about in this way. Recent

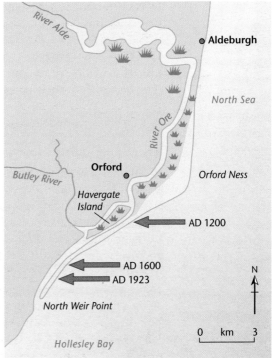

*Photograph 3.4
Aerial view of
Hurst Castle Spit*

Aerofilms

work on Chesil Beach has suggested a similar cause, although the spit was probably formed by a combination of onshore migration of sea bed materials and longshore drift.

Coastal sand dunes

Coastal sand dunes are accumulations of sand shaped into mounds by the wind (Photograph 3.5). They represent a dynamic landform. Beaches are the source of

*Photograph 3.5
Sand dunes at
Ainsdale,
Merseyside*

Malcolm Skinner

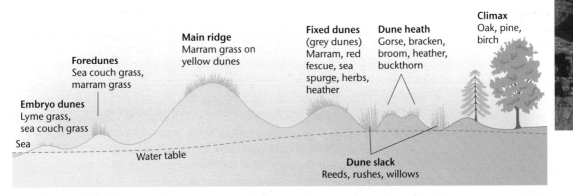

Climax
Oak, pine,
birch

Fixed dunes
(grey dunes)
Marram, red
fescue, sea
spurge, herbs,
heather

Dune heath
Gorse, bracken,
broom, heather,
buckthorn

Main ridge
Marram grass on
yellow dunes

Foredunes
Sea couch grass,
marram grass

Embryo dunes
Lyme grass,
sea couch grass

Sea

Water table

Dune slack
Reeds, rushes, willows

Figure 3.27
A typical sand-dune
transect

the sand which, when dried out, is blown inland to form dunes. Sand is moved inland by a process known as **saltation** (a bouncing action which is also seen in particles moved along by running water).

During the day, the wind on the coastal fringe is generally from the sea. Air moves in response to the small pressure differentials set up by the warmer land and the colder sea. When there is a large tidal range, large amounts of sand may be exposed at low tide, and this further contributes to dune formation. The sequence of sand-dune development (Figure 3.27) is as follows:

➤ Sand may become trapped by obstacles (seaweed, rock, driftwood) at the back of the beach, possibly on the highest berm or storm beach. Sand is not a hospitable environment for plant growth so only very hardy plants will begin to colonise here. Such plants are called **pioneers** — examples of sand-dune pioneers are sea rocket and prickly saltwort.

➤ The first dunes to develop are known as **embryo dunes**. They are suitable for colonisation by grasses such as sea couch, lyme and later (or eventually) marram. These are able to grow upwards through accumulating wind-blown sand, stabilising the surface. As a result low, hummocky dunes are formed. Marram is a robust plant which spreads vigorously by underground shoots (rhizomes). This is still a difficult environment and plants need certain features to survive. Sea couch has succulent leaves to store water, prickly saltwort has thorn-like leaves which reduce transpiration and conserve water, and marram possesses long tap roots to draw moisture from the water table. Plant growth of this kind adds organic matter to the dunes which aids water retention.

➤ Upward growth of embryo dunes raises the height to create dunes that are beyond the reach of all but the highest storm tides. These **foredunes (mobile dunes)** are initially yellow, because they contain little organic matter, but as colonisation increases, plants like marram begin to add humus to the sand. As a result, the dunes look more grey in colour and may reach heights in excess of 20 m.

➤ The dunes inland gradually become **fixed**. An organic layer develops which improves nutrient supply and water retention, allowing more plant colonisation. Lichens, mosses and flowering plants begin to appear and marram is slowly replaced by red fescue grass. Other plants include creeping willow and dewberry.

➤ In places **dune slacks** develop. These are depressions within the dunes where the water table is on or near the surface and conditions are often damp. Rushes, reeds, mosses and willows can be found, but the plants present will very much depend upon the amount of moisture.

➤ Behind the yellow and grey dunes, the supply of beach sand is gradually cut off, giving smaller dune features. This area is often referred to as **dune heath**, and heather, gorse, broom and buckthorn are the main plants. Towards the rear of the dune system, woodland may occur with trees such as pine, birch and the occasional oak. This is beginning to lead into the climatic climax vegetation for the British Isles, but in many areas the dunes may be planted with conifers to stabilise the area. If this is the case, then the vegetation is said to be a plagio-climax (short of the climatic climax because of human interference). Within this system, it is possible to find **blowouts** where wind has been funnelled through areas and has removed the sand.

Sand dunes are an example of a **succession**, a plant community in which the structure develops over time. At each stage, certain species have evolved to exploit the particular conditions present. Initially only a small number of species will be capable of thriving in a harsh environment. These hardy pioneering plants gradually modify the conditions by altering such things as the mineral and moisture content of the soil and the amount of shade. As each new plant species takes hold, the process is repeated. Changes made by the plants present allow other species, better suited to this modified habitat, to succeed the old species. When the succession has reached a point where it is in balance with the climatic conditions, a climax is said to have been reached. A succession that develops on sand is called a **psammosere**.

Salt marshes

In sheltered river estuaries or behind spits, silt and mud are deposited by rivers or gentle tides to form intertidal mudflats. Upon these, vegetation will develop which, like that of the sand-dune environment, changes through time. The succession that develops (Figure 3.28) is known in this case as a **halosere** (tolerant of salty conditions) and follows these stages:

➤ Mudflats are formed by deposition of fine material. This may be aided by the growth of eelgrass that slows currents and leads to further, uneven, deposition.

➤ **Pioneers** begin to colonise the area. These are plants able to tolerate salt and periodic submergence by the sea. They are known as **halophytes** and examples include glasswort, sea blite and *Spartina*. *Spartina* has two root systems — a fine mat of surface roots to bind the mud, and long, thick, deep roots that can secure it in up to 2 m of deposited material. This enables the plant to trap more mud than other pioneers, and thus it has become the dominant vegetation on tidal flats in the British Isles.

➤ The pioneers gradually develop a close vegetation over the mud and this allows colonisation by other plants such as sea aster, marsh grass and sea lavender. These form a dense mat of vegetation up to 15 cm high. The growth of vegetation has the effect of slowing the tidal currents even further and

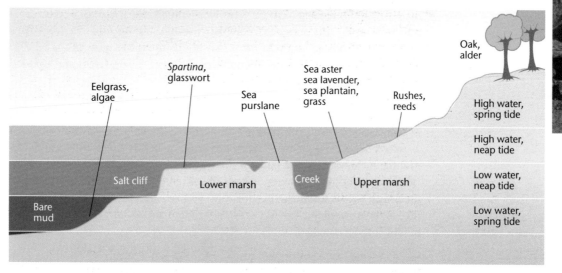

Figure 3.28
The structure of a salt marsh

this, together with the vegetation's ability to trap particles, leads to more mud and silt accumulation. Dead organic matter also helps to build up the surface, which grows in height at anywhere between 1 and 25 mm per year.

➤ As mud levels rise, complex creek systems develop that channel the tides and these deepen as the marsh becomes higher. Hollows may form where sea water becomes trapped and evaporates, leaving salt-pans in which the salinity is too great for plants to survive. As the land rises above sea level, rushes (such as the *Juncus* species) and reeds become established, eventually leading to the growth of trees such as alder, ash and then oak to complete the succession. This land is now rarely covered by the sea.

Sea-level change

Eustatic and isostatic change

Tides are responsible for daily changes in the levels at which waves break on to the land, but the average position of sea level relative to the land has changed through time. Many changes took place during the Quaternary glaciation that reflected both the advance and retreat of the ice. A typical sequence would have run as follows:

➤ **Stage 1** As the climate begins to get colder, marking the onset of a new glacial period, an increasing amount of precipitation falls as snow. Eventually, this snow turns into glacier ice. Snow and ice act as a store for water, so the hydrological cycle slows down — water cycled from the sea to the land (evaporation, condensation, then precipitation) does not return to the sea. As a consequence, sea level falls and this affects the whole planet. Such a worldwide phenomenon is known as a **eustatic** fall.

➤ **Stage 2** The weight of ice causes the land surface to sink. This affects only some coastlines and then to a varying degree. Such a movement is said to be **isostatic** and it moderates the eustatic sea-level fall in some areas.

> ➤ **Stage 3** The climate begins to get warmer. Eventually the ice masses on the land begin to melt. This starts to replenish the main store and sea level rises worldwide (eustatic). In many areas this floods the lower parts of the land to produce **submergent** features such as flooded river valleys (**rias**) and flooded glacial valleys (**fjords**).
>
> ➤ **Stage 4** As the ice is removed from some land areas they begin to move back up to their previous levels (**isostatic** readjustment). If the isostatic movement is faster than the eustatic, then **emergent** features are produced such as **raised beaches**. Isostatic recovery is complicated as it affects different places in different ways. In some parts of the world it is still taking place as the land continues to adjust to having masses of ice removed. Today, the southeast of the British Isles is sinking while the northwest is rising. This reflects the fact that the ice sheets were thickest in northern Scotland and that this was the last area in which the ice melted.

Figure 3.29 A ria

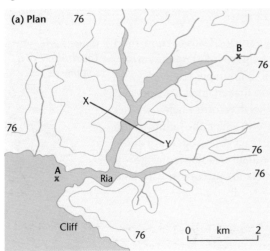

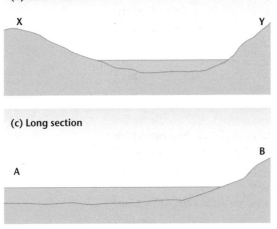

As mean global temperatures continue to rise, there is an inevitable consequence for sea levels. As more standing ice melts, particularly in Antarctica and Greenland, fresh water will be released into the oceanic store. This could have serious implications for many islands in the Pacific Ocean and for low-lying coastal areas.

Submergent features

Rias are created by rising sea levels drowning river valleys. The floodplain of a river will vanish beneath the rising waters, but on the edges of uplands only the middle- and upper-course valleys will be filled with sea water, leaving the higher land dry and producing this feature. In Devon and Cornwall, for example, sea level rose and drowned the valleys of the rivers flowing off Dartmoor and the uplands of Cornwall. Good examples are the Fowey estuary in Cornwall and the Kingsbridge estuary in south Devon. Rias have a long section and cross profile typical of a river valley, and usually a dendritic system of drainage (Figure 3.29).

Fjords are drowned glacial valleys typically found on the coasts of Norway, southwestern New Zealand, British Columbia in Canada, southern Chile and Greenland. The coast of western Scotland contains fjords which are not as well developed as those in the areas above because the ice was not as thick and did not last for the same length of time.

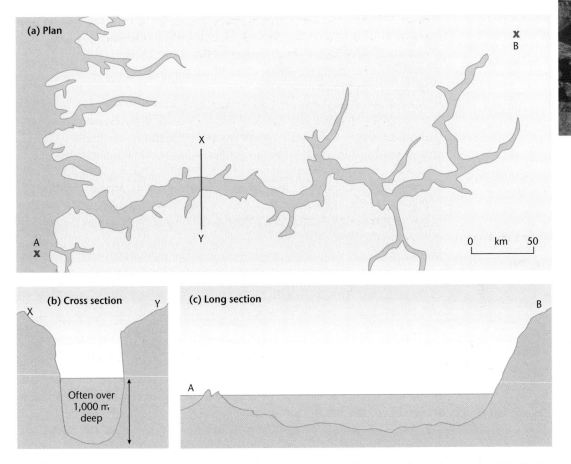

Figure 3.30 A fjord

Fjords have steep valley sides (cliff-like in places) and are fairly straight and narrow (Figure 3.30). Like glacial valleys, they have a typical U-shaped cross section with hanging valleys on either side. Unlike rias, they are not deepest at the mouth, but generally consist of a glacial rock basin with a shallower section at the end, known as the **threshold**. They were formed when the sea drowned the lower part of glacial valleys that were cut to a much lower sea level. The threshold is thought to be due to reduced glacial erosion as the glacier came in contact with the sea and the ice became thinner. Good examples include Sogne Fjord in Norway, which is nearly 200 km long, and Milford Sound in New Zealand (Photograph 3.6).

Emergent features

Raised beaches are areas of former wave-cut platforms and their beaches which are at a level higher than the present sea level. Behind the beach it is not unusual to find old cliff lines with wave-cut notches, sea caves, arches and stacks. Raised beaches are common around the coasts of western Scotland where three levels have been recognised, at 8 m, 15 m and 30 m. Because of differential uplift these are only approximate heights.

Photograph 3.6
The entrance to
Milford Sound fjord,
New Zealand

*Photograph 3.6
The entrance to
Milford Sound fjord,
New Zealand*

On the west of the Isle of Arran there is a well-developed raised beach north of Drumadoon. This has a **relict cliff**, arches, stacks and caves, including the well-known King's Cave. This beach is around 4 or 5 m above present sea level and is probably the equivalent of the 8 m beach. It was clearly produced when the sea was at that level, which initially suggests that the sea has fallen to its present level. However, we know that sea levels have *risen* considerably (eustatic) since the end of the last ice age, so the beach must have reached its raised position by isostatic rising of the land. The land locally must have risen faster than the eustatic rise in sea level to create this phenomenon.

Impacts of present and predicted sea-level increase

Sea level has been rising consistently since the end of the last ice age 15,000 years ago. In recent millennia it has risen quite slowly (about 1 or 2 mm per year), but the rate has increased recently to about 4 or 5 mm per year. The rate of rise in the future is uncertain, with predictions varying between 0.3 and 0.5 m increase by 2090.

Changes in sea level are the result of two processes: increases in the volume of the ocean and subsidence of the coast. Rising sea levels could have adverse effects, including coastal flooding and erosion, unless action is taken. In certain parts of the UK, notably the southeast, the rise in the sea relative to the land may be greater than average, owing to subsidence. Since the last ice age, glacier load removal in the north and west of the UK has resulted in a gradual uplift. At the same time, gradual subsidence has occurred on the margins of the North Sea basin in the east and southeast. This has resulted in the loss of numerous villages from low-lying east coast areas since the compilation of the Domesday Book.

A number of areas around the British coastline are potentially at risk from rising sea levels. These include major conurbations, such as London, Hull and Middlesbrough, and high-grade agricultural land. Major road and rail links near the coast are also at risk, and several power stations are situated on low-lying ground.

As well as direct effects such as coastal erosion or the flooding of coastal areas, higher mean sea levels could have an impact on underground water resources. The zone where sea water mixes with fresh water in rivers is dynamic and a rise in sea level can cause it to move upstream. A similar effect can occur between fresh water contained in rocks under the land and salt water in sea sediments, leading to intrusion of salt water beneath the land. This would adversely affect some points along the lower reaches of rivers where water is abstracted for domestic and irrigation purposes. These abstraction points would have to be moved upstream or become intermittent to avoid abstracting saline water.

Rising sea levels could also affect coastal habitats, particularly wetlands and salt marshes. The extent to which ecosystems are likely to be affected depends on the rate of sea-level rise and the ability of ecosystems to adjust, and the extent to which habitats are prevented from migrating inland by coastal defences.

Much of the east coast of Britain is at serious risk of flooding due to inadequate sea defences and the willingness of planning authorities to allow development along low-lying areas. Sea defences here need substantial investment if they are to be effective. Many were constructed in the 1950s following the storm surge of 1953 which killed over 300 people. Most at risk is the area between the River Humber and the Thames estuary. This stretch of coast has a history of flooding, and tidal surges measured at London Bridge have been increasing steadily.

The increased concentration of housing and other developments on land at risk of flooding is likely to raise insurance costs. On the other hand, high insurance premiums are an effective way of dissuading people from moving into areas at risk from sea-level rises. In rural coastal areas, under the government's Habitat Scheme, farmland is being allowed to become salt marsh. Farmers are paid up to £600 for each hectare of land that reverts to salt marsh.

Coastal flooding

Coastal flooding, which is confined to coastal plains, deltas and river estuaries, results from water levels being increased to substantially above normal high-tide levels. This can be brought about by:
➤ waves and surges generated by the passage of a tropical cyclone (hurricane)
➤ tsunamis
➤ a combination of low pressure, high tide levels and high river discharge (see case study of the North Sea storm surge in 1953, page 76)

Although coastal flooding is a natural process, the onset of global warming means that there is an increased and growing risk of extensive coastal flooding today. Among the places most at risk are many small island states in the Indian and Pacific Oceans, for example the Maldives, Seychelles, Tonga and the Cook Islands. Certain densely populated delta regions are also at great risk, including the Nile delta in Egypt and the Ganges delta in Bangladesh (see page 102). A rise in sea level of 1 m would, for example, inundate 25% of Bangladesh. The list of river estuaries at risk includes the Thames. London has been under threat of flooding for a long time. The 1953 storm surge in the North Sea prompted a debate that led to the construction

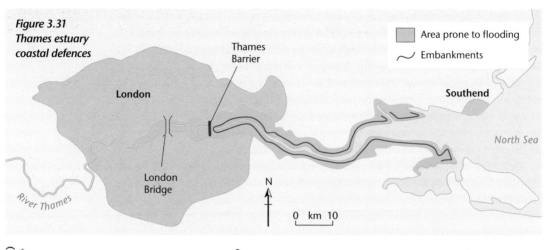

Figure 3.31 Thames estuary coastal defences

Area prone to flooding

Embankments

London

Thames Barrier

Southend

London Bridge

River Thames

North Sea

N

0 km 10

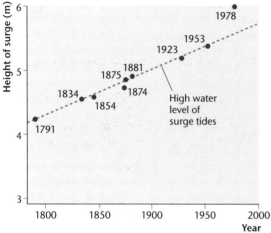

Figure 3.32 The height of storm surge events at London Bridge

Height of surge (m)

1978
1953
1923
1881
1875
1834
1854
1874
1791
High water level of surge tides

1800   1850   1900   1950   2000
Year

of the Thames Barrier. This was completed in 1982 (Photograph 3.7). Figure 3.31 shows coastal defences on the Thames estuary and Figure 3.32 the trend in the height of storm surge events at London Bridge.

Other areas of the UK that could be exposed to an increased danger of coastal flooding include the Severn, Dee and Mersey estuaries, Morecambe Bay, the Wash in Lincolnshire and East Anglia, the Solway Firth and the firths of Forth and Clyde in Scotland. Storm surges that were expected to occur only once in a 100-year period might now become one-in-50-year or even one-in-10-year events.

Imagin/Cadmium

Photograph 3.7 The Thames Barrier

Case study Towyn floods, Wales, February 1990

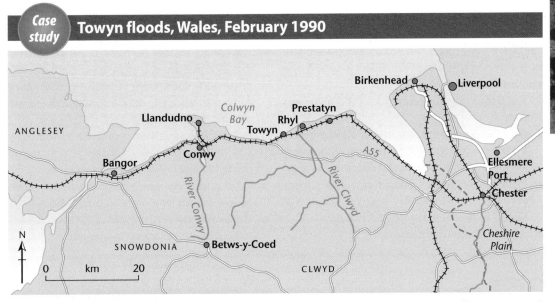

Figure 3.33 Map showing the location of Towyn

On Monday 26 February 1990, 10 m waves crashed through the 140-year-old sea wall at Towyn in north Wales. The floods that followed were a result of the breaching and erosion of the Towyn section of the railway embankment that stretches along the coastline. A severe storm on 12 February had already weakened the wall in the Towyn section, making it vulnerable to storm damage.

Towyn lies on the Chester to Holyhead railway. Where the line crosses the low-lying area known as

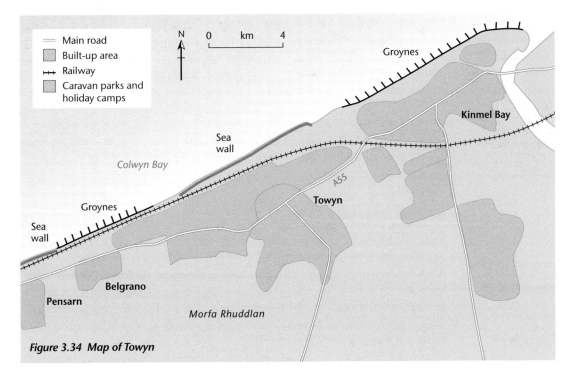

Figure 3.34 Map of Towyn

Morfa Rhuddlan, it was protected from the sea by an embankment 3 km in length. The embankment consists of a clay core, armoured on the seaward side by slate revetments. The embankment is crested by a number of sea walls.

The flooding that occurred had the following effects:

- Over 5,000 people in Towyn were affected when the floods wreaked havoc on their homes and lives, leaving a bill of £30 million for restoring the area.
- 2,800 properties were evacuated, 1,880 of them in Towyn. In Kinmel Bay and Pensarn 4,512 people were affected by flood damage.
- 6,000 caravans were damaged.

- 40% of households had no contents insurance and 15% had no buildings insurance.
- The county council (Clywd Council) estimated that £1.4 million was spent on immediate work on property and a further £3 million on structural damage to roads and other infrastructure to make the area fit to live in again.
- Insurance claims were expected to cost over £20 million, with an estimated £10.5 million needed to build new coastal defences.
- For the first few weeks after the floods 3,000 people were in temporary accommodation.
- Three months after the floods, 1,000 people were still not able to return to their homes.

Case study: Storm surges in Bangladesh

Bangladesh has the worst record in the late twentieth century for storm surges. Serious events occurred in 1970, 1985 and 1991. During a storm surge high winds, associated with cyclones forming to the south, push water northwards up the increasingly narrow Bay of Bengal. This water eventually hits the coast of densely populated Bangladesh. The country stands almost at sea level, covering most of the delta of the River Ganges. When cyclones hit, massive waves sweep water onto the land. The water level can rise by over 10 m.

Storm surges travel many kilometres inland, destroying farmland, villages and infrastructure, ruining crops and drowning livestock and people.

The estimated death toll in the cyclone of 1970 was over 300,000. Most buildings in the villages are flimsy constructions made from wood and are easily swept away by the flood waters. The influx of salt water also causes long-term problems for the country. Soils are contaminated, which greatly affects the food supply, leaving many people dependent upon aid.

Bangladesh is beginning to fight back, taking steps to protect the coastal population from such surges (see page 104). There is, however, increasing international concern about the possible effect of global warming on the country, as world sea levels are expected to rise during the twenty-first century.

Coastal protection schemes

Many of the world's coastlines are under threat of flooding. MEDCs have the resources and technical expertise to construct dams, barriers, sea walls and dykes. A low-lying country such as the Netherlands is clearly at risk from flooding, particularly on the delta of the rivers Waal, Scheldt, Lek and Maas. Forty years ago the Delta Plan was conceived in the Netherlands to control these rivers. Barriers were built to prevent the sea from inundating areas of land, as it had during the North Sea storm surge of 1953 (see case studies, below and page 76).

Case study: A national scheme, the Netherlands

Management of the Dutch coastline is divided into three main areas: the delta region, the Zuider Zee and the coastal dune area (Figure 3.35).

The delta region

In its natural state, the delta region is an area consisting of islands and peninsulas running between the distributaries of the rivers Waal (Rhine), Maas, Lek and Scheldt. Flooding has been a major problem here, but the disastrous floods of 1953 forced the Dutch government to design a scheme that would control similar events in the future. The Delta Plan (Figure 3.36) consists of:

- a series of dams that seal off the channels between the large islands to keep out the sea
- two channels to allow ships to reach the ports of Rotterdam and Antwerp
- the creation of some fresh water areas
- the East Scheldt dam, which is unlike those that had already been built (fixed dams). Pressure from environmentalists has resulted in the building of a storm surge barrier with sluice gates that can be lowered in times of need. The area behind the dam has remained as salt water, preserving salt marshes and mudflats for wildlife

The Delta Plan has reduced the length of defended coastline from 800 km to 80 km.

The Zuider Zee

The Zuider Zee was originally a long inlet of the sea that threatened large areas of low-lying coastlands when high spring tides were backed by northerly winds. A 30 km barrier was completed by 1932, which created a fresh water lake, the Ijsselmeer. This lake has been largely reclaimed as a series of polders (artificial land) providing areas for urban expansion and agriculture.

The coastal dune area

The Dutch dunes occupy an area of over 42,000 hectares, making them the largest area of continuous duneland in Europe. Currents and waves remove sand in some areas and deposit it

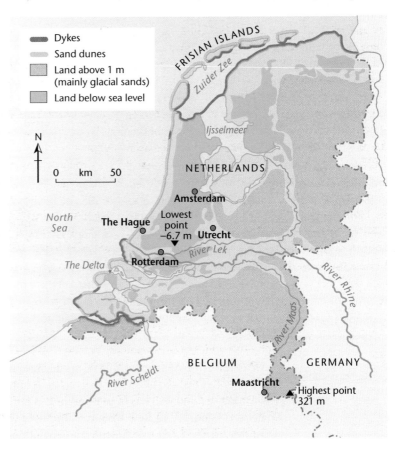

Figure 3.35 The Netherlands

Figure 3.36 The Delta Plan

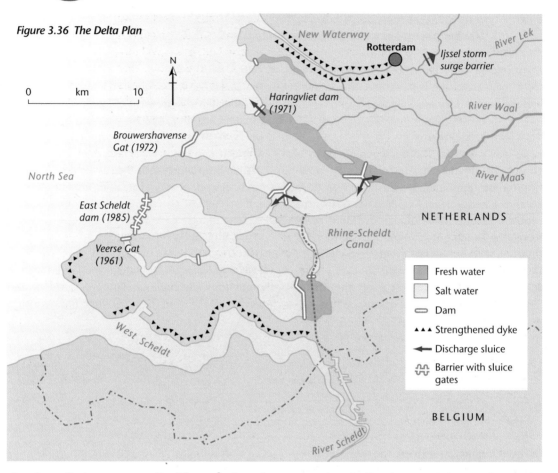

elsewhere. Each year, some 7 million m³ of sand are washed away. Only part of this is deposited elsewhere along the coast. The sand balance is therefore negative. As the nearshore underwater sand disappears, the beaches are gradually lowered, leading to damage to the dunes behind the beach. The main protective measures carried out include:

■ sand mixed with water is pumped up from the sea bed up to 20 km out at sea. It is then trans-

ported to the Dutch coast and sprayed on to the beaches. This **sand replenishment** is accompanied by the construction of groynes to hold sand on the beaches

■ grasses and trees are planted to hold the sand and reduce surface wind speeds

■ sleeper dykes are placed below the dunes to keep them bedded down

■ certain areas are fenced off to prevent access and trampling

In areas such as Bangladesh, little money has been spent on coastal defences. The policy has been to allow the delta to be inundated but to defend the capital city, Dhaka. A flood wall has been built for this purpose. However, the wall means that water is unable to flow back into the river when the flood recedes. Flood warnings are given, but it is difficult for Bangladeshis to respond to these because there is very little high ground to which they can escape. Some areas do have shelters where people can congregate in case of storm and flood. It has been estimated that over 10,000 shelters are needed but fewer than 500 have been built.

The economic disruption caused by flooding is one of the factors that contribute to Bangladesh's weak economic development. Bangladesh now has a Coastal Embankment Project — more embankments are being built, together with a series of sluices. Mangroves have been planted on the coast because mangrove swamps act as a natural buffer against sea incursions. There are some positive signs. In 1997, a tropical cyclone warning in the Cox's Bazaar area of the country allowed the evacuation of over 300,000 people. As a result, the death toll in the disaster was below 100.

Objectives and management strategies

Coastal areas contain a variety of landforms which are coming under increasing pressure from both natural processes and human activities. In response to this, a range of protection and management strategies has been put into place in many coastal areas. These solutions are often successful but, in some cases, the solutions themselves cause other problems. Coastal management has two main aims:
➤ to provide defence against flooding
➤ to provide protection against coastal erosion

Other aims of management include:
➤ stabilising beaches affected by longshore drift
➤ stabilising sand-dune areas
➤ protecting salt marshes

Management strategies can work either with or against natural processes. Working *with* nature means allowing the natural processes of erosion to occur (**managed retreat**) and not spending money on the defence of the coastal area. This is now applied to large stretches of coastline in the UK where there are few settlements. **Soft engineering** techniques such as beach nourishment are also used.

Working *against* nature usually occurs where there is significant capital investment — buildings and communications — in the coastal region and these have to be protected. Protection involves constructing sea walls, revetments, groynes and other examples of **hard engineering**. The costs of such defences are justified by the potential expense of replacing sea-damaged buildings and infrastructure if they were not in place.

There are a number of approaches to defence of the coast.

Hard engineering

Hard engineering involves building some type of sea defence with a specific purpose (Figure 3.37):
➤ **Sea walls (sometimes recurved)** aim to absorb wave energy. The recurved structure throws waves backwards. Sea walls must have a continuous facing because any slight gap will be exploited by hydraulic action. They also need drain outlets so that water does not accumulate behind them.

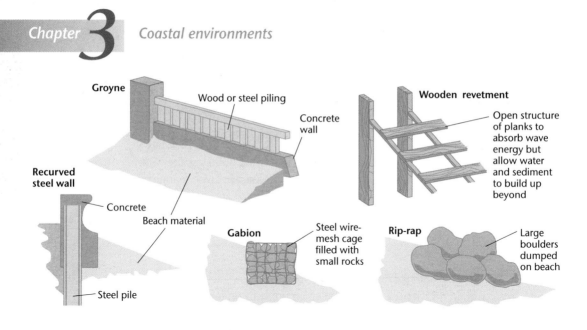

**Figure 3.37
Examples of hard
engineering
solutions**

➤ **Rock armour (rip-rap)** consists of large boulders dumped in front of a cliff or
  sea wall to take the full force of the waves.
➤ **Gabions** operate on the same principle as rip-rap, but the boulders are
  contained within a steel wire-mesh cage.
➤ **Revetments** are concrete or wooden structures placed across the beach to take
  the full force of wave energy.
➤ **Groynes** are wooden, stone or steel breakwaters built nearly at right angles to
  waves (usually 5–10° to the perpendicular to prevent scouring on the downdrift
  side of the groyne). They are built to control longshore drift but will also break
  up the waves as they hit the coast. Halting the bulk of longshore drift in an area
  may have serious effects down the coast where it will cut off the supply of beach
  material and could leave the coast exposed to erosion.
➤ **Cliff fixing** is often done by driving iron bars into the cliff face, both to stabilise
  it and to absorb some wave power.
➤ **Offshore reefs** force the waves to break offshore, which reduces their impact on
  the base of cliffs.

Barrages

A barrage is an example of a solid, hard-engineering scheme to prevent flooding
on major estuaries and other large sea inlets. It acts as a dam across an estuary and
prevents the incursion of seawater. Good examples of barrages are those that are
part of the Delta Plan in the Netherlands (see case study on page 103).

Besides controlling flooding, barrages can create large freshwater lakes behind
them, which may be associated with land reclamation schemes. Environmentalists
have opposed such schemes because they lead to the loss of valuable mudflat
areas. These include breeding grounds for a wide variety of birds. Barrages are also
expensive, in terms of both feasibility studies and construction.

The **Cardiff Bay barrage** in Wales was completed in 1999. However, there had
been strong opposition from environmental groups and local residents, who

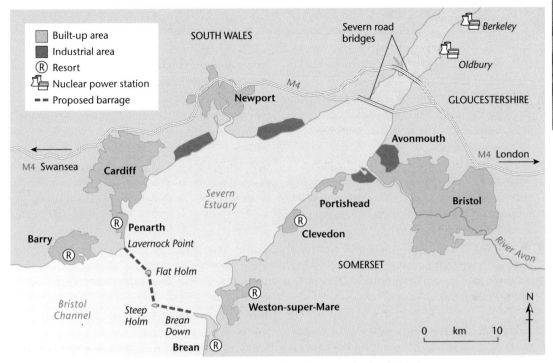

Figure 3.38
The proposed
Severn Estuary
barrage

feared damage to their houses from a higher water level. The barrage (1.1 km in length) includes a fish pass to allow salmon to reach breeding grounds in the River Taff and three locks for maritime traffic. The areas around the freshwater lake created behind the barrage (200 ha) have been regenerated, with attractions such as the Wales Millennium Centre, the National Assembly for Wales, a sports village and shopping areas on the waterfront. Over 6,000 new houses have been built.

There have been several proposals to put barrages across other major inlets in the UK, including the Wash, the Severn Estuary and Morecambe Bay. A **Severn Estuary barrage** (Figure 3.38) has been proposed in many forms. It would carry major communications across the estuary and generation of electricity using tidal power could be incorporated into the scheme. However, the estuary is an important breeding ground for many species of birds, particularly waders and waterfowl, and there are several wetland nature reserves, including the internationally renowned Wildfowl and Wetlands Trust reserve at Slimbridge. This, along with opposition from people involved in some aspects of the tourist industry, has meant that no proposals have ever been given the green light. Another stumbling block is the several billion pounds that it would cost.

Hard engineering has several disadvantages:

➤ structures can be expensive to build and to maintain (to repair a sea wall can cost up to £5,000 per metre)
➤ defence in one place can have serious consequences for another area of coast
➤ defence structures may not keep pace with rising sea levels
➤ structures are sometimes an eyesore, spoiling the landscape

The Isle of Wight Council, like all others on the UK coast, has four coastal defence options:

- **Hold the line** — retain the existing coastline by maintaining current defences or building new ones where existing structures no longer provide sufficient protection.
- **Do nothing but monitor** — on some stretches of coastline it is not technically, economically or environmentally viable to undertake defence works. The value of the built environment here does not exceed the cost of installing coastal defences.
- **Retreat the line** — actively manage the rate and process by which the coast retreats.
- **Advance the line** — build new defences seaward of the existing line.

The examples of different approaches highlighted on Figure 3.39, each of which are intended to have the potential for sustainable management, are described below.

Monk's Bay (1)

Cliff failure resulting from a combination of high-energy destructive waves and high rainfall during the severe storms of the winter of 1990/91 gave additional impetus for upgrading coastal defence here. The scheme involved constructing an **offshore breakwater**, six **rock groynes** and a **rock revetment** to reinforce the existing sea wall using 25,000 tonnes of Norwegian granite. It also required **beach nourishment** using 40,000 m³ of sand and gravel, **re-profiling** the slope and installing **land drainage** to check the active mass movement of the cliffs on the western side of the bay.

The collective value of the property far exceeded the £1.4 million cost of the scheme. It was completed in 1992 but sedimentation of the rock groynes has since been a problem.

Wheeler's Bay (2)

The ageing sea walls were in danger of collapse which would have reactivated ancient landslides.

Property on the cliff behind was becoming unsaleable. Over 15,000 tonnes of Norwegian granite was placed seaward of the existing defences to form a **rock revetment** and the coastal slopes were **regraded to make a shallower profile** before installing **land drainage**. The scheme was completed in 2000 at a cost of £1.6 million and has led to a recovery in property values. Further work from Wheeler's Bay to Ventnor's eastern esplanade is being considered

Western Cliffs (Ventnor) (3)

High-energy waves were removing chalk blocks which protected an ancient landslide complex upon which houses had been built. There was a danger that the landslides would be reactivated if sufficient chalk was removed. £1.2 million of Carboniferous limestone was brought in from the Mendip Hills in Somerset to construct a 700 m long **rock revetment** along the base of the cliffs using blocks weighing 6–8 tonnes. A series of limestone **rock groynes** was also constructed at 100 m intervals at the base of the cliffs.

Castle Cove (4)

The existing wooden revetments were becoming progressively ineffective as the clay cliffs retreated. Property valued in excess of £10 million was increasingly at risk as coastal processes activated ancient landslides. The scheme stabilised the environmentally sensitive cliffs by removing the topsoil, **stabilising the slopes** with thousands of tonnes of chalk and installing **land drainage** before replacing the topsoil. The cliff was protected by a **rock revetment** of Somerset limestone, a concrete walkway and a **gabion wall**. The defences cost £2.3 million and were completed in 1996.

Castlehaven (5)

A £6.2 million coast protection and slope improvement scheme was completed in 2004. The scheme included a 500 m **rock revetment** to protect the cliff at Reeth Bay. An extension system of drainage pipes

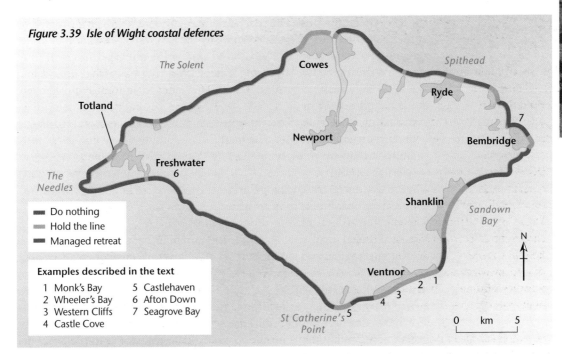

Figure 3.39 Isle of Wight coastal defences

and syphon drains was provided to reduce surface and groundwater levels, thereby reducing landslides.

East of Freshwater (6)

Where the A3055 passes over a chalk ridge at Afton Down it is now within 11 m of the cliff edge. Sea defences to prevent further cliff erosion would be economically unjustifiable and environmentally unacceptable. The council has therefore devised a scheme that **stabilises the cliff top** by anchoring the top of the cliff-face chalk on the landward side of the road. The cost is £750,000.

Seagrove Bay and Seaview (7)

The crumbling sea walls (maintained by residents)

and unstable slopes forced the council to intervene and protect property as part of its 'hold the line' policy. A scheme costing just under £1 million, and completed in 2000, included a new concrete **sea wall** with 200 m of **rock revetment** placed in front of the wall to dissipate the energy of the waves. **Rock groynes** were constructed as a further layer of protection. Mass movement on the soft clay cliffs has been significantly reduced by installing **land drainage**.

Further north at Seaview, a £4.7 million scheme was completed in 2004. This consisted of a 550 m stone-faced reinforced concrete sea wall fronted by a **rock revetment**. On the landward side a nature reserve has been developed.

Soft engineering

Soft engineering uses natural systems for coastal defence, such as beaches, dunes and salt marshes which can absorb and adjust to wave and tide energy. It involves manipulating and maintaining these systems, without changing their fundamental structures.

➤ **Beach nourishment** is the attempt to replace material that has been lost through longshore drift. It is not unknown for local councils to move material from one end of a beach to the other before the start of the tourist season.

➤ **Dune regeneration** — the fragile sand dune environment is easily disrupted by human activities. Most damage is caused by the removal of vegetation by either agriculture (overgrazing) or tourism (trampling the dunes). This can lead to blowouts during which large amounts of sand may be carried inland and deposited on valuable agricultural land. Management strategies to regenerate dunes include:
  – replanting vulnerable areas with plants such as marram grass and stabilising the surface with sacking or wire mesh
  – afforestation with conifers
  – selective grazing
  – restricting access by fencing off areas
  – providing boardwalks for tourists
  – giving tourists information about potential damage

➤ **Managed retreat** involves abandoning the current line of sea defences and then developing the exposed land in some way, perhaps with **salt marshes**, to reduce wave power. If old sea defences such as walls are abandoned, low-lying land will be flooded. This will be reclaimed naturally by marsh plants. The new area of marsh will act as a defence against rising sea levels. In this way the scale of hard sea defences can be reduced. There have been proposals in some areas to ban new developments on the coast. In California, for example, there are already requirements on some stretches of coastline that building must be a certain distance from the shore.

➤ **Do nothing** — in recent years a school of thought has grown up that asks whether the coast *should* be protected. Tens of millions of pounds are spent annually in the UK on coastal protection and it might be cheaper to let nature take its course and pay compensation to those affected. Figure 3.40 is a newspaper report on the findings of the House of Commons select committee on agriculture in August 1998. The committee suggested that large tracts of land should be 'surrendered to the sea' as trying to protect them was a waste of money.

Figure 3.40
Daily Telegraph,
6 August 1998

We must surrender our land to the sea, say MPs

Huge tracts of Britain's coastal land, especially along the east and south coast, should be surrendered to the sea as part of a 'peaceful accommodation' with nature, MPs said yesterday.

They set out a stark vision of a dramatically different coastal and riverside landscape complete with floodplains and regularly waterlogged farmlands as mankind showed more 'humility' in the face of the sea.

Describing the millions spent on flood prevention and coastal defences as an unsustainable and 'deluded' waste of money, the agricultural select committee said it was time to give up the fight along much of the East Anglian and southeast coasts.

Daily Telegraph, 6 August 1998

Soft engineering: the Sefton coast, northwest England

The Sefton coast, north of Liverpool, is the largest dune area in England, extending for over 17 km. The sand-dune system around Formby Point experienced continual erosion throughout the twentieth century, the point itself losing about 700 m between 1920 and 1970. Natural erosion levels were compounded by the effects of dredging, spoil dumping and wall construction associated with the development of the ports of Liverpool and Preston. This significantly altered the shape of the sea bed in Liverpool Bay, leading to increased wave energy focusing on Formby Point (Figure 3.41).

At present, the rate of dune erosion at Formby Point is up to 5 m per year, with significant erosion occurring when major storms coincide with high tides.

This area attracts large numbers of people to its beaches, dunes and pine forests. The forest is the home of one of the few remaining colonies of red squirrels in the British Isles, which is a further attraction. During the 1960s and 1970s, the coast was popular with holidaymakers heading for the sea. The frontal dunes suffered greatly as a result of this access. In recent years, problems have arisen with off-road vehicles breaking up the dunes and destroying the vegetation. Sand is also removed from the area by commercial contractors for the foundry trade and glass polishing.

The **Sefton Coast Management Scheme** has included:

■ close monitoring of visitor access with controls in certain areas
■ prohibiting the use of off-road vehicles in most of the area
■ controlling the extraction of sand for commercial purposes
■ suggestions that, where the natural dune landscape has been destroyed by the pine plantations, removing the tree and scrub cover from the existing frontal areas would help to re-establish and maintain a spectrum of habitats, including bare dunes and dune slacks
■ a project to recreate the natural dune landscape destroyed by the pine plantations to the north of Formby, at Ainsdale. Removal of the trees has encouraged re-colonisation by specialised plants such as yellow bartsia and animals such as the protected sand lizard and the natterjack toad
■ a determination to protect the area for future use, in other words to be sustainable

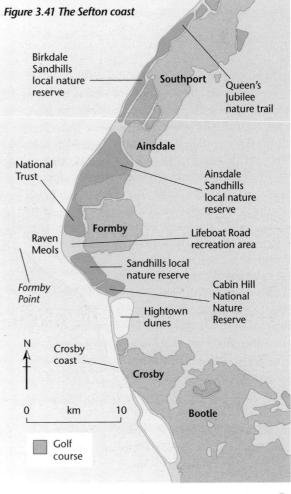

Figure 3.41 The Sefton coast

Birkdale Sandhills local nature reserve

Southport

Queen's Jubilee nature trail

Ainsdale

National Trust

Ainsdale Sandhills local nature reserve

Formby

Lifeboat Road recreation area

Raven Meols

Sandhills local nature reserve

Formby Point

Cabin Hill National Nature Reserve

Hightown dunes

N

Crosby coast

Crosby

0   km   10

Bootle

Golf course

A completely new approach to coastal management has been introduced at Pevensey Bay in East Sussex. Whereas most schemes are funded by a combination of local authorities and government agencies, the Pevensey Bay sea defences are organised and maintained as the country's first public–private partnership (PPP) coastal management scheme.

The project was begun on 1 June 2000 with a 25-year contract and a budget of £30 million. It involves the Environment Agency, HM Treasury and Pevensey Coastal Defence Ltd (PCDL), a consortium of private dredging, construction and consultancy companies. These companies work within the guidelines issued by the Department for Environment Food and Rural Affairs (DEFRA).

The Pevensey Bay sea defences stretch 9 km east from the Sovereign Harbour frontage, a marina and residential development on the outskirts of Eastbourne, towards Bexhill. They protect 50 km^2 of low-lying land, over 15,000 properties, holiday caravan sites, the A259 coast road, the railway line from Hastings to Eastbourne, Brighton and Portsmouth, two nature reserves, a wetland SSSI site and a variety of livestock and arable farms.

The defences centre on the need to manage and improve the existing shingle beach. PCDL has therefore based its management on working with the natural environment of the local sediment sub-cell. This management is environmentally and aesthetically acceptable and is an example of sustainable development which maximises opportunities for future recreational and environmental projects.

The shingle beach stretches the length of the Pevensey Bay coast. It is 6 m high and extends 45 m inland. In front of the shingle is an area of low-angle sandy beach exposed at low tide. There are 150 timber groynes, most of which were in a poor

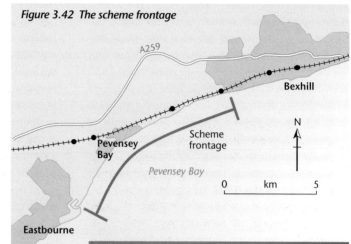

Figure 3.42 The scheme frontage

Photograph 3.8 Using bulldozers to reprofile the beach after a storm

Photograph 3.9 Use of compressed tyres to stabilise the shingle

state of repair and providing little protection. The prevailing longshore drift is from west to east, but as the source of shingle has declined, the beach has become increasingly vulnerable. In this regard Pevensey is typical of most south-coast beaches — they are no longer self-sustaining and need regular replenishment and maintenance if they are to survive.

What has been done?

- **Beach reprofiling** — a crucial part of the management at Pevensey is the use of bulldozers to re-profile the beach after a storm, and each summer ready for the winter storms, by pushing shingle back towards the beach crest (Photograph 3.8). Dump trucks also move material from areas of accretion to areas of loss along the beach. At least one bulldozer is kept on the beach all winter, with more brought in at times of need.
- **Beach replenishment** — a specially adapted barge/dredger, the *Sospan Dau*, is used to bring shingle dredged from the offshore Hastings Bank to the Pevensey Bay shore at high tide. Up to 700 m^3 of shingle can be brought each trip. As the tide falls, heavy machinery is used to move the shingle up the beach. Up to 40,000 tonnes (24,000 m^3) can be added each summer.
- **Beach monitoring** — this is used to monitor areas of accretion and loss using quad bikes, Global Positioning Systems (GPS) and computers to produce three-dimensional models of the beach.
- **Key groynes** — most of the original 150 groynes are being dismantled. Only a few key groynes (those that influence the alignment of the beach) are being replaced.
- **Wooden retaining wall** — at Herbrand Walk, a two-tier timber retaining wall 250 m long has been constructed on the landward face of the beach. This has prevented the inland migration of the beach over a local road.
- **Use of new materials** — the innovative use of non-traditional materials in the defence works has taken place, including compressed tyres and steel plates buried deep in the shingle. If successful, the plan would provide an alternative use for problematic waste and offer a sustainable alternative to dredging offshore shingle banks.

Improved sea defences were in place long before their cost was paid to PCDL. The project is being run within initial budgets, so there are savings to the taxpayer. PCDL has worked closely with local residents and businesses to ensure that they have a full understanding of what the works involve. Further information can be obtained from www.pevensey-bay.co.uk.

Assessment exercises

1 a Look at Figure A, which shows wave refraction at a headland. Identify the features labelled 1–6 by matching them to the terms in the list below:

- direction of wave energy
- waves bend to adopt the shape of the coastline
- wave energy concentrated here
- wave energy dissipated here
- headland
- wave crests

(5 marks)

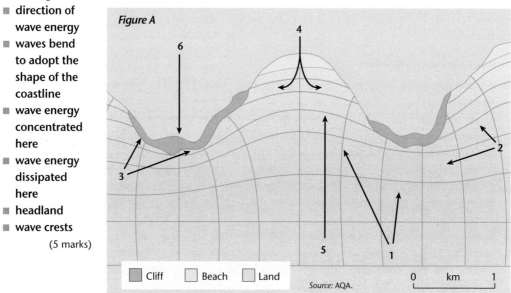

Figure A

Cliff   Beach   Land

0   km   1

Source: AQA.

b Look at Figure B, which shows the features of a beach.
   (i) Name the features marked A and B. (2 marks)
   (ii) The storm beach labelled on Figure B has been formed by destructive waves.
   Draw a labelled diagram to show the main features of destructive waves. (3 marks)

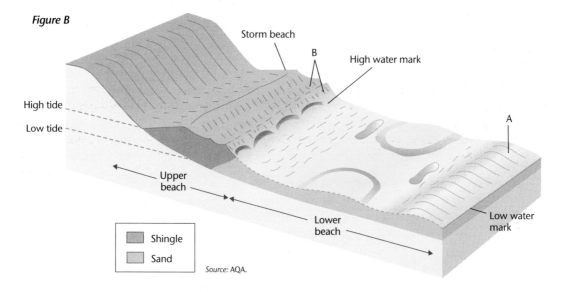

Figure B

Storm beach

B

High water mark

High tide

Low tide

A

Upper beach

Lower beach

Low water mark

Shingle

Sand

Source: AQA.

Photograph A

c Photograph A shows a cliff coastline. Describe the evidence that suggests this coastline is being eroded. In your answer you should refer to specific features on the photograph, using the grid to locate your evidence. (5 marks)

d With reference to an area that you have studied, evaluate the impact of coastal flooding on that area. (15 marks)

(30 marks)

2 Study Figure C, which is a map of Blakeney Point, a spit on the coast of north Norfolk.

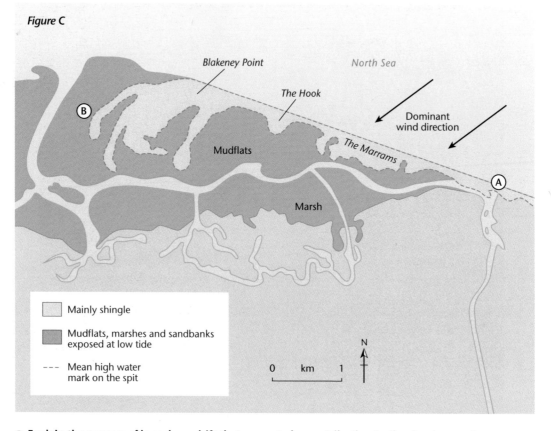

Figure C

a Explain the process of longshore drift that seems to be contributing to the development and extension of Blakeney Point between points A and B. (5 marks)

b Describe the evidence for the existence and direction of longshore drift that you would expect to find on this type of feature. (5 marks)

c Describe the characteristic features of spits. (5 marks)

d With reference to an area that you have studied, outline strategies for managing the impact of longshore drift and comment on the success of such strategies. (15 marks)

(30 marks)

Desert environments

Chapter

4

Location and characteristics

Location

Hot deserts and their margins are located within and just outside the tropics (Figure 4.1). In the southern hemisphere they occur on the western side of the continents. Major deserts are found in the following locations:

➤ North America — the Mexican Desert stretching up into southwest USA, where the Sonoran, Mojave and Colorado Deserts are found
➤ South America — the Atacama Desert of coastal Peru and northern Chile
➤ Africa — the Namib and Kalahari Deserts of the southwest and the Sahara Desert in the north, the largest in the world
➤ Asia — the Arabian, Iranian and Thar Deserts. The Thar straddles the southern part of the Indo-Pakistan frontier
➤ Australia — the Australian Desert is usually divided into two: the Great Sandy (Western) and Simpson Deserts

Figure 4.1
The location of major hot desert areas

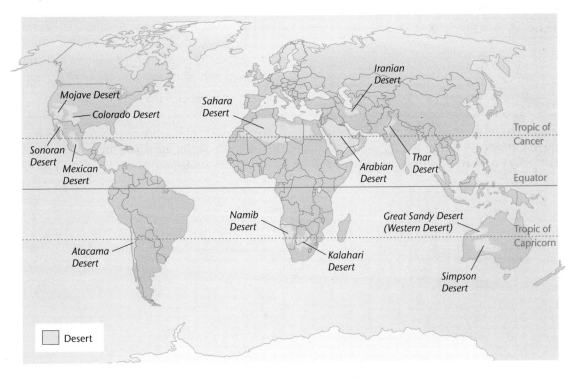

Desert

Climate

Hot desert temperatures are characterised by their extremes. There are big ranges in temperature both *annually* (between the hottest and coldest months) and *diurnally* (between night and day). During the day, especially in summer, there are high levels of insolation as the incoming solar radiation is not impeded by cloud cover. At night, the reverse happens when clear skies allow long-wave radiation to escape and ground temperatures fall rapidly, sometimes to below 0°C. Diurnal ranges of over 30°C are therefore not uncommon (Figure 4.2). Deserts close to the sea have a lower diurnal range (the coastal areas of the Atacama, for example, have highest temperatures of only 22–23°C) owing to the presence of cold offshore ocean currents. The highest shade temperatures recorded in deserts are around 45–55°C. The highest temperature ever recorded was at Al Aziziyah in Libya where the shade temperature reached 57.7°C in September 1922.

Figure 4.2 Diurnal temperature range in a hot desert

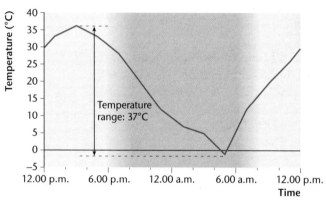

Rainfall in deserts is low and extremely unreliable. As a general rule, the lower the annual rainfall, the less reliable it is. In some places, it may not rain for long periods (Figure 4.3). At Arica in northern Chile, there was once a period of nearly 60 years when no recordable rainfall fell. Rain, when it does fall, produces rapid surface runoff which, together with low infiltration and high evaporation, minimises its effectiveness for vegetation. Deserts are also subject to extreme rainfall events during which more than the yearly average rainfall can fall in a few hours. Djibouti in northeast Africa, with an annual average rainfall of 129 mm, once had 211 mm in 24 hours.

Figure 4.3 Climate graphs for two desert areas

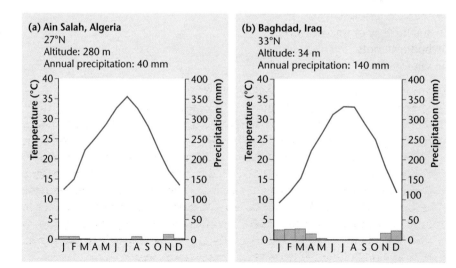

(a) **Ain Salah, Algeria**
27°N
Altitude: 280 m
Annual precipitation: 40 mm

(b) **Baghdad, Iraq**
33°N
Altitude: 34 m
Annual precipitation: 140 mm

Arid The climate of an area that receives less than 250 mm of precipitation per year.

Desertification In 1978 the United Nations defined this as 'the diminution or destruction of the biological potential of the land which can lead ultimately to desert-like conditions'.

Drought A period, usually short term, when the climate is drier than normal owing to the failure of seasonal rains, and from which the natural environment can recover quickly.

Evapotranspiration The sum of evaporation and transpiration. Evaporation is the movement of water to the air from sources such as the soil, water bodies and canopy interception. Transpiration is the loss of water from plants through their stomata. **Potential evapotranspiration** is the water loss that would occur if there was an unlimited supply of water in the soil. It is high in desert regions because the amount of water that could be lost is greater than the amount of water actually available.

Irrigation The artificial application of water to the soil. In crop production it is used mainly to replace missing rainfall in periods of drought.

Semi-arid The climate of an area that receives between 250 and 500 mm of precipitation per year.

Vegetation

Deserts have the lowest organic productivity level of any biome — an average net primary productivity (NPP) of 90 g m^{-2} yr^{-1}. Many areas of deserts have some form of vegetation, with only the sandy sea areas (constantly on the move) and the very driest places being completely barren.

Plants have adapted to arid conditions in a variety of ways:
➤ physical characteristics that prevent moisture loss
➤ the ability to store moisture in their stem or leaves
➤ deep or wide-ranging roots that maximise water gathering
➤ a short life cycle which follows sporadic rainstorms

Desert plants therefore have some of the following features to enable them to survive:
➤ fleshy stems and swollen leaves
➤ thick, waxy cuticles
➤ thick, protective bark
➤ small, spiky or waxy leaves
➤ bulbous roots
➤ salt tolerance

Desert vegetation can be categorised as follows:
➤ **Ephemerals** have a very short life cycle. They remain dormant for long periods, then come to life when it rains. They then complete their cycle by germinating, flowering and dispersing their seeds in up to 3 weeks. An example is *Boerhavia*, which is found in the southern Sahara and has a life cycle of just over 1 week.
➤ **Xerophytes** are plants which have adapted to being able to withstand drought. Within this group are **succulents**, which have various ways of resisting drought, such as the ability to close their stomata during the hottest parts of the day in order to reduce transpiration levels. They have also developed the capacity to store water in fleshy stems and leaves. The cactus is an example of a succulent, as is euphorbia (Photograph 4.1) which grows in Australia.

Photograph 4.1
Euphorbia

➤ **Phreatophytes** are plants which evade drought by having long roots. These enable them to penetrate to depth in order to tap groundwater sources. Examples include the tamarisk tree, the mesquite and the desert melon.

➤ **Halophytes** are plants such as the saltbush, which are adapted to salty conditions found in and around salt flats.

Soils

Soil development in arid environments is inhibited by:

➤ lack of moisture
➤ high rates of evaporation
➤ sparse vegetation cover

Even when soils develop they are generally poor, thin, lacking in organic content and often highly saline.

In the few places where the water table is close to the surface, moisture can be drawn upwards by capillary action. Salts and mineral bases (magnesium, calcium, sodium) are also drawn upwards and deposited in the upper layers to give a slightly alkaline soil.

The zonal soil type in these regions is the **aridosol** (Figure 4.4), which forms very slowly. Such soils range from yellow-red to grey-brown in colour and are generally very thin. The organic content is low (under 2%) and they have a high pH value, typically 7.0–8.5. Such soils may be unproductive but are not particularly infertile. When irrigated, they can yield high-quality produce.

Other soils found in desert areas include:

➤ **solonetzs** — these form in areas where there is sufficient rain to cause some leaching, but not enough to wash the mineral bases right out of the soil. Therefore, the surface layers are not saline. The B horizon is rich in sodium and very clayey, which makes this a difficult soil to cultivate

Figure 4.4
The profile of an aridosol

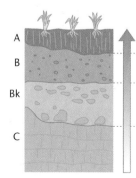

A horizon with prismatic structure, brown or grey

B horizon with clay accumulation

Bk has a thick zone of calcium carbonate accumulation

Salts are carried upwards in solution

> ➤ **solonchaks** — these are found in areas with high evaporation rates. High concentrations of salts are brought to the surface where they form a thick crust rendering the soil infertile

Causes of aridity

The arid nature of these regions arises from a number of factors including the global circulation, continentality, relief and the presence of cold oceanic currents.

Global atmospheric circulation

Hot deserts are found at 20–30° north and south of the equator in a belt where high-pressure systems tend to dominate most of the year. Figure 4.5 shows the global circulation pattern where surface air converges at or near the equator in an area of low pressure known as the **inter-tropical convergence zone (ITCZ)**. At this point, air rises and moves polewards, sinking towards the Earth's surface at around 20–30° north and south. These two pressure cells are known as **Hadley cells**. Air moving towards the equator as part of the mid-latitude circulation (**Ferrel cells**) also sinks at these latitudes and the combination of the sinking air of the Ferrel and Hadley cells creates high pressure at the surface.

Anticyclonic conditions bring clear skies and low rainfall. During the day heat builds up but at night the lack of cloud cover allows the heat to radiate back into space, resulting in high diurnal temperature ranges.

Continentality

Places in maritime regions generally have a much higher rainfall than those inland. The central parts of the Sahara Desert are the parts of Africa most distant from the sea — up to 2,000 km away.

Relief

Some very dry areas lie in the rain shadow of mountains. Moist air brought inland by prevailing winds is forced to rise over mountains, leading to condensation and precipitation on the windward side. As the air descends on the lee side it warms up, with a consequent drop in relative humidity.

In the southern hemisphere, the prevailing southeast **trade winds** meet the Andes. As it descends the western slopes, the air becomes warm and dry, leading to arid conditions (Figure 4.6). The Great Dividing Range in Australia also prevents moisture being carried to the interior of the continent.

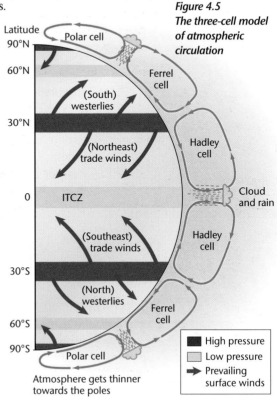

Figure 4.5
The three-cell model of atmospheric circulation

Figure 4.6
Rain shadow effect
in South America

Cold ocean currents

Some west-coast locations in tropical latitudes, such as the Atacama Desert, are extremely dry as a result of a cold ocean current off their shores. These currents are part of the global oceanic circulation and are found in the following areas:

Figure 4.7
The influence of the
Peruvian current

➤ western side of South America — Peruvian (Humboldt) current (Figure 4.7)
➤ southwestern Africa — Benguela current
➤ western Australia — western Australia current

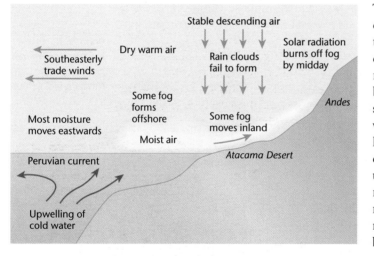

The cold water of the current cools any air that moves across the surface of the sea. Moisture is condensed offshore into fog and mist, which travel inland to be burnt off by strong tropical sunlight. Because the onshore winds have been cooled they have a low moisture-carrying capacity so precipitation is unlikely. These conditions can mean that it does not rain for many years, as was the case in northern Chile described at the beginning of this chapter.

Geomorphological processes

Weathering

Mechanical weathering

Mechanical weathering in deserts results from the extremes of temperature. By day, the air temperature may rise to above 40°C but surface layers can get much hotter — up to 80°C on exposed rock surfaces. At night, temperatures fall rapidly, usually to below 10°C but in some places to 0°C. This creates a daily rhythm of expansion and contraction of rock surfaces which are exposed to uninterrupted insolation during the day. Rock surfaces disintegrate in various ways depending on their geological structure, chemical composition and surface colouring. Several processes have been identified:

➤ **Exfoliation** — as heat does not penetrate easily into rock, the surface is heated to a much higher level than the interior. This leads to stresses being set up within the rock, which leads to cracking that runs parallel to the surface. The surface layers then peel off (Photograph 4.2).

➤ **Granular disintegration** — changes in temperature can cause different minerals within a rock to expand and contract at different rates. This is common in granites and eventually leads to a breakdown of the rock.

➤ **Shattering** — some rocks, such as basalt, which have a homogenous structure may shatter as a result of constant expansion and contraction.

➤ **Block separation** — this happens to rocks such as limestone, which are well jointed with prominent bedding planes. The surfaces break down into block structures along these lines of weakness.

These processes were once believed to operate in isolation. Research, however, has shown that the presence of moisture, even in tiny amounts, is essential for most mechanical weathering in hot deserts. Although rainfall may be limited, the rapid loss of temperature at night frequently results in dew forming and coating rock surfaces with a thin film of water.

Chemical weathering

Chemical weathering occurs in various ways but largely involves the presence of salts deposited from rainfall or brought to the surface by capillary action.

➤ **Crystal growth** — dissolved salts in water in cracks or joints form crystals as the water evaporates. Further heating causes the crystals to expand, resulting in rocks being prised apart. Eventually pieces of rock fall off.

Photograph 4.2 Granite rock in the Mojave Desert undergoing exfoliation

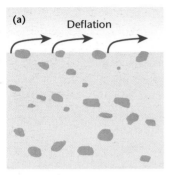

(a) Deflation

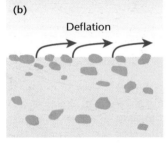

(b) Deflation

(c)

Figure 4.8
The evolution of reg

Figure 4.9
The formation of a deflation hollow

> **Hydration** — certain rocks, especially those containing salt minerals, are capable of absorbing water into their structure, causing them to swell and become vulnerable to future breakdown. Gypsum, for example, is the result of water being added to the mineral anhydrite.
> **Solution** — some minerals in rocks, such as salt, are soluble in water and dissolve when water is applied to them.

Many desert areas have an accumulation of salts near to or on their surfaces and the particles become stuck together to form **duricrusts**. Present-day arid conditions may explain some of these crusts but others may be the result of previous climatic conditions. There are several types of crusts, depending on the nature of their composition: gypcretes are gypsum-based, while calcrete is rich in lime. Under certain conditions a thin, hard and shiny dark-red surface forms where oxides of iron and manganese have accumulated on the surface. This is known as **desert varnish**.

Wind action (aeolian processes)

Wind erosion

Wind erosion takes two forms:

> **Deflation** — the wind removes loose surface material and carries it away. As the finer material is transported, deflation leaves behind a rock-strewn surface which is known as **reg** or **desert pavement** (Figure 4.8).
> **Abrasion** — material carried in the wind sandblasts exposed rock surfaces and carves them into a variety of shapes. The main factors that affect the rate of abrasion include the velocity and frequency of the wind, wind direction, the lithology of the rocks and the size of loose particles on the desert floor.

Deflation hollows (Figure 4.9) are formed when the wind removes vast amounts of surface material. In north Africa, deflation hollows can cover hundreds of square kilometres. The largest is the Qattara Depression in Egypt, which at its deepest is over 100 m below sea level and must have involved the removal of millions of tonnes of sand and other material.

Ventifacts are rocks lying on the desert floor that have been shaped by wind-driven sand. They usually have sharp edges and smooth sides.

Stage 1 Underlying basin structure within rocks is covered by a thick accumulation of sand	**Stage 2** Strong winds remove some of the loose material to reveal part of the basin shape

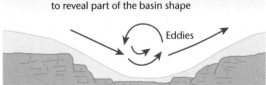

Eddies

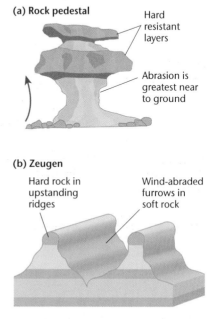

Photograph 4.3 Rock pedestals

Corel

Yardangs are extensive parallel ridges of rock separated by grooves or troughs. They are aligned in the direction of the prevailing wind (Figure 4.10). The grooves are cut by abrasion. In some areas, yardangs are impressive features over 100 m tall and running for several kilometres. The biggest concentration of such large yardangs is in central areas of the Sahara in the Tibesti mountains.

Rock pedestals (Figure 4.11 and Photograph 4.3) are mushroom-shaped rocks, formed when abrasion undercuts a tabular mass of resistant rock. Undercutting occurs as the wind is effective only up to a height of 1.5 m from the ground. When this happens on a larger scale, the wind may cut furrows through a cap rock into softer rock beneath producing a landform with long ridges. This feature is known as a **zeugen** (Figure 4.11).

(a) Rock pedestal

Hard resistant layers

Abrasion is greatest near to ground

(b) Zeugen

Hard rock in upstanding ridges

Wind-abraded furrows in soft rock

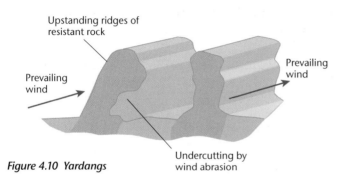

Upstanding ridges of resistant rock

Prevailing wind

Prevailing wind

Undercutting by wind abrasion

Figure 4.10 Yardangs

Figure 4.11 Features of wind erosion

Wind transport

The movement of particles by the wind is dependent on several factors:
➤ the speed and direction of the wind
➤ the amount of turbulence
➤ how long the wind blows
➤ the nature of the surface (regolith)
➤ the amount of vegetation present

The wind moves material in three main ways, the effectiveness of which depends on the velocity of the wind and the size of surface particles (Figure 4.12):

➤ **Suspension** — the finest material is picked up and carried by the wind, often over considerable distances. Saharan sand is occasionally blown as far north as the British Isles where it sometimes falls as 'red rain'. Suspension involves material with a diameter of less than 0.15 mm. When winds are high velocity, sandstorms occur.

Figure 4.12
Wind transport

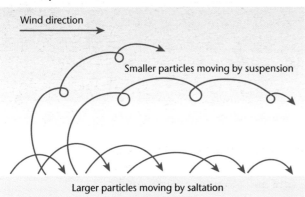

➤ **Saltation** — a process which moves sand grains forward in a series of leaps and bounds. The grains are caught by a gust of wind, move forward and then drop back to the surface. Most saltation takes place close to the surface, but it is possible for this process to raise particles up to a height of 2 m.

➤ **Surface creep** — coarser particles, which are too heavy to be uplifted, may be rolled along the surface or pushed forward as other wind-blown particles hit them.

Wind deposition

When the velocity of the wind decreases to the point where particles can no longer be transported, sediment is deposited. Dunes may form around an obstacle as the wind is slowed on the downward side of the barrier (Figure 4.13). As the wind velocity decreases, some of the sediment in suspension can no longer be held so it falls to create some form of deposit.

Figure 4.13
Wind deposition
around obstacles

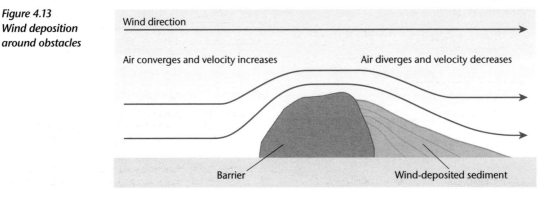

*Photograph 4.4
Dunes in the Namib
desert*

Corel

Dunes are the main feature that results from deposition. Large areas of sand dunes in arid regions are known as **ergs**. Dunes vary greatly in shape depending mainly on the direction of the prevailing wind and other winds that may be present (Photograph 4.4). They vary in height from a few millimetres to giant dunes between 500 m and 1,000 m high. Dunes also move in the general direction of the prevailing wind as material is moved by saltation on the windward side and by a series of flows, slides and slumps down the steep face of the lee side. One type of dune is the crescent-shaped **barchan** (Figure 4.14).

*Figure 4.14
Barchans and their
formation*

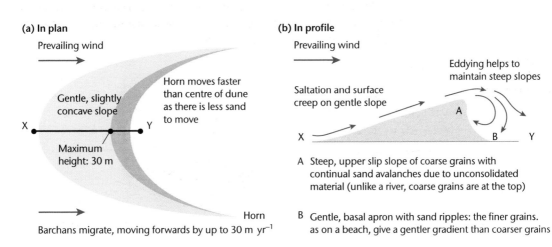

(a) In plan

Prevailing wind

Gentle, slightly
concave slope

Horn moves faster
than centre of dune
as there is less sand
to move

X   Y

Maximum
height: 30 m

Horn

Barchans migrate, moving forwards by up to 30 m yr^{-1}

(b) In profile

Prevailing wind

Eddying helps to
maintain steep slopes

Saltation and surface
creep on gentle slope

A

X   B   Y

A   Steep, upper slip slope of coarse grains with
continual sand avalanches due to unconsolidated
material (unlike a river, coarse grains are at the top)

B   Gentle, basal apron with sand ripples: the finer grains,
as on a beach, give a gentler gradient than coarser grains

Another form of dune is a **seif** which is named after an Arabic curved sword. These can run for long distances (100 km) and can be up to 200 m in height. Such dunes have serrated crests and sides resulting from the action of localised wind eddies. Modern classification of dunes includes transverse, reversing, parabolic, dome and star. Where a series of star dunes forms into a long serrated ridge (up to 5,000 m long and reaching heights of 400 m), the resultant feature is known as a **draa**.

Water action

Although most rainfall in arid areas occurs in low-intensity storms, there are occasional sudden and more isolated heavy downpours which have an effect on the landscape. In upland areas such as desert mountains and plateaux, water is often dominant as an erosional agent, whereas in lowland regions it is common to see features that result from deposition.

Rivers and streams that flow in deserts fall into the following categories:

➤ **Exogenous** — perennial rivers (they flow throughout the year) that rise in areas beyond deserts and then flow through the arid area. The best-known example is the Nile which has its origins in the Ethiopian highlands and central Africa and flows across the arid regions of north Africa to reach the Mediterranean. In North America, the Colorado River (Photograph 4.5) rises in the Rocky Mountains and then flows across the dry regions of southwest USA to the

Photograph 4.5
The Colorado River

Corel

Pacific Ocean. Both these rivers are highly managed with dams, reservoirs and irrigation schemes, reflecting their great importance to the areas across which they flow.

➤ **Endoreic** — rivers that flow to an inland lake rather than to the sea. A good example is the River Jordan which flows into the Dead Sea.

➤ **Ephemeral** — streams and rivers that are typical of desert areas as they flow intermittently after heavy rainstorms. Such streams are capable of generating a high level of discharge due to the torrential nature of the rain which exceeds the infiltration capacity of the ground, the hard ground after periods of drought which makes it difficult for water to penetrate and the lack of vegetation which means that little or no interception takes place. For these reasons most of the rainfall drains away as surface runoff.

Flooding takes place in many desert areas. After the start of a torrential downpour, it does not take long for water to start to flow across the land in the form of a sheet flood. When this runoff becomes concentrated in steep-sided valleys known as **wadis** (**arroyos** in the Americas), flash floods occur.

Water erosion

Wadis are the main feature of desert areas carved out by water. Such channels can vary from a few metres in length to complex systems over 100 km long. The valleys are generally steep-sided with broad flat bottoms where deposits have built up.

Photograph 4.6 Mesas and buttes in the Monument Valley National Park, USA

Corel

Channels on the valley floor tend to be braided because of the thick sediment and change their patterns after each flash flood.

Where the strata are formed of sedimentary rock with horizontal bedding planes, water erosion leaves behind **mesas** and **buttes**. Mesas are plateau-like features that are flat on top (the word is Spanish for table), with steep edges often falling away to a wadi or canyon. Buttes are formed in a similar way but are much smaller. Water has eroded most of the rock, leaving only a thin pillar. The lower slopes of mesas and buttes are covered in scree resulting from mechanical weathering and rockfall. The most spectacular examples are in the Monument Valley National Park in Arizona, USA (Photograph 4.6).

A more rounded type of isolated hill is known as an **inselberg**. These are found in a number of climatic areas including semi-arid regions and are formed from crystalline rocks such as granite. There has been much debate about the formation of such features but in semi-arid areas geomorphologists have suggested that they are relic features, not only of current erosional patterns but also of past climatic conditions when rainfall was higher. Inselbergs are believed to have evolved due to deep chemical weathering of crystalline rock, which then became exposed after water removed the surface deposits. This type of weathering is common in more humid environments, which helps support the theory that deserts experienced previous wetter periods (pluvials).

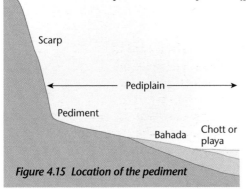

Figure 4.15 Location of the pediment

Water deposition

At the foot of highland regions lies the pediment (Figure 4.15). This gently sloping area (less than 7°) of bare rock and debris has a distinct break in the slope at its junction with the upland area. Water erosion is believed to have played some part in their formation, along with the deposition of material washed down from the uplands and deposited where the slope angle changes abruptly.

Where an ephemeral or perennial stream runs down from an upland area, material will build up

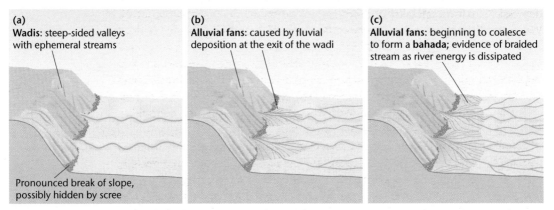

(a)
Wadis: steep-sided valleys with ephemeral streams

Pronounced break of slope, possibly hidden by scree

(b)
Alluvial fans: caused by fluvial deposition at the exit of the wadi

(c)
Alluvial fans: beginning to coalesce to form a **bahada**; evidence of braided stream as river energy is dissipated

Figure 4.16 The formation of a bahada

Photograph 4.7 A salt lake in the Namib Desert

Corel

where it meets the much gentler slopes of the lowland. This is the result of rapid energy loss on the break in slope leading to the deposition of most of the stream's load. The deposits are spread out in an **alluvial fan** by the small distributaries running from a wadi. Alluvial fans vary in size from a few metres to several kilometres in length. Within the fans the deposited material is graded, with the coarsest material on the upside of the fan and the smallest on the downside.

In areas where a number of parallel wadis arrive at a mountain front, alluvial fans may coalesce to form a much larger feature known as a **bahada (bajada)** (Figure 4.16). These may cover up the pediment or form beyond it.

At the lowest part of the desert surface, ephemeral water flows into inland depressions to form **salt lakes** or **chotts** (**playas** in the Americas) (Photograph 4.7). Water, after filling these lakes, rapidly evaporates leading to the formation of a thick crust, which cracks after long dry periods. Sodium chloride is the most common salt found in such locations; other salts include calcium sulphate (gypsum), sodium sulphate, magnesium sulphate, and potassium and magnesium chlorides. These salts can be exploited commercially. One of the best known salt lakes is the Chott el Djerid of southern Tunisia, which occupies an intermontane basin over 100 km wide and for the most part consists of bare salt flats.

In some semi-arid environments, water action creates a landscape known as **badlands** (Photograph 4.8). These are areas where soft and relatively impermeable rocks are moulded by rapid runoff which results from heavy but irregular rainfall. The aridity of the climate ensures that there is insufficient vegetation cover to hold the regolith and bedrock together, but the rainfall and subsequent runoff is

Corel

**Photograph 4.8
Badlands in South
Dakota, USA**

sufficiently powerful to create dramatic erosional and depositional landforms. General features of badlands landscapes include:

➤ extensive development of wadis of all sizes with steep sides and debris-covered bottoms

➤ gullies, which erode headwards on hillsides, cutting into them and contributing to their collapse

➤ slope failure and slumping

➤ alluvial fans at the foot of steep slopes where wadis or smaller gullies emerge

➤ pipes, which are formed when water passes through surface cracks and carves out eroded passageways. Pipes may also form caves when surface runoff is directed towards them

➤ natural arches, which are created by the erosion of a cave over a period of time

A good example of a badland landscape occurs in southern Tunisia around Matmata. This stark landscape has attracted a number of film makers and part of the original *Star Wars* film was shot there.

Desertification

The term 'desertification' has been defined in many ways. In 1978, a United Nations conference came up with the simple statement that it is 'the diminution or destruction of the biological potential of the land which can lead ultimately to desert-like conditions'. This simple definition:

➤ does not state if the cause is natural or human

➤ does not indicate whether the damage may be reversible, stating only that change has taken place

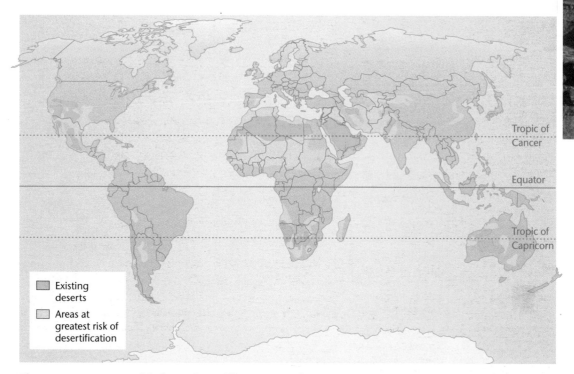

*Figure 4.17
Areas at risk from
desertification*

The areas at greatest risk from desertification are shown on Figure 4.17. This includes the desert margins and semi-desert areas in the Sahel, an area lying on the southern side of the Sahara.

There has been debate in the scientific community over many decades about the causes of desertification. Professor Andrew Goudie, a geographer at Oxford University, says:

> it is a belief that portions of the Earth's surface are drying up, leading to the spread of deserts, the depletion of groundwater reserves, the dwindling of rivers and the decline of settlement. By some it has been regarded as the result of progressive climatic deterioration in post-glacial times, while others have seen it as a result of the human mismanagement of the environment.

Semi-arid environments are fragile, and their boundaries fluctuate depending on changing patterns of rainfall and variations in the way in which people manage the land. It is difficult to separate natural causes of desertification from human ones and short-term fluctuations from long-term trends. There is no doubt, however, that severe land degradation, which can lead to desertification, is taking place and that any increase in the problem is likely to be the result of people's mismanagement of natural resources.

Climatic change

There is evidence from hot desert areas that climatic change has had considerable impacts on landscapes within the last few thousand years. Such changes are the result of:

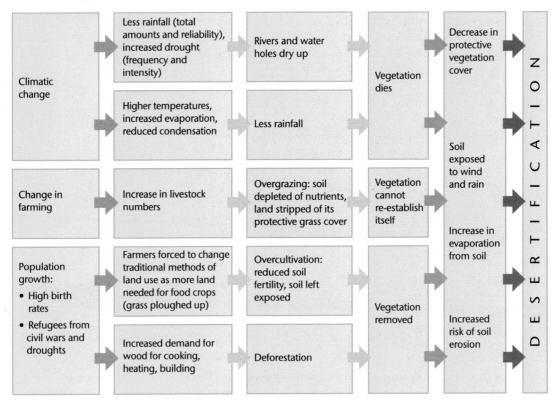

Figure 4.18
The causes of desertification in areas such as the Sahel

> reduced rainfall (total amounts and reliability)
> increased drought (frequency and intensity)
> higher temperatures leading to increased evapotranspiration and reduced condensation. Ultimately, this will lead to lower rainfall

As a result, rivers and other surface and underground water sources gradually dry up and vegetation cover decreases (Figure 4.18). The surface is then exposed to wind and occasional rain as it has lost its protective cover.

Human causes

In the past in semi-arid areas, populations were limited and well adapted to environmental conditions. Population growth, via either natural causes or migration, has led to growing pressure on the land to produce more food. This may include a change in traditional methods of farming. Overcultivation, overgrazing and deforestation all result in the removal of vegetation that cannot be re-established, the exposure of the ground surface to wind and rain and consequent soil erosion, land degradation and, ultimately, desertification.

There is also a greater demand for wood for cooking and heating in some areas.

Impacts of desertification

Desertification has an impact on the landscape, the ecosystem and on the population of an area. The main effects are:

➤ a reduction in the amount of vegetation, particularly the climax species which, with severe desertification, can make up less than 10% of the plant community
➤ severe soil erosion with, ultimately, almost all of the topsoil removed
➤ increasing soil salinity leading to the development of salt crusts
➤ deep gullies on slopes
➤ increasing amounts of sand, often formed into dunes
➤ increasing frequency of sandstorms
➤ declining fertility of soils even in irrigated areas where salt crusts may form as a result of rising water tables
➤ increase in the area of treeless zones. It is now estimated that the radius of the treeless zone around Khartoum, Sudan is 90 km
➤ decline in agricultural productivity leading to food shortages and famine
➤ movement of population away from affected areas to other regions where, because of increased population, pressure will be applied to resources such as the soil and fuelwood

Case study — Desertification in the Sahel

The Sahel is a zone between the Sahara Desert and the more fertile lands further south. The area runs from the Atlantic Ocean to the Horn of Africa and includes parts of Senegal, Mauritania, Mali, Burkina Faso, Niger, Nigeria, Chad, Sudan and Eritrea (Figure 4.19). It has a population of over 50 million people. The term 'sahel' derives from the Arabic, meaning a shore, border or coast — the edge of the Sahara.

Two periods of drought followed by famine in 1968–74 and 1979–84 brought the attention of the world to this region with news images of dry lands, dying cattle and emaciated people. These periods of poor rainfall struck particularly hard for many Sahelian farmers and pastoralists, resulting in an estimated 100,000 drought-related deaths.

The annual average rainfall of the Sahel is low (100–200 mm), with most of the rain falling in the period between June and September. The natural vegetation is a mixture of xerophytic shrubs and grasses. Traditional activities include livestock herding, cultivation (dependent on the 3-month rainfall period as well as rivers, lakes and other seasonal water courses), fishing and long-distance trading.

There is plenty of evidence of the expansion and contraction of the Sahara Desert as rainfall has varied over time. This can be seen in fluctuations in the levels of salt lakes, the past distribution of sand

Figure 4.19 The location of the Sahel

TUNISIA
MOROCCO
ALGERIA
LIBYA
EGYPT
WESTERN SAHARA
MAURITANIA
MALI
NIGER
CHAD
ERITREA
SENEGAL
BURKINA FASO
SUDAN
THE GAMBIA
GUINEA BISSAU
GUINEA
NIGERIA
ETHIOPIA
SIERRA LEONE
LIBERIA
CÔTE D'IVOIRE
GHANA
BENIN
TOGO
CAMEROON

N

0   km   1000

dunes, and in the recordings of humans such as cave paintings and the writings of European explorers and settlers. Human activities may have contributed to land degradation, including:

- civil wars in Ethiopia, Eritrea and Somalia
- population growth
- settling of the nomadic population, leading to overcultivation

Table 4.1 Energy needs in selected Sahel countries, 1980

Country	Percentage provided by wood
Burkina Faso	94
Mauritania	69
Senegal	60
The Gambia	87
Mali	93
Niger	88
Chad	89
Average	82

These factors have led to a decline in vegetation and a gradual reduction in the amount of moisture in the soil.

Another factor that contributes to desertification is the use of wood for fuel. Sahelians rarely eat uncooked food and most dishes are cooked for long periods. The Club du Sahel estimated in 1980 that 82% of the total energy needs of a number of countries in the area was supplied by wood (Table 4.1).

Attempted solutions

Initiatives to try to solve desertification and famine in the Sahel can be categorised as follows:

- Early-warning systems have been put in place to prevent the onset of drought-induced food shortages. These provide the data necessary to predict or assess potential crop loss and animal shortfalls, based partly on **remotely sensed data of vegetation cover and rainfall patterns** and partly on **food market surveys**. Such a **famine early-warning system** (FEWS) has been developed by the American aid programme USAID.
- Locally based efforts to nurture and protect the resource base are a feature of many development initiatives. These involve encouraging farmer cooperatives, small-scale non-governmental organisation (NGO) projects and other inter-

nationally funded development schemes in programmes involved in **environmental rehabilitation, soil and water conservation** and **agro-forestry**.

- Some schemes are focused on improving production technologies such as **higher-yielding drought-resistant crops, irrigation** or **improved ranching and grazing schemes**.
- Organisations that offer help and support to the Sahel include the **Sahel and West Africa Club** (formerly the Club du Sahel), which was set up by member countries of the Organisation for Economic Cooperation and Development (OECD). Its mission is to help identify and address strategic questions related to medium- and long-term development in west Africa.

Good examples of local schemes are those that operate in the central plateau of Burkina Faso, occupied by the Mossi people. The plateau is a site for some of the most innovative techniques in soil and water conservation and agro-forestry in this part of the world. For example, **contour stone lines** (Photograph 4.9) — built by farmers and consisting of lines of stones and rocks placed across the land contour — are a cheap and popular erosion control method publicised by organisations such as Oxfam. They slow the overland flow from summer rains and capture water where it is needed by the growing crops. They also encourage the deposition of sediments rich in soil nutrients. Such schemes have transformed the rural landscape around hundreds of villages in this part of Burkina Faso.

Oxfam has worked for a long time in the Sahel, bringing both short-term relief from food shortages and programmes aimed at the long-term rehabilitation of the area.

In 2005 Niger was hit by rain failure and a locust invasion. This had the effect of reducing food production by at least one third, and food prices rose sharply. Oxfam surveys noted that:

- people were eating less than normal
- people were gathering wild foods (leaves and berries) and digging up ant hills to find scraps of millet

Photograph 4.9 Building stone lines in Burkina Faso to control soil erosion

Mark Edwards/Still Pictures

- some households had earmarked almost all their income for food
- families were saving money by taking children out of school and stopping visits to health centres
- households were trying to make more income by selling household goods and cutting down trees to sell as firewood (the rate of deforestation in Niger in 2005 was noticeable)
- families were selling their livestock
- competition for scarce pasture was leading to conflict in some areas

Oxfam identified the poorest 20% of communities and began a series of programmes:
- **Cash for work schemes** whereby projects are identified within a community and Oxfam employs people to work on them in return for vouchers which they can then exchange for food. Those who are too elderly or sick are given free vouchers.
- **Destocking programmes** which aim to reduce the numbers of animals in circulation. The owners are paid a fair price for their least healthy livestock, allowing them to buy feed for those that remain.

Oxfam has worked closely with the Association to Revive Herding in Niger (AREN) on long-term activities including:
- **animal livestock fairs** where pastoralists can obtain new animals and subsidised animal feed
- **vaccination campaigns**
- **rehabilitating and constructing water points**
- **strengthening the capacity of Oxfam's partners** through training, so that they have the skills to better respond and assist people

Economic development

There has been a long history of colonisation, development of agriculture and evolution of urban areas in the arid regions of the world. The ability of such regions to continue development and to sustain a growing population has been based for a long time on the use of irrigation to maintain food supplies. Mineral wealth has been a factor in their recent development, especially in the Middle East with its oil-producing nations such as Saudi Arabia, Bahrain, Qatar, Kuwait, the UAE, Iraq and Iran. Mineral wealth has also been exploited in Chile (copper) and Australia (gold, iron ore).

Countries such as the USA have considerable wealth-generating regions outside their desert areas and some of this wealth has been invested in the development of arid regions. In recent years the southwest — the dry part of the USA — has had huge growth in both wealth and population and this phenomenon has also occurred in Australia.

Case study Southwest USA

Apart from the middle east, the southwest USA is the most economically developed area of desert in the world. Many states of the western USA have arid or semi-arid regions within them, but the core of the dry area is made up from Arizona, Colorado, Nevada, New Mexico and Utah. The water supply comes mainly from the Colorado River and its tributaries such as the Gunnison, a supply which many experts believe has reached its limit.

Although it has a low population density, this region has the fastest-growing population in the USA (Table 4.2). The sustainability of the economic growth and lifestyle of the region are issues under debate.

Water supply, irrigation and hydroelectric power

The basin of the Colorado River covers over 90,000 km² and is the most heavily used source of irrigation water in the USA. For the purposes of water extraction and management, the basin has been divided into upper and lower areas.

The basin was developed for water supplies in the early years of the twentieth century. One of the major issues has been the transfer of water from the upper to the lower basin states, which resulted in the construction of the Glen Canyon dam and Lake Powell, where water from the upper basin

Table 4.2 Population growth, southwest USA

State	Population, 1990 (thousands)	Population, 2000 (thousands)	Percentage growth
Arizona	3,811	5,131	34.6
Colorado	3,302	4,301	30.3
Nevada	1,266	1,998	57.8
New Mexico	1,520	1,819	19.7
Utah	1,749	2,233	27.7

could be stored and released when needed. In 1968 the Colorado River basin project was established. This regulated the river flow and set up plans to improve navigation, reclaim land via irrigation, improve water quality, maintain fish stocks and develop recreational facilities.

Some of the problems that have been encountered include the following:

■ The allocation of water rights was based on data collected in the 1920s which experts now agree was one of the wetter periods for the southwest, with plentiful river flows. This means that virtually all the current flow of the Colorado is allocated to various projects. As a result, the river no longer reaches the sea in the Gulf of California except for some local flood flow. This has led to arguments between the states of the upper and lower basins regarding water release.

■ There has been a marked increase in salinity downstream which has led to tensions between the USA and Mexico.

■ Conflict has occurred between farmers, the water authority and Native Americans with regard to water allocations.

Agriculture

The dry climate of the region meant that the first Europeans introduced cattle ranching, which still remains a major activity, particularly in Colorado. With the development of irrigation, more intensive forms of agriculture were introduced including cotton, grapes, nuts and vegetables. Irrigation has brought a number of problems including salinisation, the lowering of the water table and conflicts over water rights. As population growth demands more from a shrinking water supply, battles are erupting over water rights and some farm production may have to shift elsewhere because of urban growth.

Mining

The southwestern states of the USA are an important source of minerals. Copper is the major resource with mining taking place in Arizona, Utah and New Mexico. Other minerals that are exploited include silver, gold, mercury and beryllium. The evaporate crusts of the Great Salt Lake in Utah are the source of a range of salts that include potassium and sodium sulphate.

Manufacturing

There is a range of traditional industries including those related to mineral exploitation, food processing and timber extraction. In modern times the defence and associated industries have been attracted to the clear skies of the region and its open unpopulated spaces. In the Las Vegas area there are important nuclear testing facilities and electronic industries. This has led to the growth of military installations as well as the dumping of nuclear waste.

Tourism

In some areas, tourism is becoming the major source of employment. Nevada, for example, has

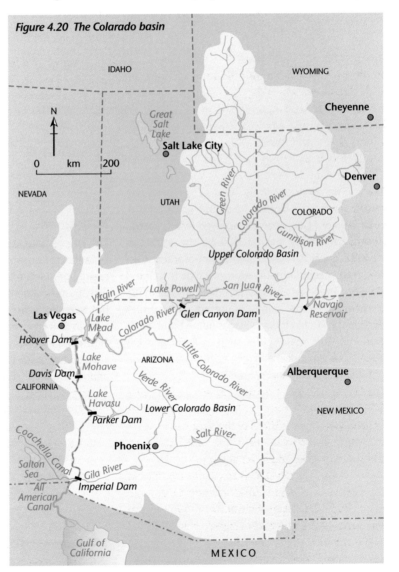

Figure 4.20 The Colarado basin

Figure 4.21 Advertisement for Sun City West

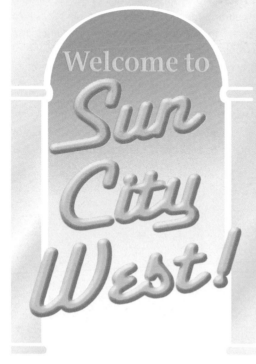

Retiring soon? Looking for a second home? Looking at active adult retirement communities? Look no further...Sun City West is the premier retirement golf community in Arizona, a mature, lush oasis nestled in the valley of the sun, near Phoenix, Arizona. With more than 320 days of sunshine, we are far away from harsh winters. The community sports four high-quality recreational complexes, nine impressive golf courses, and our own 30-lane bowling alley. We enjoy convenient local businesses, places of worship and a nationally ranked hospital.

These extensive facilities are available at a surprisingly low cost. Sun City West offers a diverse range of homes priced from $127,000 to $940,000. Our golf fees are among the lowest in Arizona....We are a self contained retirement community with shopping, healthcare facilities and recreation in one community. We even have a pet park for Rover to romp in.

Come and see for yourself! Be sure to visit our Sun City West Visitors' Center when you come to Arizona.

over 30% of its workforce employed in this sector. Tourism has been encouraged by the attractive desert scenery, the lakes along the Colorado River and the outstanding attractions such as the Grand Canyon. There has also been a significant rise in the numbers of people visiting important cultural sites such as the Pueblo Indian villages in the Mesa Verde National Park. Major cities such as Reno and Las Vegas have expanded with their economies based on gambling and live entertainment.

Retirement

The dry climate, all-year-round sunshine and the potential for outdoor activities have encouraged a rapidly growing retired population. This was originally based in the major urban centres of the region but in recent years specific retirement settlements such as Sun City near Phoenix, Arizona have grown. Figure 4.21 shows a typical advertisement for one such complex stressing the sunshine, warm winters and recreational facilities.

Assessment exercises

1 a Describe the distribution of arid and semi-arid areas as shown on Figure A. (5 marks)

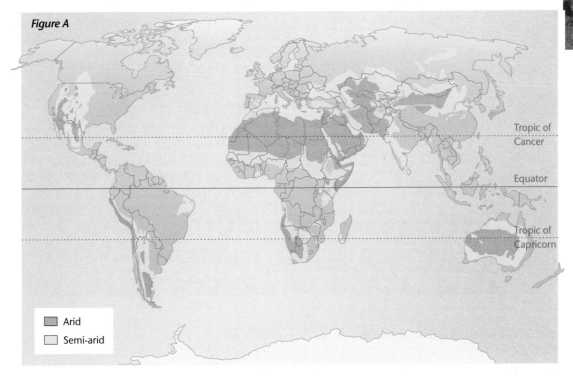

Figure A

Tropic of Cancer

Equator

Tropic of Capricorn

■ Arid
□ Semi-arid

b Show how atmospheric high pressure can be a factor in producing the low levels of precipitation in desert areas. (4 marks)
c Describe the role of mechanical (physical) weathering in the formation of desert landscapes. (6 marks)
d To what extent are the people of the Sahel responsible for desertification? (15 marks)
(30 marks)

2 a Describe the landforms shown in Photograph A. (4 marks)
b Describe the processes by which the wind is able to erode in hot desert areas. (5 marks)
c Describe, with the aid of diagrams, the formation of any landform in hot deserts that results from wind deposition. (6 marks)
d Compare and evaluate the strategies adopted with regard to land use and agriculture in two contrasting areas of hot deserts and their margins. (15 marks)
(30 marks)

Photograph A

Corel

Unit 1

Physical and human geography

Core human topic

Population change

The population of an area alters as a consequence of both natural change and migration. The annual population change of an area is the cumulative change in the size of a population after both natural change and migration have been taken into account.

Table 5.1
Global population data

Region	Birth rate (per 1,000)	Fertility (per woman)	Death rate (per 1,000)	Infant mortality rate (per 1,000)	Life expectancy at birth (years)	Population density (per km²)
World	21	2.7	9	52	67	329
MEDCs	11	1.6	10	6	77	158
LEDCs	23	2.9	8	57	65	433
Africa	38	5.1	15	84	52	205
North America	14	2.0	8	7	78	111
Latin America	21	2.5	6	26	72	184
Asia	20	2.4	7	49	68	839
Europe	10	1.4	12	7	75	212
Oceania	17	2.1	7	27	75	26

Source: World Population Data Sheet (2006)

Key terms

Birth rate A measure of an area's fertility. It is expressed as the number of live births per 1,000 people in 1 year.

Death rate The number of deaths per 1,000 people in 1 year.

Life expectancy The average number of years from birth that a person can expect to live.

Longevity The increase in life expectancy over a period of time. It is a direct result of improved medical provision and increased levels of economic development. People live longer and this creates an older population.

Natural change The change in size of a population caused by the interrelationship between birth and death rates. If birth rate exceeds death rate, a population will increase. If death rate exceeds birth rate, a population will decline.

The growth of world population

In 1999, the world's population reached 6 billion. It has grown rapidly in the last 200 years, particularly since 1950 (Table 5.2). Natural increase peaked at 2.2% globally in the 1960s. Since then, falling birth rates have reduced this increase to 1.2%. However, the global population is still expanding by 80 million every year. Estimates suggest that by 2050 the global population will be 9 billion, with zero growth occurring only towards the end of the century.

The growth in world population has not taken place evenly. The populations of some continents have grown

Year	Population (billions)
1800	1.1
1850	1.4
1900	1.8
1950	2.6
2000	6.1

Table 5.2
World population growth, 1800–2000

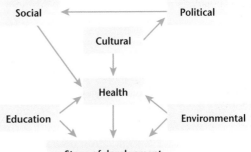

and continue to grow at faster rates than others. Europe, North America and Australasia have very low growth rates. In 1995, their share of the world's population was 20%. This is expected to fall to 12% by 2050. It is estimated that Europe's population will shrink by 90 million during this period.

Asia has a rapid, but declining, rate of population growth. Between 1995 and 2050, China, India and Pakistan will contribute most to world population growth. Indeed, it is estimated that by 2050 India will overtake China as the world's most populous country. Another potential area of rapid population growth is sub-Saharan Africa, particularly Nigeria and the Democratic Republic of Congo.

Causes of population growth

Several different factors interrelate to cause growth in the world's population (Figure 5.1):

➤ **health** — the control of disease, birth control measures, infant mortality rates, diet and malnutrition, the numbers of doctors and nurses, sexual health, sanitation

➤ **education** — health education, the age at which compulsory schooling finishes, females in education, levels of tertiary education, literacy levels (Photograph 5.1)

➤ **social provision** — levels of care for the elderly, availability of radio and other forms of media, clean water supply

➤ **cultural factors** — religious attitudes to birth control, status gain from having children, the role of women in society, sexual morality

Figure 5.1
Causes of world population growth

Photograph 5.1
A primary school in Malawi. Some of the children are late starters because the government only recently introduced primary education for all

> ➤ **political factors** — taxation to support services, strength of the economy, impact of war and conflicts, access to healthcare and contraception
> ➤ **environmental factors** — frequency of hazards, environmental conditions that breed disease

All countries and regions of the world are dynamic and changing. They develop both economically and socially and this affects population change over time.

The measurement of population characteristics

Most of the countries in the world collect data about their populations, usually in the form of a census. This is a detailed collection of information on a regular basis — for example, every 10 years. The data collected include employment characteristics, ethnicity, educational attainment, patterns of social activity, and housing type and ownership.

In the UK, the data are collated by areas of local government and by postcode. The smallest area is that covered by one census collector — an area known as an **enumeration district**.

The information collected is of use to:

> ➤ governments — to provide a basis for the allocation of resources to services such as health, education and employment
> ➤ non-governmental bodies — retailers, advertisers, financial services, property developers and utilities

Censuses are not without problems. Some people object to them on the grounds that they infringe privacy. Some people do not return their census forms. Political conditions in some countries make censuses difficult to organise.

At a national government level, a census:

> ➤ records trends over the previous 10 years which can be projected forward to enable planning in a range of social services
> ➤ helps with prediction of natural population change and migration patterns
> ➤ enables the estimation of national housing demands
> ➤ enables the planning of national transport demands
> ➤ is a snapshot of the diversity of the country

For businesses and commerce, a census:

> ➤ can be linked to other data sources, such as credit card data, to provide information on regional lifestyles
> ➤ enables targeted marketing, based on postcode areas
> ➤ enables the insurance industry to assess risk more effectively
> ➤ enables retailers to invest in optimum locations where spending power is highest
> ➤ allows firms to target goods to stores according to the profile of the population. For example, supermarkets stock more prepared foods in areas where there are greater numbers of young single adults

Indicator	Niger	Guatemala	Yemen	Haiti	Kenya	Pakistan	Botswana	USA	UK
Birth rate (per 1,000)	55	34	41	36	40	33	26	14	12
Death rate (per 1,000)	21	6	9	13	15	9	27	8	10
Natural increase (%)	3.4	2.8	3.2	2.3	2.5	2.4	–0.1	0.6	0.2
Infant mortality rate (per 1,000)	149	35	75	73	77	79	56	6.7	5.1
Fertility rate (per woman)	7.9	4.4	6.2	4.7	4.9	4.6	3.1	2.0	1.8
Contraceptive usage (% of married women)	14	43	23	28	39	28	40	73	84
% population urban	21	39	26	36	36	34	54	79	89
% population under 15 years	49	43	46	42	43	41	38	20	18
Life expectancy (years)	44	67	60	52	48	62	34	78	78
GNP per capita (US$, 2005)	800	4,410	920	1,840	1,170	2,350	10,250	41,950	32,690
% population living below US$2 per day	86	32	45	78	58	74	50	0	0

Source: World Population Data Sheet (2006)

It is easy to see, therefore, that censuses are a useful source of information for geographers and demographers. Table 5.3 shows examples of the demographic and economic indicators that are collected by censuses and other agencies.

Table 5.3 Demographic and economic indicators for selected countries

Changes in population characteristics

Fertility

In most parts of the world, fertility exceeds both mortality and migration. It is, therefore, the main determinant of population growth. Its importance has increased over time with the worldwide fall in mortality. Several African countries (e.g. Niger, Liberia, Mali) have very high birth rates of 50 and over per 1,000 per year. At the other end of the scale, Austria, Germany, Belarus (Photograph 5.2), Bulgaria, Slovenia and Ukraine have birth rates of 9 and under per 1,000 per year. Why does fertility vary?

➤ The relationship with **death rate** can be important. Countries in sub-Saharan Africa have high birth rates that counter the high rates of infant mortality (often over 100 per 1,000 live births). One study of sub-Saharan Africa concluded that a woman must have, on average, eight or nine children to be 95% certain of a surviving adult son. In contrast, in Europe, the average falls short of two children. Improvements in healthcare, sanitation and diet have led to a drop in rates of child mortality and reduce the need for large numbers of children as forms of security for the future. The USA has one of the highest birth rates among

Key terms

Fertility The number of live births per 1,000 women aged 15–49 in 1 year. It is also defined as the average number of children each woman in a population will bear. If this number is 2.1 or higher, a population will replace itself.

Infant mortality rate The number of deaths of children under the age of 1 year expressed per 1,000 live births per year.

developed countries, with a total fertility rate of 2.0. Other developed countries have fertility rates lower than 2.0.

➤ In many parts of the world, **tradition** demands high rates of reproduction. Intense cultural expectations may override the wishes of women. One useful indicator of women's ability to limit the number of children they have, and of the prospect for future fertility decline, is their desire to cease child-bearing. In Vietnam, 92% of women who had two children said they did not wish to have any more children. In Nigeria, by contrast, the figure was only 4%. Fertility among women aged 15 to 19 presents a special concern, as these young women may lack the physical development and social support needed, and child-bearing may curtail a young woman's education. In some countries, such as Chad, Bangladesh and Mozambique, more than one in four adolescent girls has given birth.

➤ **Education** for women, particularly female literacy, is a key to lower fertility. With education comes knowledge of birth control, more opportunities for employment and wider choices. Contraceptive use is becoming more widespread in developing countries to help women avoid unwanted pregnancies and to lower birth rates. A clear prerequisite is the availability of modern contraception for couples with both the knowledge and desire to use it. This objective has been generally achieved in much of Latin America and the Caribbean, but often falls short in sub-Saharan Africa and parts of Asia and Oceania. For example, in Rwanda, only 10% of women practise a modern method of family

Photograph 5.2
Belarus has a very
low fertility rate

Jane Buekett

planning, while at least 70% do in Brazil. Obstacles such as the lack of funds and supplies, and the lack of comprehensive programmes to educate couples with their choices, are significant barriers.

➤ Young **age structures** lead to developing countries far outpacing developed countries in population growth. Large proportions of young people, as there are in Mali (48%) and Bolivia (39%), ensure future population growth even when births per woman decline. This is because the 'youth bulge' is about to move through the child-bearing years. Conversely, countries with smaller proportions of youth, such as Poland (17%) and Japan (14%), face population decline even if births per woman increase.

➤ **Social class** is important. Fertility decreases from lower to higher classes or castes.

➤ **Religion** is of major significance because both Islam and the Roman Catholic Church oppose the use of artificial birth control. However, adherence to religious doctrine tends to lessen with economic development. This is particularly well illustrated in Italy. Although it is the location of the Vatican — the home of the pope — the fertility rate in Italy is very low (1.3). This suggests that some form of artificial birth control is taking place.

➤ **Economic factors** are important, particularly in less developed countires, where children are an economic asset. They are viewed as producers rather than consumers. In more developed countries, this is reversed. The length of time children spend in education makes them expensive, as does the cost of childcare if both parents work. In eastern Europe, economic uncertainty is a major factor in causing low fertility rates.

➤ There have been several cases in recent years of countries seeking to influence the rate of population growth. Such **political influences** have been either to increase the population (as in 1930s Germany and Japan, and more recently in Russia and Romania) or to decrease it (as in China, with its one-child policy).

Explosion or implosion?

There are over 6.5 billion people in the world. In the late twentieth century, the population was doubling every 30 years — this was described as the 'population explosion'. Various predictions have been made about future population growth. In 1996, one study by Earthscan estimated that the world's population would peak at around 10.6 billion in 2080 and then decline. The main reason for the slow down in population growth is that fertility rates are falling faster than had been expected.

Population growth in the less developed world

The fastest rates of population growth have been in the less economically developed world. Consequently, the greatest falls in fertility rates are expected to take place there. The average growth rate in the less developed world (excluding China) is 1.8%. Except in Africa and the middle east, where in almost 50 countries families of at least six children are the norm and the annual population growth is still over 2.3%, birth rates are now declining in less developed countries.

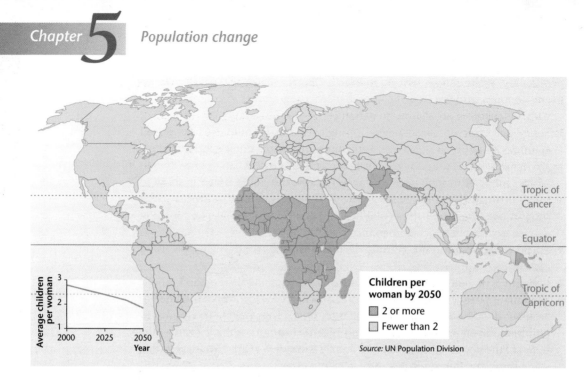

Figure 5.2 Global fertility decline

India is approaching China as the most populous country on Earth. Its population is over 1 billion and is expected to overtake that of China by 2050. This assumes an annual population growth of around 0.9% per year for India compared with 0.4% a year for China. In the southern states of India, such as Tamil Nadu and Kerala, where literacy rates are high, fertility rates have fallen sharply. However, in the impoverished Hindi belt in the north, traditional attitudes prevail, ensuring large numbers of children. Nevertheless, in India as a whole, fertility has dropped more than 50% in the last 30 years.

Fertility rates are declining in a range of less developed countries from east Asia to the Caribbean, and throughout most of South America (Figure 5.2). Although traditional religious attitudes are usually seen as a barrier to low fertility, in the Islamic world fertility is now below replacement level, at fewer than 2.12 children per woman. Tunisia, Iran and Turkey are all now in this category.

Population growth in the more developed world

In the more economically developed world, population growth has been slow for several decades. In some countries, for example Italy, Russia and Portugal, there has even been a small fall in the population — in Italy a population decrease of 4 million by 2020 is forecast. In the next 40 years, Germany could see its population drop by almost 20% and Japan by 25%. In Russia, President Putin has described the country's natural decrease as a 'national crisis'.

The fertility required to maintain the population level is 2.12 children per woman. There are already over 50 nations with fertility rates at or below this level. The United Nations (UN) predicts that by 2016 there will be 88 nations in this category — the 'Under 2.1 Club'. China is already a member of this 'club', although its population will not begin to decline until 2040 at the earliest. This is due to the time lag between reaching replacement-level fertility and actual population decline. Population growth in China will continue well into the twenty-first century.

There are very low fertility rates in many east European countries, for example Ukraine, Romania, Bulgaria, Belarus, Hungary, the Czech Republic and Latvia. Here economic collapse and uncertainty following the end of communist rule has made many women postpone or abandon having children.

Conversely, at 2.0, fertility in the USA is relatively high. Some writers suggest that this is because the American people are more religious and optimistic than those in most other rich nations, leading to a desire for more children. It is also thought that immigration will continue to be high in the USA. This gives a younger structure to the population, thereby increasing fertility.

As concern spreads about low fertility in the more developed world, governments are beginning to act. For example:

➤ the Japanese government has set aside £50 million to try to stop the fall in fertility. The money is being spent on encouraging people to have more children and on projects to assist this objective

➤ several European countries have put in place incentives to increase birth rates, with considerable financial benefits being offered for a third child (Table 5.4)

Mortality

Some of the highest death rates are found in less developed countries, particularly in sub-Saharan Africa. Liberia, Niger, Sierra Leone, Zambia and Zimbabwe all have death rates of 20 per 1,000 or more. However, some of the lowest mortality rates are also found in countries at the lower end of the development range, for example Kuwait (2 per 1,000), Bahrain (3 per 1,000) and Mexico (5 per 1,000). Why does mortality vary?

➤ **Infant mortality** is a prime indicator of socioeconomic development. It is the most sensitive of the age-specific rates. Sierra Leone has an infant mortality rate of 163 per 1,000 live births. Infant mortality is falling across the world, but there are still wide variations between nations — 142 infant deaths per 1,000 births in Liberia, but only 3 per 1,000 in Finland. Areas with high rates of infant mortality have high rates of mortality overall.

➤ Areas with high levels of **medical infrastructure** have low levels of mortality. A lack of prenatal and postnatal care, a shortage of medical facilities and trained

Country	Germany	France	Sweden	Ireland	UK
Child benefit for mother with three children (£ per month)	290	263	226	189	170
Maternity and parental leave (weeks)	170	170	78	40	52
Percentage of working women aged 25–54 with no children	7.7	7.3	8.2	6.6	8.0
Percentage of working women aged 25–54 with two children	56	59	82	41	62
Fertility rate	1.3	1.9	1.8	1.9	1.8

Table 5.4 Incentives to increase fertility

Figure 5.3
Access to improved
sanitation, 2002

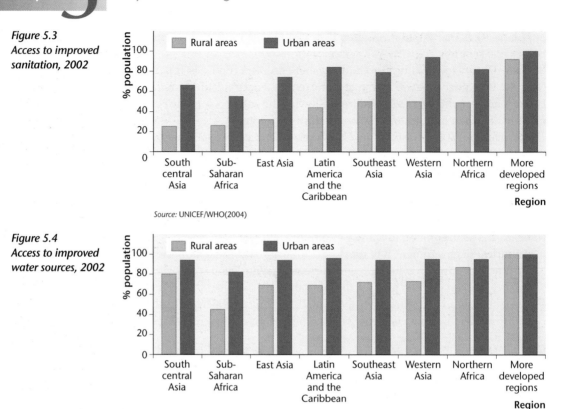

Source: UNICEF/WHO(2004)

Figure 5.4
Access to improved
water sources, 2002

Source: UNICEF/WHO(2004)

professionals, and ignorance of the need for professional care are major
contributors to high rates of mortality.

➤ Life expectancy is higher in countries with higher levels of **economic
development**. Poverty, poor nutrition, and a lack of clean water and sanitation
(all associated with low levels of economic development) increase mortality
rates. Worldwide, only 58% of the population has access to one of life's
fundamental needs: adequate or improved sanitation facilities (Figure 5.3).
There are, however, wide regional and rural/urban disparities. In developing
countries, only one-quarter to one-half of all rural residents have access to
improved sanitation. In many parts of the world, rural populations also lack
access to safe drinking water (Figure 5.4).

Table 5.5
Major causes of
death in more
developed and less
developed countries

More developed countries	Less developed countries
Heart disease and strokes	Respiratory diseases: influenza, pneumonia, tuberculosis (collectively 25% of all deaths)
Cancer	Parasitic diseases: malaria, sleeping sickness (15%)
Wars: international (e.g. two World Wars)	Wars: civil wars (e.g. Ethiopia, Sudan)
Transport-related accidents	Natural disasters (e.g. earthquakes) AIDS (greater impact than in more developed countries)

➤ The incidence of **AIDS** is having a major effect on mortality, especially in sub-Saharan Africa (Table 5.5). The number of people in the world now living with HIV/AIDS is over 40 million, with over 25 million in sub-Saharan Africa (Photograph 5.3). In some countries in southern Africa (Swaziland, Botswana, Lesotho and Zimbabwe), over 20% of the total population is affected. Out of the 7 million HIV/AIDS sufferers in south and southeast Asia, over 5 million live in India. It is estimated, however, that infection rates have begun to decline in some countries.

Sean Sprague/Still Pictures

Around the world, mortality has fallen steadily because of medical advances. People are more willing to control mortality than they are to control fertility.

The demographic transition model

The **demographic transition model (DTM)** describes how the population of a country changes over time (Figure 5.5). It gives changes in birth and death rates, and shows that countries pass through five stages of population change.

Photograph 5.3 A feeding centre for children in Namibia. Most are AIDS orphans and many are HIV positive

Stage 1 (high fluctuating) A period of high birth rate and high death rate, both of which fluctuate. Population growth is small. Reasons for the high birth rate include:

➤ limited birth control/family planning
➤ high infant mortality rate, which encourages the birth of more children

Figure 5.5 The demographic transition model

	Stage 1	Stage 2	Stage 3	Stage 4	Stage 5
	High fluctuating	Early expanding	Late expanding	Low fluctuating	Decline

Births and deaths per 1,000 people per year

High

Low

Birth rate

Natural decrease in population

Natural increase in population

Total population

Death rate

Time

➤ children are a future source of income
➤ in many cultures, children are a sign of fertility
➤ some religions encourage large families

Reasons for the high death rate include:
➤ high incidence of disease
➤ poor nutrition and famine
➤ poor levels of hygiene
➤ underdeveloped and inadequate health facilities

Stage 2 (early expanding) A period of high birth rate but falling death rate. The population begins to expand rapidly. Reasons for the falling death rate include:
➤ improved public health
➤ better nutrition
➤ lower child mortality
➤ improved medical provision

Stage 3 (late expanding) A period of falling birth rate and continuing fall in death rate. Population growth slows down. Reasons for the falling birth rate include:
➤ changing socioeconomic conditions
➤ greater access to education for women
➤ preferences for smaller families
➤ changing social trends and fashions, and a rise in materialism
➤ increased personal wealth
➤ compulsory schooling, making the rearing of children more expensive
➤ lower infant mortality rate
➤ the availability of family-planning systems, which are often supported by governments

Stage 4 (low fluctuating) A period of low birth rate and low death rate, both of which fluctuate. Population growth is small and fertility continues to fall. There are significant changes in personal lifestyles. There are more women in the workforce, with many people having high personal incomes and more leisure interests.

Stage 5 (decline) A later period, during which the death rate slightly exceeds the birth rate. This causes population decline. This stage has only been recognised in recent years and only in some western European countries. Reasons for the low birth rate in this stage include:
➤ a rise in individualism, linked to the emancipation of women in the labour market
➤ greater financial independence of women
➤ concern about the impact of increased population numbers on the resources for future generations
➤ an increase in non-traditional lifestyles, such as same-sex relationships
➤ a rise in the concept of childlessness
➤ the death rate may slightly increase because the population is ageing

Demographic change in the UK

During medieval times, both birth and death rates in the UK were high, at around 35 per 1,000. Generally, the birth rate was a little higher than the death rate, resulting in a slow rate of natural increase.

The birth rate tended to remain at a relatively stable level, but the death rate varied considerably. In 1348–49, the epidemic of bubonic plague, called the Black Death, killed one-third of the population. Other plagues followed in the seventeenth century, including the Great Plague of 1665. There was an increase in mortality between 1720 and 1740, which is attributed to the availability of cheap gin. This was ended by the introduction of a 'gin tax' in 1751.

Falling death rate

The period from the mid-eighteenth century to about 1875 was a time of rapid urbanisation, which alerted public officials and enlightened industrialists to the urgent need for improvements in public health. Factory owners soon recognised that an unhealthy workforce had a huge impact on productivity. The provision of clean, piped water and the installation of sewage systems, together with improved personal and domestic cleanliness, saw

the incidence of diarrhoeal diseases and typhoid fall rapidly. Greater disposable income from factory wages led to more food being consumed by the working class and to a wider range of food products being demanded. At the same time improvements in farming practices and transport systems allowed this demand to be met. Better nutrition played a significant role in the decline in infant mortality.

The combination of better nutrition and the general improvements in health brought about by legislation such as the Public Health Acts of 1848 and 1869 caused the incidence of common infectious diseases such as scarlet fever and tuberculosis to diminish markedly. Public perception of cleanliness was also a major factor. Soap was a well-advertised product and the availability of cheaper cotton clothing (which is easier to wash than woollen clothing) was important.

Falling birth rate

After 1875, the continued decrease in the death rate was accompanied by a reduction in the birth rate. Medical science began to play an important role in the control of mortality, with doctors being able to

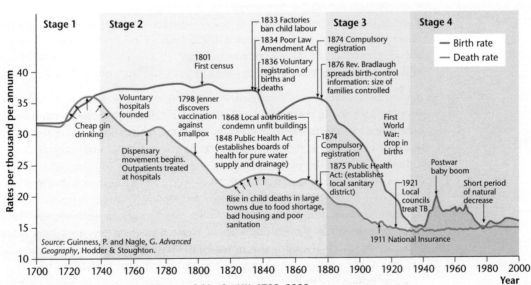

Figure 5.6 Demographic transition model in the UK, 1700–2000

administer more effective drug treatments. Surgery grew more advanced and anaesthesia became available. From the early part of the twentieth century, increasing attention was paid to maternity and child welfare, and to the health of school-children. There were further advances in nutrition — for example cheap American wheat, and refrigerated meat and fruit from Australia and New Zealand, began to be imported.

The decline in fertility began with the celebrated trial of two social reformers, Charles Bradlaugh and Annie Besant. They were prosecuted, and later acquitted, for publishing a book that gave contraceptive advice. The desire for smaller families at this time was due to the financial costs of looking after children, especially when education to the age of 13

became compulsory. Between 1890 and 1930, the birth rate fell from 32 per 1,000 to 17 per 1,000.

By 1940, the birth rate had fallen again to 14 per 1,000, partly due to the uncertainties of war. Immediately following the war, birth rates rose for a short while — the postwar baby boom. However, by 1980 birth rates had again fallen to 14 per 1,000 and have remained at this level. The introduction of the oral contraceptive pill and the wider use of condoms have meant that the relationship between desired family size and achieved family size has remained strong. The rise in the importance of women in the employment structure of the UK in the last few decades, particularly in service industries, has further impacted on birth rates, particularly in the professional classes.

The validity and application of the DTM

The DTM is useful because:
➤ it is universal in concept — it can be applied to all countries in the world
➤ it provides a starting point for the study of demographic change over time
➤ the timescales are flexible
➤ it is easy to understand
➤ it enables comparisons to be made demographically between countries

Limitations of the DTM are that:
➤ the original model did not include the fifth stage
➤ it is eurocentric and assumes that all countries in the world will follow the European sequence of socioeconomic changes
➤ it does not include the role of governments
➤ it does not include the impact of migration

In the 1960s, it was noted that many countries of the more developed world had gone through the first four stages of the model. Countries of the less developed world seemed to be in a situation similar to stage 2 — their death rates had fallen but their birth rates were still very high, leading to rapid population growth.

In the UK, as noted in the case study, stage 2 took over 100 years to complete (Figure 5.6). This was because social, economic and technological changes were introduced gradually and the death rate fell slowly. In many parts of the less developed world, the death rate has fallen much more rapidly because these changes, particularly the introduction of Western medical practices, have taken place more quickly. The birth rate, however, has stayed high and so the population has increased rapidly.

It was hoped that such countries would move into stage 3, as failure to do so could result in the population exceeding available resources. This was one of the reasons why China introduced the one-child policy, forcing its population into stage 3. Malaysia also reduced its birth rate by introducing a government-sponsored nation-wide family-planning programme. The outcomes of that programme, begun in the 1960s, are shown in Table 5.6.

Date	Birth rate	Death rate	Total population (millions)	Average population change (% per year)
1960	47	20	8	
1970	44	16	10	2.8 (1960–70)
1980	44	13	14	3.1 (1970–80)
1990	37	11	18	2.6 (1980–90)
2000	27	5	23	2.3 (1990–2000)

Table 5.6
Population change in Malaysia, 1960–2000

In summary, there are a number of important differences in the way that countries of the less developed and more developed world have undergone population change. In comparison with more developed countries, those in the less developed world:

➤ had generally higher birth rates in stages 1 and 2
➤ had a much steeper fall in death rate (and for different reasons)
➤ had in some cases much larger base populations, so the impact of high population growth in stage 2 and the early part of stage 3 has been far greater
➤ in those countries in stage 3, the fall in fertility has been steeper
➤ had a weaker relationship between population change and economic development — governments have played a more decisive role in population management

Case study **Population change in Thailand**

The birth rate in Thailand has fallen rapidly, partly as a result of the National Family Planning Programme, which has been run by the Ministry of Health since 1970. This has included:

■ public information programmes to ensure that everyone knows about contraceptive methods
■ advertising the benefits of the two-child family
■ establishing health centres throughout the country to provide mainly free contraception
■ training paramedics and midwives, who are mainly from the local villages and, therefore, are known and trusted. They provide healthcare for mothers and babies, so more babies are surviving

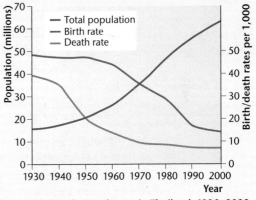

Figure 5.7 Population change in Thailand, 1930–2000

Migration

The relationship between the numbers of births and deaths (natural change) is not the only factor in population change. The balance between immigration and emigration (**net migration**) must also be taken into account. The relative

Forced migration The migrant has to migrate because of circumstances.

International migration
The UN defines international migration as the movement of people across national frontiers, for a minimum of 1 year.

Migration A permanent or semi-permanent change of residence of an individual or group of people.

Net migration The difference between the numbers of in-migrants and out-migrants in an area. When in-migrants exceed out-migrants, there is net migrational gain. When out-migrants exceed in-migrants, there is net migrational loss.

Rural–urban and urban–rural migration In less developed countries, the net migrational gain of urban areas at the expense of rural areas results in urbanisation. In more developed countries, movements from urban areas to rural areas have led to counter-urbanisation.

Voluntary migration
The migrant makes the decision to migrate.

Table 5.7 Types of migration

Criterion	Type of migration
Scale	International, regional, local
Direction	Rural–urban, urban–rural, urban–urban, MEDW to LEDW, LEDW to MEDW
Distance	Long distance, short distance, regional
Decision making	Forced (e.g. from hazards or for political safety — refugees), voluntary (e.g. for work, retirement or family reasons)
Cause of movement	Economic, social, environmental

contributions of natural change and net migration can vary both within a particular country and between countries.

Migration can be categorised using a number of criteria (Table 5.7).

Migration tends to be subject to **distance-decay** — the number of migrants declines as the distance between origin and destination increases. Refugees tend to move only short distances; economic migrants travel greater distances.

Causes of migration

Migration is more volatile than fertility and mortality. It is affected by changing physical, economic, social, cultural and political circumstances. However, the wish to migrate may not be fulfilled if the constraints are too great. The desire to move within a country is generally inhibited only by economic and social factors. The desire to move to another country is usually constrained by political factors, such as immigration laws.

Table 5.8 Examples of migration

Movement	Voluntary	Forced
Between MEDCs	The 'brain drain' of doctors and scientists from the UK and Germany to the USA The movement of east European workers into the UK following the expansion of the EU in 2004	Repatriation of East Germans into the new unified Germany after 1989
From LEDCs to MEDCs	The movement of Mexicans into the USA to work as casual employees in the farming communities of California	Movement of large numbers of refugees and asylum seekers in many parts of the world Movement of evacuees from Montserrat following the volcanic explosions in 1996
From MEDCs to LEDCs	The movement of aid workers from EU countries to the Sudan and Ethiopia	
Between LEDCs	The movement of migrant labour from Pakistan and Bangladesh to the oil-rich states of the Persian Gulf	Movement of Tutsi and Hutu peoples from Rwanda to the Democratic Republic of Congo because of the fear of genocide

Table 5.8 gives examples of some major causes of migration. It classifies such movements in terms of their origin and destination, and whether the movement is voluntary or forced.

The changing nature of international migration

International migrants make up about 3% of the world's population. Economic conditions, social and political tensions, and historical traditions can influence a nation's level of migration. Net migration rates can mask offsetting trends, such as immigration of unskilled workers and emigration of more-educated residents. Recent net migration trends raise some interesting issues, as shown in Figure 5.8.

Patterns of international migration have been changing since the late 1980s. There have been increases in:

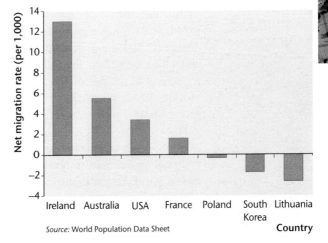

Source: World Population Data Sheet

*Figure 5.8
Net migration rate
per 1,000 people for
selected countries,
2005*

➤ attempts at illegal, economically motivated migration as a response to legal restrictions
➤ those seeking asylum (see below)
➤ migration between more developed countries, particularly between countries within the EU where restrictions have been removed to allow the free movement of labour
➤ short-term migration, as countries increasingly place limits on work permits. It is now common for more developed countries (e.g. the UK and USA) to limit the length of work permits, even for qualified migrants coming from other more developed countries
➤ movement of migrants between less developed countries, particularly to those where rapid economic development is taking place, for example the countries of the Persian Gulf and the Asian economic growth areas of Singapore and Indonesia

There has been a decline in:
➤ legal, life-long migration, particularly from less to more developed countries. Host countries provide fewer opportunities for migrants because the number of available low-skilled jobs has dropped. Many host countries have also tightened entry requirements and introduced more rigorous monitoring at the point of entry
➤ the number of people who migrate for life. Many newer migrants want to return home at some point. For example, a common feature of villages in Italy, Portugal and Greece is new housing built by returnees
➤ the number of people migrating with the purpose of reuniting family members, as the amount of long-term family separation reduces and many migrants eventually return home

Refugees

Refugees are defined by the UN as persons unable or unwilling to return to their homeland for fear of persecution, based on reasons of race, religion, ethnicity or political opinion, or those who have been displaced forcibly by other factors.

By 2003, the UN estimated that there were over 22 million refugees in the world. Many refugee movements are large-volume, non-selective and over short distances. They are often caused by war. Such migrations are often temporary — when the cause of the migration ends, the refugees return to their former homes. At the end of the twentieth century and the beginning of the twenty-first, major movements have included:

➤ 2 million from Ethiopia, Sudan and Somalia as a result of famine and civil war
➤ 6 million from Mozambique as a result of famine, civil war and flooding
➤ 1 million Kurds from northern Iraq fleeing oppression
➤ 1 million Afghans into neighbouring Pakistan fleeing civil strife and war (Photograph 5.4)
➤ 100,000 Tamils fleeing oppression and civil war in Sri Lanka
➤ 7,000 residents of Montserrat fleeing a volcanic eruption in the Soufrière Hills

Asylum seekers

One definition of asylum is 'the formal application by a refugee to reside in a country when they arrive in that country'. The numbers seeking asylum have increased steadily in recent years as countries seek to curtail immigration.

The prominence of asylum seeking has increased for the following reasons:

➤ pressure to migrate from the poorest states is increasing because of economic decline and political instability
➤ improved communications enable people to learn more about potential destinations

Photograph 5.4 Afghan girls at lessons in a refugee camp near Peshawar, Pakistan

Markus Matzel/Still Pictures

> in real terms, the cost of transport has declined
> more gangs of traffickers are preying on would-be migrants and offering a passage to a new life

It can be difficult to distinguish between those fleeing from threats to their life and liberty and those seeking to escape poverty and improve their quality of life.

Population structure

The composition of a population according to age groups and gender is known as the age–sex structure. It can be represented by means of a **population pyramid**. Figure 5.9 shows the age–sex structure for the UK in 2001.

The vertical axis of a population pyramid has the population in age bands of 5 years and the horizontal axis shows the number or percentage of males and females. The pyramid shows longevity by its height.

Population pyramids can show:
> the results of births minus deaths in specific age groups
> the effects of migration
> the effects of events such as war, famine and disease
> an indication of the overall life expectancy of a country

Age structure can also be measured by a number of indices:
> the dependency ratio
> the support ratio
> the juvenility index
> the old-age index

The **dependency ratio** shows the relationship between the economically active (working) population and the non-economically active (dependent) population.

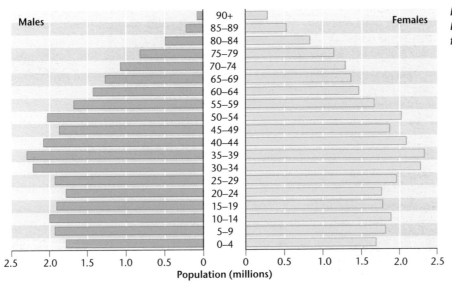

Figure 5.9
Population pyramid for the UK, 2001

In the EU, the dependent population is those people aged under 19 and over 60. The dependency ratio can therefore be calculated by:

$$\text{dependency ratio} = \frac{(\text{population } 0\text{–}19) + (\text{population over } 60)}{\text{population } 20\text{–}59}$$

The higher the dependency ratio, the more the non-economically active proportion is dependent on the working population.

The **support ratio** is the inverse of the dependency ratio.

The **juvenility index** is calculated by:

$$\text{juvenility index} = \frac{\text{population } 0\text{–}19}{\text{population } 20 \text{ and over}}$$

The higher the juvenility index, the greater the proportion of younger people in a population.

The **old-age index** is calculated by:

$$\text{old-age index} = \frac{\text{population } 60 \text{ and over}}{\text{population } 20\text{–}59}$$

The higher the old-age index, the greater the proportion of elderly people in a population.

The changing age–sex structure of the UK

The population pyramid for the UK for 2001 (Figure 5.9) shows a relatively smooth pyramidal shape, with some slight bulges and indentations. These slight variations can be explained by the circumstances at the time each age group was born and by later factors which affected that group.

The bulge of people in their 30s demonstrates that the birth rate was slightly higher in the 1960s than in the 1970s. There may be two reasons for this. First, the 1960s was a period of rising national prosperity and increasing personal income. In the 'swinging sixties', there was a lessening of sexual taboos and an increase in freedom for women. Second, this was the time at which people who themselves had been born in a baby boom following the Second World War were entering their fertile years. As there were more fertile individuals, more babies were born. Most people who were parents in the 1960s were in their 50s in 2001, and feature as a slight bulge on the pyramid. These examples demonstrate that population growth is cyclical and that to some extent changes can be predicted, so long as social norms are retained.

Two further points illustrate the changing nature of a population structure. In the 2001 pyramid, there is a relatively large number of people over the age of 80. The reasons for this are complicated. People born in the period 1910–20 were often part of large families. This was both traditional and functional. Many young children died in infancy from infectious diseases and a large family acted both as a source of income and as a form of security in old age. As the century progressed, however, death rates fell (despite the devastating impact of the First World War). Improvements in medical care and the development of new drugs and treatments have meant that some of these people, particularly women, are living into their 80s and 90s.

The second point concerns the younger part of the pyramid. As mentioned above, there was an increase in birth rates in the 1960s. The people born then became fertile in the 1980s and 1990s, so a cyclical increase in birth rates would be expected at that time. This has not happened to the extent predicted because social norms have changed. In recent decades, young adults have been less willing to have children. There are various reasons for this: the increased availability of contraception, abortion and sterilization; the growing importance of material possessions (houses, cars, holidays); and the desire of women to have careers. With hindsight, it is possible to add another factor. The economic recession of the late 1980s and early 1990s left many young adults financially insecure. A lot of women were forced to become the main breadwinners as male employment in mining and manufacturing industries fell.

The net result is that in the early part of the twenty-first century, the UK has an ageing population. The proportion of the population aged 50 and over has increased significantly since the start of the twentieth century. There has also been a rise in the 'very elderly' — people aged 80 and over. Population projections suggest that by 2021 there will be more than 3 million people over 80 — 5% of the population. At the same time the number of people aged under 16 has been falling progressively. It is anticipated that before the next census (2011) the number of people aged 65 and over will exceed those under 16 for the first time.

Links between the DTM and age–sex structure

The demographic transition model can be used to demonstrate changes in age–sex structure both spatially and over time. This can be seen in the characteristic shapes and names of the pyramids at each stage of the DTM (Figure 5.10).

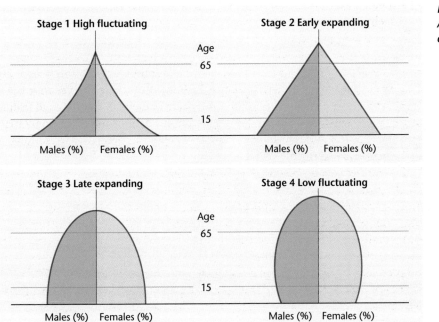

Figure 5.10
Age–sex structure and the DTM

➤ **Stage 1 (high fluctuating)** High birth rate; rapid fall in each upward age group due to high death rate; short life expectancy
➤ **Stage 2 (early expanding)** High birth rate; fall in death rate so more middle-aged people alive; slightly longer life expectancy
➤ **Stage 3 (late expanding)** Declining birth rate; low death rate; more people living to an older age
➤ **Stage 4 (low fluctuating)** Low birth rate; low death rate; higher dependency ratio; longer life expectancy

An ageing population

The population of the world is ageing significantly. In 2005, 10% of the population was over the age of 60. In the developing world this was 8% of the population, and in the developed world 20%. This proportion is expected to increase to 20% by 2050. In 2005, 670 million people were aged 60 years and over. This is projected to increase to 1 billion by 2020 and to 2 billion by 2050. The rise in the median age of the population is caused by increased life expectancy (greater longevity) and the decline in fertility. It is called **demographic ageing**. Demographic ageing has been a concern for the developed world for some time and it is now also beginning to alarm some countries of the developing world. Although ageing of the population has begun later in the less economically developed world, it is progressing at a faster rate than in the developed world. This is because the relative rates of decline in both fertility and mortality are much greater in developing than in developed countries.

The following demographic ageing features have been highlighted by the UN:
➤ The global average for life expectancy increased from 46 years in 1950 to 64 in 2000. It is projected to reach 74 years by 2050.
➤ The global median age for males was 26 in 2000 and is projected to rise to 35 years by 2050.

Photograph 5.5
Elderly men in
Shanghai, China

TopFoto

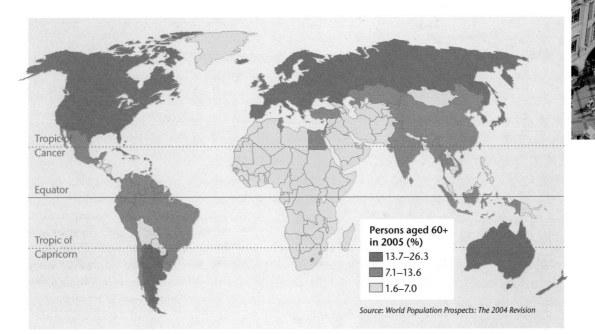

Persons aged 60+
in 2005 (%)
- 13.7–26.3
- 7.1–13.6
- 1.6–7.0

Source: World Population Prospects: The 2004 Revision

➤ In the less economically developed world, the population aged 60 and over is expected to quadruple between 2000 and 2050. The proportion of this population is projected to increase from 8% in 2000 to 22% by 2050 — to a total of 1.9 billion.

*Figure 5.11
Percentage of
population aged 60
and over in 2005*

➤ During the same time period, the proportion of children (16 and under) is projected to fall from 33% to 20%.

➤ The population aged 80 and over numbered 72 million in 2005. This is the fastest-growing section (4.2% annually) of global population and is projected to increase to 394 million by 2050.

➤ Europe is the 'oldest' region in the world. Those aged 60 and over in 2000 formed 20% of the population and this is projected to rise to 35% by 2050.

➤ Africa is the 'youngest' region in the world. Those aged 15 and under accounted for 42% of the population in 2000. This is expected to decline to 24% by 2050.

➤ The percentage of old people and their rate of increase varies among countries. In 2005, those aged 60 and over ranged from more than 25% in Japan, Italy and Germany to less than 5% in most tropical African countries and in the oil-rich countries of the middle east that attract young workers (Figure 5.11). By 2050, the range is expected to be even wider, from more than 40% in Japan, Italy, Slovenia and North Korea to even less than 5% in the African countries of Equatorial Guinea, Swaziland and Liberia.

➤ The 'oldest-old' age group (80 and over), will make up over 100 million (in India) and 50 million (in China) by 2050, and more than 15% of the populations of Italy and Japan will be this age (Figure 5.12).

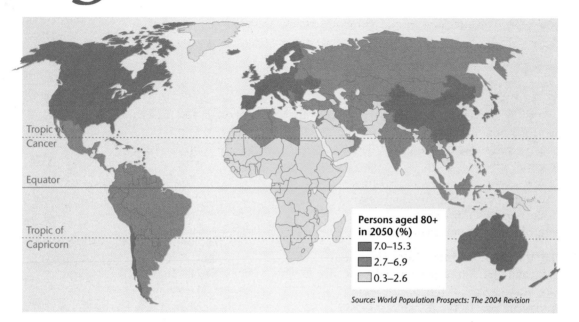

**Persons aged 80+
in 2050 (%)**
- 7.0–15.3
- 2.7–6.9
- 0.3–2.6

Source: World Population Prospects: The 2004 Revision

*Figure 5.12
Percentage of
population aged 80
and over in 2050*

➤ In 2005, globally, there were 10% more women than men aged 60 and over, twice as many aged 80 and over, and four times as many centenarians.

Demographic ageing poses problems for the world as a whole. However, it is the less economically developed world that faces the greatest challenge because:

➤ financial, health and housing resources are inadequate to meet the increasing demands of the elderly

➤ traditional support mechanisms for old people are deteriorating in an era of rapid social change

➤ the significant decline in fertility is leaving fewer children to care for elderly parents. In China, 24% of the population will be 65 and over by 2050. The first one-child generation will have to care for two parents, and up to four grandparents, without siblings to help — the '4:2:1' problem. It will be made worse by the shortage of females, the traditional carers

However, adjustments will also be needed in the more economically developed world. In the EU, it has been predicted that by 2025:

➤ there will be an increase in the number of people aged 60 and over — a further 37 million

➤ one-third of its population will be pensioners — 111 million people

➤ the working population (aged 20–59) will shrink by 13 million

➤ the numbers of over-60s will outnumber the under-20s, for the first time in recorded history

Table 5.9 Dependent and economically active populations in the EU, 1995 and 2025

Age (years)	Status	1995	2025
60+	Dependent	74 million	111 million
20–59	Economically active	203 million	190 million
0–19	Dependent	86 million	77 million

Table 5.10 Predicted change in population (%) in selected EU countries by age cohort, 1995–2025

Country	0–19 years	20–59 years	60+ years
France	−6.1	0.2	57.7
Germany	−12.1	−13.5	51.2
Ireland	−25.2	2.7	67.7
Sweden	1.2	3.7	38.1
UK	−8.2	−2.8	43.6

➤ there will be three times as many over-80s as there were in 2003

➤ there will be 9 million fewer children and teenagers — a 10% decline

These figures are summarised in Tables 5.9 and 5.10.

The impact of migration on population structure

Migration affects the population structure of both the area of origin and the area of destination. Impacts on the area of origin include:

➤ the younger adult age groups (20–34) migrate, leaving behind an older population

➤ males are more likely to migrate, causing an indentation on that side of the population pyramid

➤ birth rates fall and death rates rise

Barra, an island in the Outer Hebrides (Scotland), has long experienced depopulation as a result of the poor economic prospects in this remote location (Figure 5.13). Impacts on the area of destination are that:

➤ the proportions of the younger adult age groups (20–34) increase

➤ males are more likely to migrate, causing an expansion on that side of the pyramid

➤ birth rates rise and death rates fall

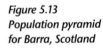

Figure 5.13
Population pyramid for Barra, Scotland

Dar-es-Salaam, the largest city in Tanzania, is a thriving international port and has long been a magnet for those seeking employment in that area of east Africa (Figure 5.14).

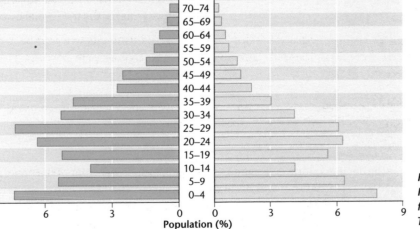

Figure 5.14
Population pyramid for Dar-es-Salaam, Tanzania

The balance between population and resources

Demographic ageing in the UK

Demographic ageing is one of the greatest challenges facing the UK today as the contrasting population pyramids for 2001 and 2050 show (Figures 5.15 and 5.16).

*Figure 5.15
Distribution of the
UK population by
age, 2001*

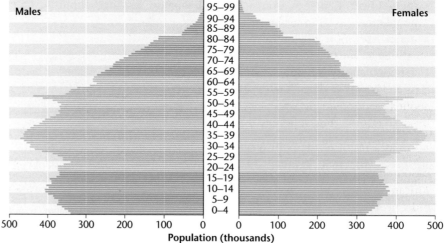

Note: The paler area highlights those aged 20–64
Source: GAD 2002-based Pensions Commission analysis

*Figure 5.16
Projected
distribution of the
UK population by
age, 2050*

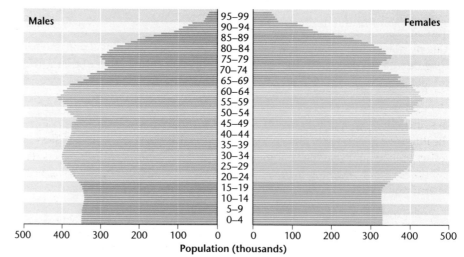

Note: The paler area highlights those aged 20–64
Source: GAD 2002 projection, Pensions Commission

The demographic trends predict that by 2050 the proportion of the population aged 65 years and over will have almost doubled. The main impacts will be on healthcare, pensions and housing. The UK government predicted in its most recent review that:

- the ratio of people 65 years and over to those aged 20–64 will rise from 27% in 2001 to 48% in 2050. This marks a considerable change from the very slow increase in the previous 20 years
- average male life expectancy at 65, which rose from 12.0 years in 1950 to 19.0 in 2001, will increase further to 21.0 by 2030 and to 21.7 by 2050. Female life expectancy is higher, but will increase at a slightly slower rate
- the current low fertility rate of 1.7 children per woman will increase only slightly to 1.75 by 2025, levelling off thereafter

Figure 5.17 Distribution of people aged 65 and over in the UK, 2003

The 2001 census enumerated more than 1.1 million people (1.9% of the population) aged 85 and over. There were more than 300,000 aged 90 or more.

Life expectancy is influenced by socioeconomic class and by ethnic group. Men in social class 1 have about 4 years longer life expectancy at 65 than men in social class 5. Thus, longevity is greater in more affluent parts of the country. The white Irish and white British populations have the highest proportions of people aged 65 and over; the black African population has the lowest proportion of older people.

Christchurch in Dorset is the pensioners' 'capital' of the UK with one in three residents of retirement age. Eastbourne, another popular retirement centre, has the highest ratio of elderly women to elderly men (100:90). However, it is not just coastal areas that attract retirees — the growing elderly population is migrating to the countryside too (Figure 5.17).

% of population
- 18.0+
- 16.0–17.9
- 14.0–15.9
- 12.0–13.9

0   km   200

N

Ageing and health

An ageing population places increasing pressure on health resources but it is important not to overstate this impact. Average healthcare costs do rise with age, but the cost of this trend could be significantly offset by people becoming healthier. Retired people continue to pay income tax and other taxes. Health costs tend to be compressed into the last years or even months of life — a process termed the **compression of morbidity**.

Ageing and pensions

The state pension system transfers resources from the current generation of workers to the current generation of pensioners. As the population has aged the level of resource transfer required has increased. The system cannot be sustained in the future without significant change. Four options have been suggested:
- pensioners become poorer relative to the rest of society
- taxes and National Insurance contributions devoted to pensions increase
- the rate at which individuals save for retirement increases
- the average retirement age increases

Public responses to these options will feature in political debate. However, the Pensions Act 2007 stated that the state pension age will be equalised at 65 for men and women between 2010 and 2020. It will be raised to 68 over the 22-year period from 2024.

Another feature of demographic ageing is that the voting power of the older age group increases. The 'grey vote' is of major significance to political parties and the needs of the elderly cannot therefore be ignored by those in power.

The economic and purchasing power of the 'grey pound' is also increasing. This is beneficial to companies that specialise in providing goods and services to older people. For example:

➤ in the tourist industry, cruising is a popular type of holiday with this age group
➤ some companies, for example Saga, provide a wide range of leisure services for older people, in this case for the over 50s
➤ some companies, for example B&Q and Homebase, target this age group for their workforce
➤ the growing number of elderly people who live alone has led to the provision of a range of support services, such as health visitors, meals on wheels, home-help cleaners and drivers for hospital visits

Ageing and housing

As the number of elderly people and the age to which they live increases, so some degree of segregation has taken place, particularly in terms of housing. Many elderly people have to decide whether or not to leave the family home when they are left on their own or have difficulty caring for themselves. Old people living alone in council and Housing Association houses have found that very often they do not have a choice. Housing departments move them out into sheltered accommodation or nursing homes because their houses are required for families.

Segregation based on age has manifested itself in a number of ways in towns in the UK.

➤ On council estates, it is common to see clusters of purpose-built bungalows occupying one small part or parts of the estate. In some areas maisonettes with security access have been built. This type of housing for elderly people is provided in the belief that it is best for them to live in the community for as long as they are fit enough. They are often people who have lived in the area for many years. They have friends and relatives living locally and they are integrated into social functions such as the church or social clubs.
➤ A more recent provision has been sheltered accommodation — a complex of flats or units with some shared facilities, overseen by a warden or manager. In some cases purpose-built blocks of flats, some for single people and some for married couples, have been constructed. A mobile warden may oversee a number of complexes. The location of these facilities is only just beginning to establish a pattern in some urban areas.
➤ Nursing homes have been increasing in number to cater for the growing number of elderly people who have difficulty looking after themselves.

Initially, both local authorities and private developers provided such housing, but local authorities have been cutting back their provision. In many urban areas, concentrations of nursing homes are becoming clear. They are often in both inner and outer suburbs, in areas where large Georgian, Victorian and Edwardian houses can either be converted or extended for this purpose. Close links with medical provision are also a factor, and some of the most financially successful nursing homes are located on a main road in a town so as to facilitate the arrival of ambulances.

Less developed countries with youthful populations

In many less developed countries:

➤ the population pyramid has a broad base, indicating a youthful population with a large proportion of children and high fertility
➤ the pyramid tapers rapidly, indicating high mortality with a significant reduction in numbers in each 5-year group
➤ the pyramid has a narrow apex, suggesting a small proportion of elderly people
➤ as mortality falls in large less developed countries (e.g. India and China), the huge numbers of over-60s will cause major problems
➤ the working population is reduced by migration to more developed countries, particularly by those with skills
➤ there may be few relatives to act as carers (due to migration and deaths from AIDS), so the costs of care for the elderly will rise

Case study — Iran

The main characteristics of the age–sex structure of Iran are shown in Figure 5.18.

There is evidence that the population growth rate in Iran is slowing down, even though it currently has a youthful population.

Writers who have studied the country state that there have been four revolutions for women, each of which has influenced the birth rate:

■ **The urban revolution** — women who have moved to the cities (e.g. Tehran) usually have fewer children than those who stay in the rural areas. Sixty-seven per cent of Iran's population is now classed as urban.

■ **The education revolution** — there has been a slow but steady increase in education for girls and women. Women who are educated are likely to marry later, become more

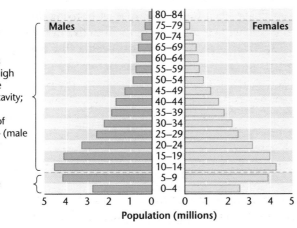

High birth rates together with high death rates give consistent concavity; also reflects out-migration of those aged 20+ (male and female) for employment

Fall in birth rate

Population (millions)

Figure 5.18 Age–sex structure of Iran, 1999

aware of family planning (74% of Iranian women between the ages of 15 and 49 used contraception in 2006) and gain paid employment.

■ **The working revolution** — women who work in the cities find it more difficult to arrange childcare, and hence have fewer children.

■ **The migration revolution** — women who migrate from Iran to other Persian Gulf states and to Europe

have a more Westernised lifestyle with smaller families and more consumer goods. By remaining in contact with friends and relatives, they have influenced social attitudes in the country.

The fertility rate in Iran has fallen to 2.0 per woman — one of the lowest in the Arab world. As fertility decreases, there will be a greater proportion of people in the economically active age range. Economists have matched the declining dependency ratio to rising rates of investment and savings. This is likely to encourage foreign investment into the country. Both factors are favourable for economic growth over the next 30 years although political concerns about Iran may counteract this.

Table 5.11   Population statistics for Iran, 2006

Population	70.3 million
Age structure:	
0–14 years	29% (male, 11 million; female, 9 million) Estimated to fall to 27% by 2015.
15–64 years	66% (male, 23 million; female, 23 million)
65 years and over	5% (male, 1.8 million; female, 1.7 million)
Population growth rate	1.2%
Birth rate	18 births per 1,000 population
Death rate	6 deaths per 1,000 population

Social, economic and political effects of migration

*Table 5.12
The effects of migration on the area of origin*

Migration affects both the area of origin and the area of destination. The effects of migration are social, economic and political (Tables 5.12 and 5.13).

Issues of economic migration: source country

Impact	Effect
Social	Marriage rates fall
	Family structures can break down
	Departure of males and young families causes a loss of cultural leadership and tradition
Economic	Those with skills and education leave, causing labour shortages or reduced pressure on resources such as farmland
	The area benefits from remittances sent back — an economic gain
	On their return migrants bring back new skills
	Farming declines and land is abandoned

Economic costs include:
➤ the loss of the young adult labour force
➤ the loss of those with skills and entrepreneurial talents, which may slow economic development
➤ regions where out-migration takes place may suffer from a spiral of decline that is difficult to halt
➤ the loss of labour may deter inward investment by private organisations, increasing dependence on governmental initiatives

Economic benefits include:
➤ reduced under-employment in the source country
➤ returning migrants bring new skills to the country, which may help revitalise the home economy
➤ many migrants send remittances home and much of this money is reinvested in the home economy in projects such as new buildings and services

➤ there is less pressure on resources in the area, including basic supplies such as food and essential services such as healthcare

Social costs include:

➤ the perceived benefits of migration encourage more of the same generation to migrate, which has a detrimental effect on social structure

➤ there is a disproportionate number of females left behind

➤ the non-return of migrants causes an imbalance in the population pyramid

➤ returning retired migrants may impose a social cost on the community if support mechanisms are not in place to cater for them

Social benefits include:

➤ the population density is reduced and the birth rate decreases, as it is the younger adults who migrate

➤ remittances sent home by economic migrants can finance improved education and health facilities

➤ returning retired migrants increase social expectations in the community, for example, the demand for better leisure facilities

Political effects include:

➤ policies to encourage natural increase

➤ policies to encourage immigration to counteract outflow or to develop resources

➤ requests for international aid

Table 5.13
The effects of migration on the area of destination

Impact	Effect
Social	Marriage rates rise
	Arrival of a new group of people can cause friction, especially if their cultural identity is retained
	Attitudes of local people to new migrants may be both negative and positive
	Social tension may increase
	New food, clothes, music etc. are introduced into the area
Economic	There is a labour surplus; those with skills and education fuel a new drive to the economy; there is a greater take-up of menial jobs
	Remittances are sent back to the area of origin — an economic loss
	On returning to the area of origin, migrants export the skills they have learned — a kind of reverse 'brain drain'
	Pressure on resources

Issues of economic migration: destination country

Economic costs include:

➤ the costs of educating the migrants' children have to be borne

➤ there is an over-dependence of some industries on migrant labour, e.g. the construction industry in the UK

➤ much of the money earned, including pension payments, is repatriated to the country of origin

➤ increased numbers of people add to the pressure on resources, such as health services and education

Economic benefits include:

➤ economic migrants tend to take up the less desirable jobs

➤ the host country gains skilled labour at reduced cost

➤ the 'skills gap' that exists in many host countries is filled by qualified migrants

➤ costs of retirement are transferred back to the source country

Social costs include:

➤ the dominance of males is reinforced, especially in countries where the status of women is low — for example, in the Persian Gulf states

➤ aspects of cultural identity are lost, particularly among second-generation migrants

➤ segregated areas of similar ethnic groups are created, and schools are dominated by migrant children

Social benefits include:

➤ creation of a multiethnic society increases understanding of other cultures

➤ there is an influx of new and/or revitalised providers of local services — for example, Turkish baths and local corner shops

➤ there is a growth of ethnic retailing and areas associated with ethnic food outlets — for example, the 'curry mile' in Rusholme, Manchester

Political effects include:

➤ discrimination against ethnic groups and minorities which may lead to civil unrest and extremism

➤ calls for controls on immigration

➤ entrenchment of attitudes which may encourage fundamentalism

Case study — Economic migration: the USA

Immigration has been a dominant trend in the demography of the USA for nearly 200 years. During this time migrants have entered the country from many parts of Europe (including Britain, Ireland, Italy, Germany), and from China, west Africa and Latin America.

In 1965, an act was passed that set an annual limit of 120,000 immigrants from the western hemisphere (the Americas) and 170,000 immigrants from the eastern hemisphere (Europe and Asia). In 1990, these quotas were raised by 40%.

In the 1990s, a considerable influx took place, which reopened the immigration debate. More than 5 million immigrants arrived between 1991 and 1996. Some Americans argued that recent immigrants were taking jobs that should be theirs, others voiced concern about racial tension and the impact on the welfare system.

This immigration has been spatially selective. In 1995, 55% of all immigration was to just four states — California, New

TopFoto

Photograph 5.6 US border patrol with illegal Mexican migrants in the desert, Arizona

York, Florida and Texas. The main reasons for such concentrations are:

- the location of existing immigrant communities
- the availability of employment in these, the four most populous states
- the land border with Mexico for California and Texas, and Florida's proximity to Caribbean countries

In 1997, over 25% of the population of California were born outside the USA. For the city of Los Angeles the proportion is almost 40%, compared with 16% for New York.

For obvious reasons, it is difficult for the authorities to be precise about numbers of illegal immigrants. Estimates vary from 2.5 to 4 million in the 1990s. In the early 1990s, more than 1 million undocumented migrants were apprehended coming from Mexico each year (Photograph 5.6). In 1996, Congress increased the number of guards on the border with Mexico, tightened asylum rules and made it harder for illegal immigrants to become legal.

There is debate as to whether these migrants are beneficial to the American economy in the long term. Some facts are:

- foreign-born residents are 35% more likely to receive public assistance than native Americans
- immigrants on average pay 32% less tax during their lifetimes than native Americans
- over a period of 40 years, the children of immigrants will pay far more to the state in taxes than they will take from it (assuming they stay in the country)
- for the public purse, the most lucrative immigrant is a 21-year-old with a higher-level education

Case study · Economic migration: Germany

Following the end of the Second World War, Germany became two separate countries:

- West Germany — a capitalist country supported by the USA and western European countries, which became a powerful economic force. It had large resources of coal and developed prosperous industries of steel, chemicals, engineering, electronics, motor vehicles and consumer goods. The standard of living of the people became high.
- East Germany — a communist country supported by the former Soviet Union, which became reliant on out-dated heavy industries. Living standards were low, although there was full employment and everyone received state housing. Individual enterprise and initiative were not encouraged.

During the 1960s and 1970s, rapid economic growth led to labour shortages in West Germany. The government encouraged migration from East Germany. However, in 1963, East Germany built a fortified fence between the two countries and constructed the Berlin Wall to separate East and West Berlin (the city was inside East Germany but West Berlin was part of West Germany).

The pull of West Germany's economy attracted workers from many other countries including unemployed building workers from the UK and large numbers (over 2 million) from Turkey.

As West Germany continued to grow economically and East Germany did not, the difference in their standards of living became greater. By the late 1980s, large numbers of East Germans (Ossies) were travelling to other east European countries such as Czechoslovakia (now the Czech Republic and Slovakia) and then crossing the border into West Germany. Their movement became symbolised by old-fashioned Trabant cars loaded with possessions passing through border controls.

Following brief but mass protests in East Germany, the communist government collapsed and the Berlin Wall came down in 1989. East and West Germany were re-united. At first the East Germans were delighted and many moved west. The old East German factories could not compete with their modern western counterparts. Many were deemed too polluting and were closed.

Germany is still a 'country divided'. Although there has been massive development in some parts of the east, especially around Berlin, other parts still suffer from high unemployment and poor housing. Despite these problems, Germany is still seen as an attractive destination by people from Asia (mainly Iraq and Afghanistan) and Europe (former Yugoslavia, Albania, Greece and Turkey). Germany has over four times as many migrants as the UK each year and the numbers show no sign of falling. Surprisingly, there are relatively few migrants from nearby countries such as Poland and Lithuania.

The German economy is relatively strong and it has extensive land borders with its neighbouring countries, which make it easy for migrants to enter.

Case study Economic migration: Dubai, United Arab Emirates

In 2007, Dubai was the world's fastest-growing city. It is a landscape of building sites full of workers feverishly constructing the highest, the largest and the deepest buildings in the world. Half of the world's cranes are at work here on projects worth US$100bn — double the total foreign investment in China, the world's third largest economy. Among the developments are:

- Flower City, which aims to take over the international flower trade from Amsterdam
- Hydropolis, a large underwater hotel
- Chess City, with buildings the shape of chess pieces
- Dubailand, which will become the world's largest theme park
- 300 man-made islands in the Arabian Gulf, in a variety of shapes, which will become the homes of the rich and famous

Dubai's oil reserves are dwindling, and the ruling family, the Maktoums, want to reinvent their personal fiefdom as a financial and transport centre using the profits, while stocks last, of their oil revenues. For many visitors, Dubai is a high-rise paradise rising out of a barren desert fringed with beaches, where there is no income tax. It is a favoured destination for wealthy Britons wishing to work and play abroad.

Migrant workers

Nearly 10 million foreigners, most of them unskilled or semi-skilled migrants, work in the Gulf states. Migrants comprise 90% of the workers in the UAE. Dubai itself (one of the states of the UAE) has over 1 million migrants within a total population of 1.5 million.

Migrants come from over 160 different countries, but mainly from south and southeast Asia (Photograph 5.7). The average pay for an unskilled labourer is US$4 a day, and that is enough of a lure for the impoverished people of India, Pakistan, Sri Lanka and Bangladesh. Migrants also come from the Philippines, Egypt, Jordan, Lebanon and Morocco. Remittances sent home exceed US$100bn and are important sources of finance for developing countries. The jobs are arranged through contractors and many migrant workers have to take out loans to pay for their passage.

On arrival in Dubai, migrants face a number of problems:

- their passports are often confiscated to prevent them absconding while they are on contract
- exit visas typically cannot be obtained without the approval of either their sponsor or their employer
- cramped and remote workers' camps have been constructed in the desert, adding long daily journeys to the 12-hour shifts
- there are many accusations of discrimination, intimidation and violence at the hands of employers, supervisors, police and security forces, including sexual assault of the large numbers of women employed as domestic servants
- trafficking of children occurs for a variety

Photograph 5.7 *Construction workers from the Indian subcontinent working on the Burj Dubai, planned to be the world's tallest building*

of purposes, including begging and as camel jockeys
- accident and suicide rates among migrant workers are high — there were 84 known suicides in 2006

Strikes and demonstrations by migrant workers complaining of unpaid wages and demanding better working conditions have become more common-place. In response, the police and the labour ministry have set up a hotline for foreign workers who have complaints. Civil servants visit factories and labour camps to listen to grievances and have occasionally ordered compensation from the firms involved.

Implications of population change

Overpopulation, underpopulation and optimum population

Overpopulation exists when there are too many people in an area relative to the amount of resources and the level of technology available locally to maintain a high standard of living. It implies that, with no change in the level of technology or natural resources, a reduction in a population would result in a rise in living standards. The absolute number or **density** of people need not be high if the level of technology or natural

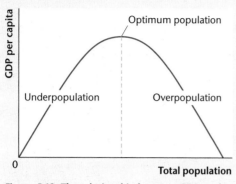

Figure 5.19 The relationship between GDP and population

resources is low. Overpopulation is characterised by low per capita income, high unemployment and underemployment, and outward migration.

Underpopulation occurs when there are too few people in an area to use the resources efficiently for a given level of technology. In these circumstances an increase in population would mean a more effective use of resources and increased living standards for all of the people. Underpopulation is characterised by high per capita incomes (but not maximum incomes), low unemployment and inward migration.

Optimum population is the theoretical population which, working with all the available resources, will produce the highest standard of living for the people of that area. This concept is dynamic — when technology improves, new resources become available which mean that more people can be supported.

Figure 5.19 shows the relationship between GDP and population.

An optimistic approach to population change

Ester Boserup, in *The Conditions of Agricultural Change: The Economics of Agrarian Change under Population Pressure* (1965), stated that environments have limits that restrict activity. However, these limits can be altered by the use of appropriate technologies which offer the possibility of resource development or creation. People have an underlying freedom to make a difference to their lives.

Boserup stated that food resources are created by population pressure. With demand, farm systems become more intensive, for example by making use of shorter fallow periods. She cited certain groups in tropical areas of Africa who reduced the fallow period from 20 years, to annual cropping with only 2–3 months fallow, to a system of multi-cropping in which the same plot bore two or three crops in the same year.

The pressure to change comes from the demand for increased food production. As the fallow period contracts, the farmer is compelled to adopt new strategies to maintain yields. Thus necessity is the mother of invention.

Evidence to support this approach

The following two changes in agricultural practice support this view:

➤ The increasing intensity of shifting cultivation systems in various parts of the world. These move from 'slash and burn' systems in areas of very low rural population density, to systems making use of irrigation in areas of higher rural population density. People are adapting to their changing circumstances by adopting more intensive forms of agriculture.

➤ The Green Revolution — the widespread introduction of high-yielding varieties of grains, along with the use of fertilisers and pesticides, water control and mechanisation. The increased yields from these processes allow more people to be fed.

More recently, other writers, notably Julian Simon and Bjørn Lomborg, have contributed to these optimistic views. They refer to a number of so-called environmental scares of recent years. In the 1960s it was pesticides, carcinogens and the population explosion. In the 1970s there was the oil crisis, the imminent failure of the world's food supply and the fear of nuclear power. In the 1980s the deserts were advancing, acid rain was killing trees, the ozone layer was thinning and the elephant was on the point of extinction. The 1990s brought retreating rainforests, falling sperm counts, new diseases such as ebola and genetically modified crops.

Photograph 5.8
Optimists argue that food production per head has increased

They argue that the alarmists were wrong. In their opinion none of these predictions has been fulfilled — there has been no rise in cancer caused by pesticides, population growth has slowed, oil reserves have increased, food production per head has increased even in the poorer countries of the world (Photograph 5.8), nuclear accidents have been rare, deserts have not advanced, acid rain has killed no forests, the elephant has never been in danger of extinction, sperm counts are not falling and rainforests are still 80% intact. They think people are being made to indulge in environmental guilt when technology should in fact be encouraged, to improve living standards throughout the world, rather than just for a rich minority.

More recently Lomborg has argued against the costs of combatting climate change. He argues that resources should be channelled into adjusting to climate change, and fighting global poverty and disease.

A pessimistic approach to population change

In *An Essay on the Principle of Population as it Affects the Future Improvement of Society* (1798), Thomas Malthus suggested that the environment dominates or

Table 5.14 Changes in population and resources (food supply) over time

Time periods (25-year intervals)	1	2	3	4	5	6	7
Population	1	2	4	8	16	32	64
Food supply	1	2	3	4	5	6	7

determines patterns of human life and behaviour. Our lives are constrained by physical, economic and social factors.

His argument was that the population increases faster than the supporting food resources. If each generation produces more children, the population grows geometrically (1, 2, 4, 8 etc.) while food resources only develop arithmetically (1, 2, 3, 4 etc.) and cannot keep pace (Table 5.14). He believed the population/resource balance was maintained by various checks:

➤ increased levels of misery through war, famine and disease
➤ increased levels of moral restraint such as celibacy and later marriages
➤ increased incidence of abortion, infanticide and sexual 'perversions'

Malthus asserted that the power of a population to increase its numbers was greater than that of the Earth to sustain it. This view is still held by so-called **neo-malthusians**. For example, in 1972 the Club of Rome (an international team of economists and scientists) predicted in a book entitled *The Limits to Growth* that a sudden decline in population growth could occur within 100 years if present-day trends continued. They argued that environmental degradation and resource depletion were not only related to population growth but were also a function of the technologies and consumption patterns of greater numbers of people. They suggested greater control and planning of both population and resource use to create more stability.

Evidence to support this approach

Neo-malthusians believe that a number of recent issues support their views:

➤ They believe the wars and famines in Ethiopia, Sudan and other countries of the Sahel region of Africa in recent decades suggest that population growth has outstripped food supplies. On a global scale, the Food and Agriculture Organization of the United Nations (FAO) suggests that over 800 million people are chronically malnourished, while 2 billion lack food security.
➤ Population growth accelerated rapidly in less developed countries after their mortality rates began to fall. Rapid population growth impedes development and brings about a number of social and economic problems. In recent decades, however, population growth has slowed. In 2006, the population growth rate was 1.2% per annum compared with 2.4% in 1960.
➤ Water scarcity is predicted to be a major resource issue this century. The UN predicts that by 2050, 4.2 billion people (45% of the world's population) will be living in areas that cannot provide the required 50 litres of water a day to meet basic needs.

One of the most prominent neo-malthusians in recent years has been the American writer Paul Ehrlich. In the 1960s he suggested that India should not receive Western emergency aid because of its environmental state. He said then that 'sober analysis shows a hopeless imbalance between food production and population'. However, optimists have since pointed out that India now more than feeds its population due to the advances of the Green Revolution.

The most recent scare from the pessimists is global warming, which cannot be proven either right or wrong within our lifetime. In response to this threat, at the 1997 Kyoto conference on the environment, the industrialised countries agreed to cut their carbon dioxide emissions by 30% by 2010. In the UK this was to be achieved by a switch away from coal-fired power stations to alternative sources, increases in public transport and taxes on fuel consumption. However, the USA, under President Bush, refused to comply with the agreement at that time. The 2007 UN Climate Change Conference in Bali aimed to negotiate a successor to the Kyoto Protocol. The 'Bali roadmap' was adopted as a 2-year process to reaching a binding agreement in 2009 in Denmark. Environmentalists were disappointed by the lack of firm emissions-reduction targets.

In 2002, at the World Summit on Sustainable Development held in Johannesburg, key issues were sustainable management of the global resource base, poverty eradication and better healthcare. The last two were seen as ways in which population growth could be reduced. The population–resources debate continues.

Population change and sustainable development

Sustainability: the principles

The concept of sustainable development dates from the first Global Environmental Summit held in Stockholm in 1972. It was first expressed as a set of environmental objectives, for example to:

➤ maintain ecological processes
➤ preserve genetic diversity
➤ ensure the sustainable utilisation of species and ecosystems

It was later defined by the *Brundtland Report* in 1987 as 'development that meets the needs of the present without compromising the ability of future generations to meet their own needs'.

Economic sustainability takes this further by considering the ability of economies to maintain themselves when resources decline or become too expensive, and when populations dependent on these resources are growing.

Various international summits, held in Rio (1992), Kyoto (1997), and Johannesburg (2002), have endeavoured to produce international agreements on sustainable development, with varying degrees of success. There has been further development of the principles of sustainability at these summits, as described below.

Environmental
➤ People should be at the heart of concerns regarding development.
➤ States should have the right to exploit their own environments, but they should not damage the environments of other states.
➤ Laws should be enacted regarding liability for pollution and compensation.

> States should pass on information about natural disasters and notify neigh-bours of any foreseen and accidental consequences of their own activities that might cross boundaries.

Economic

> The right to development must be fulfilled to meet equitably the needs of present and future generations.
> All states should cooperate in eliminating poverty in order to decrease disparities in standards of living.
> The special needs of developing countries, particularly the least developed and environmentally most vulnerable, should be given priority.
> Unsustainable production and consumption patterns should be eliminated and appropriate demographic (i.e. population) policies should be promoted.

Population policies

A variety of social policies aimed at the control of population growth have been established around the world:

> Policies that aim to tackle rapid population growth by reducing fertility are known as **anti-natalist**. An example is the Chinese one-child policy (see case study). Family-planning programmes are usually the main strategy.
> For economic and political reasons, a few countries have **pro-natalist** policies designed to increase population. Examples include France after the Second World War and Russia and Romania in the 1980s. These policies may be either voluntary or imposed on the people.
> Other countries try to manage population numbers by controlling immigration (e.g. Australia and the USA) or by encouraging emigration (e.g. the Philippines) or transmigration (e.g. Indonesia, see case study, page 184).
> Many countries that do not have population policies try to influence fertility indirectly through fiscal measures such as child allowances and tax concessions for young married couples.

Examples of national policies

Thailand

In 1969, women in Thailand averaged 6.5 children each, 16% of the population used contraception and population growth was 3% a year. The government tried to reduce the birth rate through a nationwide family-planning programme that began in 1970. It included free contraception, trained family-planning specialists and government campaigns, especially among rural communities. By 1999, contraceptives were being used by 72% of people, women averaged 1.7 children and population growth was only 0.8% a year. The policy is community-based rather than coercive.

The Philippines

Opposition to birth control from the Roman Catholic Church (83% of the pop-ulation are Catholic) has countered government encouragement of contraceptive use in the Philippines. In 1999, only 47% of the population used contraceptives and the population growth rate was 1.7% per year. Women now average 3.4 children each and the population is expected to double by 2027. The government is seeking to increase food production through the Green Revolution, while at the same time not discouraging the out-migration of labour to Singapore, Malaysia and the UK.

Case study — The Chinese one-child policy

During the second half of the twentieth century the Chinese government became concerned about population growth for two main reasons:

- the Chinese wanted to avoid a malthusian-type disaster in the future
- they realised that China could only have a rising living standard if the population was controlled

Chinese population policies have gone through a number of stages:

1950–59 The philosophy of the government under Chairman Mao was that 'a large population gives a strong nation'. The government encouraged people to have children. In 1959, there was a serious famine and 20 million people died.

1960–73 After the famine there was a population boom. The population increased by 55 million (equivalent to the population of the UK) every year. Nothing was done to reduce the spiralling birth rate.

1974–79 There was a policy change and people were encouraged to reduce the birth rate by the slogan 'wan-xi-shao' (later, longer, fewer):
- later marriages
- longer gaps between children
- fewer children

1979–90 The wan-xi-shao policy did not work well and the population went on increasing. In 1979 the government introduced the one-child policy which set strict limits on who was allowed to have children, and when. Strong pressure was put on women to use contraception. Special family-planning workers in every workplace, and 'granny police' in housing areas, were instructed to make sure women were practising contraception, and to report on pregnancies. Enforced abortions and sterilisation became common.

The policy was successful in urban areas, but less so in rural areas where disobedience was more common. A disturbing effect of the policy was the practice of female infanticide. Couples wanted sons and many baby girls were killed or 'disappeared'. The dominance of male babies also led to the spoilt 'little emperor' syndrome — the attention of the extended family fell on the one child.

1990 onwards The one-child policy has been relaxed slightly. It was difficult to enforce, and the Chinese government was concerned about the economic implications of a population with far more older people than younger ones (see page 166). In addition, the revolution in global communications (the internet, satellite phones) has opened up the country to much greater social influence from the West. In more remote parts the policy is still encouraged. For example, the authorities in Guangdong, the state capital, ordered 20,000 abortions and sterilisations by the end of 2001 in the mountainous region of Huaiji.

By 2006, annual growth rate had fallen to 0.6%, and yet the fertility rate was still 1.6. The Chinese government has moved away from coercion to a more health-orientated policy and committed itself to implement international agreements promoting mother and child welfare. However, the long-term aim is still to stabilise population growth by 2050.

Migration controls and schemes

In some parts of the world, migration is a means by which populations can be managed, either by preventing people entering a country (e.g. immigration controls on the USA–Mexico border), or by moving people from an overpopulated area to an under-populated area (e.g. transmigration in Indonesia, see case study below).

Immigration controls

The border between the USA and Mexico is the most closely monitored in the world. Every day, 800,000 people arrive in the USA from Mexico. In 2001, over 300 million two-way border crossings took place at 43 crossing points. In the same year there were over 19 million pedestrian crossings in Texas alone.

There are currently around 9,150 border patrol agents working along the 3,200 km border. After the events of 9/11, President Bush asked Congress to approve funding for an additional 280 border-patrol agents in 2002 (Photograph 5.6).

The US Immigration and Naturalization Service (INS) has four operations to apprehend unauthorised border crossers as part of its southwest border-control strategy: Operation Hold-the-Line in El Paso, Operation Gatekeeper in San Diego, Operation Rio Grande in El Paso and Operation Safeguard in Tucson. They use electronic detection devices and heat sensors, night vision telescopes, ground vehicles and aircraft, including Blackhawk helicopters.

In 2000, over 1.6 million immigrants were caught at the border, 100,000 more than in 1999. This includes those who may have been caught several times.

Elsewhere in the world, policies that have been introduced to deal with the numbers of migrants include:

➤ limiting the number of migrant workers at source — for example by making it more difficult to satisfy visa requirements
➤ insisting on pre-boarding arrangements — for example a return ticket
➤ preventing illegal crossings — for example sea patrols between Florida and Cuba
➤ returning ineligible asylum seekers immediately and requiring the carrier to pay for the return
➤ fast-track procedures to enable entry for genuine asylum seekers
➤ the use of holding bases in third countries where checks are made on visas — as used by Germany in collaboration with Bulgaria, Poland, Romania and the Czech Republic
➤ proposals to charge people who have foreign visitors a deposit that is returnable once their guests have gone home

 Case study **Transmigration in Indonesia**

Transmigration was a scheme by which the Indonesian government provided transportation to a new settlement site in a less populated part of the country. In addition, a house and a farming plot were provided, together with basic infrastructure and a living allowance intended to support

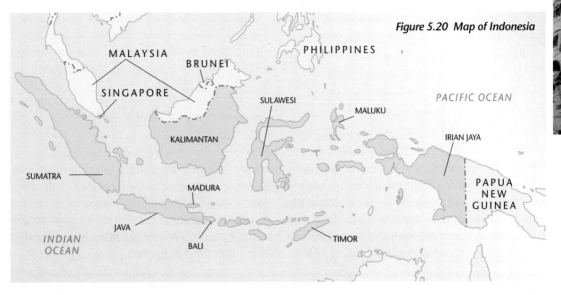

Figure 5.20 Map of Indonesia

the transmigrant family, usually for the first 18 months.

Transmigration was not a new policy. It was begun under Dutch colonial rule during the early twentieth century and was taken over by the Indonesian government after independence. The three main goals of transmigration were:

■ to move millions of Indonesians from the densely populated inner islands (Java, Bali, Madura) to the less densely populated outer islands, to achieve a more balanced demographic development
■ to alleviate poverty by providing land and new opportunities for poor landless settlers to generate income
■ to exploit more effectively the potential of the outer islands

Objections to the policy

In the 1980s, transmigration increased dramatically and large numbers of people were resettled, mainly to Kalimantan, Sumatra, Sulawesi, Maluku and West Papua (Irian Jaya) (Figure 5.20). Massive financial support from the World Bank and bilateral donors (other countries) helped to boost the programme.

The expansion of the programme alerted environmental and human rights critics both inside and outside Indonesia, who exposed transmigration as a development fraud and an environmental disaster.

Important criticisms of the transmigration policy included:

■ Indonesia's outer islands contain 10% of the world's remaining rainforest and transmigration led to loss of forest.
■ Resettlement was political and intended to control the indigenous population of the outer islands (e.g. Irian Jaya, East Timor, Kalimantan).
■ Transmigration violated customary land rights and was aimed at the forced assimilation of indigenous people and forest dwellers.
■ With average resettlement costs of US$7,000 per family in the mid-1980s, the programme was an economic disaster, increasing Indonesia's national debt.
■ Transmigration failed to reach its core goals. Rather than alleviating poverty, the programme redistributed poverty. Most transmigrants were actually worse off in their new locations because of inadequate planning and site preparation, poor access to markets and neglect of the soil and water necessary for a prosperous agricultural economy.
■ Transmigration made virtually no dent in the population pressure in Java.

Recent changes

The course of transmigration policies has changed

dramatically over recent years. Foreign financial assistance has switched to a new strategy to improve existing resettlement projects. The financial crisis which hit Indonesia in mid-1997, and the struggle to rebuild the economy and transform the corrupt political system, have resulted in major changes in the transmigration programme.

Today the picture is both reassuring and alarming. On the positive side, the official transmigration programme appears to have been dropped quietly by the current government. Forced transmigration — so damaging to indigenous communities in receiving areas, and to those Javanese peasants who had to move out after losing their own lands to development — is no longer possible.

However, there is a real danger that transmigration in a new guise may take over where the old programme left off. Both the central government and the newly empowered local governments are relying on exploitation of natural resources — logging, mining, industrial timber and pulpwood plantations, oil palm, and industrial shrimp farming — to generate revenue. Large-scale commercial exploitation of these resources, aimed at export markets, is being encouraged by Indonesia's international creditors, led by the International Monetary Fund (IMF) and the World Bank. If this continues, the demand for labour in areas of low population will increase, fuelling a new migration — and possibly transmigration — boom.

Sustainability: the dilemma

The dilemma facing supporters of the concept of sustainability is that developed countries continue to demand resources for their populations in increasing amounts while less developed countries are supplying the resources that make the developed countries more affluent. Further, the rapidly increasing populations of the developing countries, especially China and India, are demanding more and more resources themselves.

Supporters of sustainability believe that in order to satisfy this dilemma a number of over-riding supra-national policies should come into force:

➤ States should support an open economic system.
➤ Trade policies should not involve arbitrary or unjustifiable discrimination.
➤ Unilateral actions to address issues should give way to international consensus.
➤ The environmental and natural resources of people under oppression, domination and occupation should be protected.
➤ National authorities should endeavour to promote the internationalisation of environmental costs, taking into account that the polluter should pay.

For any of these schemes to work, political principles need to be agreed at future global summits. Given the current global political situation, this looks unlikely.

Agenda 21

Agenda 21 is a UN sustainable development programme agreed at the various Earth summits. Governments are obliged to formulate national plans or strategies for sustainable development. Agenda 21 states that it is people, not governments, who engage in development, and therefore sustainable development is essentially a local activity. Everyone, however poor, has some ability to change what they do in a small way.

ImageDJ/Cadmium

*Photograph 5.9
Tram service in
Rome, Italy.
Improving public
transport is part of
Agenda 21 for
many local
authorities*

Local authorities in many parts of the world are beginning to translate Agenda 21 into local action. Just as global sustainability cannot exist without national sustainable policies, national Agenda 21 is incomplete without a local Agenda 21.

Suggested strategies by local authorities include:
➤ effectively monitoring air and water quality
➤ promoting energy efficiency
➤ establishing effective recycling systems
➤ introducing efficient forms of public transport (Photograph 5.9)
➤ placing population management at the heart of any activity

Authorities in developing countries, such as most sub-Saharan African countries, can introduce local population management by:
➤ training community nurses to be responsible for all elements of care: prenatal, midwifery, childcare, educating adolescents about AIDS, inoculations and care for the elderly
➤ increasing levels of female literacy, thereby raising aspirations and improving levels of prevention and care within families

Authorities in developed countries can:
➤ train sufficient medical care workers to look after the rising numbers of elderly people, especially those too old or infirm to look after themselves. This would reduce the need to recruit medical workers from overseas
➤ recognise that birth rates are falling and consider the issues that may arise from having smaller numbers of children and eventually a reduced workforce

Population change in rural and urban areas

The population changes that are taking place in countries at different stages of development also occur in smaller communities within those countries. The issues associated with ageing populations in more developed countries and those of youthful populations in less developed countries appear at local as well as national scales. Most, if not all, rural and urban areas show the effects of population growth or loss, and of immigration or emigration. It is not possible or desirable to categorise certain areas as areas of loss and others as areas of gain. Some urban areas are losing population while others are gaining. A similar situation exists in rural areas.

Whatever the population change, from either natural growth or migration, there are effects on the areas themselves, and in particular on the provision of services.

Changes in rural settlements in the UK

Population characteristics

Remote rural populations in the UK are declining whereas accessible rural–urban fringe areas are expanding (Figure 5.21).

The consequences of decline include:

➤ many of the people left behind are elderly and of limited means
➤ houses are bought as second homes, creating a ghost-town effect for much of the year

*Figure 5.21
Population pyramid
for two types of
rural areas*

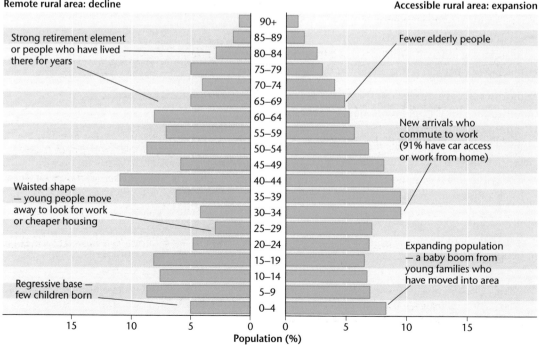

Remote rural area: decline   **Accessible rural area: expansion**

Strong retirement element or people who have lived there for years

Fewer elderly people

New arrivals who commute to work (91% have car access or work from home)

Waisted shape — young people move away to look for work or cheaper housing

Expanding population — a baby boom from young families who have moved into area

Regressive base — few children born

Population (%)

➤ deprivation sets in — many of the people left cannot move away and lead restricted lives
➤ a sense of isolation becomes pervasive
➤ breaking the spiral of decline and deprivation is the key issue

The consequences of expansion include:
➤ creation of several small, new housing estates, often with houses that local people cannot afford
➤ many families have two or more cars, so there is increased traffic congestion, particularly at peak times
➤ villages are often dormitory villages, with little life during the day
➤ conflicts can occur between established villagers and newcomers — local people may not feel that their values are respected
➤ maintaining the rural identity in an increasingly urban environment is a key issue

Services

The main changes to services in rural settlements in the UK are summarised in Table 5.15.

Table 5.15
Changes to services in rural settlements

Service	Changes for the worse	Changes for the better
	ower s	New types of village shop have been created, such as farm shops and garage shops
	wall' n	There is cooperation between some rural post offices and banks to offer combined services
	ties e .	Grants are available for community buses and taxis, such as the postal bus service that combines transport with letter delivery
	ool ls t	Opening more nurseries has increased the total number of children in school. Grants exist to support small schools. Shared headships allow smaller schools to remain open
		The number of mobile libraries has increased
Primary healthcare	Some GP surgeries have closed. There is a decline in dental facilities	Mini-health centres have been set up in larger villages. Grants are available for rural GP practices and pharmacies
Village halls	There is a general decline in village-centred activities. Funds for youth clubs and social facilities for the elderly have been withdrawn	Grants are available for the refurbishment of village halls

Case study

The Isle of Purbeck, Dorset

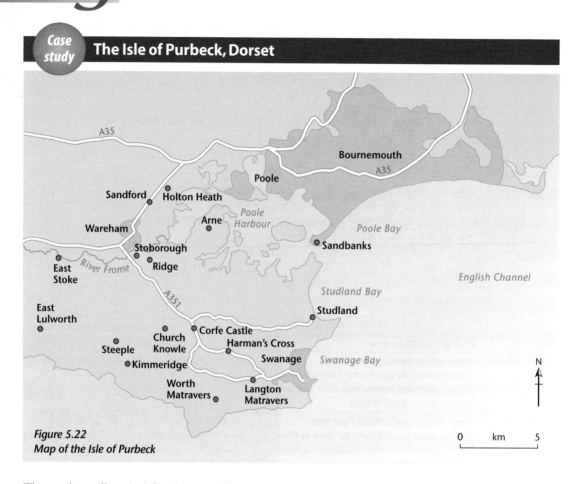

Figure 5.22
Map of the Isle of Purbeck

'The modern village is defined as a small group of houses, none of which can get pizza delivered' (Dorset Rural Facilities Survey, 2002).

The Isle of Purbeck forms the southeastern part of the Purbeck District in Dorset. It is an area of about 200 km² bounded by the sea to the south and east, and by the River Frome and Poole Harbour to the north. The isle does not constitute a formal administrative area and its western boundary is open to debate.

The area is classed as a remote rural district. There is only one town, Swanage, a seaside resort, and a number of villages, Corfe Castle being the largest. The A351, sometimes referred to as the spine of Purbeck, runs from Wareham south through Corfe Castle and then to Swanage. This road provides a direct link to the Poole-Bournemouth conurbation, an area with a population of almost 500,000. This has had an increasing influence on the Isle of Purbeck, which has developed an important dormitory function. The resulting commuter traffic at peak periods presents particular problems in the peninsula.

The population of the area has increased over the last 40 years, reaching 44,400 in 2001. Comparison with the UK average shows that the population of Purbeck is considerably older than that of the country as whole, mainly because of the popularity of the area for retirement. The out-migration of young adults in search of economic opportunities and lower-cost housing is also a factor. In 2001, the birth rate for the district was 10.1 per thousand while the death rate was 11.9 per thousand, resulting in a natural decrease in the population. In Corfe Castle and Studland the death rate was even higher, at 19.6 per thousand. Clearly, in-migration by significant numbers of older age groups is an important factor.

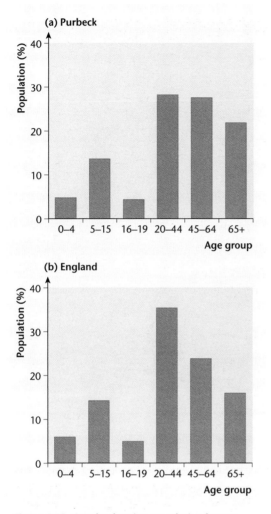

(a) Purbeck

(b) England

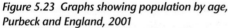

Figure 5.23 Graphs showing population by age, Purbeck and England, 2001

Table 5.16 Selected census statistics: Purbeck and England, 2001

Statistic	Purbeck	England
Population		
Total population	44,416	49,138,831
Males	21,521	23,922,144
Females	22,895	25,216,687
Density (people per hectare)	1.10	3.77
Age groups (%)		
0–4	4.73	5.96
5–15	13.55	14.20
16–19	4.30	4.90
20–44	28.14	35.31
45–64	27.50	23.75
65+	21.77	15.89
Ethnic groups (%)		
White	98.8	90.9
Mixed	0.4	1.3
Asian/Asian British	0.1	4.6
Black/black British	0.1	2.3
Chinese/other	0.6	0.9
Employment status people aged 16–74 (%)		
Full-time	36.8	40.8
Part-time	14.2	11.8
Self-employed	11.4	8.3
Unemployed	1.9	3.3
Retired	18.6	13.5
Qualifications people aged 16–74 (%)		
No qualifications	27.4	28.9
Level 1	18.5	16.6
Level 2	20.9	19.4
Level 3	7.4	8.3
Levels 4/5	17.6	19.9
Housing (%)		
Owner-occupied	73.7	68.7
Rented from council	7.7	13.2
Rented from Housing Association	4.0	6.1
Rented from private landlord/ letting agency/other	14.7	12.0

Source: Office for National Statistics

Ethnic minorities are significantly low in proportion compared to the rest of the country.

The rural housing problem

House prices in the area have risen at a rate above the national average over the last decade. This has been due largely to competition from a number of different groups:

- out-of-area commuters
- retirees
- second homeowners
- in-migrants

This high level of competition for a limited number of available properties has pushed the cost of housing to a level well beyond the reach of most local people. The problem is compounded by the

Photograph 5.10 Worth Matravers

fact that local employment opportunities are limited and wages are low. The average weekly wage for people in this district is 6% below the national average. The right to buy local authority housing has reduced the potential stock of moderately priced rental properties.

Most housing in the area is owner-occupied but there is some private and public rented housing. Two small Housing Association developments have been completed recently in Corfe Castle but this has not been enough to satisfy demand.

Rural service decline

Dorset County Council sees access to services as a key issue. The Dorset Rural Facilities Survey (2002) found a continuing decline in rural services in the Isle of Purbeck and throughout Dorset. Some of the major findings were:

- a sharp decline in the number of shops selling general produce, whether incorporated in a post office or petrol station or as a stand-alone general store
- three out of four villages had no general store, including four villages with a population of over 500
- 38 rural post offices had closed since 1991
- eight villages had lost their only public house since 1991
- 35 rural petrol stations had closed since 1991

However, the survey also noted some positive points. Six village-based doctors' surgeries had opened since 1991 and there had been no rural school or village hall closures. There had been a trend whereby parishes were grouped together and served by one minister or priest, often on a rota basis, which meant some churches in smaller villages were less regularly used.

Table 5.17 shows the availability of rural services in the Isle of Purbeck in 2004. Corfe Castle has by

far the best level of service provision, despite having a similar population to Langton Matravers. Clearly, Corfe's tourism function has been an important positive influence on services, whereas Langton Matravers's close proximity to Swanage has deterred some services that might otherwise have located there. Other anomalies stand out. For example, the village of Ridge, with a population of almost 300, lacks a village hall, whereas some smaller villages, such as Church Knowle, have one.

Privately owned services are lost more quickly than public services because social and political considerations as well as economic ones play a part in maintaining public services. Service decline makes people more reliant on transport, both public and private, to gain access to basic services. In terms of causal factors for rural service decline, the Dorset survey pointed to:

- increased competition from urban supermarkets, which can undercut prices and provide a greater range of produce than small rural retail outlets
- increased personal mobility of most of the rural population as the proportion of people who have access to a private vehicle has risen over the years. This enables most of the rural population to shop weekly and in bulk

Public transport in the Isle of Purbeck is limited. It exists in the form of the 150 bus from Poole to Swanage via the Sandbanks/Studland ferry, and the 142/143/144 buses via Holton Heath, Sandford, Wareham, Corfe and various other villages. There is extra minibus coverage through volunteer schemes but this is limited in extent. Wareham is on the Waterloo (London) to Weymouth rail line. The line between Wareham and Swanage was cut in 1972. A steam railway exists in Swanage but this is basically a tourist operation.

The area is a retirement centre but it is also a commuter area for Swanage and Wareham, and beyond for Bournemouth and Poole. In the deep rural areas, agriculture is still a major industrial activity, though more for self-employed farmers than for general employees. Some farmers have diversified their activities in response to the tourist trade.

Table 5.17 The Isle of Purbeck: village facilities, 2004

Village	Population (2001)	Churches/chapels	Village halls	Schools	Combined post offices/shops	Post offices	General stores	Food shops	Other shops	Petrol stations	Banks	GP surgeries	Public houses
Arne	20	1											
Church Knowle	120	1	1										1
Coombe Keynes	60		1										
Corfe Castle	980	3	1	1		1	1	2	13	1		1	4
East Holme	30	1											
East Lulworth	170	1											1
East Stoke	60												
Furzebrook	60		1										
Harman's Cross	340	1	1			1				1			
Kimmeridge	70	1	1										
Kingston	100	1											1
Langton Matravers	910	1	1	1	1								2
Ridge	290												
Steeple	30	1											
Stoborough	800		1	1	1					1			1
Stokeford	180		1										1
Studland	540	1	1		1								1
Worth Matravers	240	1	1		1								1

Further case studies

One way in which you can study the impact of population change on different localities is by comparing two or more areas through either primary research and/or fieldwork. The specification requires you to study two or more of the following:

➤ an inner-city area
➤ a suburban area
➤ an area of rural–urban fringe
➤ an area of rural settlement (see Isle of Purbeck case study)

Your study should look at characteristics such as housing, ethnicity, age structure, wealth and employment, and the provision of services. These characteristics may impact on the social welfare of people in those localities.

In the UK the census is a valuable source of information and detailed information can be obtained from www.neighbourhood.statistics.gov.uk. Such internet-based research can be supported by fieldwork in the area.

Census-based (2001) information for three urban areas in the UK is given in Tables 5.18–5.20, pages 196–198. This may form the basis for investigation.

Using census data

The census is a rich seam of geographical data for use in fieldwork enquiries. Local census data can provide the backbone of secondary data which can be used in a report to support, challenge or add value to primary findings.

When dealing with census data, the hierarchy of data available (known as the **NeSS hierarchy**) needs to be understood. The smallest units in the 2001 data are **output areas (OAs)**. These are geographical areas based on groups of postcodes. In previous censuses the smallest areas were called enumeration districts. You need to be aware of this for any study that considers change over time. The next three layers up the hierarchy are called **super output areas (SOAs)** and these vary in size from the lower layer SOA (minimum population 1,000) through the middle layer SOA (minimum population 5,000) to the upper layer SOA (minimum population 25,000). Each geographic area of the census is given a numerical and letter code, for example 024C.

The top of the hierarchy is made up of regions and counties which are subdivided into **wards**, **local authority districts** or **unitary authorities**. Wards are areas used for electoral purposes. They usually conform to a collection of OAs and SOAs but often there is not an exact boundary match. They are also subject to regular boundary changes, making comparisons over time difficult. Wards are also used as the base unit for parliamentary constituencies and for primary care trusts (PCTs) for the National Health Service.

When choosing census data, be careful to select the most appropriate scale for your study. The most useful scales are OA, SOA (lower and middle), ward and district.

The main source for obtaining secondary data is the National Statistics website at www.statistics.gov.uk. Go to the home page and then click on *Neighbourhood*.

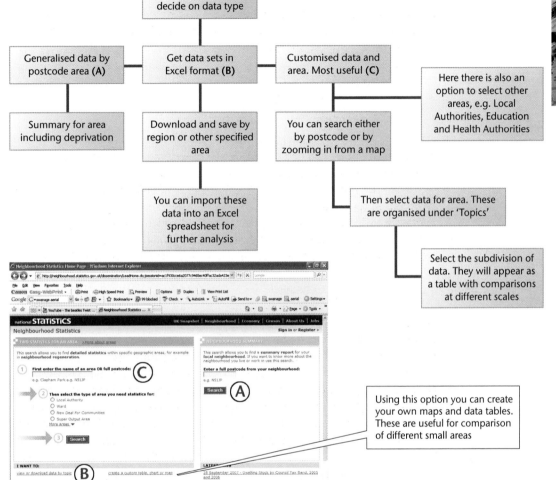

Figure 5.24 explains some of the options.

The main topics in *Neighbourhood Statistics* are:

➤ 2001 census (census area statistics and key statistics)
➤ access to services
➤ community wellbeing/social environment
➤ crime and safety
➤ economic deprivation
➤ education, skills and training
➤ health and care
➤ housing
➤ people and society (income and lifestyles; population and migration)
➤ physical environment
➤ work deprivation

Figure 5.24 How to use the National Statistics website

Table 5.18 *Selected census area statistics: Manchester area 024C lower layer SOA (an inner-city area), Manchester metropolitan district, and England, 2001*

Statistic	Manchester area 024C	Manchester metropolitan district	England
Population			
Total population	1,576	392,819	49,138,831
Males	740	191,570	23,922,144
Females	836	201,249	25,216,687
Density (people per hectare)	50.0	34.0	3.77
Age groups (%)			
0–4	9.6	6.3	5.96
5–15	19.3	14.8	14.20
16–19	5.8	6.2	4.90
20–44	34.3	41.2	35.31
45–64	17.4	18.3	23.75
65+	13.5	13.2	15.89
Ethnic groups (%)			
White	37.8	81.0	90.9
Mixed	10.0	3.2	1.3
Asian/Asian British	4.3	9.1	4.6
Black/black British	46.5	4.5	2.3
Chinese/other	1.4	2.2	0.9
Employment status people aged 16–74 (%)			
Full-time	17.5	33.0	40.8
Part-time	9.0	8.8	11.8
Self-employed	2.2	4.6	8.3
Unemployed	9.6	5.0	3.3
Retired	12.5	10.2	13.5
Qualifications people aged 16–74 (%)			
No qualifications	45.4	34.0	28.9
Level 1	13.2	12.4	16.6
Level 2	12.9	14.2	19.4
Level 3	6.8	13.1	8.3
Levels 4/5	15.8	21.4	19.9
Housing (%)			
Owner-occupied	13.1	41.8	68.7
Rented from council	48.2	28.6	13.2
Rented from Housing Association	27.2	10.8	6.1
Rented from private landlord/ letting agency/other	11.6	18.8	12.0

Source: Office for National Statistics

Summarise the main characteristics of this area.

Statistic	Doncaster area 025A	Doncaster metropolitan district	England
Population			
Total population	1,538	286,866	49,138,831
Males	711	140,114	23,922,144
Females	827	146,752	25,216,687
Density (people per hectare)	38.0	5.0	3.77
Age groups (%)			
0–4	4.2	5.9	5.96
5–15	14.2	15.0	14.20
16–19	4.9	5.0	4.90
20–44	24.8	33.4	35.31
45–64	28.2	24.4	23.75
65+	23.7	16.4	15.89
Ethnic groups			
White	96.9	97.7	90.9
Mixed	0.5	0.6	1.3
Asian/Asian British	1.8	1.1	4.6
Black/black British	0.3	0.4	2.3
Chinese/other	0.5	0.3	0.9
Employment status people aged 16–74 (%)			
Full-time	33.0	36.5	40.8
Part-time	13.7	13.5	11.8
Self-employed	9.5	6.0	8.3
Unemployed	2.7	4.2	3.3
Retired	21.4	15.3	13.5
Qualifications people aged 16–74 (%)			
No qualifications	23.0	38.1	28.9
Level 1	15.1	18.6	16.6
Level 2	21.5	18.5	19.4
Level 3	8.3	5.4	8.3
Levels 4/5	25.8	11.8	19.9
Housing (%)			
Owner-occupied	84.6	69.6	68.7
Rented from council	0.9	19.1	13.2
Rented from Housing Association	8.8	1.9	6.1
Rented from private landlord/ letting agency/other	5.8	9.5	12.0

Source: Office for National Statistics

Table 5.19 *Selected census area statistics: Doncaster area 025A lower layer SOA (a suburban area), Doncaster metropolitan district, and England, 2001*

Summarise the main characteristics of this area.

Table 5.20 Selected census area statistics: Southern Parks ward (an area of rural–urban fringe), Doncaster metropolitan area, and England, 2001

Statistic	Southern Parks ward	Doncaster metropolitan district	England
Population			
Total population	14,502	286,866	49,138,831
Males	7,086	140,114	23,922,144
Females	7,416	146,752	25,216,687
Density (people per hectare)	10.2	5.0	3.77
Age groups (%)			
0–4	4.7	5.9	5.96
5–15	13.0	15.0	14.20
16–19	4.8	5.0	4.90
20–44	28.8	33.4	35.31
45–64	31.0	24.4	23.75
65+	17.8	16.4	15.89
Ethnic groups (%)			
White	98.9	97.7	90.9
Mixed	0.5	0.6	1.3
Asian/Asian British	0.3	1.1	4.6
Black/black British	0.1	0.4	2.3
Chinese/other)	0.2	0.3	0.9
Employment status people aged 16–74 (%)			
Full-time (%)	38.6	36.5	40.8
Part-time (%)	13.9	13.5	11.8
Self-employed (%)	9.8	6.0	8.3
Unemployed (%)	2.2	4.2	3.3
Retired (%)	17.7	15.3	13.5
Qualifications people aged 16–74 (%)			
No qualifications (%)	24.5	38.1	28.9
Level 1 (%)	16.5	18.6	16.6
Level 2 (%)	21.0	18.5	19.4
Level 3 (%)	6.6	5.4	8.3
Levels 4/5 (%)	23.3	11.8	19.9
Housing (%)			
Owner-occupied	87.4	69.6	68.7
Rented from council	6.1	19.1	13.2
Rented from Housing Association	0.4	1.9	6.1
Rented from private landlord/ letting agency/other %	6.1	9.5	12.0

Source: Office for National Statistics

Summarise the main characteristics of this area.

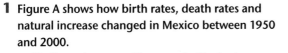

Assessment exercises

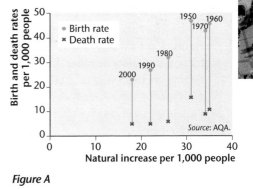

1 Figure A shows how birth rates, death rates and natural increase changed in Mexico between 1950 and 2000.

  a (i) State the natural increase in Mexico's population in 1970 and 1990. *(2 marks)*

  (ii) With reference to Figure A, state the stages of the demographic transition model into which Mexico fitted in 1950 and 2000. *(3 marks)*

  (iii) Outline reasons for the variations in natural increase shown in Figure A between 1950 and 2000. *(6 marks)*

Figure A

  b Define the terms: fertility, infant mortality rate. *(4 marks)*

  c Explain why the pattern of population change in some countries does not follow that predicted by the demographic transition model. *(15 marks)*

(30 marks)

2 Figure B illustrates the population structure of Afghanistan in 2000 and the projected structure for 2050.

  a (i)   These pyramids show absolute numbers on the horizontal axes but percentages are more commonly used. Give advantages of using a percentage scale. *(2 marks)*

  (ii) Identify the ways in which the population structure is expected to change between 2000 and 2050. *(3 marks)*

  (iii) Explain why the changes identified in (ii) will occur. *(5 marks)*

  b Describe the impact that emigration can have on a population structure. *(5 marks)*

  c In recent years, many refugees have fled Afghanistan to seek safety in the UK. Examine the factors that can lead to refugee migrations. *(15 marks)*

(30 marks)

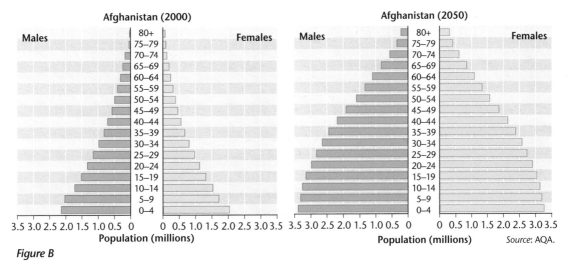

Figure B

3 Table A shows census information for two areas of Bolton: Burnden (an inner-city area) and Hulton Park (a suburban area), for 2001.

  a Describe the differences between Burnden and Hulton Park as shown in the census statistics in Table A. (5 marks)

  b Identify and describe other socioeconomic differences that could exist between these two types of areas in a city. (5 marks)

  c Explain why a census is useful to national governments. (5 marks)

  d With reference to two or more areas you have studied, discuss the impact of age structure, ethnicity, wealth and employment on the provision of services. (15 marks)

(30 marks)

Table A

Census characteristic	Burnden	Hulton Park
Population	12,969	16,370
Ethnic group (%)		
White	70.3	95.5
Asian or Asian British	23.6	1.8
Black or black British	1.3	0.2
Managerial/professional	1,485	4,065
Self-employed	580	899
Routine occupations	1,163	843
Unemployed or never worked	660	187

Unit 1

Physical and human geography

Optional human topics

Chapter 6

Food supply issues

Global agricultural patterns

Global food supply and consumption

At a global level, agricultural production has been increasing steadily, outstripping world population growth by a widening margin since the 1960s (Figure 6.1). In developing countries, production and consumption of the main agricultural products have been growing at much higher (and increasing) rates than in the developed world. This is a result of higher population growth rates, increasing GDP and a greater responsiveness of demand to income growth in less developed countries. In contrast, a slower growth of demand has occurred in the developed world because high per capita consumption and slow growth of population have had a dampening effect on the growth in demand for many commodities. Figure 6.2 shows that countries such as China and Brazil have high growth rates, while North America, Europe and Russia have lower growth rates and, in some cases, production has declined.

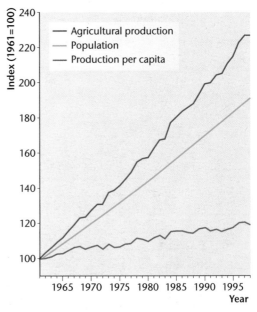

Figure 6.1 Global agricultural production, 1961–98

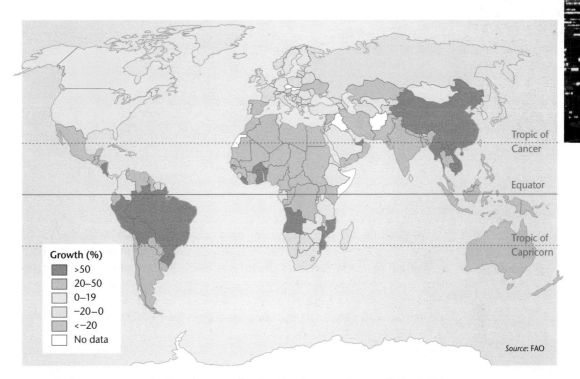

Source: FAO

In the last 15 years agricultural net production has increased annually by 2.2%. The growth in the developing world was almost 3.4% per year while developed countries increased by just over 0.2%. Both crops (63% of total production) and livestock (37% of total production) showed increases. Gross production of crops for food went up 2% per year, but the most important of them, cereals, increased by just 1% (Photograph 6.1). Oil-bearing crops increased by 4%, fruit and

Figure 6.2 Growth of agricultural production per capita, 1993–2003

Photograph 6.1 Sorghum growing in Zimbabwe

Corel

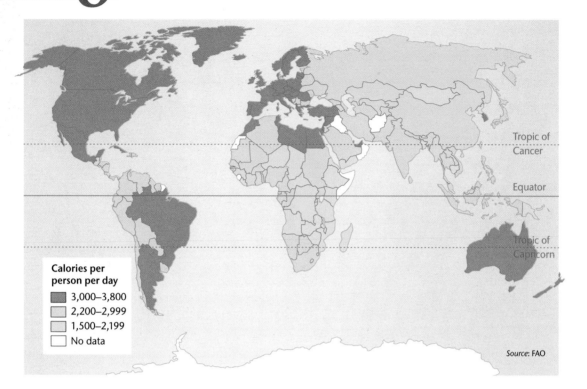

Figure 6.3 Food consumption, 1999–2001

vegetables by 3.8%, eggs by 3.7%, meat by 2.7% and milk by 1.2%. Developing countries now account for 67% of the world's agricultural net production whereas 25 years ago they produced only half of the total.

In terms of food consumption there is still a problem in sub-Saharan Africa. As Figure 6.3 shows, the number of calories consumed per day in the period 1999–2001 was high throughout the developed world, with many countries having an average consumption of over 3,000 calories per person per day. In sub-Saharan Africa and parts of southeast Asia, consumption was below 2,200 calories per person per day. The situation was improving, as many of the countries with a low calorie intake showed a growth in food consumption over a similar period (Figure 6.4). There are, however, a number of areas where calorie consumption actually fell during the period, the Sudan being one example.

Global trade

Global trade in agricultural products has grown in the last 50 years but only at about the rate of global economic output. Reasons for this include:

➤ failure to include agriculture fully in the multi-trade negotiations under the General Agreement on Tariffs and Trade (GATT), which were so successful in reducing industrial tariffs. Agricultural tariffs are as high now as industrial ones were in the 1950s
➤ domestic support policies in developed countries
➤ in developing countries, policies that promoted import substitution at the expense of international trade

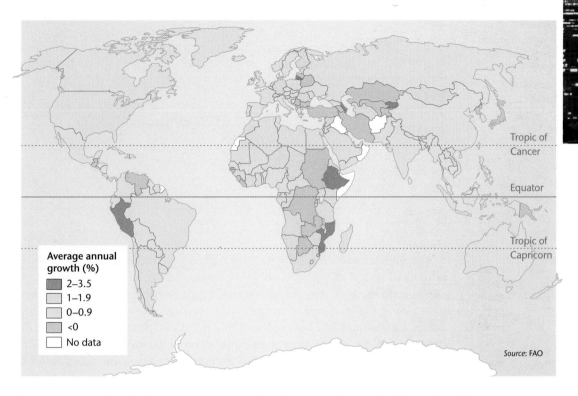

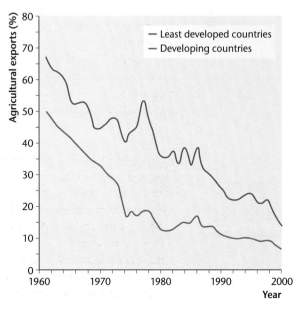

> the growth of agricultural exports in developing countries was held back by the limited absorption capability of their export markets. Most of their produce was aimed at saturated markets in developed countries. Many tropical products were seriously affected by these limitations, including tea, coffee, cocoa and rubber

Figure 6.4
Growth in food consumption, 1995–2001

The result of the rapid export growth in manufactured goods in the last 50 years has been a dramatic decline in the relative importance of agricultural exports (Figure 6.5). The structure of agricultural trade has also changed markedly. In the early 1960s, developing countries had an overall agricultural trade surplus of over US$6 billion, but this gradually disappeared. By the 1990s it was roughly in balance. The least developed countries have been at the forefront of this shift. Their trade deficit has increased so rapidly that by 2000 they were importing almost twice as much as they were exporting (Figure 6.6).

Figure 6.5 *Agricultural exports as a percentage of total exports*

Figure 6.6 Least developed countries' trade balance for agricultural products

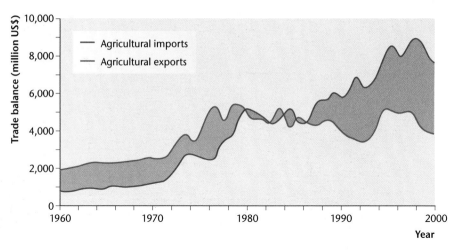

Agricultural trade is less important for high-income countries but it remains a substantial source of export earnings for some, such as Australia, France, New Zealand and the USA. Around one-third of international agricultural trade takes place among the countries of Europe. The once-large import market of western Europe has declined and been replaced by a net export position for a number of commodities (e.g. cereals, sugar, meat) due largely to the success of the **Common Agricultural Policy (CAP)**. Some Pacific rim countries have growing agricultural imports due to high income growth based on manufacturing and almost the whole of Africa is in a position where imports exceed exports (Figure 6.7).

Figure 6.7 Net trade in food, 2000–02

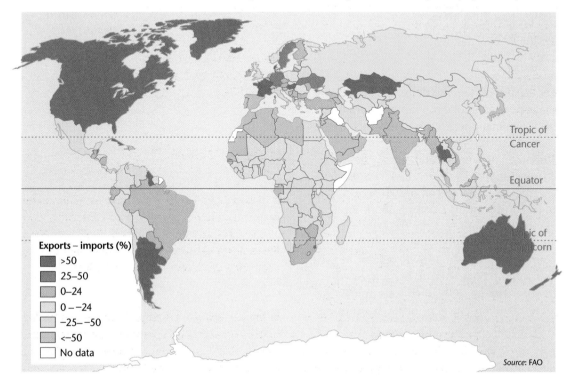

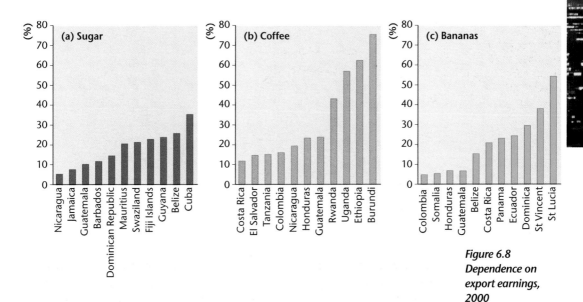

Figure 6.8
Dependence on export earnings, 2000

Despite the declining importance of agricultural exports for developing countries as a whole, some of them still rely heavily on agricultural exports for their foreign earnings. Heavy reliance on a few crops often shows that these economies are small. Figure 6.8 shows the export earnings for three crops in a selection of countries.

One aspect of international trade in food in recent years has been the emergence of **fair trade**. Under fair-trade agreements agricultural products such as bananas, coffee, nuts, orange juice, tea and wine are sold to companies in the developed world at a rate above market price. This extra money is used to provide a better standard of living for the producers. The global market for fair-trade produce was worth over £350 million in 2005, with sales in countries that license the Fairtrade brand growing at about 20% per year. In 2005, Fairtrade coffee accounted for 5% of all coffee consumed in the UK.

Case study   Cereals

Cereal crops are mostly grasses cultivated for their edible grains and seeds. They are a rich source of carbohydrate and continue to be overwhelmingly the major source of food for direct human consumption. In developing nations, grain constitutes almost the entire diet of many families, whereas in richer countries cereal consumption is more moderate but still substantial. In addition, around 35% of production is used as animal feed.

World production has increased substantially since the 1950s because most producers have increased their yields by using fertilisers. This can be seen in Figure 6.10, which shows the growth in cereal yield over a 50-year period. Table 6.1 shows the relative importance of the world's major cereals, comparing production in 1961 and 2005.

Trade in cereals

In the 1970s and 1980s import growth was fuelled by the oil-exporting countries of the middle east, North Africa and a few rapidly industrialising countries such as South Korea, Taiwan and

Photograph 6.2 Canada is traditionally an exporter of wheat

Corel

Table 6.1 The production of cereals, 1961 and 2005

Grain	1961 (tonnes)	2005 (tonnes)	Notes
Maize	205,004,683	711,762,871	A staple food of peoples in North America, South America and Africa, and livestock worldwide. Called 'corn' or 'Indian corn' in North America, Australia and New Zealand
Wheat	222,357,231	630,556,602	The primary cereal of temperate regions
Rice	284,654,697	621,588,528	The primary cereal of tropical regions
Barley	72,411,104	139,220,431	Grown for malting and livestock feed on land too poor or too cold for wheat
Sorghum	40,931,625	59,722,088	An important staple food in Asia and Africa, popular worldwide for livestock
Millet	25,703,968	30,302,450	A group of similar but distinct cereals that form an important staple food in Asia and Africa
Oats	49,588,769	24,032,521	Formerly the staple food of Scotland, popular worldwide for livestock
Rye	35,109,990	15,202,142	Important in cold climates
Triticale	0	12,962,777	A hybrid of wheat and rye, grown similarly to rye
Buckwheat	2,478,596	2,127,823	Used in Europe and Asia, major uses include pancakes and groats
Fonio	178,483	284,578	Several varieties are grown as food crops in Africa
Quinoa	32,435	58,443	Grown in the Andes

Malaysia. There was also a huge leap in demand from the USSR and Japan. In the 1990s many of these countries reviewed their import levels, with some even becoming exporters. Japan rapidly increased meat imports instead of importing grain to feed livestock.

Between the mid-1970s and the end of the twentieth century, the net annual imports of the cereal-importing nations nearly doubled, from 89 million tonnes to 167 million tonnes. Cereal exporters coped well with the spurt in demand, doubling their export levels, with the traditional exporters such as Australia, the USA, Canada, Argentina and Uruguay playing their part. The EU, from being an annual net importer of 21 million tonnes of grain in the mid-1970s, became a net exporter of 24 million tonnes per year by the end of the century. Initially, much of this turnaround depended on heavy price support and protectionist policies.

Developing countries, however, have increased their imports as agricultural production could not keep pace with the growth in population and the expansion of many economies. Imports increased substantially through the 1980s and 1990s and are projected to increase further in the early part of the twenty-first century (Figure 6.11).

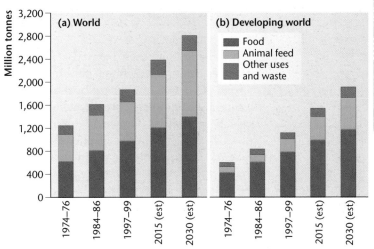

Figure 6.9 Consumption of cereals by category, projected to 2030

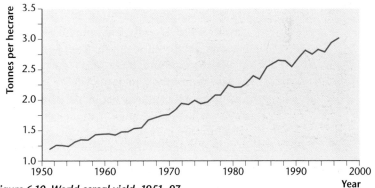

Figure 6.10 World cereal yield, 1951–97

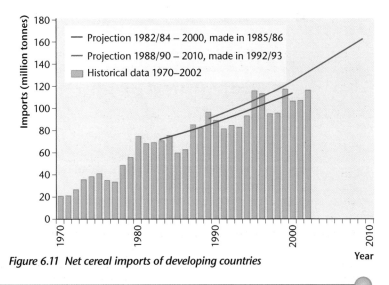

Figure 6.11 Net cereal imports of developing countries

The geopolitics of food

Most countries do not grow enough food to feed their own populations but others produce more than their internal markets demand. Food, therefore, is either bought as part of international trade or supplied as aid.

Food aid is sometimes used by more developed countries to get rid of their surplus agricultural produce. Sometimes this food is sold at low prices in less developed countries (known as 'dumping') in order to create markets in those countries and a possible dependence on food imports. This kind of aid has a tendency to perpetuate the existing political and social structures in a country, structures that often helped to create the need for aid in the first place. Food aid can also be used as a political tool — it can help to keep a government sympathetic to the West in power or be used to maintain good relations with the recipient country. For example, in 1974 the USA withdrew its food aid from Bangladesh to try to 'persuade' that country not to trade with Cuba.

Agriculture is often the driving force in developing countries. World Trade Organization (WTO) statistics show that agriculture accounts for over one-third of export earnings for around 50 developing countries. Significant agricultural subsidies provided by governments to farmers in more developed countries, however, compromise the ability of farmers in developing countries to participate in global agricultural trade. This reduces their income and keeps them in poverty. As well as protecting their markets, richer countries, through the WTO, have been forcing poorer countries to open up their markets. Since India was forced to open up its markets, food imports to the country have quadrupled. As a consequence, rural incomes in many parts of India have fallen sharply, with foreign imports of soya and palm oil undercutting local producers and virtually wiping out the production of edible oil.

Many transnational agribusinesses based in the developed world have the financial resources to buy up land in poorer countries. They also have the political influence to be able to use this land for the exclusive production of cash crops for sale to the developed world. This may squeeze poor farmers off more productive lands with obvious impacts on food production.

Agricultural production systems

Agriculture can be regarded as a system with inputs that have physical, cultural, economic and behavioural elements. The variations in the inputs are responsible for the different types and patterns of agriculture around the world (Figure 6.12). This leads to classifications of agriculture in which contrasts between the different types of farming are clear.

Subsistence and commercial

Subsistence agriculture occurs when a plot of land produces only enough food to feed the family working it or the local community (group, tribe etc.), pay taxes and sometimes leave a little surplus for barter or to sell in better years. The main priority is self-sufficiency, which is achieved by growing a wide range of crops

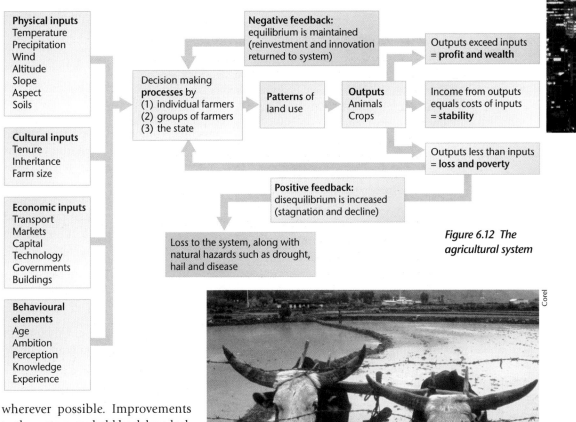

Physical inputs
Temperature
Precipitation
Wind
Altitude
Slope
Aspect
Soils

Cultural inputs
Tenure
Inheritance
Farm size

Economic inputs
Transport
Markets
Capital
Technology
Governments
Buildings

Behavioural elements
Age
Ambition
Perception
Knowledge
Experience

Negative feedback:
equilibrium is maintained (reinvestment and innovation returned to system)

Decision making **processes** by
(1) individual farmers
(2) groups of farmers
(3) the state

Patterns of land use

Outputs
Animals
Crops

Outputs exceed inputs
= **profit and wealth**

Income from outputs equals costs of inputs
= **stability**

Outputs less than inputs
= **loss and poverty**

Positive feedback:
disequilibrium is increased (stagnation and decline)

Loss to the system, along with natural hazards such as drought, hail and disease

Figure 6.12 The agricultural system

Photograph 6.3 Wet rice farming: ploughing with oxen in western Bhutan

wherever possible. Improvements to the system are held back by a lack of capital to provide fertilisers, pesticides and other farming technology. Animals are kept, although where land is limited it is generally too valuable to allow grazing or growth of fodder crops.

Where the climate is too extreme to support permanent settled agriculture, farmers become **pastoral nomads**, moving in search of food for their animals. Depending on their location, animals provide milk, meat and blood for consumption; wool and skins for shelter and clothing; dung for fuel; bones for utensils and weapons; and mounts for transport. Other examples of subsistence farming are **shifting cultivation**, which is practised in parts of the Amazon basin and in southeast Asia, and **wet rice agriculture**, also in southeast Asia and the Indian sub-continent (Photograph 6.3).

Commercial farming usually takes place on a large, profit-making scale. It may be carried out by individual farmers or by companies, with both groups trying to maximise the return on inputs and seeking maximum yields per unit of land. This is often achieved by growing a single crop or by raising one type of animal. Commercial farming develops in places where there are good communications and markets are large, often both domestically and on a global scale. Europeans

Photograph 6.4
A tea picker on a plantation in Kenya

have developed large-scale **plantations** in the tropics (Photograph 6.4) to supply the markets of Europe and North America with crops that include rubber, sugar cane, coffee, tea, palm oil, bananas, pineapples and tobacco. Other types of commercial farming include **cattle ranching**, **commercial grain farming** and the intensive cultivation of fruits, flowers and vegetables (sometimes referred to as **market gardening**). A growing number of farmers throughout the world are now abandoning the growth of staple food crops in order to produce for the emerging **biofuels** market.

Extensive and intensive farming

Extensive and intensive refer to the relationship of inputs to each other, particularly labour, capital and land.

Extensive farming occurs where the amounts of capital and labour are small in relation to the amounts of land being farmed. Shifting cultivation is an example of farming in which labour and capital are both low but large areas are covered. Labour is limited and capital higher in cattle ranching and extensive grain cultivation in the USA, Canada and Australia.

Figure 6.13 Selected agricultural types

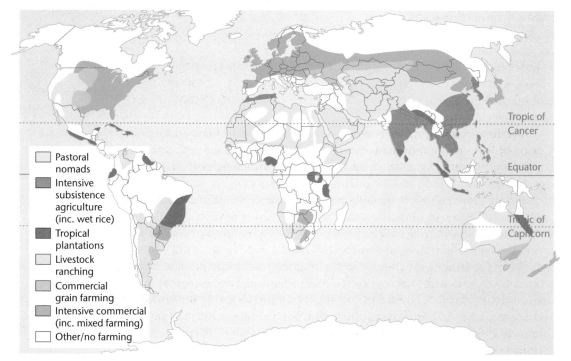

Pastoral nomads

Intensive subsistence agriculture (inc. wet rice)

Tropical plantations

Livestock ranching

Commercial grain farming

Intensive commercial (inc. mixed farming)

Other/no farming

Tropic of Cancer

Equator

Tropic of Capricorn

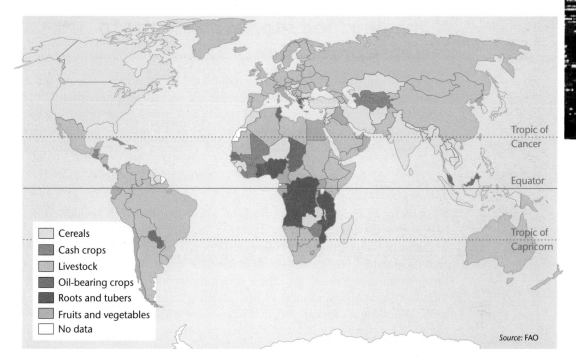

Cereals
Cash crops
Livestock
Oil-bearing crops
Roots and tubers
Fruits and vegetables
No data

Tropic of Cancer

Equator

Tropic of Capricorn

Source: FAO

Intensive farming occurs where the amount of labour is high, even if the amount of capital is low in relation to the area being farmed. An example is intensive wet rice cultivation. Labour input can be low but capital input high, allowing high levels of mechanisation and technological input. This occurs in intensive fruit, flower and vegetable production in the Netherlands.

Figure 6.14 Highest value agricultural production by commodity group, 1999–2001

Arable and livestock farming

Arable refers to growing crops, whether on an intensive scale (e.g. rice and market gardening) or on an extensive scale (e.g. grain farming on the Canadian prairies). Arable farming usually takes place on the more favoured land which is flatter and has higher quality soil.

Livestock farming involves animals and usually takes place in areas less favourable to arable farming (wetter, steeper, colder, higher). This can be at an extensive scale (e.g. pastoral nomadism and cattle ranching) or intensive (e.g. dairy farming).

Mixed farming occurs when farmers grow crops and rear animals on the same farm. It tends to take place in more developed countries where it reduces the commercial risk of relying on one type of farming. It is typical of farming in many parts of the British Isles. In subsistence areas it reduces the risks of food shortages.

Figure 6.13 shows the general global distribution of certain types of farming based on those described above. It should be remembered that there is no widely accepted consensus on how the major types of farming should be recognised and classified. Figure 6.14 indicates the highest value type of agricultural production for each country, as recognised by the Food and Agriculture Organization of the United Nations (FAO).

Managing food supply: strategies to increase production

Much of the increase in agricultural production since the 1950s was the result of the intensification of farming through the use of fertilisers to produce increased yields and healthier crops. Pesticides and herbicides were also applied to control pests, diseases and weeds. More recently a number of strategies have been used in both developed and developing countries to increase agricultural output.

The Green Revolution

The package of agricultural improvements known as the Green Revolution has been seen as the answer to the food problem in many parts of the less developed world. India was one of the first countries to benefit, when a high-yielding variety seed programme (HVP) commenced in 1966. In terms of production it was the turning point for Indian agriculture, which had reached stagnation. The HVP introduced new hybrid varieties of five cereals: wheat, rice, maize, sorghum and millet. With the exception of rice, the cereals were drought-resistant. All were responsive to fertilisers and had a shorter growing season than the traditional varieties they replaced. Advantages of the Green Revolution are:

➤ yields of new varieties are two to four times greater than those of traditional varieties
➤ the shorter growing season has allowed the introduction of an extra crop
➤ farming incomes have increased, allowing the purchase of machinery, better seeds, fertilisers and pesticides
➤ the diet of rural communities is now more varied
➤ local infrastructure has been upgraded to accommodate a stronger market approach
➤ employment has been created in industries supplying farms with inputs
➤ areas under irrigation have increased in number
➤ by intensifying production on existing croplands, large tracts of wilderness have been spared from agricultural encroachment in Africa, Asia and Latin America

Disadvantages of the Green Revolution are:

➤ high inputs of fertiliser and pesticide are required to optimise production, which is costly in both economic and environmental terms
➤ in some areas, rural debt has risen sharply as farmers borrow money to pay for these inputs
➤ high-yielding varieties (HYVs) require more weed control and are often more susceptible to pests and diseases
➤ middle- and high-income farmers have often benefited much more than those on low incomes, widening the income gap in rural communities
➤ increased rural–urban migration has often been the result
➤ mechanisation has increased rural unemployment
➤ some HYVs have inferior flavour

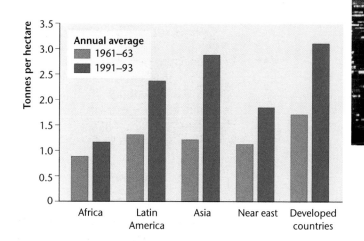

- salinisation (soils becoming increasingly saline) has increased with the expansion of irrigation
- dependence of countries on transnationals (which supply the seeds, fertilisers, pesticides, machinery and markets) has increased significantly

In Asia, the Green Revolution has had an enormous impact. Almost 90% of wheat fields have been planted with modern varieties and the planting of HYVs of rice has increased from 12% to 67%. Between 1970 and 1990, fertiliser application in more developed countries rose by 360% while pesticide use increased by 7–8% per year. The amount of land under irrigation increased by one-third. The gains in productivity were also dramatic, with world cereal production increasing from 1.4 tonnes per hectare in the early 1960s to 2.7 tonnes per hectare by 1991 (Figure 6.15) Over a 30-year period the volume of agricultural production has doubled, with world trade in agricultural products increasing three fold.

Figure 6.15 Improving cereal yields

Recent concerns

In recent years great concern has arisen about the Green Revolution. In the 1990s nutritionists noticed that even in countries where average food intake had risen, incapacitating diseases associated with mineral and vitamin deficiencies remained commonplace and in some cases had increased. A UN report linked some of these deficiencies to the increased consumption of Green Revolution crops. It seems that HYV crops are usually low in minerals and vitamins. The new crops have displaced the local fruits, vegetables and legumes that traditionally supplied vitamins and minerals in people's diets. Therefore, the diet of many people in developing countries has become low in zinc, iron, iodine and vitamin A. This threatens to lock people into a cycle of ill health, low productivity and underdevelopment.

The International Food Policy Research Institute has suggested that there should be an effort to breed new crop strains for the less developed world that are both high yielding and rich in vitamins and nutrients. However, in order to do this, scientists may enter the uncertain world of genetically modified crops.

The genetic modification of crops

The latest revolution in plant breeding is a result of the genetic modification (GM) of seeds. All living things contain DNA, a complex molecule that holds a genetic code for each plant or animal. DNA contains the instructions, inherited from previous generations, for building the organism. Genetic modification involves taking some of the DNA from one species and adding it to the DNA of another species. When a plant is genetically modified, one or more characteristics of the donor species are transferred to the new plant.

Some examples of the methods by which new varieties can be developed include:

➤ adding the genes of a herbicide-resistant weed to a wheat seed to produce a type of wheat that is not harmed by herbicides. A field of wheat can then be sprayed to kill weeds without affecting the crop
➤ adding the genes of a species resistant to a particular pest to soya bean seed, so that the plant is not damaged by that pest
➤ adding a gene from a plant that grows well in an arid environment to the DNA of a rice plant. This could produce a plant that grows better in drier areas than traditional rice plants

Arguments in favour

Those in favour of GM crops claim that newly engineered crops could solve food shortages throughout the world and could reduce the input of chemicals into farming. Trials of GM soya and maize have done well in the USA and some produce has been imported into the UK and used as animal feed.

China has invested a great deal into researching GM rice and cotton crops. Rice is the staple diet for its huge population and cotton is an essential raw material for its clothing industry. Such developments are therefore important for both feeding its people and improving its level of development. It is no surprise that there is little opposition to GM crops in China.

Arguments against

Trials in the UK have been conducted since 1999 but they have been controversial. Critics of GM have the following objections:

➤ The pollen from GM plants might pollinate nearby plants and crops, spreading the modifications in an uncontrolled way.
➤ Crops on organic farms might be contaminated by pollen from GM crops, causing farms to lose their organic status.
➤ The long-term effects of GM crops on human health are unknown.

Protestors have destroyed GM field trials in the UK because of these fears. Campaigners want GM crops to be banned completely and point to agricultural innovations that have had serious health and economic effects, such as BSE. On the other hand, some farmers and companies see a great opportunity to make profits from GM crops. The UK government is encouraging further testing in laboratories, along with carefully controlled field trials. In the meantime, all GM crops that are sold to the public have to be labelled.

The future

On a global scale, GM production is continuing in countries such as the USA and China. International seed companies and food manufacturers are unlikely to be influenced by protestors in one country. Similarly, within a free-trade environment such as the EU, it will be increasingly difficult for governments to regulate the import of GM seeds or products.

In less developed countries, farmers may well face similar problems to those caused by the Green Revolution. GM seeds will be available only from large seed companies and it will not be possible to save seeds from one year to the next because many crops are designed to produce infertile seeds. Poor farmers will not be able to compete with their richer neighbours.

In 2005 the Institute of Genomic Research (TIGR) announced that it had finally unravelled the genetic code of rice. In previous years researchers had uncovered part of the sequence but after private companies Monsanto and Syngenta made figures available to TIGR, it was possible to complete the code. It is estimated that the DNA of rice has over 400 million base pairs holding around 40,000 genes, far more than are found in humans.

Rice is a staple food for around half the world's population but growing most varieties requires large volumes of water and, compared with similar crops, it is inefficient. Rice is also vulnerable to drought. The genomic data should speed up the breeding of tougher and higher-yielding varieties that can help feed the world's expanding population. Consumption trends suggest that 4.6 billion people will be reliant on rice crops by 2025, necessitating a 30% increase in production.

As the crop is closely related to other major cereal grasses including maize, wheat, barley, rice, sorghum and millet, it is hoped that this discovery will allow researchers to access the DNA of a range of cereal crops. As one scientist stated, 'Rice is the Rosetta Stone for crop genomes.'

Photograph 6.5 Knowledge of the rice genome will be a boon for plant breeders

Integrated pest management

Integrated pest management (IPM) is a pest-control strategy that uses an array of complementary methods, natural predators and parasites, pest-resistant varieties, cultural practices and biological controls. Pesticides are used only as a last resort and must present the least possible hazard to people, property and the environment. The following strategies have been used against pests:

➤ mechanical trapping devices
➤ natural predators
➤ insect growth regulators
➤ mating disruption substances (pheromones)

In the 1990s, IPM was used in Pennsylvania (USA) on several crops, with maize the focus of attention. Using pheromone traps on insects reduced pesticide application by up to 50%, saving farmers over US$20 million per year.

Irrigation

Irrigation has been used since agriculture began but many traditional systems are regarded as inefficient and not always beneficial to the environment. Flooding and furrow irrigation are not efficient in water conservation and can be responsible for soil erosion, while sprinklers may waste water.

Research has developed new methods, particularly drip irrigation, which address these problems. Drips deliver water at or near the root zone and are water efficient as evaporation and runoff are minimised.

Micro-propagation

Micro-propagation in agriculture is not new. However, the modern method of using tissue culture to allow rapid multiplication of plantlets is becoming well established. The advantages of tissue culture over earlier forms of propagation are that the planting materials can be replicated quickly, and the properties of these materials can be fixed and assured. Other advantages include disease-free plants and the fact that rooted plantlets are ready for growth, unlike seeds or cuttings, resulting in a more robust plant. Disadvantages include the fact that micro-propagation is an expensive process, particularly in terms of labour costs, and infections can be easily passed on. The banana industry in parts of the Caribbean has benefited from this process in recent years.

Growth hormones

Although this is banned in the EU, steroid hormones can be implanted in beef cattle to improve weight gain, feed conversion efficiency and carcass quality. Hormones can also be used to increase milk yields in dairy cattle by as much as 10%. This technology is used widely in the USA, but many countries have not approved the use of growth hormones, citing worries over public health and animal welfare. The ban in the EU is the subject of a long-standing dispute with the USA, which currently has retaliatory sanctions on some imports from Europe.

Case study   Infrared technology in Kenya

Over the last four decades, more than half of the land on the plains of Lake Victoria in western Kenya has been abandoned as a result of soil degradation due to removal of plant cover. When vegetation is removed the physical structure of the soil starts to degrade and collapse, depleting vital nutrients. Scientists have determined that the key is to identify the problem early enough to prevent switches that

occur from a healthy ecosystem to a degraded state. Until recently, analysis of soil samples in the laboratory cost over US$50 per sample, rendering it unavailable to farmers.

Representing a major advance in field diagnostics, new infrared (IR) technology offers a low cost and accurate method of quality diagnosis. Although the scanner costs US$75,000, it can cost-effectively analyse samples at less than a dollar per sample. The process, known as **infrared spectroscopy**, works by shining a light on a soil sample. The reflections from a range of wavelengths are collected to create a digital scan which is used to determine soil composition and type. This offers a rapid and non-destructive soil analysis and can predict potential shifting points in the soil, allowing restoration before its structure is entirely degraded. Low nutrient levels can be redressed using specific fertilisers. The analysis can also predict soil and plant performance, so that recommendations can be made about how to boost crop productivity.

Infrared technology is used along with tree planting and advice on a sustainable economy as part of the UN Millennium Villages project, which is working in conjunction with the World Bank to halt desertification in this part of Africa. A popular leguminous tree, *Gliricidia sepium*, produces leaves containing 3–4% nitrogen. By capturing nitrogen from the air, the plant is capable of producing nitrogen-rich biomass that can double, or even triple, maize yields.

Appropriate/intermediate technology

Appropriate technology is the use of small-scale, sustainable low-tech ideas which are appropriate to the local climate and environment, and the wealth, skills and needs of the local population. Such schemes could include the following elements:

➤ **water supply** — efficient water is supplied using methods such as drip irrigation instead of dams and complex irrigation schemes. Projects also include water conservation measures such as contour stone lines (see case study of desertification in the Sahel, Chapter 4) and small check dams. Such schemes can increase crop yields by more than half

➤ **fertilisers** — farmers rely on cheap organic fertilisers such as animal dung instead of chemical fertilisers

➤ **mechanisation** — tools are built and maintained locally instead of importing expensive machinery

➤ **produce** — farmers are encouraged to produce a balance of cash and subsistence crops

Wu Yuabin, Director General of the China Rural Technology Development Centre, said recently with regard to Chinese agriculture that 'it is essential to put emphasis on appropriate science and technology in the process of promoting agricultural production, raising the income of farmers and encouraging sustainable rural development'.

Land colonisation

Areas that were not previously developed for agriculture have been exploited, sometimes on a massive scale. The purpose of this expansion has been to provide new land for subsistence farmers or or to grow commercial crops for domestic consumption or exports to bring in foreign earnings.

Apart from the examples described below, land colonisation can involve draining marshes, reclaiming land from the sea and extending cultivation into dry areas through the provision of irrigation.

*Photograph 6.6
A soya-bean
plantation in the
Amazon rainforest,
Brazil*

Brazil

In the 1970s the government opened up vast tracts of the Amazon basin to provide farmland for the landless people of Brazil, particularly those in the impoverished northeast. This caused considerable damage to the rainforest and such migration programmes have now ended. In recent times, however, large areas have been deforested in order to provide pasture and land for soya bean farming (Photograph 6.6). Pasture is the most inexpensive agricultural use as it requires a relatively small and unskilled workforce. Clearing forest for soya beans, particularly in the south of the region, is considered by the government to be an effective use of the land. Brazil has become a leading producer of grains, accounting for more than one third of the country's GNP. Increasing the cultivated area has been a way of increasing agricultural production to meet the demand of a rapidly growing population — but at what cost to the environment?

Indonesia

Transmigration schemes (see case study, Chapter 5) were developed in Indonesia to move people from the highly populated islands of Java, Bali and Madura to less populated islands. Migrants were provided with a house and a plot to farm. The scheme was begun under Dutch colonialism, but the Indonesian government developed it in the 1970s and 80s, moving millions to the less densely peopled outer islands (Kalimantan, Sumatra, Sulawesi). The provision of farming plots, as in Brazil, led to the destruction of tropical forests and the scheme has now been dropped by the government.

Land reform

Land reform is essentially the redistribution of land and can be used to overcome the inefficiencies in the use of land and labour. It includes:

- expropriation of large estates, redistributing land to individual farmers, landless people or communal groups
- consolidation of small fragmented farms
- increasing security of tenure for the farmer
- attempting land colonisation projects
- moving land into state ownership

In Brazil, thousands of impoverished farmers have joined the Movimento dos Sem Terra (MST) (the Landless Movement). This group has organised protests and property invasions, sometimes risking violent confrontation, because so much of the arable land in the country is controlled by a handful of wealthy families. As a result of such pressure, the Brazilian government began to redistribute land on an unprecedented scale in the 1990s.

Commercialisation

An increasing number of transnational corporations (TNCs) and supermarkets in more developed countries are sourcing more of their food products from less developed countries. Small farmers are being drawn into contracts to supply customers in the developed world, increasing their output by intensification, but such developments often lead to a decline in the production of staple foods for the local population.

Many fresh vegetables sold in British supermarkets are grown in Kenya. Crops include summer salads, mange touts and baby sweetcorn, and Kenya also has a thriving flower industry. It has been estimated that this type of agriculture supports at least 100,000 smallholders in the country.

When people see a commercial market for produce they often respond by intensifying their production. In Kibera, a shanty town in Nairobi, enterprising people with access to waste sewage water have developed thriving areas of urban farming, selling their produce in Nairobi's markets. Many are now so successful that they employ casual labourers to work the farms.

Managing food supply: strategies to control the level and nature of production

In 1957 the signing of the Treaty of Rome by the original six members (Italy, France, West Germany, Belgium, the Netherlands and Luxembourg) created the European Economic Community (EEC, later the EU). One of the first areas for which policies were proposed was agriculture. In 1960 the EEC set up the Common Agricultural Policy (CAP).

The Common Agricultural Policy

The aims of the CAP were to:
- increase agricultural productivity within member states
- ensure a fair standard of living for farmers
- stabilise agricultural markets within and between member states

➤ ensure reasonable consumer prices
➤ maintain employment in agricultural areas

These aims replaced existing national agricultural policies and often caused conflict between member states. Several mechanisms were established through which the policy operates:

➤ **Import tariffs** are applied to specific goods imported into the EU. These are set at a level to raise world market prices up to the EU target price. The target price is chosen as the maximum desirable price for those products within the EU. For example, in 2004 the EU set new import tariffs for rice. Brown rice was put up to €65 per tonne and milled rice to €175 per tonne. Import tariffs for basmati rice from India and Pakistan were set at zero.

➤ **Quotas** are used to reduce production from one country or area. Internally, they are used in an attempt to reduce certain types of production. Quotas were introduced for milk production in the early 1980s but although this reduced the amount produced, it was still more than the market required. Further restrictions were placed on the dairy industry in 1992 and 1999 when quotas were reduced. An example of external tariffs concerned banana production (Photograph 6.7). In the late 1990s, the EU was accused by Ecuador, Guatemala and Honduras of operating a quota and tariff system that discriminated against them and in favour of higher cost producers in former European colonies in the Caribbean and Pacific. The protestors were joined by the USA, which claimed that the EU system was unfair trading and took retaliatory action by imposing tariffs on certain European produce. The World Trade Organization (WTO) supported the protestors and ordered the EU to drop the restrictions. The EU eventually backed down and opened its markets fully to Latin American producers. It tried to to reimpose quotas in 2005, which the WTO again ruled to be illegal. One result of this action has been the demise of some West Indian banana producers.

Photograph 6.7
Bananas growing in
Jamaica

➤ **Intervention prices** are set. These are guaranteed prices for each commodity. If the internal market price falls below the intervention level, the EU buys up produce to raise the price to the intervention level. The internal market price can vary only within the range between the intervention price and the target price.

➤ **Subsidies** are paid to farmers growing particular crops. This policy was intended to encourage farmers to grow certain crops, therefore maintaining home-grown supplies. Subsidies are usually paid on the amount of land growing the crop rather than on crop yields. Later reforms have phased out specific crop subsidies in favour of payments based on the total amount of land in cultivation and the adoption of environmentally beneficial farming methods. This will reduce further, but not eliminate, the economic incentive to overproduce.

Case study **EU chicken quotas and Thailand**

After the outbreaks of bird flu in southeast Asia, the EU banned the import of fresh chicken meat from that region. In response, producers in Thailand began to increase their exports of cooked chicken to the EU. Exports grew from 61,000 tonnes in 2003 to over 106,000 tonnes in 2005, and this attracted a tariff of 10.9%. The EU also had in place a quota arrangement to cover this trade.

Observing the considerable surge in trade, the EU decided it would leave the quota in place, but all imports above that level would attract an import tax of 53%. This was considered to be within the WTO rules. Not surprisingly, the Thai producers were not happy with these arrangements and stated that 'the new tariff at a level of 53% has never been expected by any WTO members, especially by those developing countries that have been dependent upon agricultural exports'.

In November 2005, the EU and Thailand agreed that the new quota for cooked chicken imports should be 160,033 tonnes. Furthermore, the EU agreed to reduce the in-quota tariff from 10.9% to 8% but out-of-quota imports would have to pay a tariff of €1,024 per tonne.

The result of the CAP's policies was that farmers in the EU tended to overproduce. This created surpluses in a range of products, sometimes known as 'mountains' or 'lakes'. Over the last 40 years, these surplus products have included cereals, butter, beef, apples, oranges, tobacco and wine.

Agriculture provides only 5% of the EU's total income, but at one time 70% of its budget went on supporting farmers. The net gainers from the CAP were countries such as France and those in southern Europe with smaller, less efficient farms. The net losers tended to be those countries with a smaller agricultural sector but with efficient farms, such as the UK. By the mid-1980s it was accepted that the CAP had brought great benefits, such as close to self-sufficiency in food production, but it had also caused problems:

➤ surplus production as described above
➤ over-intensive farming, especially the use of fertilisers, which was damaging the environment

*Photograph 6.8
In 2004 Poland, a
highly agricultural
country, joined
the EU*

> growing tension between the EU and some of its main trading partners, such as the USA, Australia and New Zealand, over the impact of EU-subsidised produce on world markets
> large, prosperous farmers benefiting more than medium- to small-scale farmers. This caused many smaller farmers to leave the land and migrate to urban areas

CAP reform

In 1992 radical reforms to the system were introduced:
> the support for cereals, beef and sheep was reduced
> quotas were introduced, particularly in dairy farming
> there were to be more set-aside policies
> environmentally sensitive farming was encouraged, decreasing the use of fertilisers and pesticides
> early retirement plans for farmers aged 55 and above were implemented

Although surpluses fell dramatically through the mid-1990s, several member governments were not happy with the way in which the CAP operated. Germany, which was the CAP's main paymaster, was particularly anxious to reduce its net contributions. There was also the problem of accommodating the agricultural economies of the countries of central and eastern Europe that were lining up to join the EU (Photograph 6.8).

Germany and the UK were aware that the CAP could not sustain this level of funding without financial problems. There was a move to curb open-ended production-based subsidies in order to prevent the collapse of the CAP. The other major factor driving reform was the need for the EU to comply with World Trade Organization (WTO) requirements to work towards freer trade in food commodities. Import tariffs and export subsidies were cut and European farmers were forced to rely more on world prices. Consumers in Europe benefited from cheaper food and the environment benefited from a shift in emphasis from agricultural production to rural stewardship.

These reforms, which were agreed in March 1999, did not go as far as many people wanted. Some member states voted to reduce the level of changes, claiming that the effect on their agriculture and farming communities would be too great. In 2002 a new plan was put forward by the European Commission to switch funds gradually from intensive production to schemes that promote rural life, safer food, animal welfare and a greener environment. Farmers will no longer be subsidised on the basis of crop area or head of livestock, ending the incentive that leads to over-production. No farming operation will receive more than £200,000 per year, ending the anomaly in which 80% of CAP funds go to big farmers while the smallest producers receive nothing.

These plans were adopted by EU farm ministers in June 2003. The new CAP is geared towards consumers and taxpayers, but gives EU farmers the freedom to produce what the market wants. In applying the new regulations in the UK in early 2005, the Department for Environment Food and Rural Affairs (DEFRA) website informed farmers that:

the CAP reform will simplify arrangements for subsidy payments by replacing eleven major CAP payment schemes with one new single payment. Farmers will have greater freedom to farm to the demands of the market, as subsidies will be decoupled from production. At the same time, environmentally friendly practices will be better acknowledged and rewarded.

Table 6.2 Schemes available to UK farmers, 1987–2000

Start date	Scheme
1987	In Environmentally Sensive Areas (ESAs) farmers are offered financial incentives to encourage them to maintain or reintroduce environment-friendly management practices
1988	Set-aside applies to the arable sector — compensation payments are given for reducing the cropping area but the land can be used to create nature reserves etc.
1989	The Farm Woodland Premium Scheme encourages the planting of woodland on land currently used for agriculture to enhance the landscape, provide new habitats to increase biodiversity and provide farmers with an alternative productive use — hence the large areas of broadleaved woodlands now being planted
1990	Farmers in Nitrate Sensitive Areas (NSAs) are given grants towards adopting practices to reduce nitrate leaching and to promote extensive uses of land. As part of the grant, environmental features must be retained
1991	The Countryside Stewardship Scheme aims to restore and conserve traditional landscapes and wildlife habitats such as stone walls and hay meadows
1994	The Habitat Scheme gives grants to create and protect wildlife habitats such as water fringes and salt-marsh areas The Organic Aid Scheme gives aid to farmers wishing to convert to organic production, which helps to improve soil quality and avoids use of pesticides
1995	The Moorland Scheme protects heather moorland by paying farmers to reduce sheep stocking densities (known as 'bringing back the purple [heather]') The Farm and Conservation Grant Scheme provides grants for planting hedgerows or establishing shelterbelts on farms
1998	The Arable Stewardship Scheme aims to bring back wildlife to arable areas, for example by building beetle banks (earth ridges across fields)
2000	The England Rural Development Programme (ERDP) is a 7-year programme providing an umbrella for existing agri-environmental schemes such as Countryside Stewardship and Organic Aid with four new schemes: ■ the Rural Enterprise Scheme (includes farm diversification and envouragement of tourist and craft activities) ■ Processing and Marketing Grants to support farm businesses ■ the Energy Crops Scheme to support short rotation coppice and miscanthus (a perennial woody grass) to provide biomass ■ the Vocational Training Scheme (VTS) to support improved expertise for farm and forestry workers

Support from both national governments and the EU has included grants for farmers for a whole range of schemes. Table 6.2 shows the schemes that were available to UK farmers between 1987 and 2000.

Case study   Set-aside

As a result of agricultural incentives, farmers in the EU produced more cereals than were needed by its own consumers. It is expensive to store and export these surpluses to other markets, and the subsidies needed to do so were costly to the taxpayer and disruptive to world trade. Subsidised EU exports can also undermine the development of local agriculture in developing countries.

Set-aside was originally established on a voluntary basis in the late 1980s as a response to this over-production of cereals. Farmers who took over 20% of their cultivated land out of production were paid an initial £200 per hectare, providing the land was left fallow under grass, planted with woodland or put to some non-agricultural use. By the early 1990s cereals were still in over-production, so the EU declared that if farmers with over 20 hectares wished to keep receiving subsidies they had to take 15% of that land out of production. The UK government would have preferred to use price cuts alone to reduce over-production, but accepted that set-aside acts more quickly and provides environmental benefits.

UK farmers have a choice between moving their set-aside area around the farm each year or setting the same piece of land aside for a number of years. Land must be managed, however, so that it can be brought back into agricultural production if necessary. The rules (which in the DEFRA handbook run to 153 paragraphs and 5 appendices) are kept under review in consultation with environmental groups.

Cutting of the set-aside plant cover is prohibited between mid-April and early July to protect ground-nesting birds such as stone curlews, lapwings and skylarks. Farmers are allowed to set aside strips 10 m wide next to water courses and lakes. These act as a buffer zone for pesticide spray drift, set up a wildlife habitat for beetles and other insects and provide a wildlife corridor around farms.

Set-aside land can be used to grow oilseed rape (used in pharmaceuticals and lubricants) and willow coppice (used for fuel).

In response to the low EU cereal harvest in 2006, which led to higher cereal prices and falling stocks, the EU set the obligatory set-aside rate for 2008 at 0%. This means farmers may grow crops or keep livestock on previously eligible land. It does not oblige farmers to cultivate their land — they can set land aside on a voluntary basis. Cereal production was expected to increase in 2008 and the set-aside rate would be reviewed.

Environmental stewardship

Farmers in the UK have an important part to play in protecting and managing the environment. DEFRA's Entry Level Stewardship Scheme (ELS) aims to encourage a large number of farmers to deliver simple yet effective management. Farmers receive £30 per hectare per year (£8 if over 15 hectares are involved) and there are over 50 options to choose from. These include hedgerow management, stone wall maintenance, creating buffer strips, ditch and pond management, infield tree protection, management of rush pastures, stubble control, management of archaeological sites, and bird and flower conservation. There is a similar scheme for organic farmers as DEFRA recognises that they are able to deliver greater environmental benefits.

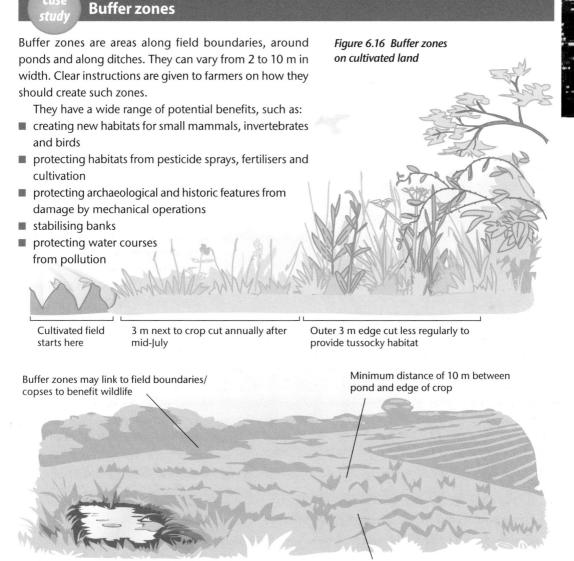

Case study

Buffer zones

Buffer zones are areas along field boundaries, around ponds and along ditches. They can vary from 2 to 10 m in width. Clear instructions are given to farmers on how they should create such zones.

They have a wide range of potential benefits, such as:

- creating new habitats for small mammals, invertebrates and birds
- protecting habitats from pesticide sprays, fertilisers and cultivation
- protecting archaeological and historic features from damage by mechanical operations
- stabilising banks
- protecting water courses from pollution

Figure 6.16 Buffer zones on cultivated land

Cultivated field starts here

3 m next to crop cut annually after mid-July

Outer 3 m edge cut less regularly to provide tussocky habitat

Buffer zones may link to field boundaries/copses to benefit wildlife

Minimum distance of 10 m between pond and edge of crop

Vegetation cut no more than 1 year in 5 to provide tussocky habitat

Figure 6.17 Buffering infield ponds in arable land

Changes in demand

Growing demand in more developed countries

A major development in world trade in the last decade has been the growth of imports into richer countries of high-value agricultural products from the developing world. In the UK, this drive has been led by major supermarkets such as Tesco, Waitrose, Asda, Morrisons and Sainsbury's — companies that will

Table 6.3 Cut flower imports into the UK

Source country	Imports (tonnes) 2001	2006
Kenya	10,183	16,509
Colombia	8,017	9,453
Ecuador	222	449
Costa Rica	218	401
Ethiopia	2	130
Zambia	1	83

bring produce thousands of kilometres onto their shelves. One source of asparagus, for example, is Peru, involving a journey of over 10,000 km to the UK market. Table 6.3 shows the growth of cut flower imports into the UK in recent years. Figure 6.18 shows the source of vegetables imported into the EU in 2005, highlighting the importance of the developing world in this trade.

There is no doubt that the growth in this trade has been beneficial to some farmers in the poorest countries, but concerns have been expressed on the following points:

➤ horticultural crops compete with subsistence crops in developing countries for scarce land and water resources

➤ some land has been cleared to grow cash crops, including tracts of rainforest

➤ food production for domestic consumption might decline in the exporting countries

➤ the use of chemical fertilisers and pesticides could damage the environment

➤ poorer farmers may not take the same precautions when handling chemical fertilisers and pesticides as those in richer countries

➤ the transport of produce over long distances to market contributes to carbon dioxide emissions and climate change

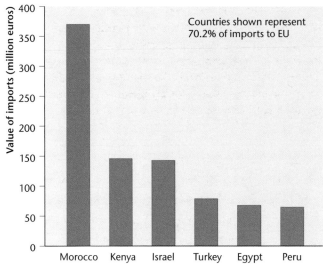

Figure 6.18 Major importers of vegetables into the EU, 2005

Countries shown represent 70.2% of imports to EU

Photograph 6.9 An experimental jatropha plot in Gujarat, India

Joerg Boethling/Still Pictures

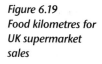

The growth of crops for biofuel production has also expanded rapidly in recent years. In Brazil sugar is grown for the production of ethanol, and jatropha (a drought-resistant oil-bearing plant) has become a major crop in Malawi and Zambia (Photograph 6.9). The EU has a target that 5.75% of transport fuels should come from biological sources by 2010. It has been calculated that growing crops to provide such fuel would consume over 15% of EU agricultural land. As this is unrealistic, the EU would have to rely on fuels derived from imported palm oil and sugar cane grown in less developed countries to meet its target. This has raised the question of competition for land with food production in those areas.

All-year demand for seasonal foodstuffs

Seasonal products are now available in UK supermarkets all year round thanks to sources in tropical and southern hemisphere countries. Many of these products travel thousands of kilometres to reach the UK market. One of the problems highlighted by British consumer groups is that in order to maintain contracts overseas, the supermarkets also import such produce when it is in season in the UK and other parts of Europe. Figure 6.19 shows the results of a survey taken in a UK supermarket showing the distance travelled by some of the produce.

Figure 6.19 Food kilometres for UK supermarket sales

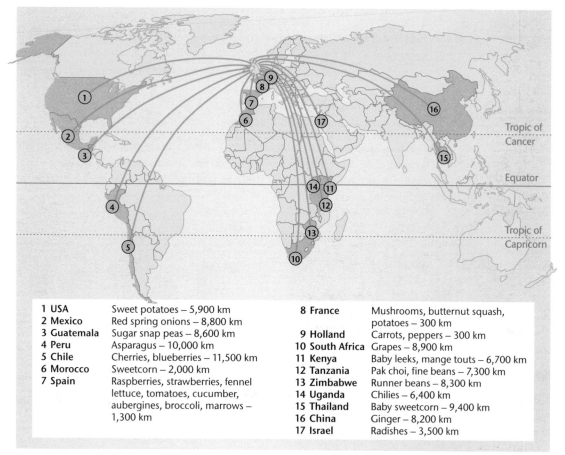

1 USA	Sweet potatoes – 5,900 km
2 Mexico	Red spring onions – 8,800 km
3 Guatemala	Sugar snap peas – 8,600 km
4 Peru	Asparagus – 10,000 km
5 Chile	Cherries, blueberries – 11,500 km
6 Morocco	Sweetcorn – 2,000 km
7 Spain	Raspberries, strawberries, fennel lettuce, tomatoes, cucumber, aubergines, broccoli, marrows – 1,300 km

8 France	Mushrooms, butternut squash, potatoes – 300 km
9 Holland	Carrots, peppers – 300 km
10 South Africa	Grapes – 8,900 km
11 Kenya	Baby leeks, mange touts – 6,700 km
12 Tanzania	Pak choi, fine beans – 7,300 km
13 Zimbabwe	Runner beans – 8,300 km
14 Uganda	Chilies – 6,400 km
15 Thailand	Baby sweetcorn – 9,400 km
16 China	Ginger – 8,200 km
17 Israel	Radishes – 3,500 km

Another way to meet this demand is to develop new crops in the UK. In 2005, Wight Salads of the Isle of Wight produced its first cherry tomatoes for the UK winter market. Tomatoes in the UK are usually imported from Spain or Israel in the winter. In order to cope with the long journey, these tomatoes tend to have thicker skins and are picked while green. The tomatoes produced by Wight Salads, as they are grown near the market, have thinner skins and a better flavour. They are produced in heated greenhouses and have not been exposed to artificial light.

Increasing demand for organic produce

In the last 20 years, a small but increasing number of UK farmers have converted their operations to organic farming. The use of the term 'organic', when applied to food, has a legal meaning. Food has to be grown (or reared) and processed according to certain rules, known as **standards**, which are legally enforceable in the UK and across Europe. The standards cover every aspect of organic food production, from farm to shop. Organic farmers operate in the following ways:

➤ Farmers build up their soil fertility using clover, manure, rock salt, fish and bonemeal. Natural fertilisers like these increase the organic content of the soil, enabling it to retain more moisture during dry periods and allowing better drainage and aeration when it is wet.

➤ Herbicides are not allowed and only an extremely restricted use of pesticides is permitted.

➤ Animals must have enough room to express their behaviour and access to pasture when conditions allow.

➤ Some form of crop rotation is usually involved, meaning that pests and diseases do not have a chance to build up from season to season.

Conversion of a farm to an organic system normally takes at least 2 years. This type of farming is intensive in terms of both land and labour and less damaging to the environment than conventional modern farming, as no chemical fertilisers or herbicides are used.

*Figure 6.20
Registered organic
producers in the UK,
1997–2005*

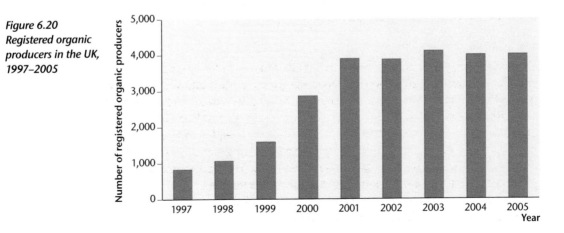

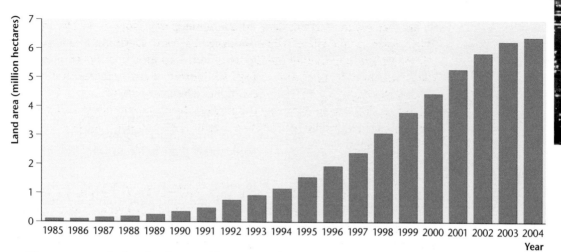

Figure 6.21 Organic certified and in-conversion land area in Europe, 1985–2004

However, organic farming is not without its problems:

➤ In the early years of conversion, yields fall as artificial fertilisers are not permitted.
➤ Farmers in the process of conversion cannot sell as 'organic' any produce until their farms have been certified as organic.
➤ Weeds may have to be controlled by hand.
➤ Labour costs per unit of land are much higher than for conventional farming.
➤ Lower yields are obtained which means the produce is more expensive than conventional produce.

The number of farmers converting to organic has continued to increase in the early years of the twenty-first century. Figure 6.20 shows this rise and the small drop in 2004 and 2005 reflecting amalgamations and closures, something which is replicated in the conventional farming system. The market for organic products is buoyant and expanding, with retail sales in the UK now worth approximately £1.2 billion per year. The total amount of land under organic management has increased ten-fold since 1997 (60,000 hectares in 1997 compared with 686,000 in 2005). This is reflected in the growth of organic farming in Europe (Figure 6.21), where German sales now exceed £2 billion per year.

Local and regional sourcing of foodstuffs

The restructuring of supermarkets in the 1980s consisted of more than just the growth of out-of-town superstores; it led to the growth of the multiples' power in the food chain. The largest five supermarkets now sell over 70% of food in the UK. With this power they have been able to out-compete smaller independent stores. Their quest for easily transportable, cosmetically attractive and broadly acceptable produce has favoured the cultivation of uniform varieties over the more locally distinct, quirky and genetically diverse varieties of fruit and vegetables that prevailed as part of former farming practices and food traditions.

The benefits of smaller independent food stores include:
➤ promotion of local diversity and food culture

Photograph 6.10 Riverford organic farm, near Totnes, Devon

➤ fresher produce

➤ boosting the local economy by supporting local food producers and employment and, indirectly, other local businesses (the multiplier effect)

Apart from local independent stores, a number of initiatives for sourcing local produce have gained a small market share in recent years. Two of them are:

➤ **farmers' markets** — markets where farmers, growers and producers from a defined local area are present in person to sell their own produce direct to the public. Public support has been good and there are now over 400 such markets nationwide that supply regional and local food to customers on a regular basis

➤ **direct marketing** — produce delivered to the customer's door on a weekly basis. One scheme, Riverford in Devon, delivers 3,500 boxes of organic vegetables every week

Most supermarket chains are aware of the potential that locally sourced food offers, and claim they want to increase the number of locally and regionally produced food lines. Some groups, such as Booths in the north of England, have gone further (see case study).

Case study | **Booths supermarkets**

Booths has 27 stores in the northern counties of Lancashire, Cheshire, Cumbria and Yorkshire. The company has a clear policy of sourcing a large percentage of its produce from a defined region. Promotions are often based on regional and local foods, stressing their provenance, variety and quality.

Booths maintains a large supplier base in order to provide choice for the company and its customers, and has built up strong links between buyers and suppliers. The organisation estimates that it has over 100 local suppliers and sources at least 20–25% of produce from the four counties in which it has stores. Suppliers include Bonds of Elswick (ice-cream manufacturers), Island Spice of Kirkby Lonsdale (herbs and spices) and Farmhouse Fare of Clitheroe (puddings and biscuits).

Booths provides a good example of how supermarket chains can operate by keeping a strong local or regional identity, reducing the flow of produce into and out of regions, and allowing more store autonomy.

Food supplies in a globalising economy

The role of transnational corporations

A small number of **agribusinesses** now dominate each part of the food chain in developed countries. Chemical companies that produce seeds are increasingly linked to grain traders and food processors in the production chain. The same companies buy, ship and mill grain, then feed it to livestock or turn it into cereal, often crossing several national borders in the process.

Horizontal integration occurs when a small number of firms effectively control a given market. Such concentrations increase the market power of the dominant firms, enabling them to secure large profits.

 Case study 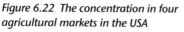 **Agricultural markets in the USA**

In the USA, certain agricultural subsectors are controlled by very few firms. Figure 6.22 shows the concentration in four agricultural markets.

The companies involved are:
- **terminal grain-handling facilities** — Cargill, Cenex Harvest States, ADM, General Mills
- **corn exporters** — Cargill, ADM, Zen-Noh
- **beef packers** — Tyson, ConAgra, Cargill, Farmland National
- **flour-milling facilities** — ADM, ConAgra, Cargill, General Mills

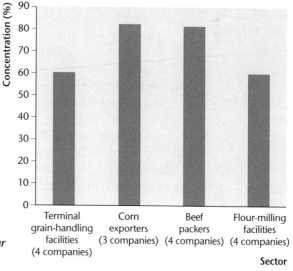

Figure 6.22 The concentration in four agricultural markets in the USA

On a global scale, there are many examples where a small number of firms control large parts of trade in an international commodity. For example, three companies control around 90% of world coffee exports, each of them having an annual turnover larger than the economy of many countries. The dominant transnational agribusinesses are characterised not only by horizontal integration in a given sector but also by their dominance of multiple sectors of agricultural production, shipping and processing. Cargill (see case study) is the largest grain exporter in the USA. It is dominant in wheat, soya beans, corn and cotton and is ranked in the top ten in the world as a food and beverage company. It is also a major player in beef packing and ethanol and fertiliser production, and

Tesco

*Photograph 6.11
Food is travelling
increasing distances
between farmer
and consumer*

operates a large financial division which manages risks in the commodity market.

Vertical integration is where one company either owns, or controls through joint ventures, multiple stages in a production chain. For example, the company Dole owns plantations and canning facilities, and has the marketing power to bring pineapples from plantations in the Philippines to consumers around the world.

The role of large agribusinesses in the agricultural market is therefore increasing. However, many critics are unhappy with the amount of power these companies wield and their influence on governments and international organisations such as the WTO and World Bank. Critics argue that:

➤ the global nature of their operations gives agribusinesses a political voice in many countries, creating a powerful force for policies that reflect their interests
➤ they have been accused of allocating labour-intensive processes to low-wage economies and environmentally damaging processes to countries with lenient environmental regulations
➤ their operations use large amounts of pesticides and fertilisers
➤ their operations have led to the destruction of traditional agricultural communities and family farms
➤ they impose uniformity on agricultural production, undermining the long-term sustainability of agriculture in some parts of the world
➤ many agricultural products grown in developing countries are not directed at local needs but at the markets of richer developed countries, leading to possible food shortages in poorer countries
➤ some agribusinesses have been at the forefront of the promotion and use of GM crops

Environmental impacts

Over the past 50 years, food has travelled increasing distances between farmer and consumer (Photograph 6.11). This is a result of the globalisation of the food industry, the trend towards bigger farms at home, the centralisation of supermarket distribution networks, and out-of-town shopping by car. Mode of transport makes a big difference. Large volumes of food can be imported vast distances by sea at a low environmental cost whereas air transport produces high amounts of pollution for the low volumes it carries and has tripled since 1992 (Figure 6.23).

*Figure 6.23
Air transport of UK
food, 1992–2004*

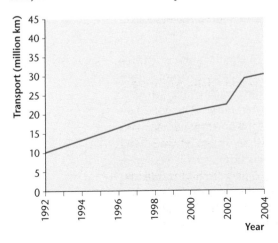

Figure 6.24 shows the carbon dioxide emissions associated with the transport of UK food, indicating that transport by HGV is by far the biggest source of air pollution. Some research, however, suggests that growing food in other parts of the world and importing it into the UK may not be as damaging to the environment as it first seems. A recent report maintained that it takes less energy to import tomatoes from Spain, where the climate is warmer and no heating is used, than to grow them out of season in gas-heated greenhouses in the UK.

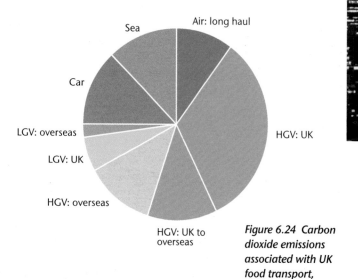

Figure 6.24 Carbon dioxide emissions associated with UK food transport, 2002

The potential for sustainable food supplies

Sustainable agriculture refers to the ability of a farmer to produce food indefinitely without causing irreversible damage to the local ecosystem. Two key issues in promoting sustainability are:

➤ **biophysical** — the long-term effects of various practices on the soil and other aspects of the environment
➤ **socioeconomic** — the long-term ability of farmers to obtain inputs and manage resources such as labour

A number of practices can lead to irreversible soil degradation including excessive tillage and over-irrigation leading to salt accumulations. Farmers remove nutrients from the soil when they grow crops and without replenishment the land would be unable to support agriculture. Sustainable practice replaces those nutrients while minimising the use of non-renewable resources and avoiding chemicals that could damage the environment. In sustainable farming, the nitrogen that farmers are seeking to replace can be obtained from:

➤ recycling crop waste
➤ using animal or human manure
➤ growing legume crops and forages such as peanuts and alfalfa which have bacteria in their roots that fix nitrogen in the soil

The Food and Agriculture Organization of the United Nations (FAO) has identified five causes of unsustainable agricultural practice and degradation of the rural environment:

➤ **policy failure** — inadequate or inappropriate policies including pricing, subsidy and tax policies which have encouraged the excessive (and often uneconomic) use of inputs such as fertilisers and pesticides, and over-exploitation of land. Policies may also favour farming systems which are inappropriate to both the circumstances of the farming community and the available resources

- ➤ **rural inequalities** — rural people often know best how to conserve their environment, but they may need to overexploit resources in order to survive. Meanwhile, commercial exploitation by large landowners and companies often causes environmental degradation in pursuit of higher profits
- ➤ **resource imbalance** — almost all of the future growth in the world's population will be in developing countries and the biggest increases will be in the poorest countries of all — those least equipped to meet their own needs or invest in the future
- ➤ **unsuitable technologies** — new technologies have boosted agricultural production worldwide, but some have had harmful side effects which must be contained and reversed. Such side effects include resistance of insects to pesticides, land degradation through wind and water erosion, nutrient depletion or poor irrigation management, and the loss of biological diversity
- ➤ **trade relations** — as the value of raw materials exported by developing countries has fallen, their governments have sought to boost incomes by expanding crop production and timber sales, and this has damaged the environment

The FAO suggests four strategies to obtain sustainable agriculture and rural development:

- ➤ **intensification through specialisation** — cautious use of inputs such as pesticides and fertilisers combined with improved agricultural and related practices (soil management, integrated pest management, efficient waste management)
- ➤ **intensification through diversification** — minimising environmental and socioeconomic risks, assisting waste recycling and reducing the need for external inputs
- ➤ **combining on-farm and off-farm activities** — promoting additional sources of income can limit pressure on natural resources
- ➤ **extensive systems** — applicable to low population density areas where there is only light pressure on natural resources

Assessment exercises

1 a Compare the main characteristics of capital-intensive farming and labour-intensive farming.

(4 marks)

b Figure A shows processed milk production and dried milk imports in Kenya.
An FAO report of 2003 stated that 'falling prices can lead to import surges that displace domestic production'. To what extent is this true for milk production in Kenya? (5 marks)

c The introduction of capital-intensive farming of cash crops in developing countries can lead to food shortages. Explain why this occurs. (6 marks)

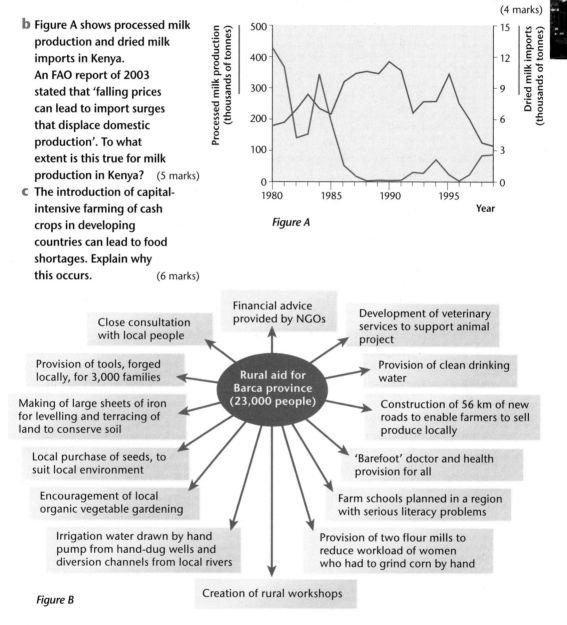

Figure A

Figure B

d Figure B shows the elements of a scheme in Eritrea whose purpose is to bring improvements to an agricultural region of 23,000 people. What evidence is there that this scheme is sustainable?

(15 marks)

(30 marks)

Figure C

2 a Describe the global distribution of irrigated farm land as shown in Figure C. (4 marks)

b What do you understand by the term 'appropriate technology'? What are the benefits of using such technology in developing countries? (6 marks)

c Describe *one* method by which some areas such as the EU have sought to control agricultural production. (5 marks)

d Assess the success of the Green Revolution in improving agricultural output in a country or countries you have studied. (15 marks)

(30 marks)

Energy issues

Types of energy

Energy resources and reserves

A **resource** is defined as any aspect of the environment that can be used to meet human needs. Energy resources are classed as either renewable or non-renewable.

➤ **Non-renewable energy resources** (also known as finite, stock or capital resources) are those that have been built up, or have evolved, over time. They cannot be used without depleting the stock because their rate of formation is so slow that it is meaningless in terms of human lifespan. There is no theoretical limit on the rate of use of non-renewable resources — it depends on the capacity of society to exploit them. Non-renewable energy resources are primarily fossil fuels (oil, natural gas, coal) but they also include nuclear energy.

➤ **Renewable energy resources** (also known as flow or income resources) have a natural rate of availability. They yield a continuous flow that can be consumed in any given period of time without endangering future consumption, as long as current use does not exceed net renewal during the same period. Renewable energy resources include solar power, hydroelectric power, geothermal energy, wave and tidal power, wind power and biomass sources (Photograph 7.1). Renewable resources can be subdivided into:

  – **critical** — sustainable energy resources from forests, plants and animal waste, which require prudent management
  – **non-critical** — everlasting resources such as tides, waves, running water and solar power

Renewability may not be automatic and certain resources may be depleted by heavy use or misuse. In such cases the life cycle of the resource is curtailed. Resource management is the control of the exploitation and use of resources in relation to the associated economic and environmental

> ### Key terms
>
> **Flow** A term used to describe renewable resources.
>
> **Reserve** That part of a resource that is available for use.
>
> **Resource** Any part of the environment that can be used to meet human needs. Resources can be classed as renewable (infinite) or non-renewable (finite).
>
> **Stock** A term used to describe non-renewable resources.
>
> **Sustainable development** Development that meets the needs of the present generation without compromising the needs of future generations.

Photograph 7.1
Wind power is a renewable source of energy

costs. A key element of this is the concept of **sustainable development**. This involves a carefully controlled system of resource management to ensure that the current level of exploitation does not compromise the ability of future generations to meet their own needs.

A **reserve** is the proportion of a resource that can be exploited under existing economic conditions and with available technology. Reserves can be classified as recoverable or speculative.

➤ **Recoverable reserves** are the amounts of a mineral likely to be extracted for commercial use within a certain time period and at a certain level of technology. They:
  – are known to exist
  – can be estimated on the basis of information and judgement
  – are in unexplored areas near established areas of production
➤ **Speculative reserves** are deposits that may exist in a geological basin or terrain where no exploration has yet taken place. They occur where the geological makeup of the Earth's crust is similar to regions that have yielded comparable deposits.

Primary and secondary energy

Primary energy resources are raw materials used for power in their natural form such as coal, oil, wood and uranium. They can be converted into secondary energy sources such as petrol or diesel and used to run vehicles, or into electricity and used to power domestic, industrial and commercial premises (Figure 7.1). In more developed countries energy sources such as oil, natural gas, coal, hydroelectric power and uranium provide the main sources of power. A continual supply of this energy is necessary for the survival of such advanced

Key terms

Electricity A form of energy created from primary fuel sources. The National Grid supplies electricity throughout the UK. This is a network of high-voltage electric power lines between major power stations and cities, which can supply power on demand.

Fossil fuels Oil, natural gas and coal, formed from plant and animal remains in previous geological periods. All are non-renewable sources of energy.

Primary energy Energy sources in raw form such as oil, natural gas or running water. They are used to produce secondary energy.

Secondary energy Manufactured sources of power such as electricity or petroleum.

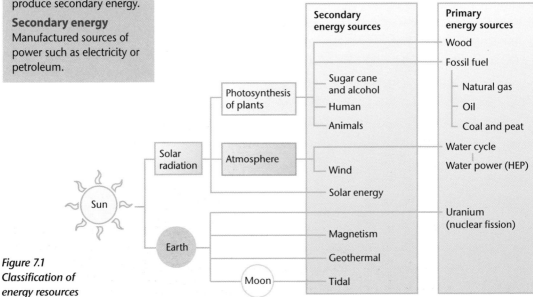

Figure 7.1
Classification of
energy resources

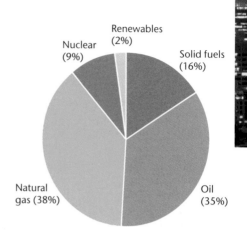

technological nations. In contrast, most less developed countries rely on sources of energy such as wood, peat and animal waste.

Demand for and consumption of energy has grown dramatically worldwide over the last 200 years due to:

➤ rapid population growth, initially in more developed countries but in the last 50 years more markedly in less developed countries

➤ economic development and wealth — in more developed countries the rate of demand for energy has outstripped population growth. With increased wealth comes increased personal mobility and the demand for more goods, services and labour-saving devices in the home

➤ technological change, initially as a result of the development of the steam engine fuelled by coal during the Industrial Revolution of the nineteenth century. In the twentieth century demand for oil outstripped that of coal as combustion and jet engines were developed

Figure 7.2 Primary energy supply in the UK, 2004

Primary energy in the UK

Until recently the UK was self-sufficient in terms of primary energy resources, producing considerable quantities of its own coal, oil and natural gas (Figure 7.2). Although there are still significant coal reserves, these are not considered to be economically viable at present. In addition, clean air legislation has led to the increase in demand for cleaner sources of fuel. The coal industry was privatised in the 1990s and since then almost all pits in the UK have closed down (Photograph 7.2).

Photograph 7.2 Miners at the end of a day's work in the 1940s. The board shows the amount of coal mined

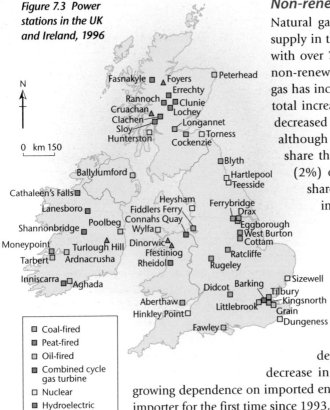

Figure 7.3 Power stations in the UK and Ireland, 1996

N

0 km 150

Fasnakyle ◻ ▲Foyers   ◻Peterhead
Errechty
Rannoch◻ ◼Clunie
Cruachan▲ ◼Lochey
Clachen◻ Longannet
Sloy ◻ ◻Torness
Hunterston◻ Cockenzie

◻Blyth

Ballylumford ◻ ◻Hartlepool
◻Teesside

Cathaleen's Falls◼

Lanesboro ◼   Heysham   Ferrybridge
Fiddlers Ferry ◻   Drax
Poolbeg Connahs Quay ◻Eggborough
Shannonbridge◼ ◻ Wylfa◻ ◼West Burton
Moneypoint▲ Dinorwic▲ Cottam
Tarbert◻ Turlough Hill Ffestiniog ◼Ratcliffe
Ardnacrusha Rheidol◼ Rugeley
Inniscarra◻◻Aghada

◻Sizewell
Didcot Barking
◻ Tilbury
Aberthaw◻ Kingsnorth
Hinkley Point◻ Littlebrook◻ Grain
◻Dungeness
Fawley◻

◻ Coal-fired
◼ Peat-fired
◻ Oil-fired
◼ Combined cycle gas turbine
◻ Nuclear
◼ Hydroelectric
▲ Pumped storage scheme

Non-renewable sources

Natural gas and oil dominate UK primary energy supply in the first decade of the twenty-first century, with over 70% of the total coming from these two non-renewable sources of fuel. The share of natural gas has increased significantly in recent years, with a total increase of around 85% since 1990. Coal has decreased in importance by 40% since 1990 and although renewable resources have increased their share they still provide only a small proportion (2%) of the total primary energy supply. The share of nuclear power has not changed much in the recent past, although the government is considering its expansion to reduce dependence on potentially shrinking supplies of fossil fuels.

Although the UK is still the largest producer of oil and natural gas in the EU (with proven oil reserves of 4 billion barrels and natural gas reserves of 0.53 trillion m^3 at the end of 2005), the depletion of these reserves coupled with the decrease in domestic coal production has led to a growing dependence on imported energy. In 2004 the UK became a net energy importer for the first time since 1993, although it is still a net exporter of oil and maintains one of the lowest import dependencies in the EU. Natural gas is now overtaking coal as the primary fuel for Britain's power stations (Figure 7.3). In the future it is likely that increasing amounts of natural gas will need to be imported. At present Norway is a significant source of imported natural gas but Russia is likely to become increasingly important.

Renewable sources

In 2005, approximately 76% of the UK's energy was generated from fossil-fuel sources, just over 19% from nuclear sources, and just over 4.5% from renewable sources. As part of its goal to reduce carbon dioxide emissions, the UK government has set a target for the generation of electricity from renewable resources. By 2010, 10% of the UK's electricity should come from renewable sources, and the aim is to double this by 2020. To reach this target, approximately 10,000 MW of energy will need to be created from renewable sources, which equates to between 3,000 and 5,000 wind turbines, or 200 biomass power stations generating 50 MW each.

Until recently hydroelectric power (HEP) was the most important source of renewable energy in the UK (Photograph 7.3). By 2000 this had been overtaken by biofuel. Most HEP stations are large-scale schemes in the Scottish highlands. Opportunities to increase the numbers of large plants are limited as most commercially attractive and environmentally acceptable sites have already been used, although many smaller-scale schemes may be feasible. If small-scale HEP from all the streams and rivers in the UK could be tapped, it would be possible to produce just over 3% of total energy needs.

In 2006, biomass used for both heat and electricity generation accounted for 82% of renewable energy sources in the UK. Most of this energy was generated from landfill gas and waste combustion (47%) with smaller amounts from sewage gas, domestic wood and industrial wood. Biomass has the potential to make a significant contribution to the UK's energy needs in the future.

Photograph 7.3
The HEP scheme at Coniston in the Lake District

Wind is the third largest contributor of renewable energy in the UK and in 2007 there were 1,769 wind turbines in operation at 137 sites, producing enough energy to supply electricity to around 400,000 households. By 2010 it is expected that wind power will make the main contribution towards the government's 10% renewable energy target, with more offshore wind farms.

Energy consumption in the UK has remained fairly constant over recent years. Transport consumes over 30% of the total energy supply and has shown the largest growth in demand over the past 20 years. Although domestic consumption has also increased during this period, this has been balanced by a decrease in demand from the industrial sector. Most of the energy used by transport, domestic and industrial consumers is secondary in nature. Within the energy industry, losses during conversion to secondary fuels and during distribution accounted for just over 30% of the total energy consumption in 2005. In future improved methods of conversion could result in better efficiency and less overall waste.

Global patterns of energy supply, consumption and trade

There is a marked energy gap between the rich and poor nations of the world.

➤ Nearly a third of the world's people — those living in low-income countries — have no electricity or other modern energy supplies and depend almost entirely on wood or other biomass for their energy needs. The use of wood for fuel is usually damaging to the environment.

➤ In more developed countries oil provides the bedrock for modern life. Ninety per cent of transport relies on oil products and they are vital components in the pharmaceutical, chemical and food industries. The more developed countries consume around 75% of the total supply of the three major fossil fuels, although as China and India industrialise their consumption will continue to increase rapidly.

The International Energy Agency (IEA) predicts that the world will need almost 60% more energy in 2030 than in 2002, and that fossil fuels will still meet most of these needs. Although there is plenty of coal, it is not likely to grow in popularity because it is so polluting — so that leaves oil and gas. Oil industry experts predict that current reserves will only last for another 40 years or so and although gas supplies will last longer they are finite. However, if governments deliver on promises to push cleaner and more efficient supplies, growth in demand could be restrained by about 10% according to the IEA. A report commissioned by the agency considered two scenarios:

➤ **Business as usual** — referred to in the report as the 'reference scenario', this projects how the world's energy mix would look in 2030 if current trends continue to be followed (Figure 7.4). The demand for fossil fuels, and their related carbon emissions, will grow by around 83%.

➤ **Alternative policies** — this projects how the world's energy mix would appear in 2030 if the package of policies and measures currently being considered by governments is adopted (Figure 7.5). The projected reduction in increased demand by 10% is the equivalent to China's total energy consumption and would result in a 16% cut in carbon emissions.

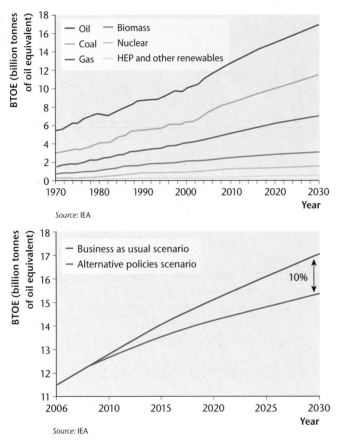

Figure 7.4
Business as usual
scenario

Figure 7.5
Primary energy
demand projections
for both scenarios

The supply of non-renewable sources of energy

Globally, energy supplies are distributed unevenly. This means that energy sources are often long distances from the point of consumption. Two hundred and fifty years ago virtually everyone would have depended on the fuel they could find within a few kilometres of their home. In the modern world, fuel often travels vast distances to reach its consumers (Photograph 7.4). These distances create many challenges, from the environmental risks of long-distance pipelines to oil-related problems linked to political instability in the middle east.

Fossil fuels, which provided the foundations for industrial and economic development in more developed countries, are not present in great quantities in the least developed countries. Recoverable amounts of uranium, used in the production of nuclear energy, are also distributed unevenly.

➤ It has been estimated that the very poorest countries in the world contain 14% of the world's coal reserves, 5% of the oil reserves and 8% of the natural gas reserves.

➤ The middle-income countries, including many middle eastern states such as Iran and Iraq, and other newly industrialising nations such as China, India and Brazil, possess 45% of the world's coal reserves, 70% of oil reserves and 68% of natural gas reserves.

➤ In total the developed world has fewer fossil fuels than the developing world (42% of the world's coal, 25% of oil and 24% of natural gas), but more than those countries in the low-income category. As in the developing world, however, most of these resources are concentrated in only a few countries.

Oil

Most of the oil reserves in the world are in the middle east, which is why the region is so politically important. Saudi Arabia alone possesses 25% of the world's proved reserves. The North Sea and Canada still have substantial reserves, but they would be expensive to extract.

No one really knows how long oil reserves will last, but even the oil industry suspects that the world peak is now approaching. It says that at the moment it has 40 years of proven reserves left. However, it also said that 30 years ago (Figure 7.6). In fact, this estimate has increased in recent years even as production has fallen. Cutting consumption would clearly preserve the oil supply.

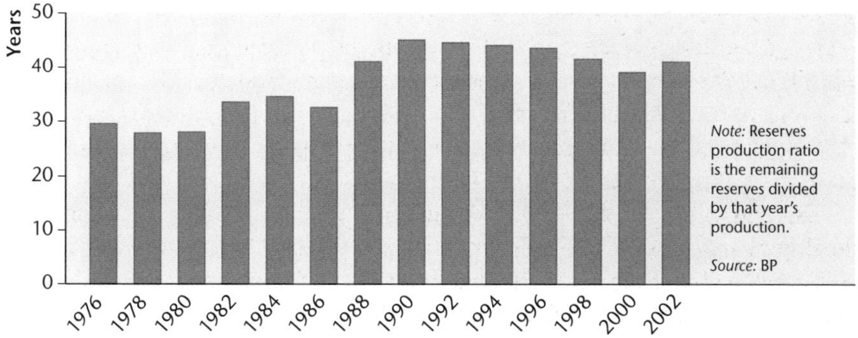

Corbis/Cadmium

*Photograph 7.4
An oil pipeline: fuel often travels vast distances to consumers*

*Figure 7.6
World reserves: production ratio*

Note: Reserves production ratio is the remaining reserves divided by that year's production.

Source: BP

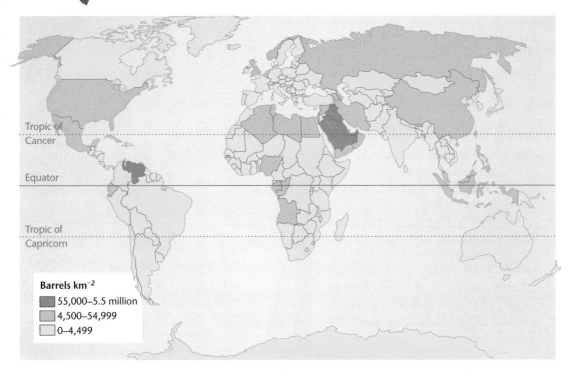

Figure 7.7 International distribution of oil reserves, 2001

Barrels km^{-2}
- 55,000–5.5 million
- 4,500–54,999
- 0–4,499

Photograph 7.5 A BP liquefied natural gas plant in Australia

The middle east is the biggest oil producer, currently providing nearly one-third of the world's total. However, Eurasia (mainly Russia and the UK) and North America are also big producers. With the exception of Nigeria, Libya and Angola most African countries appear to possess limited oil reserves (Figure 7.7).

Natural gas

The world's reserves of natural gas, although finite, are enormous and are widely distributed around the globe. It is estimated that there are still significant amounts of natural gas undiscovered, but at current levels of production the known reserves will last between 60 and 70 years. Russia holds the world's largest natural gas reserves — 38% of the total. Together with countries like Iran that make up the middle east, which holds 35% of the world's total, they account for 73% of natural gas reserves (Figure 7.8).

Natural gas is a much cleaner fuel than oil as it produces virtually no sulphur dioxide and less than half the carbon dioxide released by other fossil fuels. However, it is a volatile product and because of its flammable nature must be transported by pipeline or as

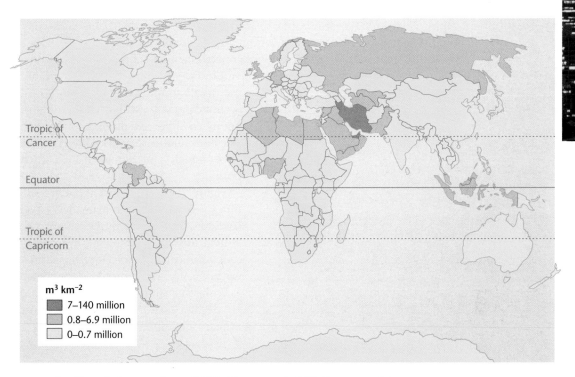

expensive liquefied natural gas (LNG, Photograph 7.5). Because of these transportation problems, the main areas of production tend to be near to their markets.

At present the middle east supplies only a very small percentage of demand, although this is increasing more rapidly than elsewhere in the world. The largest producers in 2005 were the Russian Federation (22.5% of world production) and the USA (22.9% of world production) but in the future if more pipelines are constructed this picture could change (Figure 7.9).

*Figure 7.8
International
distribution of
natural gas
reserves, 2001*

Coal

Coal resources are available in almost every country in the world, with recoverable reserves in around 70 countries. At current production levels,

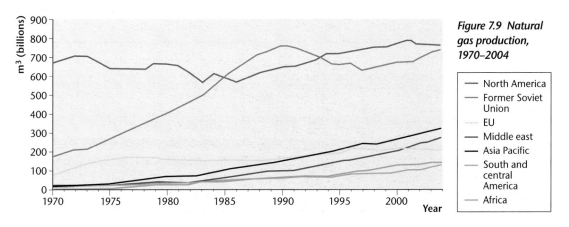

*Figure 7.9 Natural
gas production,
1970–2004*

— North America
— Former Soviet Union
— EU
— Middle east
— Asia Pacific
— South and central America
— Africa

proven coal reserves will last for at least 150 years. After oil, coal is the second most widely used energy source. At present its use is falling in more developed countries but rising in less developed countries and in countries such as China and India, which are experiencing rapid industrialisation. In China and India coal is abundant and relatively cheap to mine, but much of the coal produced has a high sulphur content so is hazardous to the environment and human health when burnt.

Figure 7.10 shows that there are significant coal reserves in many developed countries, in particular the USA, Germany, Poland, Russia and Australia. The future of coal is difficult to predict, because cleaner ways of using it might be developed, such as coal gasification. As supplies of oil and gas decline, coal might well become the primary fossil fuel.

Key terms

Geopolitics The study of the relationships between a country and the rest of the world. Each nation has a sphere of influence it exerts over surrounding nations in areas such as trade, economic aid and military intervention.

Globalisation The close economic interdependence between the leading nations of the world in trade, investment and cooperative commercial relationships.

OPEC The Organization of the Petroleum Exporting Countries was set up in the 1960s to coordinate trade and production policies relating to oil. There are 13 member countries, of which 8 are located in the middle east and north Africa.

Transnational corporations (TNCs, multinationals) Large companies that operate in more than one country.

Uranium

Uranium is the major source of fuel for the nuclear power industry. Only 35 countries in the world possess uranium reserves. The largest amounts are located in the industrialised nations of the USA, Canada and Australia (46% of

Figure 7.10 International distribution of coal reserves, 2001

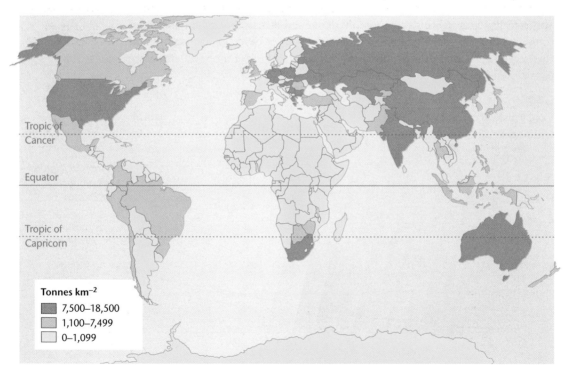

Tonnes km^{-2}
- 7,500–18,500
- 1,100–7,499
- 0–1,099

total global reserves of uranium combined), with other major reserves in Niger, Brazil, Kazakhstan, Russia and South Africa. As worldwide demand for energy grows, greater use of nuclear power is considered an option by the International Energy Agency's (IEA) *World Energy Outlook*. It forecasts that the total global generation capacity of nuclear power plants could almost double by 2030. This would help many industrialised countries to reduce their dependence on imported natural gas and would help to curb carbon dioxide emissions.

Consumption of and trade in non-renewables

Oil

Western Europe and Japan are heavily dependent on oil imports because production cannot meet massive domestic demand. The USA is the world's largest per-capita oil consumer. However, it produces much of its own requirements. Producers in the middle east, where oil is cheap, are also heavy users. Poorer countries consume much less oil per head (Figures 7.11 and 7.12). Rapid industrialisation in China has resulted in a similarly rapid rise in demand for oil, for both industrial and transport uses.

The Organization of Petroleum Exporting Countries (OPEC) is a trading group set up to represent 13 countries, mainly in the middle east, in which over half of the world's oil reserves are located. In the 1970s, OPEC had great power because

North America
14,163

Europe and Eurasia
16,222

Asia Pacific
7,987

Tropic of Cancer

Africa
7,937

Equator

Middle east
20,973

Tropic of Capricorn

Central and South America
6,654

Note: Figures in thousand barrels a day.   *Source:* BP

Figure 7.11 World oil production, 2002

Figure 7.12 World oil consumption and imports, 2002

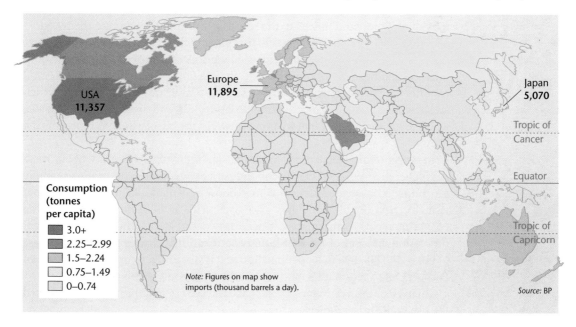

Europe
11,895

Japan
5,070

USA
11,357

Tropic of Cancer

Equator

Tropic of Capricorn

Consumption (tonnes per capita)
- 3.0+
- 2.25–2.99
- 1.5–2.24
- 0.75–1.49
- 0–0.74

Note: Figures on map show imports (thousand barrels a day).

Source: BP

*Photograph 7.6
Oil pumps*

Corbis/Cadmium

it controlled 90% of the world's crude oil exports. Acting as a cartel, OPEC was able to introduce quotas in order to control oil prices and as a result prices rocketed, sending developed countries into economic recession. Its influence has since been reduced as the high price of oil has allowed more expensive fields, such as those in the North Sea and Alaska, to be brought into production. However, most of the world's recoverable reserves still lie in OPEC countries and trade in oil is predominantly between these countries, North America, Europe and China. Oil is transported by pipeline across short distances or by ocean-going tankers over long distances. The transportation of oil has huge potential environmental problems.

In the early part of the twenty-first century there have been some significant trends in oil production and consumption. These are reflected in the rapid rise in oil prices that took place from 2005, accompanied by fears of political instability, risks of pollution and threats to the security of the industry around the world.

In oil-importing countries, rises in the price of oil and therefore energy can have a damaging economic impact. Higher fuel prices can cause unwelcome rises in inflation and restrict economic growth, and are unpopular with voters. Major oil exporters are divided between those such as Saudi Arabia and Kuwait, which favour increasing output in an attempt to ease prices, and those such as Venezuela, which argue against conciliatory moves towards the big consumers, especially the USA.

In simple terms, global economic expansion is driving up the price of oil. There is a higher than expected demand in industrialised countries and China's rapidly expanding economy has created a huge boost in demand, increasing at 20% per year. In the USA, demand has also risen. This is because of strengthening economic recovery and a greater need for higher grade crude oil suitable for processing into petrol for fuel-hungry sport utility vehicles (SUVs). These are popular with US drivers, a phenomenon that is spreading to consumers in western Europe. Only Saudi Arabia has the capacity to respond to this increase.

There are, however, other factors than increased demand that have influenced the rise in the price of oil:

➤ In recent years, oil companies have tried to become more efficient and to operate with lower stocks of crude oil than previously. This means there is less of a cushion against interruptions in supply.

➤ Terrorist threats in the middle east from militants inspired by Al-Qaeda, ethnic tensions in Nigeria and strikes in Venezuela have all affected prices.

➤ In Saudi Arabia and Iraq, sabotage attacks on oil facilities have had a limited impact on supplies. However, they have raised questions over the long-term stability of the area. Any substantial attack on Saudi Arabian oil facilities would have a major impact on global oil markets.

➤ OPEC accounts for 50% of the world's crude oil exports. It attempts to keep prices roughly where it wants them by reducing or increasing supplies to the market, thereby preventing a fall in either price or demand.

➤ The actions of analysts and speculators have had a significant effect. Analysts in some major oil companies have made incorrect forecasts of demand, thereby lowering output. Speculators on the world's stock markets have exacerbated price pressures.

Natural gas

Natural gas accounts for almost a quarter of the world's total energy consumption, and this consumption has increased considerably over the past 30 years. The USA consumed 27.2% of total natural gas in 2005, followed by the Russian Federation with 25.7%. Europe consumed 19.1%, so these three industrialised regions accounted for some three-quarters of global consumption (Figure 7.13). It is likely that there will be continued increases in demand for this source of energy over the next 20 years, and the largest increments in future gas use are likely to be in developing countries.

Despite its importance only 26.3% of the marketed natural gas in 2005 was internationally traded. The low share of international trade is due to high transportation costs. Natural gas is complex to transport and requires enormous investment. Liquefied natural gas (LNG) tankers accounted for most internationally traded gas but a small proportion was transported by pipeline. The construction and management of pipelines is not only expensive but it also poses

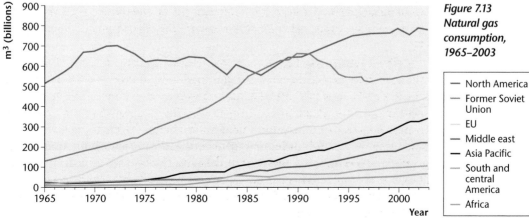

Figure 7.13 Natural gas consumption, 1965–2003

— North America
— Former Soviet Union
— EU
— Middle east
— Asia Pacific
— South and central America
— Africa

legal, logistical and environmental problems. The main exporting countries by pipeline in 2000 were the Russian Federation, Canada, Norway, the Netherlands, Algeria and the UK. The main importing area by pipeline — apart from the USA, which took all of Canada's exports — was Europe.

Case study   Natural gas reserves in western Europe

Reserves of natural gas in western Europe are limited, accounting for only 5% of global resources. The main producing countries within western Europe are the Netherlands, Norway and the UK. Privately owned transmission and distribution companies dominate the European gas industry. More than 30% of gas consumption in western Europe is met by pipeline imports from the former Soviet Union and Algeria, with some LNG imports from north Africa. Before the break-up of the Soviet Union, most of the gas it exported went to eastern Europe. Since then, although Russia has continued to supply this area, it has diversified, with more than 62% of its natural gas exports being sold to non-traditional destinations, in particular to western European countries. It is unlikely that import dependence will cease in the future.

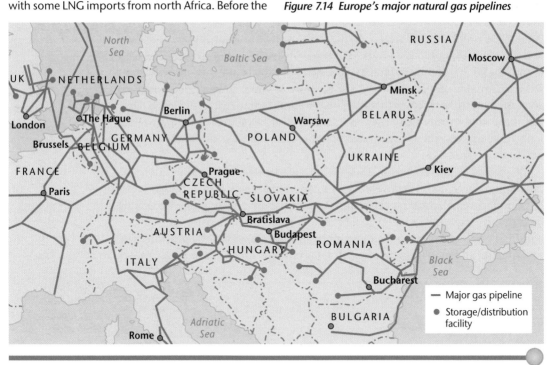

Figure 7.14 Europe's major natural gas pipelines

Coal

Coal remains a major fuel source used for generating electricity worldwide. For example, 92% of the total electricity generated in Poland and South Africa comes from coal, 78% in China and 50% in the USA. Coal is used to generate almost 40% of the world's electricity.

There has been a marked change in the pattern of coal consumption and trade over the past 30 years (Tables 7.1 and 7.2). The three most important producers

— China, the USA and Russia — are still in lead position but Australia and South Africa in the southern hemisphere, and Indonesia (a developing country), have grown in importance. In these locations coal is relatively cheap and easy to mine using modern methods of production. The coal industry in many European countries, particularly in the UK and Germany, suffered decline largely as a result of domestically produced coal becoming more expensive than that imported from abroad.

The future use of coal in the electricity market is closely linked to the availability of oil and natural gas. If prices of these commodities continue to rise unchecked as supply diminishes, it is possible that use of coal for electricity generation in the UK will increase.

Uranium

Nuclear power is predominantly associated with the advanced industrial nations of the world, and its possible expansion as a source of electricity in these nations is a major debate in the early years of the twenty-first century.

In the 1960s and 1970s nuclear power generation increased tenfold. The USA assumed dominance and other important producers were the UK, Japan, Germany, France, Canada, Sweden, Russia and Belgium. In recent decades less developed countries such as India, China and South Korea have also developed their nuclear power industry (Figure 7.15). Nuclear power lost support in more

Table 7.1 Top five coal-exporting countries, 2006

Country	Exports (millions of tonnes)
Australia	231
Indonesia	108
Russia	76
South Africa	73
China	72

Table 7.2 Top five coal-importing countries, 2006

Country	Imports (millions of tonnes)
Japan	178
South Korea	77
Taiwan	61
UK	44
Germany	38

Figure 7.15 Nuclear power consumption, 2000

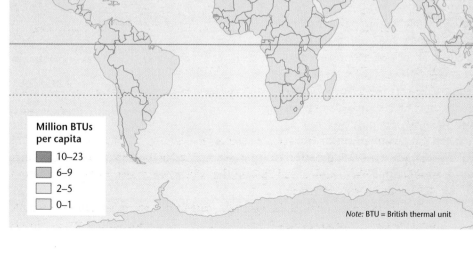

Million BTUs per capita
- 10–23
- 6–9
- 2–5
- 0–1

Tropic of Cancer

Equator

Tropic of Capricorn

Note: BTU = British thermal unit

developed countries following major accidents in 1979 at Two Mile Island (USA) and in 1986 at Chernobyl (Ukraine).

On a global scale the nuclear future does not appear promising. Nuclear power accounts for 16% of worldwide electricity generation and in 2006 output rose by 1.4%, but by 2020 that contribution is expected to decline to just 10%.

Case study · UK government policy and nuclear power

The UK government's 2007 White Paper on energy not only backed renewable energy and improved efficiency measures, but the preliminary view supported the expansion of the nuclear industry. This was a U-turn in policy because just 4 years earlier, in 2003, the government had declared that nuclear power was 'an unattractive option' for the future.

The argument presented to support the expansion of nuclear power was threefold. The White Paper stated that:

- The UK needs to reduce its dependence on imported fossil fuels at a time when global demand is accelerating.
- The UK is committed to addressing the issue of climate change and nuclear power could play a vital part in this due to its low carbon emissions.
- A third of current electricity-generating capacity is due to close in the next 20 years, and there is a pressing need for investment in new low-carbon sources of energy. Although renewable energy is set to produce up to 15% of the UK's total needs by 2015, it will not be enough to bridge the energy gap.

All but one of the UK's current nuclear power stations are due to be phased out by 2023, and many traditional oil- and coal-fired power stations are also reaching the end of their lives. The government supported the construction of up to ten new nuclear power stations, at a cost of £1.2 billion each, through private investment. A number of possible locations were earmarked, the most appropriate of which were considered to be those next to existing reactors around the south coast of England.

Two sites in particular, at Hinkley Point in Somerset and Sizewell in Suffolk, are best suited to accommodate giant 3,200 MW twin-reactor stations. Seven further coastal sites have been selected for single reactors: Bradwell, Dungeness, Hartlepool and Heysham in England; Hunterston and Torness in Scotland; and Wylfa in Wales. Engineered flood defences might be necessary to protect some of these sites from rising sea levels and storms caused by predicted climate change.

Figure 7.16 Map showing the location of nuclear power stations in the UK

The geopolitics of energy

Oil is a global commodity, vulnerable to any event that impacts on its supply and demand. All countries that depend on oil imports are defenceless against external events affecting its supply.

The global energy system faces three major strategic challenges in the twenty-first century:

➤ the growing risk of disruptions to energy supply
➤ the threat of environmental damage caused by energy production and use
➤ persistent energy poverty in the less developed nations of the world

By 2020 energy consumption in less developed countries is set to surpass that of more developed countries. By 2025 China's economy will be bigger than the USA's and India's will be much larger than that of any individual European country. As these and other newly industrialising countries develop, so will their appetite for natural resources, leading to fierce demand for ever-diminishing supplies of non-renewable energy.

As reserves of non-renewable fossil fuels continue to diminish, the following scenarios are likely:

➤ European dependence on middle east oil will remain significant
➤ Asian dependence on Gulf oil will increase
➤ US oil imports will continue to grow
➤ natural gas will continue to be the fastest-growing primary energy source
➤ the growth of natural gas will require major infrastructure investments
➤ the USA will become more reliant on imported natural gas
➤ Russia is likely to expand its exports to Europe
➤ the use of sustainable renewable sources of energy will increase

It is unlikely that the pattern of oil production will change significantly in the near future; the major producers at the start of the twenty-first century will still be major suppliers in 2020. Saudi Arabia is projected to be in the lead, followed closely by Russia, Iran, Iraq and Venezuela.

The developed countries must manage their dependence on imported oil and the risks associated with this. There are a number of threats regarding the future security of oil supplies:

➤ Saudi Arabia at present has strong links with the USA and other Western countries, but this could change with leadership transition, economic reform and terrorism threats.
➤ Iraq faced UN economic sanctions, which constrained the oil industry under Saddam Hussein's rule. Although these sanctions have been lifted since the US invasion, civil unrest and internal economic problems since the war have continued to disrupt supplies.
➤ Iran has an elected government but its politics are influenced strongly by religious leaders. This can hamper relations with the Western world. For example, the USA has imposed economic sanctions on Iran.

BP plc

*Photograph 7.7
BP's Andrew
production platform
in the North Sea*

> OPEC has been successful in the past in manipulating fuel supply in an effort to hold prices within a particular range. This might lead to future price hikes similar to those of the 1970s.

> Russia's President Putin warned the West that its energy dependence on Russia could create obstacles if Moscow was not treated as an equal partner in future trade agreements.

Political developments in the middle east are of great importance to the energy security of the rest of the world because the region possesses most of the reserves of oil and gas. The West has an obvious interest in supporting political and social stability in the region. It is believed by some observers that once trade restrictions and sanctions have been removed in the middle east, liberalisation of political systems and economic growth will follow. In the future it is likely that the resource-rich middle eastern countries will want to develop their gas and oil reserves so that they can maximise their value. In the short term production decisions are likely to be taken within the framework of OPEC agreements, but in the long term it is likely that global oil corporations will be involved as they are needed in the exploration and production stages.

Tremendously wealthy and powerful transnational corporations (TNCs), such as Shell, BP and Exxon, dominate the international oil trade (Photograph 7.7). Oil companies have considerable power in today's globalised world and they help fund development projects and even presidential campaigns in many countries. A number of NGOs are working together to uncover payments that have been made to governments by international companies and to expose corruption, but transnational oil giants are effectively the neo-colonial masters of the world.

The role of TNCs in world energy production and distribution

A transnational corporation (TNC) is one that operates in at least two countries. Many have their centres of production in one or more countries, while the headquarters and research and development (R&D) department are in a different part of the world. The organisation therefore tends to be hierarchical, with the headquarters and R&D in the home country (country of origin) and branch manufacturing plants overseas. As the organisation becomes more global, regional headquarters and, in some cases, regional R&D departments, develop in manufacturing areas.

TNCs take many different forms and cover a wide range of companies involved in the primary, secondary (manufacturing) and tertiary (service) industries. Table 7.3 shows that six out of the top ten of the largest TNCs in 2007 were oil companies.

TNCs control and coordinate economic activities in different countries and develop trade within and between units of the same corporation in different countries. Because of this, they can control the terms of trade and can reduce the effects of quota restrictions on the movement of goods.

They are able to take advantage of spatial differences in production at a global scale. They can exploit differences in the availability of capital, labour costs, and land and building costs — for example, they can take advantage of cheaper labour costs in less developed countries. TNCs exert considerable political influence on governments in both more and less developed countries.

Table 7.3 The world's largest companies, 2007

Rank	Company	Home country	Total revenue (US$ billion)
1	Wal-Mart	USA	351.14
2	Exxon Mobil	USA	347.25
3	Royal Dutch/Shell	Netherlands	318.85
4	BP	UK	274.32
5	General Motors	USA	207.35
6	Toyota Motor	Japan	204.75
7	Chevron	USA	200.57
8	Daimler Chrysler	Germany	190.20
9	ConocoPhillips	USA	172.45
10	Total	France	168.36
11	General Electric	USA	168.31
12	Ford	USA	160.13
13I	NG Group	Netherlands	158.27
14	Citigroup	USA	146.78
15	AXA	France	139.75
16	Volkswagen	Germany	132.32
17	Sinopec	China	131.64
18	Credit Agricole	France	128.48
19	Allianz	Germany	125.35
20	Fortis	Benelux	121.20

Case study BP

BP is the largest UK-owned TNC, with a workforce of nearly 100,000 employees operating in more than 100 countries across six continents. Its annual income in 2006 was $26,172 million, demonstrating continued healthy growth. Brands associated with BP include Castrol, ARCO, Aral, Ultimate, Connect and am/pm and reach nearly as many consumers globally as Wal-Mart, the world's largest retailer. BP is organised into the following main business segments:

- exploration and production
- refining and marketing
- gas, power and renewables

Exploration and production

The main activities in this sector are the exploration, production and transportation of oil prior to refining. Exploration involves geologists employing seismology to detect the presence of oil or gas. In 2005 BP had active exploration sites in 26 countries in locations as diverse as Angola and Azerbaijan and in the deep waters of the Gulf of Mexico. Production is the process of drilling and extracting the oil from the ground.

In 2005 BP's proven reserves of oil and gas equivalent stood at 18.3 billion barrels of oil, and daily oil and gas production reached 4 million barrels of oil equivalent per day. BP is also undertaking

Photograph 7.8 Liquefied natural gas (LNG) carrier Northwest Shearwater *carries gas from Australia to customers in the far east*

Photograph 7.9 A BP service station in Poland

BP plc

exploration and production of oil in partnership with the Russian company TNK. A further 100,000 people are employed by BP-TNK.

BP has its own pipelines and ships to transport oil and gas around the world (Photograph 7.8). Oil pipelines generally run along the ground and oil is moved along by a system of pumping stations along the pipeline. One important oil pipeline, in which BP has a 30% stake, stretches some 1,700 km from the Caspian Sea in Azerbaijan to the Mediterranean coast of Turkey. BP is also helping to fund the construction of a deep-water pipeline some 700 km in length in the Gulf of Mexico. This Mardi Gras pipeline at times runs 2 km below the sea surface and will be capable of transporting 1 million barrels of crude oil a day when completed.

BP Shipping operates its own international fleet of crude oil tankers, product tankers and LNG carriers. Fifteen new tankers were added to the fleet in 2003 and 40 more since then, bringing the total to over 100 operational vessels. They are crewed by around 1,000 seafarers and 400 onshore staff.

Refining and marketing

Oil refining separates the various components of crude oil to produce different types of fuels and lubricants. The oil is heated to varying temperatures to extract petroleum gas, gasoline, kerosene and other valuable energy sources. BP owns, wholly or in part, 17 refineries worldwide, with a processing capacity of 2.8 million barrels of oil a day. Five of these refineries are in the USA, seven are in Europe and the rest are spread around the globe.

BP fuels are sold under a number of brand names including ARCO, Castrol, Amoco, Aral and BP itself (Photograph 7.9). In Europe, BP is the second largest fuel retailer overall, with its biggest market in Germany where there are over 2,700 outlets. Under its various brand names BP is also the second largest fuel retailer in North America. In China its retail presence is growing rapidly and by the end of 2007 it had more than 1,400 retail outlets.

Environmental impacts of energy production

One of the main differences between renewable and non-renewable sources of energy is their impact on the environment. Renewable sources of energy on the whole are 'cleaner' and less harmful to the atmosphere than non-renewables. However, renewables can have some environmental impacts. Some people think wind farms are visually polluting, and burning biomass can have serious environmental consequences in terms of deforestation and the release of carbon dioxide. In less developed countries clearing trees for fuel often damages an area's ecological balance and can lead to desertification.

Non-renewable sources of energy release harmful pollutants, such as carbon and sulphur compounds, into the atmosphere when they are burnt. Transporting fuels from the area of production to the area of consumption has environmental impacts. An obvious example is the movement of crude oil from one part of the world to another by means of tanker or pipeline. There is the danger of an oil spill contaminating the environment where it occurs and transport by tanker uses fuel, which releases carbon dioxide and other pollutants into the atmosphere.

Another difference between renewables and non-renewables lies in the scale at which they are used. Renewable resources can often be exploited on a smaller, more localised scale than non-renewable resources. An example is the mini-hydro systems used for electricity generation in remote Himalayan villages in Nepal. However, this is a generalisation; most hydroelectric power (HEP) and tidal barrage schemes are as large scale as oil-fired power stations.

Table 7.4 People relying on biomass resources as their primary fuel for cooking, 2004

Region	Total population %	Total population Million	Rural %	Rural Million	Urban %	Urban Million
Sub-Saharan Africa	76	575	93	413	58	162
North Africa	3	4	6	4	0.2	0.2
India	69	740	87	663	25	77
China	37	480	55	428	10	52
Indonesia	72	156	95	110	45	46
Rest of Asia	65	489	93	455	35	92
Brazil	13	23	53	16	5	8
Rest of Latin America	23	60	62	59	9	25
Total	52	2,528	83	2,147	23	461

Fuel-wood gathering

In developing countries, particularly in rural areas, 2.5 billion people rely on biomass such as fuel wood to meet their energy needs for cooking (Table 7.4). This figure is projected to increase to over 2.6 billion by 2015 and to 2.7 billion by 2030 because of population growth. In most less developed countries use of fuel for cooking accounts for over 90% of household energy consumption because most rural dwellers have no access to electricity (Figure 7.17).

Figure 7.17 Map showing domestic biomass consumption in developing countries

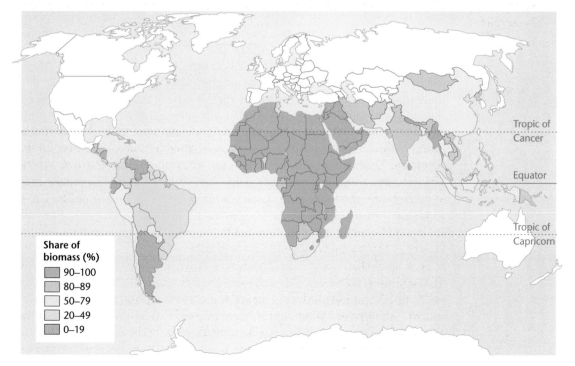

Share of biomass (%)
- 90–100
- 80–89
- 50–79
- 20–49
- 0–19

*Photograph 7.10
Woman carrying
fuel wood in
southern Nigeria*

Corel

The use of biomass is not in itself a concern unless fuel is harvested unsustainably. In many countries reliant on biomass, such as those in east Africa, women and children bear the burden of fuel-wood collection — a time-consuming and exhausting task (Photograph 7.10). In Tanzania the average distance travelled to collect wood is between 5 and 10 km per day. Many children, especially girls, are withdrawn from school to attend to this task.

In addition to the human costs of fuel-wood gathering in less developed countries, there are also environmental factors to consider. Increased population pressure in relation to the carrying capacity of the land has led to overuse of the land through a combination of activities, including fuel-wood gathering, over-cultivation and overgrazing. The scarcity of fuel supplies has led to the widespread removal of woodland for firewood. This results in less interception of rainfall, reduced infiltration, faster runoff and greater soil erosion by water and wind.

Nuclear power and its management

Nuclear power stations produce high-level radioactive waste in the form of used fuel rods which have been removed from reactors. In the UK, these are taken to the Thorp nuclear reprocessing plant at Sellafield in Cumbria (Figure 7.18). Here, reusable uranium and plutonium are separated out to leave unusable radioactive waste. This is currently stored at Sellafield in steel-clad or lead-lined glass containers.

Disposal of nuclear waste

Nuclear waste has a long half-life (the measure of how long it takes to lose half its radioactivity). The half-life of uranium is measured in millions of years. The material will therefore remain highly radioactive for a very long time and this has to be borne in mind when disposing of it safely. Transport of the waste from one part of the country to another is also a problem. Specially designed railway containers have been constructed and extensively tested.

In the UK, the Nuclear Decommissioning Authority (NDA), formerly Nirex, has responsibility for disposing of all forms of nuclear waste, some of which does not originate in this country. It has tried unsuccessfully to find enough sites for disposal. When examining the potential of a site it is necessary to consider the following factors:

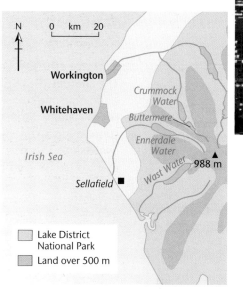

Figure 7.18
The location of Sellafield

➤ the geology of the area — the ground must be geologically stable so that there is little chance of underground displacement
➤ unemployment figures in the area — jobs will be created by the activity
➤ the availability of land, which has to be bought for the site
➤ transport links to the site, both locally and for transporting the waste long distances from nuclear power stations and ports
➤ the potential strength of local pressure groups
➤ the design features that will be necessary to make the site safe for many years
➤ the technology that will be necessary to ensure safe transport, storage and security

The construction of a site for the safe storage of nuclear waste raises a number of issues, which include:

➤ noise and disruption during construction
➤ short-term and longer-term safety concerns, with particular emphasis on leukaemia and cancer
➤ potential contamination of water supplies, again both in the short and longer term
➤ the effect on farming activities — will crops be safe to consume in the area and will animals become contaminated by grazing on grass, which may be affected by the waste?
➤ the potential risk of accidents and the worry that the site may become the target of terrorism
➤ the effects on tourism — will the site destroy the tourist industry of the area or increase visitor potential?
➤ the 'hiding and forgetting' syndrome — what future problems may arise, which are difficult to predict and plan ahead for?
➤ if it is located in Cumbria, will the area become too economically dependent on the nuclear industry?

Chapter **7** *Energy issues*

The use of fossil fuels

See case study of the trans-Alaskan oil pipeline, chapter 2, page 64.

Climate change

The continued rise in the consumption of oil means a predicted 60% rise in carbon dioxide emissions between 2004 and 2030, mostly from cars, trucks and power stations. More than two-thirds of the increase will come from developing countries as a consequence of fast economic growth and a massive rise in car ownership. This rise will be in addition to that which has already taken place over the last 50 years (Figure 7.19).

Figure 7.19 Carbon emissions from fossil fuel burning, 1950–2003

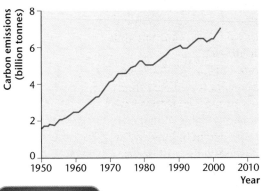

Views still differ over the degree to which human activity has contributed to global warming. However, there is a growing international consensus that human-induced emissions of carbon dioxide and other gases, for example methane and nitrous oxide, are a major factor causing climate change. These emissions come from, among other sources, burning ever-greater quantities of oil, coal and petrol. The gases trap the sun's energy in the atmosphere and cause what is known as the greenhouse effect. Carbon dioxide occurs naturally and the greenhouse effect keeps temperatures on the planet at a level that makes it habitable, but current carbon dioxide levels are about 40% higher than they were before the Industrial Revolution.

Most observers agree that the less developed world is more susceptible to the effects of climate change than the more developed world. This is because poorer countries do not always have the infra-structure and resources to counter the effects of climate change. It is not uncommon for single weather events, such as tropical cyclones and floods, to kill thousands of people in regions such as south Asia, southern China and central America. In Africa the UN reports a 40–60% decrease in total water in the large catchment basins of Niger, Lake Chad and Senegal. In a continent already struggling with poverty and famine, climate change is a matter of life and death.

As the risks of manmade climate change became better known, the international community began to negotiate a treaty that would define mandatory limits for greenhouse gas emissions. The Kyoto Protocol, adopted in 1997, required that by 2008–12 developed countries should have reduced carbon dioxide emissions by 5% from 1990 levels. This was considered minimal because many scientists claimed that a 50% reduction would be needed to achieve climate stabilisation.

When the Kyoto Protocol was developed, poorer countries felt that the rich countries should take responsibility for solving problems of

Key terms

Carbon trading Rich, economically developed countries can buy carbon credits from poorer countries, for example by helping them to modernise old, inefficient power stations.

Greenhouse effect The way that the atmosphere absorbs long-wave radiation from the Earth and is warmed. The effect is increasing because of the release of gases such as carbon dioxide into the atmosphere by human activity.

Kyoto Protocol An agreement signed in 1997 by most of the more developed countries (a major exception being the USA). The aim of this treaty is to cut harmful emissions by 5% by 2012.

AQA AS Geography

which they had been the primary cause. Reductions in emissions for developing countries were, therefore, to be phased in over time; targets for richer countries were to be imposed sooner. At the insistence of the US government, several 'flexibility mechanisms' were added to the treaty. These measures included trading carbon emission credits between nations so that some could emit more if they helped others to emit less. Different countries were given different emission-reduction targets, for example 8% for the EU countries and 6% for Japan.

Although carbon dioxide emissions from developing countries such as China and India are rising rapidly, developed countries are still the biggest emitters. For example, the USA puts nearly 25% of global greenhouse gases into the atmosphere. The US decision to drop out of the Kyoto treaty in 2001 was therefore a major setback. When leaving the treaty, the Bush administration claimed it would take its own steps to reduce greenhouse gases. It was worried that meeting its target of a 7% reduction in emissions would affect economic growth.

US absence aside, the Kyoto Protocol came into force in February 2005, after Russia's accession to the treaty. Meeting the commitments to reduce carbon dioxide emissions will not be easy because emissions in most countries have risen since 1990.

In December 2007 the UN held a climate-change convention in Indonesia. The main outcome was the 'Bali roadmap', which started a 2-year process of negotiations on a new set of emissions targets. Other points agreed were:

➤ the transfer of clean technology to developing countries
➤ aims to halt deforestation
➤ helping less developed nations to protect themselves against the impacts of climate change, such as falling crop yields and rising sea levels
➤ a framework for developed nations and transnational companies to earn 'carbon credits' by paying for forest protection in less developed countries

The final text of the 'Bali roadmap' acknowledged that 'deep cuts in global emissions will be required to achieve the ultimate objective of avoiding dangerous climate change.' It was seen as the first step towards a binding deal to be finalised in Copenhagen in 2009.

Acid deposition

The major causes of acid deposition are the burning of fossil fuels in power stations, the smelting of metals in older industrial plants and exhaust fumes from motor vehicles. Acid deposition consists of the dry deposition of pollutants released by these activities: sulphur dioxide and nitrogen oxide. These chemicals mix with precipitation, mist and clouds to produce wet deposits of sulphuric acid, nitric acid and compounds of ammonia (acid rain).

Acid deposition causes damage to trees, particularly conifers. It produces a yellowing of the needles and strange branching patterns. It also leads to the leaching of toxic metals (aluminium) from soils, and their accumulation in rivers and lakes. This in turn kills fish. Acid deposition is blamed for damage to buildings, particularly those built of limestone. It can cause health problems in people, such as bronchitis and other respiratory complaints.

Various ways of reducing acid deposition exist:

➤ the use of catalytic converters on cars to reduce the amount of nitrogen oxide emitted in exhaust fumes

➤ burning fossil fuels with a lower sulphur content

➤ replacing coal-fired power stations with nuclear power stations

➤ the use of flue-gas desulphurisation schemes and other methods of removing sulphur either before or after coal is burnt

➤ reducing the overall demand for electricity and car travel

Case study — Acid deposition in Scandinavia

Scandinavia is one area of the world where forests and lakes have been severely damaged by acid rain. Scientists found that most of the pollution came from outside the region, mainly from the UK (Figure 7.20). The UK has now recognised its responsibility and has made significant moves to reduce sulphur emissions.

By 1999 total acid deposition on Scandinavia had fallen by 30%, but the residual effects mean that it will take time to repair the

environmental damage. Today, much of the pollution affecting this area comes from eastern Europe where countries have weak economies and cannot afford anti-pollution measures.

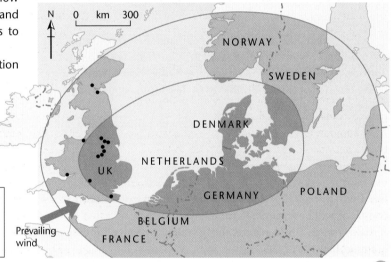

Figure 7.20 Acid rain over Scandinavia

- UK coal-fired power station
- Acidity in rain above average
- Acidity in rain well above average

The potential for sustainable energy supply and consumption

Current patterns of energy supply and consumption are unsustainable in the long term. Fossil-fuel reserves are finite and their consumption is polluting.

The UK is currently responsible for the release of about 3% of the world's global greenhouse gases, despite having only 1% of the world's total population. The UK's energy industries are its largest single contributors to greenhouse gas emissions. The increased use of renewable energy resources is thought to be vital if sustainable energy supply and consumption are to be a feature of the future.

Types of renewable energy

Biomass energy

Living plants and decaying vegetable matter comprise the greatest bulk of the Earth's biomass. Biofuel is that part of the biomass that can be converted into energy. At its simplest this involves burning fuel wood, dung and crop residues for cooking in less developed countries, but this is quite inefficient. Modern techniques involve gasifying the biomass and burning the gas released. In more developed countries biofuels also include the methane that is harvested from landfill sites and municipal waste. Biofuels create lower levels of pollution than traditional fossil fuels.

Case study — Bioethanol in Brazil

Sugar cane has been cultivated in Brazil for hundreds of years but until the twentieth century virtually all production was used to make sugar. In 1973, the price of petroleum rose from US$2.84 to US$12.27 per barrel, causing important changes in the world energy market. Brazil had become dependent on imported fuel and suffered greatly, so the government implemented a series of strategic measures to reduce its reliance on fuel imports.

In addition to exploration for oil and gas within Brazil's boundaries and developing large-scale hydro-electric power schemes, emphasis was placed on the use of alternative energy sources. Ethanol, derived from sugar cane, was introduced as vehicle fuel, combined with petrol or used on its own.

Government policy (the PROALCOOL programme) in the 1970s and 1980s determined that all sugar cane produced was destined for ethanol production. The government banned the use of diesel-powered vehicles, required government agencies to buy only ethanol-powered cars and ensured that import duties on petrol kept the price

of ethanol below that of imported fuel. It also assisted with the purchase of ethanol-powered cars through tax incentives and subsidised the price of ethanol to consumers.

By 1988, 90% of the 800,000 cars produced in Brazil each year ran on ethanol, and in 1994 Brazil had more than 4.6 million cars powered totally by ethanol. However in the 1990s low oil prices and a decline in the supply of sugar-based fuel meant that sales fell rapidly. During this period the government also slackened its hold on the sugar industry.

However, global oil prices rose steeply again in 2002 and the development of 'flexible-fuel' cars helped to re-ignite ethanol production in Brazil. More than half of all cars in Brazil are now flexible-fuel cars with the option of running on petroleum, ethanol or a combination of the two.

Brazil is no longer dependent on imported fuel and is now a net exporter of energy. Countries like Sweden and Japan have begun to import Brazilian ethanol to help fulfil Kyoto Protocol environmental obligations.

Solar power

The Earth receives massive amounts of energy from the sun as incoming radiation. Some of this is lost on passing through the atmosphere but overall the surface has a net gain of energy. There are variations in energy and heat between different latitudes. The tropics have a net surplus of energy, mainly due to their relative proximity to the sun, but high latitudes (polewards 40°N and 40°S) have a net

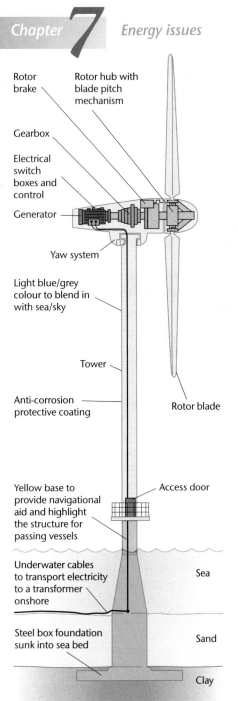

Rotor brake

Rotor hub with blade pitch mechanism

Gearbox

Electrical switch boxes and control

Generator

Yaw system

Light blue/grey colour to blend in with sea/sky

Tower

Anti-corrosion protective coating

Rotor blade

Yellow base to provide navigational aid and highlight the structure for passing vessels

Access door

Underwater cables to transport electricity to a transformer onshore

Sea

Steel box foundation sunk into sea bed

Sand

Clay

Figure 7.21 An offshore wind turbine

Photograph 7.11 Photovoltaic (PV) cells convert light into electricity: a BP Solar array on the roof of the Lufthansa terminal at Munich airport

deficit. Overall, although the potential for harnessing the sun's energy is enormous, the locations where the greatest amounts of solar energy could be harvested are often great distances from major centres of population.

At present the initial investment required for solar energy is high and conversion efficiency is relatively low. Although development is ongoing, solar power is most viable on a small scale. Many householders living in sunny Mediterranean climates use solar roof panels to heat their water and homes and large-scale solar power stations have been built in California and Spain (Photograph 7.11). However, in the UK sunshine is less reliable and the potential for large-scale development of this power source is limited under current levels of technology.

Wind energy

Wind power is the fastest-growing renewable energy source. Many countries, particularly in Europe and North America, are seeking ways of developing wind power as one of their major sources of renewable energy.

Electricity is generated from the wind using a wind turbine. It is more economical if several turbines are sited in the same place in the form of a wind farm. As objections are sometimes raised to building wind farms in upland areas, wind energy companies have started to look for offshore sites where larger capacity turbines can be used (Figure 7.21).

Wind energy is pollution-free and does not contribute to global warming. In Europe and North America, winds tend to blow strongly in winter when demand for electricity is at its highest. Wind farms do not take up a lot of space (only 1% of the land on which they are sited), which allows farmland or natural habitats to exist around them. Electricity generation by wind energy is becoming increasingly competitive with coal-fired power plants and is cheaper than nuclear fuel. It is still not as cheap as gas-fired power stations, but wind energy costs are likely to go down in the future. Supporters of wind energy maintain that it represents an excellent example of sustainability.

Opponents of wind farms claim that many of the windiest sites are also areas of natural beauty. They argue that wind turbines are an unwelcome intrusion into the landscape and an eyesore. Some people are worried about the noise the turbines create, particularly as wind farms are often sited in quiet locations; the damage that they could inflict on wildlife (especially birds); and the potential effect on property prices. Critics also point out that wind farms require large areas to produce only small amounts of energy. It can take over 7,000 wind turbines to produce the same amount of energy as one nuclear power station. If wind energy is to be viable, a lot of wind turbines will have to be built.

Case study Wind energy in the UK

The UK is the windiest country in Europe. In 2004, renewable energy sources in the UK generated just over 3% of the total electricity supply, 30% of which was derived from wind energy. The government's target is to generate 10% of the UK's total electricity supply from renewable sources by 2010 and it has announced that it intends to increase this to 15% by 2015. Wind energy is probably best placed to meet these targets.

Although many wind farms are well established in the UK, there have been objections to both existing and planned developments. Even though he supports wind power, Jonathon Porritt, former director of Friends of the Earth, has his reservations: 'the real problem is that people building the things have been insensitive. They have put some of them in the wrong places and have not consulted local people or involved them in the benefits. The result is a growing anti-wind power lobby'.

As a result of these objections, the industry is locating many of its new developments offshore. The North Hoyle Offshore wind farm, off the coast of north Wales, has 30 turbines which generate enough electricity to power 50,000 homes. It has been

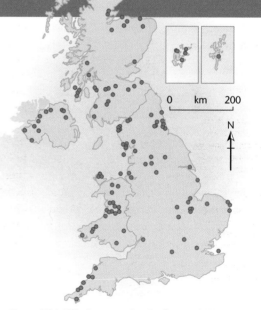

Figure 7.22 Wind energy sites in the UK, 2007

estimated that this station will offset the release of 160,000 tonnes of carbon dioxide into the atmosphere every year. David Bellamy, the well-known naturalist, is however campaigning against offshore wind farms, warning of 'plans that will make the British coastline ugly and impossible for birdlife'.

Case study Manchester City Football Club

Manchester City Football Club is to become one of the greenest sporting stadiums in the world. The club occupies a brownfield site, formerly used by heavy industry, which was redeveloped initially for the Commonwealth Games in 2002. The stadium will be powered by an 85 m tall, 2.6 MW wind turbine. This will be sited at the front of the stadium and will reduce the club's carbon dioxide emissions by 3,500 tonnes per year. It will generate more electricity than the club can use itself, allowing the excess to flow into the local grid and be used by local homes and businesses.

Wave energy

Wave power is one of the least developed renewable energy sources and is thought to be 10 years behind wind power in development terms. Although offshore devices have tremendous potential in terms of the amount of electricity that could be generated, at present they are too expensive to implement on a large scale. In addition, the development of such schemes could create negative environmental changes in tidal basins.

A number of small-scale schemes have been developed in the UK, including the Pelamis device off the Orkney Islands and Limpet off the island of Islay, Scotland.

Case study Wave energy in Scotland

The Limpet device began operating in 2004 and at that time was the only fully operational wave power project in the UK, supplying power to the National Grid. To install Limpet, a gully was excavated into the shoreline and a concrete chamber was constructed to capture onshore waves. Air trapped in this chamber by the waves is forced through a pair of turbines, each of which is connected to a 250 kW generator.

In September 2007 ScottishPower was granted planning permission to build the world's largest generating capacity commercial wave farm off the Orkney Islands. This will be the first wave farm in the UK and is expected to be operational by 2008. It will cost around £10 million, and will consist initially of four floating 160-m long Pelamis devices, otherwise known as 'sea snakes'. These are expected to provide 3 MW of renewable electricity, enough to power around 3,000 homes.

Photograph 7.12 The Islay Wave Bus was the first electric bus in the world to be powered by wave energy (Limpet)

Tidal energy

This renewable source of energy uses the movement of the tides to create power. Areas with the greatest tidal range offer the best potential for development and several sites have been suggested for the UK including the Severn and Mersey estuaries, Solway Firth and Morecambe Bay. Schemes with reversible blades could harness the power of both incoming and outgoing tides. The major drawback of tidal power is cost, in both economic and environmental terms, and this might explain why few sites are in operation. A tidal barrage has been built across the estuary of the River Rance close to St Malo in Brittany, France and another large-scale scheme, which began generating electricity in 1984, exists in Nova Scotia, Canada in the Bay of Fundy.

The arguments for tidal power include:
- it is renewable
- it is reliable and predictable
- its large size — the projected Severn barrage would provide the same energy as five nuclear power stations
- it is non-polluting
- it benefits the estuary as erosion rates are reduced behind the barrage

The arguments against include:
- flooding of wetlands bordering estuaries, often the home of many species of migrating birds, is damaging
- it could have an adverse effect on spawning fish such as salmon
- construction costs are extremely high

Geothermal energy

Geothermal power is derived from the hot rocks beneath the surface of the Earth. Although it is a renewable source of energy with tremendous potential for energy generation in the future, geothermal power is not an entirely 'clean' resource as pollutants such as hydrogen sulphide are present in the steam and heated water.

At present, most large-scale geothermal power stations operate on the steam that occurs naturally in geysers and hot springs. Steam can also be created artificially. Cold water is pumped down boreholes, where it becomes heated by contact with hot underlying rocks and turns to steam. This steam then returns to the surface and is used to generate electricity.

Geothermal power is used in a variety of locations around the world, particularly in areas that are active tectonically such as the USA, Iceland and New Zealand. In Iceland geothermal heat is provided to homes, open-air swimming pools and greenhouses.

In the UK small-scale projects, such as the Southampton District Energy Scheme, have been developed. In 1986 the council began pumping heat from a geothermal borehole, commissioned initially by the Department of Energy, and started to use this to provide heating and cooling services. The scheme, which started with a single customer (the civic centre) now has thousands of consumers. It provides heating and cooling to over 1,000 homes, several large office buildings, a hospital, BBC television studios, one of Europe's largest shopping centres, and a swimming and diving complex. Southampton City Council is committed to the implementation of alternative sources of energy and aims to substantially reduce its greenhouse gas emissions. The further expansion of local geothermal power will help it to do so.

Appropriate technology for sustainable development in more developed countries

Sustainable development is defined as 'development that meets the needs of the present without compromising the ability of future generations to meet their needs'. Energy resources should be seen as an asset, a stock of available wealth. However, if the present generation spends this wealth without investment for the future, the world will run out of resources. If some of the wealth amassed from finite resources is used on research and development, sustainable development can be achieved. Ways in which this might happen include:

➤ the development of renewable sources of energy
➤ increasing the efficiency of existing technology
➤ paying attention to environmental degradation and pollution caused by energy production
➤ government policies to encourage sustainable development

The term **appropriate technology** is generally used in relation to less developed countries. It means the technical expertise and equipment being used are suited to the economic and technological levels of development in a country. Sudan in east Africa is one of the poorest places in the world in terms of its economic and social development, and intermediate technology might be more appropriate to the needs of its people than high-tech energy generation.

In more developed countries, where levels of wealth are much higher, it is the responsibility of governments and large-scale corporations to invest in sustainable methods of energy production for the future.

Energy conservation

Energy conservation refers to the variety of methods by which the use of all types of energy, but in particular electricity and motor vehicle fuels, is limited or reduced. It may be achieved by:

➤ greater efficiency — for example, more economic fuel consumption in motor vehicles, cavity wall and roof insulation, and low-energy light bulbs in the home
➤ the use of alternative sources of energy that are less wasteful or are renewable

The UK Sustainable Development Strategy recognises that everyone has the right to a clean, healthy and safe environment. This can be achieved by reducing pollution. The use of non-renewables such as fossil fuels cannot be stopped overnight, but they can be used more efficiently and sustainably, and the development of alternatives should be used to help to phase them out. The

UK Sustainable Development Strategy recognises the need to develop more environment-friendly transport, energy production and waste management schemes.

The UK government's 2007 White Paper on energy set out a range of energy conservation initiatives, including:

➤ the introduction of 'smart' electricity meters using real-time displays in people's homes by 2010 so that people can see how much electricity they are using
➤ tougher environmental standards for new-build homes and other products
➤ working with industry to phase out inefficient goods, such as televisions with energy-consuming standby modes
➤ tripling the amount of electricity produced from renewable sources by 2015
➤ setting up the world's first carbon trading scheme for large companies and organisations, such as banks, supermarkets and local authorities
➤ providing £20 million of funding for public procurement of low-carbon vehicles and £35 million for green transport research

Designing homes for sustainability

In 2004 more than a quarter of the UK's carbon dioxide emissions came from energy used in the home. The government's Code for Sustainable Homes was introduced to provide guidelines for the design and construction of new sustainable homes. The code is intended as a single national standard for industry. It will complement the system of Energy Performance Certificates, introduced in 2007, which provide key information about energy efficiency and carbon performance of the home. Although compliance with the code is voluntary, the government intends to make it mandatory in 2016. Zero carbon homes costing less than £500,000 will be exempt from stamp duty.

The code measures sustainability of a home against the following design categories:

➤ energy use and carbon dioxide emissions
➤ water use
➤ use of materials
➤ surface water runoff
➤ waste production
➤ pollution
➤ health and wellbeing
➤ management
➤ ecology

The code will ensure the following benefits to the environment:

➤ reduced greenhouse gas emissions
➤ better adaptation to climate change
➤ reduced overall impact on the environment

To be awarded the highest-level status according to the code, a home will have to produce zero carbon dioxide emissions from all energy use. This could be achieved by:

- improving thermal efficiency of the walls, windows and roof by using more insulation or triple-glazed windows
- installing a high-efficiency condensing boiler or being part of a district heating system such as the one set up by Southampton District Council
- carefully designing the fabric of the home to reduce heat loss between the inner and outer walls
- using low and zero carbon technologies, such as solar panels, biomass boilers, wind turbines, and combined heat and power systems. Electricity taken from the National Grid would have to be replaced by low or zero carbon-generated energy so that over the course of a year the net emissions were zero
- installation of energy-efficient domestic appliances and lighting
- improved daylighting by fitting larger windows
- using environment-friendly building materials

In June 2007 the UK government proposed the building of five eco-towns, each with up to 100,000 homes. The first eco-villages announced by the English Partnerships Regeneration Agency are to be constructed on brownfield sites at Hanham Hall in Bristol (a 6.1 hectare former hospital) and Glebe Road in Peterborough (more than 10 hectares in size). These settlements will feature solar and wind power and will also use district heating systems.

Designing workplaces for sustainability

Businesses are under pressure to reduce their carbon footprint and their unsustainable energy use. There are a number of ways that businesses can be run more sustainably, such as car-sharing schemes and incentives to encourage employees to work from home.

The Carbon Trust is working with businesses and the public sector in the UK to help them cut carbon emissions. It provides practical expertise and resources, including funding.

 Marks and Spencer

Marks and Spencer has taken the management of energy seriously for a number of years and was a signatory to early government initiatives. Nearly every store operates a remote half-hourly energy monitoring system. The  company has also invested in the most up-to-date refrigeration systems for its chilled foods, resulting in significant energy savings. Working with the Carbon Trust, Marks and Spencer has spent a significant amount of time training its store designers and builders, as well as the teams who maintain the stores, on the opportunities for saving energy. It has also run a number of energy-awareness campaigns targeting employees, including posters, stickers and a staff competition. The company now has 30% fewer carbon emissions than in 2002.

Manchester United Football Club

Manchester United has an annual turnover of £170 million and employs 500 full-time and 800 part-time staff on match days.

A big modern stadium like Old Trafford uses a huge amount of electricity, and its energy bill in 2004 was more than £400,000, with carbon emissions calculated to be somewhere in the region of 1,500 tonnes for that year. Much of this energy goes on the lighting needed in the stadium, which seats 70,000 fans and broadcasts matches to millions of people around the world.

The Carbon Trust was commissioned to identify where energy savings could be made. It identified several areas, including introducing new electricity sub-meters in the north and south stands, employing wardens to ensure equipment is turned off, instigating an employee energy-awareness campaign and reducing the running time of heating and air-conditioning systems. Lighting in the hospitality suites and concourse areas is also more carefully controlled using photocells and timers.

By September 2006 the club had implemented changes that saved 265 tonnes of carbon a year, representing 18% of its total emissions. It intends to do more in the future and is investigating the potential for the development of onsite renewable energy generation at its Carrington training ground, 8 km west of Old Trafford.

Designing transport for sustainability

In the UK government's White Paper on energy, published in 2007, plans were set out for a low carbon transport innovation strategy. This allows £20 million of funding for public procurement of low-carbon vehicles and up to £35 million for green transport research.

In addition to national measures, many local authorities have transport strategies that include reintroducing public transport systems such as electric tramways and implementing congestion charging. An example of a successful light-rail transport scheme is the Metrolink, developed in Manchester in 1991. Sections of the Metrolink run parallel to the existing road network and it is seen as a viable alternative to private transport in the city. The Greater Manchester Passenger Transport Authority plans to extend the Metrolink and to encourage even more than the 19.9 million passengers who used the system in 2005/06. Eight additional trains are due to come into service in 2009.

The financial incentives that support green cars and fuels in the UK include:

➤ **Reduced tax on fuels** such as liquified petroleum gas (LPG) — fuel duty on petrol and diesel in 2007 was 49.6 pence per litre compared to 29.6 pence per litre for biodiesel, 8.8 pence per litre for LPG used as road fuel and zero for electricity.

➤ **Vehicle excise duty (road tax)** — the amount levied depends on the type of fuel used and the level of carbon dioxide emissions produced. Cars with small engines producing carbon dioxide emissions lower than 100 g km^{-1} are exempt from this tax and cars with the largest engines, producing more than 225 g km^{-1}, pay over £300 per year.

➤ London **congestion charge discounts** — these are available for the greenest cars, with up to 100% discounts for hybrid electric, battery electric and fuel-

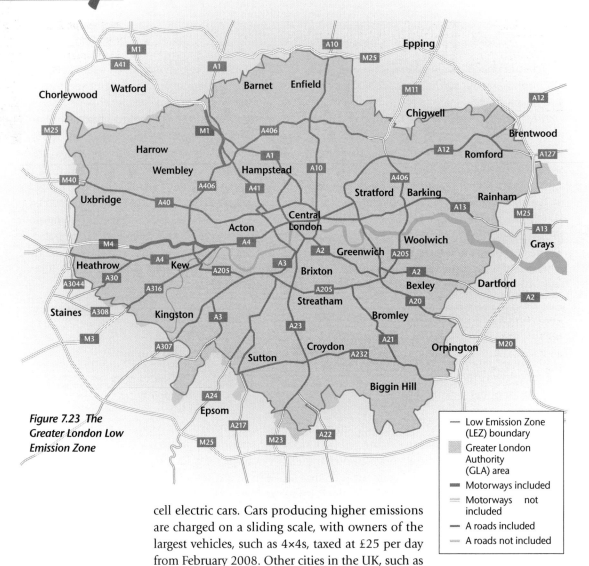

Figure 7.23 The Greater London Low Emission Zone

Legend:
— Low Emission Zone (LEZ) boundary
Greater London Authority (GLA) area
Motorways included
Motorways not included
A roads included
A roads not included

cell electric cars. Cars producing higher emissions are charged on a sliding scale, with owners of the largest vehicles, such as 4×4s, taxed at £25 per day from February 2008. Other cities in the UK, such as Cardiff, Birmingham, Manchester and Cambridge, are considering similar schemes. In addition to congestion charging, a wide range of measures has been introduced in London designed to make public transport faster, cheaper and more reliable.

➤ **The Greater London Low Emission Zone (LEZ)** was introduced in February 2008 — a specified area in Greater London within which the most polluting vehicles will be required to pay a daily charge (Figure 7.23). Although only lorries will be charged at first, it will apply to all heavily polluting vehicles by 2012. The aim of the LEZ is to improve the quality of the air in London.

Most major car manufacturing companies are developing new models with 'green' credentials. Toyota developed its hybrid Prius 10 years ago and plans to go 100% hybrid in the future. Saab introduced its BioPower flexi-fuel cars in 2006.

Volkswagen UK

They run on petrol and bioethanol, and carbon dioxide emissions are reduced by up to 70%. Volkswagen has developed a 'tax-free' Polo, the BlueMotion — a conventional fuel car with carbon dioxide emissions of 99 g km^{-1}, placing it in the road tax exempt band (Photograph 7.13).

Assessment exercises

1 Study Figure A, which shows the trends in world use of selected energy resources and total population through the twentieth century.

a Comment on the trends in energy resource and population that are shown in Figure A. **(4 marks)**

b Outline the connections that exist between the use of energy resources and economic development. **(4 marks)**

c To what extent are the trends shown in Figure A compatible with sustainable development? **(7 marks)**

d Examine the role of transnational companies in the production and distribution of energy at the global scale. **(15 marks)**

(30 marks)

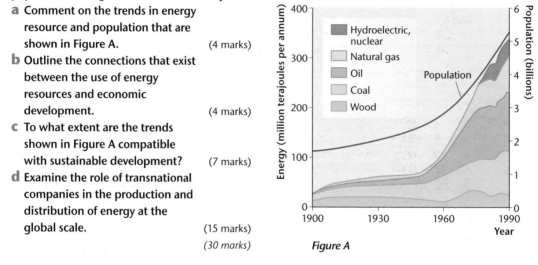

Figure A

2 a Explain the meanings of the following terms:

(i) stock **(2 marks)**

(ii) flow **(2 marks)**

b Outline the contribution that stocks make to the UK's primary energy mix. **(5 marks)**

c Study Photograph A, which shows a small-scale hydroelectric power station in the Lake District National Park in Cumbria.

Examine the reasons why the development of small-scale renewable energy projects, such as this, are more sustainable than large-scale projects in an area like the Lake District. **(6 marks)**

d Discuss the environmental impacts related to the production and use of one or more sources of non-renewable energy you have studied. **(15 marks)**

(30 marks)

Photograph A

Chapter 8

Health issues

Health is a state of complete physical, mental and social well-being and not merely the absence of diseases and infirmity. (World Health Organization 1946)

Why is the geographical study of health issues important?
➤ The geography of health investigates topics such as the pattern and spread of disease.
➤ Physical and human factors can greatly influence the health of people.
➤ Disease and infection have profound social, economic and environmental effects.
➤ Each society responds differently to the challenge of providing healthcare and welfare for its members.
➤ The twenty-first century has new challenges in the form of virulent new diseases and a rapidly ageing population.

Global patterns of health

Global patterns of mortality

Some of the highest **crude death rates** are found in the less developed countries, particularly in sub-Saharan Africa. Liberia, Niger, Sierra Leone, Zambia and Zimbabwe all have death rates of 20 or more per 1,000. However, some of the lowest **mortality** rates are also found in countries at the lower end of the development range, for example Kuwait (2 per 1,000), Bahrain (3 per 1,000) and Mexico (5 per 1,000).

Infant mortality is falling across the world, but there are still wide variations between nations —142 infant deaths per 1,000 births in Liberia, compared to 3 per 1,000 in Finland. Areas with high rates of infant mortality have high rates of mortality overall.

HIV/AIDS is having a major impact on mortality around the world but especially in sub-Saharan Africa. More than 40 million people are now living with HIV/AIDS, over 25 million of them in sub-Saharan Africa. In Swaziland, Botswana, Lesotho and Zimbabwe, over 20% of the total population of the country are affected. Asia is also badly affected and of the 7 million HIV/AIDS victims in south/

Key terms

Attack rate The number of cases of a disease diagnosed in an area, divided by the total population, over the period of an epidemic.

Case-mortality rate The number of people dying from a disease divided by the number of those diagnosed as having the disease.

Crude death rate The number of deaths per 1,000 people in 1 year.

Infant mortality The number of deaths of children under the age of 1 year expressed per 1,000 live births per year. It is useful as a barometer of social and environmental conditions and is sensitive to changes in either.

Morbidity Illness and the reporting of disease. In the UK 2001 census respondents were asked how well they felt and whether they had a limiting long-term illness. Some diseases are so infectious that by law they must be reported; these are usually included in international surveillance programmes. Plague, cholera and yellow fever are the most serious, but malaria, influenza and typhoid are other examples.

Mortality The death of people. It is measured by a number of indices including death rate, infant mortality, case mortality and attack rate.

southeast Asia, over 5 million live in India. It is estimated, however, that infection rates have begun to decline in a number of countries.

Global patterns of morbidity

Patterns of **morbidity** vary according to the nature of the illness. Detail of two examples of the most serious causes of illness around the world is given below.

Influenza

Influenza is caused by a virus that attacks the upper respiratory tract — the nose, throat and bronchi and sometimes also the lungs. The infection usually lasts for about a week. It is characterised by sudden onset of high fever, headache and severe malaise, non-productive cough and sore throat. Most people recover within 1–2 weeks without requiring any medical treatment.

In the very young, the elderly and people suffering from chronic medical conditions such as lung diseases, diabetes, cancer, kidney or heart problems, influenza poses a serious risk. In these high-risk people, the infection may lead to severe complications, pneumonia and death.

Influenza spreads around the world in seasonal epidemics and imposes a considerable economic burden in the form of hospital and other healthcare costs and lost productivity. In annual influenza epidemics 5–15% of the population are affected with upper respiratory tract infections. Hospitalisation and deaths mainly occur in high-risk groups. Although difficult to assess, these annual epidemics are thought to result in between 3 and 5 million cases of severe illness and between 250,000 and 500,000 deaths every year around the world. Most deaths currently associated with influenza in industrialised countries occur among those over 65 years of age.

Much less is known about the impact of influenza in the developing world. However, influenza outbreaks in the tropics, where viral transmission normally continues year-round, tend to have high **attack** and **case-mortality** rates. For example, during an influenza outbreak in Madagascar in 2002, more than 27,000 cases were reported in 3 months and 800 deaths occurred despite rapid intervention. An investigation of the outbreak, coordinated by the World Health Organization (WHO), found that there were severe health consequences in poorly nourished populations with limited access to adequate healthcare.

Three times in the last century, influenza viruses have undergone major genetic changes resulting in global pandemics and large tolls in terms of both disease and deaths. The most infamous pandemic was 'Spanish flu' which affected large parts of the world population and is thought to have killed at least 40 million people in 1918–19. Two other influenza pandemics occurred in 1957 ('Asian influenza') and 1968 ('Hong Kong influenza') and caused significant morbidity and mortality globally. In contrast to current influenza epidemics, these pandemics had severe outcomes among healthy younger persons, although not on such a dramatic scale as the 'Spanish flu' where the death rate was highest among healthy young adults. Limited outbreaks of a new influenza subtype (H5N1) directly transmitted from birds to humans occurred in Hong Kong Special Administrative Region of China in 1997 and 2003 and there have been fears that this could cause a pandemic (Photograph 8.1).

Yellow fever

Yellow fever is a viral disease that has caused epidemics in Africa and the Americas. It can be recognised in historic texts stretching back 400 years. Infection causes a wide spectrum of disease, from mild symptoms to severe illness and death. The 'yellow' in the name is explained by the jaundice that affects some patients. Although an effective vaccine has been available for 60 years, the number of people infected over the last two decades has increased and yellow fever is now a serious public health issue again.

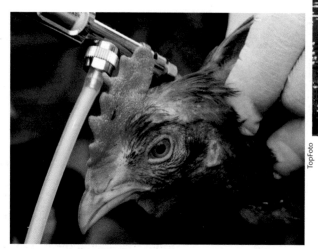

Photograph 8.1
Poultry in Russia being vaccinated against bird flu

The virus remains silent in the body during an incubation period of 3–6 days. There are then two phases. Some infections have no symptoms whatsoever, but the first, 'acute', phase is normally characterised by fever, muscle pain (with prominent backache), headache, shivers, loss of appetite, and nausea or vomiting. Often, the high fever is associated with a slow pulse. After 3–4 days, most patients improve and their symptoms disappear.

However, 15% enter a 'toxic phase' within 24 hours. Fever reappears and several bodily systems are affected. The patient rapidly develops jaundice and complains of abdominal pain with vomiting. Bleeding can occur from the mouth, nose, eyes and stomach. Once this happens, blood appears in the vomit and faeces. Kidney function deteriorates; this can range from abnormal protein levels in the urine to complete kidney failure with no urine production. Half of all patients in the 'toxic phase' die within 10–14 days.

The virus is constantly present at low levels of infection (i.e. endemic) in some tropical areas of Africa and the Americas. This viral presence can amplify into regular epidemics. Yellow fever outbreaks have also occurred in Europe, the Caribbean islands, and Central and North America. Thirty-three countries, with a combined population of 508 million, are at risk in Africa. These lie within a band from 15°N to 10°S of the equator. In the Americas, yellow fever is endemic in nine South American countries and in several Caribbean islands. Bolivia, Brazil, Colombia, Ecuador and Peru are considered at greatest risk. There are estimated to be 200,000 cases of yellow fever (with 30,000 deaths) per year. However, due to under-reporting, only a small percentage of these cases are identified. Small numbers of imported cases also occur in countries free of yellow fever. Although yellow fever has never been reported in Asia, this region is at risk because the appropriate primates and mosquitoes thought to transmit the disease are present.

Health in world affairs

Health geography can make an important contribution to future global and national plans and policies. This can include:

➤ advising on planning for healthcare staffing in southern African countries devastated by the HIV/AIDS crisis
➤ analysing the global correlation between income and welfare
➤ monitoring the effects of climate change on the emergence of new infectious diseases
➤ investigating the optimum pattern of healthcare provision in primary health-care trusts

An infectious disease: HIV/AIDS

HIV is the human immunodeficiency virus which causes the illness AIDS. HIV is a slow retrovirus, which means that it takes years to show symptoms and that it invades the white cells in the blood by literally writing the structure of itself backwards (retro) into them and reproducing itself inside the cells. White cells produce the antibodies that are the body's main defence against disease and without them the body becomes the target of everyday infections and cell changes that cause cancers. This is what happens to someone suffering from AIDS.

There is some controversy over the source of the disease. Some people believe that it is manmade and was produced by a chemical weapons laboratory or by medical research gone wrong. However, the generally accepted view is that it evolved in sub-Saharan Africa, crossing over from the chimpanzee population in contaminated meat or by a bite from a pet, possibly in the 1930s. Some scientists have suggested that the virus was present in the human population of central Africa for a long time but on a local scale. Developments in the twentieth century such as international travel, blood transfusions and intravenous drug use brought it onto the world stage and produced a pandemic.

The spread of HIV

Today, the virus is spread in the following ways:

➤ exchange of body fluids during sexual intercourse
➤ contaminated needles in intravenous drug use (IDU)
➤ contaminated blood transfusions
➤ from mother to child during pregnancy

Evidence shows that the disease started in small high-risk groups such as gay men, drug users and prostitutes, and then spread into the population as a whole. This meant that in the early stages of the disease in developed countries, AIDS was regarded by many as a 'gay plague' (Photograph 8.2). The heterosexual community took little notice of it and education about safe sex was disregarded. In developing countries, mainly in Africa, the transfer of the virus was more commonly through heterosexual sex, but this was not known in most of the developed world. Three distinct patterns of distribution therefore developed:

> **Pattern 1** covers areas which began to see a spread of HIV in the late 1970s, first among the homosexual, bisexual and drug-using communities and later in the general population. This includes North America, western Europe, Australia and some parts of Latin America.

> **Pattern 2** covers those countries where the spread has been essentially through heterosexual contact. This includes the bulk of sub-Saharan Africa, where more women than men are infected (in the proportion of 60:40). In 2005 over 0.5 million children were infected as a result of mother-to-child transmission.

> **Pattern 3** covers those regions where the disease appeared later (in the 1980s) and was brought in by travellers and sometimes by blood imported for transfusions. This includes eastern Europe (including the former USSR), Asia, the middle east and north Africa.

Photograph 8.2
A candlelit AIDS vigil in Trafalgar Square

By 2006, it was estimated that over 39 million people worldwide were living with HIV or full-blown AIDS (Table 8.1). In every global region the number of people living with HIV is rising. The steepest rises have been in east Asia, central Asia and eastern Europe, but the situation is most serious in sub-Saharan Africa. Over 62% of people living with HIV/AIDS (24.7 million people) in 2006 were in the countries of sub-Saharan Africa. It has been estimated that 6% of the adult

Region	Number of people living with HIV	New HIV infections (2005)	AIDS deaths (2005)	Adult HIV prevalence (%)
Sub-Saharan Africa	24.7 million	2.8 million	2.1 million	6.1
Asia	8.5 million	960,000	700,000	0.5
Latin America	1.7 million	140,000	65,000	0.5
North America and western and central Europe	2.1 million	65,000	30,000	0.5
Eastern Europe and central Asia	1.7 million	270,000	64,000	0.9
Middle east and north Africa	460,000	70,000	37,000	0.2
Caribbean	250,000	27,000	19,000	1.2
Oceania	80,000	7,200	4,000	0.4
Total	39.5 million	4.3 million	2.9 million	1.0

Table 8.1 HIV/AIDS: global statistics, 2006

Source: UNAIDS (2007)

population of sub-Saharan Africa is HIV-positive. The area has over 13 million infected women, which represents 76% of all women in the world living with HIV. Ten countries have 10% or more of their adult population infected: Swaziland (33%), Botswana (24%), Lesotho (23%), Malawi, Mozambique, Namibia, South Africa, Zambia, Central African Republic and Zimbabwe. The United Nations has estimated that, by 2020, 70 million people in the world will have died from AIDS.

Evidence for frequency and scale

Figures can be obtained from medical records (from doctors and hospitals), national government health department records, the World Health Organization (WHO) and the media. These statistics, however, can never be totally accurate for the following reasons:
- medical records are confidential
- many people with HIV are not aware that they are infected
- the social stigma of AIDS means that many sufferers do not report the illness until it is into its later stages
- AIDS is not always given as the cause of death because the sufferer usually dies of another disease, such as pneumonia, that they have succumbed to because of the effects of HIV on their immune system
- it has been alleged that the disease has been overestimated in parts of Africa so that countries can obtain more overseas aid

Effects

The United Nations has estimated that only one in ten sufferers knows they have the virus in the early days of infection. Apart from the physical effects of the disease, sufferers may experience prejudice in their employment and social life. This may even extend to the immediate family: in some societies children are ostracised if one of their parents has the disease.

Life expectancy in much of sub-Saharan Africa will soon fall to levels not seen since the nineteenth century (Table 8.2). Some authorities estimate that by 2010 people in many southern African countries will not be expected to live beyond their 30s. Populations of some of these countries will have started to shrink. HIV/AIDS has also reversed the decline in infant mortality that was seen across southern Africa in the 1980s and early 1990s. Rates in certain countries are now close to double what they would have been without the pandemic.

In Africa, the effects on families include loss of income-earning opportunities, the diversion of effort and income into care and medicine, and the withdrawal of children from school, either because of lack of money or because they are needed for agricultural work. There has been a huge effect on farming, with HIV/AIDS threatening food-growing and income-earning potential

Table 8.2 Estimated life expectancy in selected African countries, 2010

Country	Without AIDS (years)	With AIDS (years)
Angola	41.3	35.0
Botswana	74.4	26.7
Lesotho	67.2	36.5
Malawi	59.4	36.9
Mozambique	42.5	27.1
Namibia	68.8	33.8
Rwanda	54.7	38.7
South Africa	68.5	36.5
Swaziland	74.6	33.0
Zambia	58.6	34.4
Zimbabwe	71.4	34.6

Source: US Census Bureau

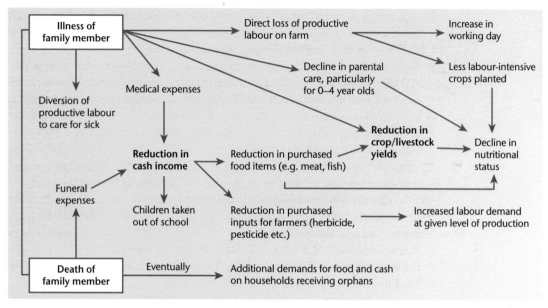

in areas already facing food shortages. Some countries have large numbers of orphans as a result of HIV/AIDS, and this has put a great strain on local resources (Figure 8.1).

Figure 8.1 Effects of HIV/AIDS on families in Africa

Management

Management of HIV/AIDS takes the following forms:

➤ **Trying to find a vaccine** — the hope of this seems remote, but research is continuing, particularly in trying to find groups that might possess some degree of natural immunity through their white cells.

➤ **Prolonging life through drugs** — such drugs are available but expensive: a typical course of AZT cost US$10,000 a year per individual in 2000, but costs are now much lower at $300 for generic drugs such as Nevirapine. This is still beyond the reach of most governments in less developed countries. In 2001, however, a court case against the South African government by a group of multi-national pharmaceutical companies was dropped because of massive public pressure on the companies. This means that the South African government can now manufacture and import cheap generic versions of anti-retroviral drugs instead of having to buy the expensive brand-name products. In 2003, South Africa announced that it would make available free HAART (highly active anti-retroviral therapy) treatment to everyone who was HIV-positive. In 2005, 17% of those needing HAART around the world were receiving it, funded by donations from Western countries. Some people argue that this is leading to complacency, as HAART is not a cure.

➤ **Plotting the course** of an outbreak, making it possible to predict the future spread of the disease and identifying areas where resources should be concentrated.

➤ **Screening blood** for HIV antibodies before it is used for transfusions in developed countries, leading to a negligible risk of infection. This was not always the case. Blood plasma products, such as factor eight (for haemophiliacs), are now treated to remove the virus.

➤ **Education and advertising** — education is seen as the main way in which HIV/AIDS infection can be combated in sub-Saharan Africa. However, this assumes that humans are rational and their behaviour is under individual control. Often, due to social norms and prejudices, they are not. Education is aimed at increasing the use of condoms, but, in Africa in particular, they are not popular. In developed countries, education and advertising have been aimed at vulnerable groups such as homosexuals and intravenous drug users to try and prevent the spread of the disease. Raising the profile of the disease in schools through sex education has been a major feature in the UK government programme. Other campaigns in the UK have included free needles for drug users, free condoms, and warnings to travellers about their sexual behaviour in foreign countries.

➤ **Caring for victims and families**, which involves charities such as the Terrence Higgins Trust and London Lighthouse in the UK.

It is now believed that the spread of HIV/AIDS is rooted in problems of poverty, food and livelihood insecurity, sociocultural inequality, and poor support services and infrastructure. Although responses to HIV/AIDS have grown and improved over the past decade, they still do not match the scale or pace of a steadily worsening epidemic. Indeed, in a report published in 2005, UNAIDS said that 'the AIDS epidemic continues to outstrip global efforts to contain it'.

Case study: AIDS in sub-Saharan Africa: Botswana

The AIDS pandemic has had a huge impact on Botswana. The country has a total population of 1.6 million and it has been estimated that 24% of adults are infected with HIV. In the northeast of the country and among expectant mothers in urban areas, rates are over 50%. The government has tried to manage the spread of the disease by focusing on prevention, but in 2002 Botswana became the first African country to provide free anti-retroviral drugs. It is able to do this because it has the most lucrative diamond mines in the world and, as a result, per capita income is seven times the average for sub-Saharan Africa.

Life expectancy in the country has dipped to below 40 years of age for the first time since 1950 and in 2006 stood at just under 34 years. It would have been expected to rise to 74 years and 5 months by 2010 if there had been no AIDS pandemic, but the

Figure 8.2 Map showing the location of Botswana

current projected figure for that year is only 26 years and 8 months.

The economy of the country has been affected because AIDS is destroying the workforce. It is predicted that the economy of the country will be one-third smaller by 2021 than it would have been without AIDS, while government expenditure will have to increase by 20%.

Case study AIDS in Asia: Thailand

Figure 8.3 Map showing the location of Thailand

Towards the end of the twentieth century, Thailand had the most serious AIDS problem in Asia. The first case there was diagnosed in 1984 and from that point there was a rapid increase in infection rates, particularly among vulnerable groups such as intravenous drug users and commercial sex workers. Prostitutes were extremely vulnerable, with infection rates reaching 30% by the early 1990s.

HIV spread rapidly to the heterosexual and non-intravenous drug-using population as a result of low condom use and a high rate of premarital and extra-marital male contact with sex workers. By 1995, over 5,000 HIV-infected babies were being born each year. It was clear that in Thailand infection would not be limited to a few isolated high-risk groups as it had been in North America and Europe. In 1999, it was estimated that 1 million people were infected with HIV, of whom over 100,000 had developed AIDS. In that year, 66,000 people died of AIDS-related conditions.

As the scale of the problem became clear, the Thai government responded in a positive way. It had already launched a '100% condom programme' in 1991, but it now established a National AIDS Committee that came up with a hard-hitting campaign on television, radio and poster sites. Commercial sex workers were targeted with a supply of 60 million free condoms a year. One of the results was that condom use among men visiting prostitutes rose to over 90%. The programme has been so successful that HIV infection rates in Thailand now appear to be in decline. This success stands out against the record of other countries in southeast Asia.

A disease of affluence: coronary heart disease

A heart attack occurs when the blood vessels supplying the heart muscle become blocked, starving it of oxygen and leading to the heart muscle's failure or death. A wide range of risk factors can be responsible for a heart attack, often acting in combination. The incidence of these factors varies around the world and so does the occurrence of the disease.

Table 8.3
Variations in impact of coronary heart disease in selected countries

Country	Population (millions)	Heart disease: DALYs lost per 1,000 people, 2003	Heart disease deaths, 2002
Afghanistan	23	36	33,157
Argentina	38	6	34,292
Burkina Faso	13	11	5,877
China	1,294	4	702,925
Denmark	5	5	10,013
France	60	3	46,132
India	1,049	20	1,531,534
Russian Federation	144	27	674,881
South Africa	45	9	27,013
UK	59	7	120,530
USA	291	8	514,450
Zambia	11	8	4,153

Source: World Health Organization

Country	% change in coronary heart disease death rates of females aged 35–74	% change in coronary heart disease death rates of males aged 35–74
Croatia	61	62
Kazakhstan	36	56
Ukraine	38	49
Romania	26	20
Japan	–10	8
Hungary	–2	2
Greece	–15	–11
USA	–29	–30
Netherlands	–29	–39
Sweden	–40	–43
Australia	–52	–46
Denmark	–46	–49

Source: World Health Organization

Table 8.4
Changes in heart disease death rates in selected countries, 1988–98

The impact of heart disease is measured both by deaths and by disability-adjusted life years (DALYs) (Table 8.3). DALYs are an indication of the number of healthy years of life lost. The measures indicate the total burden of a disease, as opposed to just the number of deaths. Since 1990, more people around the world have died from coronary heart disease than from any other cause. Its disease burden is projected to rise from around 47 million DALYs globally in 1990 to 82 million DALYs in 2020.

Variations in death rates are marked: they are lower in populations with short life expectancy (Table 8.4). Coronary heart disease is decreasing in many more developed countries due to improved prevention, diagnosis and treatment, and in particular reduced cigarette smoking and lower than average levels of blood pressure and cholesterol. However, it is increasing in less developed countries, partly as a result of increasing longevity, urbanisation and lifestyle changes. The World Health Organization (WHO) states that more than 60% of the global burden of coronary heart disease occurs in newly developing countries. Is this a disturbing sign of development?

What are the risk factors?

Over 300 risk factors have been associated with coronary heart disease. Many of these are significant in all populations. In MEDCs, there are five major risk factors:

- tobacco use
- alcohol use
- high blood pressure
- high cholesterol
- obesity

In developing countries with low mortality, such as China, the same risk factors apply, with the additional risks of under-nutrition and communicable

Risk factor	Developed countries (%)	Low mortality developing countries (5%)	High mortality developing countries (%)
Tobacco use	12.2	4.0	2.0
High blood pressure	10.9	5.0	2.5
Alcohol use	9.2	6.2	< 1.0
High cholesterol	7.6	2.1	1.9
Obesity	7.4	2.7	< 1.0
Under-nutrition	No importance	3.1	14.9
Unsafe sex	0.8	1.0	10.2

Source: World Health Organization

diseases. In developing countries with high mortality, such as those of sub-Saharan Africa, low vegetable and fruit intake are also important factors. The relative impact of these risk factors is shown in Table 8.5. Some major risks are modifiable in that they can be prevented, treated and controlled. There are considerable health benefits at all ages, for both men and women, in stopping smoking, reducing cholesterol levels and blood pressure, eating a healthy diet and increasing physical activity.

Table 8.5
Relative importance of risk factors

Economic costs

The economic costs of heart disease include the cost to the individual and to the family of healthcare and time off work, the cost to the government of healthcare and the cost to the country of lost productivity. All of these are difficult to quantify. Some statements about costs are:

- 'If only 10% of adults began walking regularly, Americans could save US$5.6 billion in costs related to heart disease' (President George W. Bush, 2002).
- 'The direct costs of physical inactivity accounted for an estimated US$24 billion in healthcare costs in 1996' (WHO).
- 'Healthcare costs associated with smoking-related illnesses result in a global net loss of US$200 billion per year, with one-third of those losses occurring in developing countries' (WHO).
- 'Health problems related to obesity, such as heart disease, cost the USA an estimated US$177 billion a year' (WHO).
- 'Cholesterol-reducers were the top-selling medications in 2003, generating US$14 billion in sales' (WHO).
- 'The direct cost of obesity to the NHS is £0.5 billion per year, while the indirect cost to the UK economy is at least £2 billion' (Liam Donaldson, UK Chief Medical Officer, 2003).
- 'The cumulative Medicare costs of treatment of heart diseases in people aged 65 and over in the USA amounted to US$76 million in 2000' (WHO).
- 'Expenditure in OECD countries on heart disease medications increased from 9.4% in 1989 to 11.0% in 1997' (WHO).
- 'The number of people who die or are disabled by coronary heart disease could be halved with wider use of a combination of drugs that costs just US$14 a year' (WHO).

Region	Availability of equipment for treatment of high blood pressure (%)	Availability of suitable drugs (%)	Number of medical professionals working in disease control per 100,000 people	Countries with tobacco legislation (%)
Africa	81	70	111	22
Americas	96	88	310	50
Eastern Mediterranean	93	92	259	75
Europe	97	100	772	80
Southeast Asia	88	71	151	70
Western Pacific	96	96	516	69

Source: World Health Organization

Table 8.6 Approaches to coronary heart disease prevention and treatment, 2001

Photograph 8.3 World Heart Day was created to increase public awareness of the risks of heart disease and stroke

Prevention strategies

Significant health gains in the treatment of heart disease can be made within a short period of time through public health and treatment interventions (Table 8.6). Governments are stewards of health resources and have a fundamental responsibility to protect the health of citizens. They can do this by educating the public, making treatments affordable and available and advising patients on healthy-living practices. Some examples of prevention strategies are:

➤ In the UK, dieticians promote the benefits for heart health of eating oily fish, more fruit and vegetables, and less saturated fat.
➤ In Finland, community-based interventions, including health education and nutrition labelling, have led to population-wide reductions in cholesterol levels closely followed by a sharp decline in heart disease.
➤ In Japan, government-led health education campaigns and increased treatment of high blood pressure have reduced blood-pressure levels in the population.
➤ In New Zealand, the introduction of recognisable logos for healthy foods has led many companies to reformulate their products. The benefits include greatly reduced salt content in processed foods.
➤ In Mauritius, a change from palm oil to soya oil for cooking has brought down cholesterol levels, but obesity has been unaffected.

Health education

The above strategies are not effective without public understanding, support and demand. Health education is essential to promote healthy choices. Schools are an ideal venue for health education as they can provide a healthy diet, prohibit smoking and allow opportunities for exercise. WHO has initiated a number of activities to assist schools around the world, and since 2000 has coordinated World Heart Day events and activities, including:

➤ medical activities such as blood-pressure testing
➤ activities to engage the public in physical activity
➤ scientific conferences
➤ activities to promote a heart-healthy diet (Photograph 8.3)

World Heart Day

World Heart Federation. © Lois Greenfield

The number of countries taking part in World Heart Day increased from 63 in 2000 to 120 in 2006.

Policies and legislation

Only governments can legislate for the prevention and/or control of disease. The most common legislation involves reducing tobacco smoking, which has clear links to reducing heart disease. Legislation can include advertising bans, smoke-free areas, health warnings on packets, taxation and outright bans in public places (Table 8.6). A smoking ban was first introduced in Singapore in 1970 and 37 years later the idea was implemented in the UK.

Another interesting form of legislation was introduced in the USA in 2004. The House of Representatives banned lawsuits against fast-food restaurants by obese customers who argue that they have become overweight by eating there.

Food and health

The Food and Agricultural Organization (FAO) of the UN insists that there is sufficient food for everyone in the world. Food is not in short supply — globally, we produce enough to feed everyone 2,700 calories per day. However, an estimated 30 million people die every year from starvation and a further 800 million suffer from chronic malnutrition. Some of these people live in countries that export food products to the developed world.

Malnutrition is defined as a condition resulting from some form of dietary deficiency. This may be because the quantity of food, measured in calories per day, is too low or because certain important nutrients are absent. Malnutrition weakens immunity and makes people more vulnerable to diseases. It may also lead to deficiency diseases such as beriberi or anaemia. Some authorities refer to the condition that results from consuming too little food over a period of time as **undernourishment**.

Famine

➤ Most famines result from a combination of natural events and human misman-agement. Some authorities refer to famine as a decline in the access to food, rather than to there not being enough food.

➤ Famines are not always widespread. They can be localised and can affect only one group or social class.

➤ In areas affected by famine, it is not uncommon to see food available in markets and some agricultural produce being exported.

The decline of food availability is said to be the result of a deterioration in the enti-tlements of certain sectors of society. Poorer people have limited access to food as a consequence of weaker purchasing and bargaining powers. They have low status, menial occupations and limited land ownership.

Famines on a large scale occur as a result of one or more of the following factors:

➤ **Drought** — lack of rainfall causes soil and groundwater sources to decline, which ultimately leads to a reduction in the supply of water. The soil moisture will not meet the needs of particular plants and agricultural crops, creating serious problems for areas that depend on farming, both arable and pastoral.

➤ **A population increase greater than the rate of crop (food) production** — this often occurs in areas where there is a sudden influx of refugees fleeing a war zone or an area of civil unrest. It can also occur as people migrate from one drought zone to another.

➤ **A rapid rise in the price of foodstuffs and/or animals** — this can occur when the quality of farmland and grazing land declines (often during a drought). It is further compounded by a breakdown in the local economy and marketing systems. Control mechanisms react too slowly and inflationary price rises fuel panic buying, which rapidly leads to shortages of basic foodstuffs.

Case study   Drought in southern Ethiopia and Somalia, 2000

Ethiopia's worst drought of the twentieth century occurred in 1984–85. Dramatic pictures of starving refugees were brought to the television screens of richer Western countries and a massive aid appeal was launched, including Bob Geldof's Live Aid. Fifteen years later, in 2000, the rains failed again, leading to another severe drought that affected 43% of the population. The drought had the following effects:

- It led to unusual movements of people and live-stock as herders moved in search of water and fresh pasture.
- As a result of these migrations, too much pressure was put on those areas that had sufficient water and pasture.
- The lack of food and water took a heavy toll on herders and thousands of cattle, sheep, camels and goats died.
- The death of livestock led to a deterioration in people's nutritional status.
- Milk, one of the main components of the diet (particularly that of women and children) became scarce.

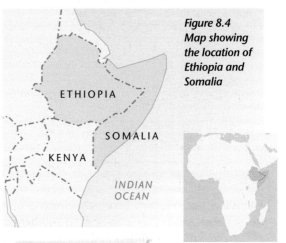

Figure 8.4 Map showing the location of Ethiopia and Somalia

- Food prices began to rise.
- Thousands of families abandoned their lands and headed for the cities. Many camps for these internally displaced persons had to be set up. One camp, on the outskirts of the town of Denan, contained at least 13,000 people.
- Large amounts of foreign aid were required to run these camps; the rate of malnutrition was estimated at over 50%.

Solutions to famine

Famine relief is a **short-term aid** that takes the form of distributing food (Photograph 8.4). It is usually carried out by a combination of non-governmental organisations (NGOs, e.g. Oxfam, Red Cross and Save the Children) and government. Much of this aid is temporary in nature. It is usually given with caution because it could result in overdependence by the receiving country and might damage the local agricultural economy.

Issues related to famine relief include:

➤ The **cost** of providing relief — all NGOs have overheads, the costs of which have to be met from the money raised through charitable donations. Donors to charities often question these internal costs, although they are generally very low.

➤ **Disaster fatigue** — modern communication systems publicise disasters quickly but can lead to a feeling of helplessness in donors as yet another famine occurs.

➤ The type of **food** provided — it must be available, non-perishable and easily transported. It must also be consumable, reflecting local tastes. Sending powdered milk to the drought-stricken area of Ethiopia in the mid-1980s was a classic food-aid error because there was no clean water with which to make it up.

➤ **Infrastructure** to deliver aid — there should be international-standard entry facilities into an area (a port or an airport) as well as adequate roads for delivery by lorry.

➤ **Coordination** between aid agencies and national governments — this is essential when famine relief is necessary in an area of civil unrest.

➤ **Targeting aid** — how can those most in need be identified?

Photograph 8.4 Malnourished children at a nutrition centre in Ouagadougou, Burkina Faso

The **long-term response** involves helping people to develop a more productive system of farming in order to prevent another famine. Such aid could involve:

➤ increased use of fertilisers and new technologies such as high-yielding varieties of seeds

➤ improvements to systems to ensure that produce gets to markets more efficiently

➤ easing international trade and cancelling national debts

Obesity and overweight

Overweight and obesity are defined as abnormal or excessive fat accumulation that may impair health. Body mass index (BMI) is a simple index of weight-for-height that is commonly used in classifying overweight and obesity in adult populations and individuals. It is defined as the weight in kilograms divided by the square of the height in metres.

The World Health Organization (WHO) defines 'overweight' as a BMI equal to or more than 25 and 'obesity' as a BMI equal to or more than 30. These cut-off points provide a benchmark for individual assessment, but there is evidence that the risk of chronic disease in some populations, such as people in Asia, increases progressively with a BMI of 22 and over.

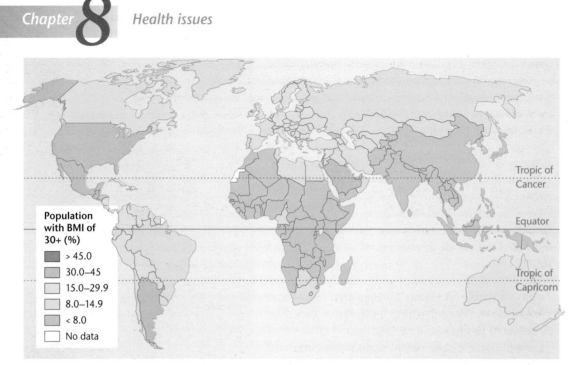

Figure 8.5
Prevalence of
obesity in males
aged 30+, 2005

Figure 8.6
Prevalence of
obesity in females
aged 30+, 2005

The new WHO Child Growth Standards, launched in April 2006, include BMI charts for infants and young children up to age 5. However, measuring overweight and obesity in children aged 5–14 years is challenging because a standard definition of childhood obesity is not applied worldwide. The WHO is currently developing an international growth reference for school-age children and adolescents.

WHO's global figures indicate that in 2005:

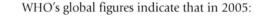

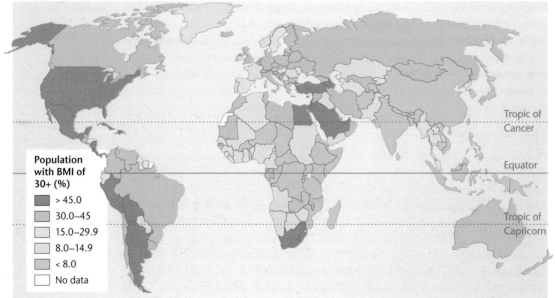

> approximately 1.6 billion adults were overweight
> at least 400 million adults were obese (Figures 8.5 and 8.6)
> at least 20 million children under the age of 5 years were overweight. Childhood obesity is a big problem in the USA where over 35% of children are overweight

WHO further projects that, by 2015, approximately 2.3 billion adults will be overweight and more than 700 million will be obese. Overweight and obesity were once considered to be problems of high-income countries, but are dramatically on the rise in low- and middle-income countries, particularly in urban areas.

Causes of obesity and overweight

The fundamental cause of obesity and overweight is an energy imbalance between calories consumed and calories expended (Figure 8.7). Global increases in overweight and obesity can be attributed to a number of factors, including:

> a global shift in diet towards increased intake of energy-dense foods that are high in fat and sugars but low in vitamins and minerals
> a trend towards decreased physical activity due to the increasingly sedentary nature of many forms of work, changing modes of transportation and increasing urbanisation

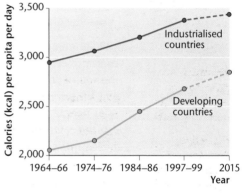

Health consequences

Overweight and obesity can have serious health consequences. Risk increases progressively as BMI increases. Raised BMI is a major risk factor for chronic diseases such as:

Figure 8.7
Trends in food consumption, 1964–99

> cardiovascular disease (mainly heart disease and strokes) — already, the world's number one cause of death, killing 17 million people each year
> diabetes, which has rapidly become a global epidemic. WHO projects that diabetes deaths will increase by more than 50% worldwide in the next 10 years
> musculoskeletal disorders, especially osteoarthritis
> some cancers (endometrial, breast and colon)

Childhood obesity is also associated with a higher chance of premature death and disability in adulthood. Life expectancy is reduced by an average of 14 years for obese smokers compared with non-smokers of normal weight.

More than 60% of adults in the USA are overweight or obese. Triple-width coffins, capable of holding a 300 kg body, are in increasing demand. Worldwide, airlines are having to recalculate their passengers' payload weight. There are 70 million overweight people in China and the south Pacific now has some of the world's highest rates of obesity.

Many low- and middle-income countries are now facing a 'double burden' of disease. While they continue to deal with the problems of infectious disease and undernutrition, they are at the same time experiencing a rapid upsurge in chronic disease risk factors such as obesity and overweight, particularly in urban settings.

It is not uncommon to find undernutrition and obesity existing side by side in the same country, the same community and even the same household. This double burden is caused by inadequate prenatal, infant and childhood nutrition followed by lack of physical activity and exposure to high-fat, energy-dense, micronutrient-poor foods.

Reducing overweight and obesity

Overweight and obesity, as well as their related chronic diseases, are largely preventable. At an individual level, people can:

➤ achieve a healthy weight by reducing calore intake and exercising more
➤ limit energy intake from fats and shift fat consumption from saturated to unsaturated fats
➤ increase consumption of fruit and vegetables, as well as legumes, whole grains and nuts
➤ limit the intake of sugars
➤ increase physical activity — at least 30 minutes of regular, moderate-intensity activity on most days. More activity may be required for weight loss

The implementation of these recommendations requires sustained political commitment. Governments, NGOs and the private sector have vital roles to play in shaping healthy environments and making healthier diet options affordable and accessible. This is especially important for the most vulnerable in society — poor people and children — who have limited choices about the food they eat and the environments in which they live.

The following initiatives by the food industry could accelerate health gains worldwide:

➤ reducing the fat, sugar and salt content of processed foods
➤ reducing portion sizes
➤ introducing innovative, healthy and nutritious choices
➤ reviewing current marketing practices

Contrasting healthcare approaches

A model by Field (1989), which attempts to classify health service types, is shown in Table 8.7. The groupings emphasise the roles of the individual doctor, any medical organisations to which the doctor may belong, the ownership of facilities such as clinics and medical equipment, how the patient pays for the healthcare and the influence of the state. The level of economic development of the country is also an important factor.

Emergent

In India, healthcare is highly diversified, with both Western and traditional practitioners operating. Most hospitals are in cities, where patient:doctor ratios are 500:1. In rural areas, the ratio is 7,000:1. Many rural areas lack clinics and in several states, e.g. Tamil Nadu, the state government has sponsored mobile clinics and local health workers who deal with a wide range of ailments, and give inoculations and advice on basic hygiene. National government spending on health is low (< 2% GDP), but there is help from the World Bank to increase it.

Pluralistic

In the USA, the health system is provided by thousands of independent doctors, pharmacies, clinics and hospitals. The consumer pays for out-patient treatment, doctors' fees, hospitalisation, surgery, equipment and appliances. The federal government recently established the following systems, but both of these provide only basic care:

➤ Medicaid — to provide medical care for the poor
➤ Medicare — to provide medical care for the poor elderly

Most people have insurance cover to pay for treatment, although it is estimated that there are 44 million inhabitants without such insurance.

Insurance/social security

WHO judged the healthcare system in France to be the most effective in the world. Others have been less complimentary: 'French patients can choose their doctors, see them as often as they like, consult specialists at will, even check themselves into hospital…a hypochondriac's paradise' (Michael Moore's film *Sicko*). It functions using the social security system backed up by private insurance schemes. The patient pays on the spot and is reimbursed later to varying degrees. There are three doctors for every 1,000 citizens, but the system is expensive (10% of GDP) and costs are increasing rapidly with an ageing population.

National health service

For the UK, see page 305.

Canada's aim is to provide its citizens with equal access to healthcare regardless of their ability to pay. Its system is known as Medicare and

Table 8.7 Contrasting healthcare approaches in selected countries at different stages of development

Type of healthcare	Main characteristics	Examples
Emergent	Healthcare viewed as an item of personal consumption Physician operates as a solo entrepreneur Professional associations are powerful Private ownership of facilities Direct payment to physicians State's role in healthcare is minimal Development of local health workers	Bangladesh Brazil India Kenya Pakistan Sierra Leone South Africa
Pluralistic	Healthcare viewed as consumer product Physician operates as a solo entrepreneur Professional associations are powerful Private and public ownership of facilities State's role in healthcare is minimal and indirect	USA
Insurance/social security	Healthcare is an insured and guaranteed consumer product Physicians operate as a solo entrepreneurs and as members of professional associations, which are strong Private and public ownership of facilities Payment for services mostly indirect State's role in healthcare is evident but indirect	France Japan Spain
National health service	Healthcare is a state-supported service Physicians operate as solo entrepreneurs and as members of professional associations, which are strong Facilities are mainly publicly owned State's role in healthcare is central and direct	Canada UK
Socialised	Healthcare is a state-provided public service Physicians are state-employed Professional associations are weak or non-existent Facilities are wholly publicly owned Payments for services are entirely indirect State's role in healthcare is total	China Cuba

Photograph 8.5
A state-sponsored
exercise class for
senior citizens in
Cuba. Fitness is part
of the Cuban
government's
health service

it provides comprehensive coverage that allows patients to take their benefits with them from one province to another. The system is financed by national government taxation, supplemented by provincial government taxation, although provincial authorities reserve the right to divert some of the funds to other services. It ensures that indigenous groups (e.g. Inuits) and people living in remote rural areas (e.g. the Yukon) are well served.

Socialised

Cuba's health service is very effective — WHO ranks it at a level just below that of the USA despite spending ten times less per person (Photograph 8.5). Cuba has the second highest life expectancy in the Caribbean (77 years against an average of 69 years), and for a population of 11 million it has over 30,000 family doctors and 10,000 dentists. It aims to improve mobile medical assistance to reduce hospital bed demand for less serious cases. There are 21 medical schools providing free training, and many doctors are 'exported' to other countries.

Health matters in a globalising world

Transnational corporations

A **transnational corporation** (TNC) is a company that operates in at least two countries. It is common for TNCs to have a hierarchical structure, with the headquarters and R&D department in the country of origin, and manufacturing plants overseas. As the organisation becomes more global, regional headquarters and

R&D departments may develop in the manufacturing areas. TNCs take on many different forms and cover a wide range of companies involved in the following primary, secondary (manufacturing) and tertiary (service) activities:

➤ resource extraction, particularly in the mining sector, for materials such as oil and gas

➤ manufacturing in three main sectors:

(1) high-tech industries such as computers, scientific instruments, microelectronics, pharmaceuticals

(2) large-volume consumer goods such as motor vehicles, tyres, televisions and other electrical goods

(3) mass-produced consumer goods such as cigarettes, drinks, breakfast cereals, cosmetics, branded goods

➤ services such as banking/finance, advertising, freight transport, hotels and fast-food operations

> **Key terms**
>
> **Globalisation** The close economic interdependence between the leading nations of the world in trade, investment and cooperative commercial relationships.
>
> **Transnational corporations (TNCs)** Capitalist enterprises that organise the production of goods and services in more than one country. TNCs include the largest companies in the world and many have total sales that are greater than the GNP of a small country.

TNCs are the driving force behind economic **globalisation**. As the rules regulating the movement of goods and investment have been relaxed and the sources and destinations of investment have become more diverse, such companies have extended their reach. There are now few parts of the world where the influence of TNCs is not felt and in many areas they are a powerful influence on the local economy. TNCs tend to be involved in a web of collaborative relationships with other companies across the globe.

The significance of TNCs

➤ TNCs control and coordinate economic activities in different countries and develop trade within and between units of the same corporation in different countries.

➤ TNCs can exploit differences in the availability of capital, and costs of labour, land and building.

➤ TNCs can locate to take advantage of government policies in other countries, such as reduced tax levels, subsidies/grants or less strict environmental controls. They can get around trade barriers by locating production within the markets where they want to sell.

➤ The large size and scale of operations of TNCs means they can achieve economies of scale, allowing them to reduce costs, finance new investment and compete in world markets.

➤ Large companies have a wider choice when locating a new plant, although governments may try to influence decisions as part of regional policy or a desire to protect home markets. Governments are often keen to attract TNCs because inward investment creates jobs and boosts exports which assist the trade balance. TNCs have the power to trade off one country against another in order to achieve the best deal.

➤ Within a country, TNCs have the financial resources to research several potential sites and take advantage of the best communications, access to labour, cost of land and building, and government subsidies.

Pharmaceutical transnationals

Modern pharmaceutical drugs can be seen as authority in pill form. Effectively encapsulated in each pill is a long, expensive chain of scientific research and marketing. Each pill embodies the faith which doctors and patients place in Western medicine. Each pill promises a chance of better health. Each pill, in a way, symbolises power.

(Samantha Madell)

Table 8.8 The ten largest pharmaceutical companies in the world by sales, 2006

Rank	Company	Location	Sales ($m)
1	Pfizer	USA	45,083
2	GlaxoSmithKline	UK	37,034
3	Sanofi-Aventis	France	35,638
4	Novartis	Switzerland	28,880
5	Hoffmann La Roche	Switzerland	26,596
6	AstraZeneca	Sweden/UK	25,741
7	Johnson & Johnson	USA	23,267
8	Merck	USA	22,636
9	Wyeth	USA	15,638
10	Eli Lilly	USA	14,814

The modern pharmaceutical industry is a lucrative one. The largest ten pharmaceutical companies in the world each feature in the top 400 companies in the world (Table 8.8). The geographical distribution is interesting: five have headquarters in the USA, two in Switzerland, one in France and two in the UK. They are all successful examples of globalisation. For example, Johnson & Johnson has more than 190 operating companies in 52 countries, selling products to 175 countries.

Photograph 8.6 GlaxoSmithKline has its headquarters in the UK, but facilities all over the world, such as the corporate offices in Philadelphia (left) and R&D facility in Harlow (inset)

Branded pharmaceuticals

Pharmaceuticals can be sold under two broad categories: generic or branded. Branded medicines, as with branded clothes, are more expensive than their generic counterparts. However, the generic name of a drug is its chemical description. This means that generic drugs are chemically identical to their brand-named equivalents. The generic name for a drug tends to be long and hard to remember whereas the brand name is often catchy. For example, the generic drug fluoxetine hydrochloride is marketed successfully as Prozac by its manufacturer Eli Lilly. The same drug is also marketed by other companies under the names of Erocarp, Lovan and Zactin. Branded drugs may be three to thirty times more expensive to purchase, making them prohibitive for much of the world's population. For any brand-name drug to be more well-known and popular than the generic equivalent, marketing forces must be involved.

Essential drugs

WHO regularly publishes updated lists of 'essential drugs'. These are generic drugs that can provide safe, effective treatment for most communicable and non-communicable diseases such as diarrhoea, tuberculosis and malaria. These lists are widely regarded as an important tool in increasing access for the world's populations to effective healthcare. They are, however, unpopular in countries with strong pharmaceutical industries. The WHO essential drugs list is not implemented in the USA or any EU country. This is because of the business goals (i.e. profit) of manufacturers. In the USA the federal government is now prevented from encouraging the use of generic drugs following legal action from the Pharmaceutical Manufacturers' Association.

Drug development

The largest profits in the pharmaceutical industry come from the sale of brand-name drugs in developed countries. Research into tropical diseases affecting hundreds of millions of people in less developed countries receives only a small proportion of the sum spent on cancer research. Most money is spent on developing drugs to control 'diseases of affluence' such as heart disease, cancer and high blood pressure. Patents for new drugs are viewed as 'intellectual property' and it is illegal to make generic 'copies' of them for 20 years. Therefore, many new drugs that WHO may regard as 'essential' are not available in generic form. Pharmaceutical companies are criticised for this but point out the enormous investment in R&D required to develop a new drug. The money to fund this research comes partly from their profits.

Marketing and distribution

Branded drugs are unusual among consumer goods in the developed world in that their consumers tend to have little choice in the drug they purchase and use. Patients tend to use what their doctor prescribes for them. Therefore, the industry heavily targets doctors with its marketing, providing free samples of drugs, giving away everyday items (pens, calendars etc.), advertising in medical journals and arranging visits of sales representatives to surgeries and offices.

Another criticism aimed at pharmaceutical companies and WHO is that they tend to treat the symptoms rather than the root cause of the problem. For example, iron folate, a vitamin supplement, is on WHO's list of essential drugs. It is included because of its ability to prevent anaemia in pregnant women, a common problem in both the underdeveloped and developed world. However, a similar compound, with the same anaemia-preventing properties, is found in leafy green

*Photograph 8.7
A doctor giving an
antiparasitic drug
to a child in Sri
Lanka. This is part
of GlaxoSmithKline's
humanitarian
programme to
help eliminate
lymphatic filariasis
(elephantitis)*

vegetables. It is possible that encouraging the growth of these vegetables would be more valid than promoting vitamin supplements.

Tobacco transnationals

Philip Morris, R. J. Reynolds and British American Tobacco (BAT), the world's largest non-state owned tobacco producing TNCs, own or lease plants in more than 60 countries. These three companies have a total revenue of more than US$70 billion, a sum greater than the combined GDP of Costa Rica, Lithuania, Senegal, Sri Lanka, Uganda and Zimbabwe.

Of the 1.2 billion smokers in the world, 800 million are in the developing world. Countries where consumption is growing the fastest are also among the world's poorest, and it is these countries that the major tobacco TNCs are targeting with their advertising and marketing campaigns. China's increase in tobacco consumption has been the most dramatic. Nearly 70% of Chinese men smoke, compared with just 4% of Chinese women. This means that China alone accounts for 300 million smokers, almost the same number as in all the developed world.

India

BAT has targeted the expanding market in India. According to the International Non-Governmental Coalition Against Tobacco (INGCAT):

➤ each day 55,000 children in India start using tobacco in some way
➤ about 5 million children in India under the age of 15 are already addicted to tobacco
➤ although cigarettes form only about 20% of the Indian tobacco market, BAT is engaged in campaigns to convert 250 million tobacco users, particularly the young, to cigarette smoking
➤ the Indian government has relaxed investment rules so that TNCs can now have 100% ownership of their manufacturing plants (previously they had to be joint ventures)

Production in developing countries

Tobacco TNCs are turning to developing countries not only to expand their markets but also as a source of cheaper tobacco. The danger with this is that tobacco cultivation will replace food crops. In Kenya, food production in tobacco-growing districts has decreased as farmers have shifted from food crops to tobacco. BAT is the largest agribusiness company in Kenya, contracting over 17,000 farmers to cultivate tobacco in an area of around 15,000 hectares. The situation is similar in Brazil, the world's largest exporter of tobacco. Brazilian tobacco is primarily used by Philip Morris to make less expensive brands. Cigarettes made with tobacco grown in the USA cost twice as much.

Like many other international companies, tobacco TNCs are shifting production overseas to take advantage of cheaper labour costs. They have all started production in Asian countries. For example, R. J. Reynolds has a factory in Vietnam which is used to supply German and Canadian markets. Damon, one of the world's largest tobacco-leaf dealers, also has an office in Vietnam, where it is developing new crop varieties for what it hopes to be a growing market. Vietnam sells most of its tobacco for less than US$3 per kg.

Regional variations in the UK

Life expectancy

Life expectancy in the UK is increasing. Across the country as a whole, men aged 65 can expect to live a further 16.6 years and women a further 19.4 years if mortality rates remain the same as they were in 2005. Women continue to live longer than men, but the gap is decreasing. In 1985, there was a difference of 4 years between male and female life expectancy at age 65 in the UK (13.2 and 17.2 years respectively). By 2005 this had narrowed to 2.8 years.

There are slight variations in life expectancy between the constituent countries of the UK, as shown in Table 8.9. English men and women have the highest life expectancy at age 65, at 16.8 and 19.6 years respectively. Scotland, at 15.5 and 18.4 years respectively, has the lowest life expectancy at this age.

There are also more local variations. The southeast, southwest and east of England have the highest life expectancies. Scotland, the northeast and northwest of England have the lowest.

Table 8.9
Life expectancy in years, 2005

Country	At birth		At age 65	
	Males	Females	Males	Females
England	76.9	81.2	16.8	19.6
Wales	76.3	80.7	16.4	19.2
Scotland	74.2	79.3	15.5	18.4
Northern Ireland	76.0	80.8	16.4	19.3
UK	76.6	81.0	16.6	19.4

Source: Office for National Statistics

All the ten local authorities with the highest male life expectancy at birth are in England: five in the southeast, three in the east of England and one each in the southwest and London. Eight of the ten local authorities with the lowest male life expectancy are in Scotland (Table 8.10). Glasgow City (69.9 years) is the only area in the UK where life expectancy at birth is less than 70 years. Kensington and Chelsea is the local authority with the highest male life expectancy. A similar situation exists for female life expectancy (Table 8.11).

Table 8.10
Local authorities with the lowest life expectancy at birth, 2005

Males			Females		
Local authority	Rank order	Years	Local authority	Rank order	Years
Glasgow City	432	69.9	Glasgow City	432	76.7
West Dunbartonshire	431	71.0	West Dunbartonshire	431	77.5
Inverclyde	430	71.1	North Lanarkshire	430	77.6
Comhairle nan Eilean Siar	429	72.1	Inverclyde	429	77.9
Manchester	428	72.5	East Ayrshire	428	78.0
Renfrewshire	427	72.6	Liverpool	427	78.1
North Lanarkshire	426	72.7	Renfrewshire	426	78.2
Dundee City	425	73.0	Halton	425	78.3
Blackpool	424	73.2	Hartlepool	424	78.3
Clackmannanshire	423	73.2	Manchester	423	78.3

Source: Office for National Statistics

Table 8.11
Local authorities with the highest life expectancy at birth, 2005

Males			Females		
Local authority	Rank order	Years	Local authority	Rank order	Years
Kensington and Chelsea	1	82.2	Kensington and Chelsea	1	86.2
East Dorset	2	80.9	Epsom and Elwell	2	84.5
Hart	3	80.2	East Dorset	3	84.1
Uttlesford	4	80.0	South Cambridgeshire	4	83.9
Wokingham	5	80.0	Rutland	5	83.8
South Norfolk	6	80.0	Purbeck	6	83.7
Chiltern	7	80.0	Guildford	7	83.6
Horsham	8	79.9	New Forest	8	83.6
Brentwood	9	79.9	North Dorset	9	83.5
Crawley	10	79.9	Horsham	10	83.4

Source: Office for National Statistics

Morbidity

A considerable amount of research has been conducted into regional variations in morbidity in the UK. The purpose of this research is to try to identify patterns of morbidity and the factors that contribute to these patterns, with a view to targeting elements of healthcare to combat them. The results are far from clear; variations exist for some aspects of morbidity but not for others. The links between factors such as age, income, occupation, education and environment and types of morbidity are also difficult to establish. They tend to be based on speculative association rather than clearly established causal links.

The research so far has shown that, at a country level:

➤ Scotland has the highest rates of lung cancer, heart disease, strokes, and alcohol and drug-related problems
➤ Wales has the highest incidence of breast, prostate and bowel cancer
➤ Northern Ireland has the highest rate of respiratory diseases
➤ England has the lowest rates for most of these

At regional level within England, a north–south divide in health is evident in some cases but not in others. Regions in the north have a higher mortality from heart disease, strokes and lung cancer. London has the highest rates for infectious and respiratory diseases. Alcohol-related problems do not show a regional pattern (Figures 8.8 and 8.9). There is little variation in the incidence of bowel cancer, whereas breast and prostate cancer rates are higher in the south than in the north. Age appears to be a factor for some aspects of morbidity. For example, in London heart disease incidence at ages 45–64 is below average, whereas the incidence of strokes for this age group is high.

A central finding of the research is that differences *between* countries and regions of the UK are less important than the wide differences than exist *within* regions. Urban areas tend to have higher levels of morbidity. Deprivation is often given as the main reason for this, but many areas of deprivation exist in rural parts. The examples in Figures 8.8 and 8.9 illustrate the problems of trying to establish clear patterns of morbidity.

Blackpool tops drink deaths table

Blackpool has a higher number of alcohol-related deaths per head of population than anywhere else in England and Wales, new figures show. Out of every 100,000 people who died in the resort from 2001 to 2003, 30 died from drinking, the Office for National Statistics (ONS) said. Manchester, Liverpool, Preston and Barrow had the next highest figures. Brighton and Hove, Salford, Corby, Sandwell and Camden were also in the top ten. The ONS said that in 2003 there were 6,580 deaths from alcohol-related illnesses, such as liver disease, in England and Wales, up from 5,970 in 2001.

The figures also showed wide variations between different regions. In the northwest, there were 15.1 deaths per 100,000, compared to 7.7 in the east. The northeast, the West Midlands and London also had high rates.

Source: BBC News

Figure 8.8

Figure 8.9

Coast areas 'heart disease risk'

People living near the coasts of Devon, Norfolk and Dorset have the highest risk of heart disease, experts say. The University of Portsmouth and market researchers TNS analysed national healthcare data to find out who was at risk. In the south and east of Dorset, nearly 14% of the population were at risk compared to under 6% in areas of London. Researchers put the risk down to the age of populations, access to health services and lifestyle.

The five areas most at risk were: south and east Dorset, north Norfolk, Bexhill and Rother, east Devon and east Lincolnshire.

The five areas least at risk were: Wandsworth, Hammersmith and Fulham, Westminster, Kensington and Chelsea, Haringey, all in greater London.

A spokesman said, 'It's thought that age and deprivation that are the biggest predictors of heart disease rather than a north–south divide, though we do have misconceptions about what areas are deprived. Rural deprivation is also significant.'

Source: BBC News

Factors affecting regional variations

One explanation put forward for regional differences in health and morbidity is that they simply reflect a concentration of people of lower socioeconomic status. However, other factors also appear to influence patterns in the UK.

Socioeconomic status does appear to be significant. In all regions of England, babies born to fathers in social class 5 (unskilled and unemployed) have higher infant mortality rates than those born to fathers in social class 1 (professional and managerial). Men aged 20–64 within social class 5 themselves have higher mortality than those in social class 1. Furthermore, men in this class in the north of England have higher mortality and morbidity than those in the same class in the south of England. It is believed that the explanation for this lies in material deprivation particularly in terms of employment and housing. In addition, people in this social class display different behaviours towards health — more smoking, less uptake of healthcare, lower ability to maintain health — and there is a cumulative effect of disproportionate numbers of disadvantaged people living in deprived areas. There is little geographic difference in mortality among those in social class 1.

Health-related behaviours may also affect geographic variations in health. Levels of smoking vary considerably across the countries of the UK and within the regions. It is well known that those of lower economic status are more likely to be heavy smokers, and it is this that drives the pattern of lung cancer by deprivation. Levels of education may also be a factor. Alcohol consumption and diet vary only a little between regions and therefore are likely to have limited influence on patterns of health. Attitudes to health, and in particular to **exercise** (again a reflection of education), may have an effect, but it is far from straightforward to quantify the effects.

Environment is also cited as a factor. The relationship between the **weather** and various aspects of health has been studied in great detail. Relationships have been found between:

- temperature, heart disease and pneumonia, but these are more associated with seasonal variations of temperature than regional variations
- rainfall and heart disease, which may impact on regional variations

Seasonality of mortality has declined in the UK since the 1960s, possibly due to the increased use of central heating. Air pollution was responsible for high morbidity and mortality from respiratory diseases before this period, and has declined.

Other smaller-scale aspects of the environment have an influence on morbidity. The impact of background radiation may be a factor in some diseases. For example, some rocks in the southwest of England contain high amounts of radon, and the radioactivity from this is thought to be responsible for a higher risk of lung cancer in the area. Issues of water quality are significant. Hard water is found in the south and east, soft water in the north and west. A consistent relationship has been shown between soft water and high levels of heart disease. Deficiencies and excesses of certain trace elements in water are known to be harmful. Excesses of nickel, cadmium, mercury and lead are hazardous and high concentrations of aluminium in water have been suggested as an explanation for the geographic distribution of Alzheimer's disease.

The influence of age, gender and wealth

One way in which you can study the impact of age, gender and wealth on access to healthcare and exercise facilities is to study one or more small-scale areas through primary research and/or fieldwork.

The specification requires you to study two or more such areas, as detailed in Chapter 5. This could be extended to consider healthcare, exercise and nutrition. For the first time in 2001, the UK census asked people to describe their health over the previous 12 months as 'good', 'fairly good' or 'not good'.

Tables 8.12 and 8.13 give general health information from census data for an inner-city area and a suburban area. A greater range of general statistics for these census areas is given in Tables 5.18 and 5.19, pages 196 and 197. The health data may reflect the access to facilities for exercise and healthcare of people in those localities, as well as nutrition levels. They could form the basis for investigation, possibly by using a questionnaire with residents, businesses and healthcare or exercise providers. We recommend you complete an investigation in a locality of your choice.

Table 8.12 Health statistics: Manchester area 024C lower layer SOA (an inner-city area), Manchester metropolitan district and England, 2001

General health (%)	Area 024C	Manchester metropolitan district	England
Good	60.6	64.6	68.7
Fairly good	23.2	22.9	22.2
Not good	16.2	12.5	9.0

Source: Office for National Statistics

Table 8.13 Health statistics: Doncaster area 025A lower layer SOA (a suburban area), Doncaster metropolitan district and England, 2001

General health (%)	Area 025A	Doncaster metropolitan district	England
Good	67.0	64.5	68.7
Fairly good	23.1	23.5	22.2
Not good	9.9	12.0	9.0

Source: Office for National Statistics

Implications for the provision of healthcare systems

Healthcare in the UK is provided within the context of the National Health Service (NHS). You are advised to study healthcare systems in an area of your choice. However, the following gives some background information on the NHS and illustrates its operation in two specific areas: a larger area (the Wirral in northwest England) and a city (Sheffield).

The NHS

The NHS was founded in 1948 by Aneurin Bevin, who was determined to make good health a priority for all citizens: 'The essence of a satisfactory health service is that rich and poor are treated alike.'

*Photograph 8.8
An oncologist
studying CT scans of
a patient's chest
and abdomen at
Newcastle General
Hospital*

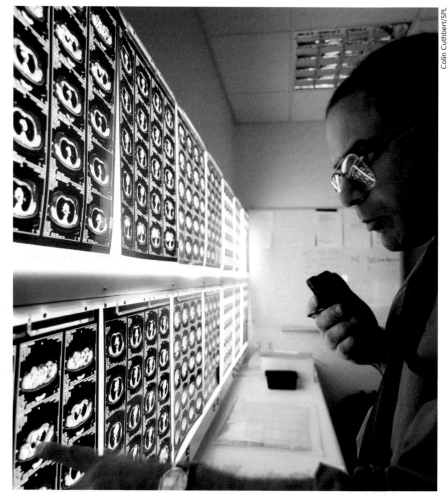

Colin Cuthbert/SPL

There have been profound changes in the NHS since 1948. Successive governments have found it difficult to manage, and costs have risen as people live longer and medical advances take place.

In 2000, the government produced the NHS Plan. A number of reforms were implemented based around the creation of primary care trusts (PCTs). Primary care is the care provided by the people you see when you first have a health problem, including doctors, dentists, opticians and pharmacists. NHS walk-in centres and the phone service NHS Direct are also parts of primary care (Photograph 8.8). All of these are managed by a local PCT. These trusts are at the centre of the NHS and control about 80% of its budget. Their aims are to:

➤ engage with the local population to improve health and well-being
➤ commission a comprehensive and fair range of high-quality, responsive and efficient services, within allocated resources
➤ directly provide high-quality, responsive and efficient services where this gives the best value

Case study — Healthcare in the Wirral

Four NHS trusts provide services to the people of the Wirral:

- Wirral Primary Care Trust (PCT)
- Wirral Hospital NHS Trust
- Cheshire and Wirral Partnership NHS Trust
- Clatterbridge Centre for Oncology NHS Foundation Trust

Wirral Primary Care Trust

The PCT is responsible for deciding on the health service needs of the population of the Wirral and securing the continual provision of the services required. It achieves this by providing primary care and community services itself and commissioning secondary care from the other three trusts.

Primary care and community services provided by the PCT are doctors, dentists, opticians, pharmacists, health visitors and physiotherapists. Its headquarters is at St Catherine's Hospital in Tranmere. There are more than 60 GP surgeries in the region. The formation of the PCT allows local GPs to manage health services in their own districts. They can use the knowledge they have gained from working in a neighbourhood to influence, for example, which operations are bought from the Wirral Hospital NHS Trust and which illnesses are focused on.

Wirral Hospital NHS Trust

The Hospital Trust is responsible for most operations and major specialist treatments for Wirral residents. This may occur when the patient is referred to the trust by his or her family doctor, or brought into the Accident and Emergency department. Although it has departments on various sites around the peninsula, the best-known part of the Hospital NHS Trust is Arrowe Park Hospital.

Cheshire and Wirral Partnership NHS Trust

This is a specialist trust working across Wirral and Cheshire. The PCT commissions specialist mental health, learning disabilities, drug and alcohol services from the Partnership Trust for the people of the Wirral.

Clatterbridge Centre for Oncology NHS Foundation Trust

This is a specialist regional cancer centre. It provides cancer services to patients in Cheshire, Merseyside and the Isle of Man. The PCT commissions services from the Clatterbridge Centre so that Wirral residents can benefit from the centre's expertise.

At a national level, NHS North West oversees the four Wirral trusts. It reports to the Department of Health, which is headed by the secretary of state for health.

Case study — Healthcare in Sheffield

The Sheffield PCT serves a population of 520,000 and covers the same area as Sheffield City Council. Its headquarters are in the centre of the city at Don Valley House.

Secondary care is provided by three hospital NHS trusts:

- Sheffield Children's NHS Foundation Trust
- Sheffield Teaching Hospitals NHS Foundation Trust
- Sheffield Care Trust

Sheffield Children's NHS Foundation Trust

This is a major provider of healthcare for children and young people in Sheffield, South Yorkshire and beyond. Its services are located at Sheffield Children's Hospital on Western Bank and throughout the city at Beighton Community Hospital, Centenary House, Flocton House, Oakwood Young People's Centre, Ryegate Children's Centre, Shirle Hill Hospital and St Peter's Close.

Sheffield Teaching Hospitals NHS Foundation Trust

This manages the five adult hospital services in the city. It provides around 900,000 appointments and operations a year and offers almost every kind of treatment. Its hospitals are Northern General Hospital, Royal Hallamshire Hospital, Jessop Wing, Weston Park Hospital and Charles Clifford Dental Hospital.

Sheffield Care Trust

This delivers mental health services for adults, older people's services, psychology and therapy agencies and specialist learning disability services.

At a national level, the Yorkshire and Humber Strategic Health Authority oversees the three Sheffield trusts. It in turn reports to the Department of Health which is headed by the secretary of state for health.

What is the role of other providers?

The role of **private healthcare** has increased in recent years. Private health organisations such as BUPA offer a quick and efficient service to people who can pay insurance premiums, which are often met by their employers. Private companies tend to offer a more speedy response to elective surgery whereas acute situations are still dealt with by the NHS.

Charitable organisations offer wider support than the NHS. They tend to concentrate on welfare as much as on health. Examples include:

➤ the Down Syndrome Educational Trust
➤ Macmillan Cancer Support
➤ the hospice movement
➤ organisations such as Shelter and Help the Aged

People who work for these organisations are a necessary part of the total provision of health and welfare in the UK. Many of them are unpaid volunteers.

Assessment exercises

1 a Figure A shows the relationship between melanoma (skin cancer) deaths and latitude for selected states in the USA and Canada.
 (i) Draw a sketch copy of the figure and insert a best-fit line to indicate the relationship shown. **(2 marks)**
 (ii) State the nature of the relationship indicated by your best-fit line. **(2 marks)**
 (iii) Suggest reasons for this relationship, and for possible anomalies to it. **(6 marks)**

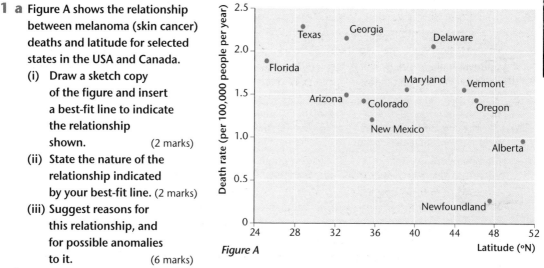

Figure A

b Describe the impact of one disease of affluence on economic development. **(5 marks)**

c For one infectious disease you have studied, describe its impact on health, economic development and lifestyle in the area(s) affected. **(15 marks)**

(30 marks)

2 a Describe the different approaches to healthcare in *two* countries you have studied. **(7 marks)**

b Figure B shows the percentage availability of basic medical equipment for the diagnosis and management of high blood pressure and diabetes by WHO region. Describe and comment on the differences in the availability of medical equipment shown. **(8 marks)**

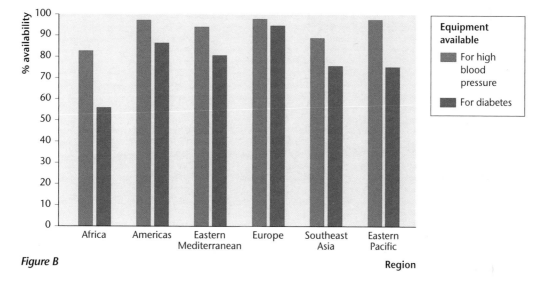

Figure B

c Table A summarises the main attitudes in response to the question: should poorer countries have access to cheap generic drugs?

Table A

No	Yes
Unless controlled, the generic drugs business will inevitably undermine research and development into new drugs	Millions die each year from preventable, treatable diseases. It is immoral to deny them access to the cheapest drugs
The problem is poverty not the high cost of patented drugs. Most poor nations cannot even afford the cost of generic drugs	Poor nations should not have to foot the bill for research and development into drugs aimed at richer nations
The drugs industry is a commercial business not a charity. If we were to subsidise the poor, the taxpayer would foot the bill	Allowing poorer countries to undercut patent medicine prices will have a minimal effect on the profits of the drugs industry

Using Table A and your own knowledge, discuss the view that 'drugs companies are conducting an undeclared war against the world's poorest people'.

(15 marks)

(30 marks)

Unit 2

Geographical skills

Geographical skills

This unit assesses your ability to apply your knowledge and skills to unseen information and resources, with reference to fieldwork that you have undertaken. A range of skills from at least three of the six categories — **basic**, **investigative**, **cartographic**, **graphical**, **statistical** and **ICT skills** — will be examined in each exam series. You need to develop an awareness of the appropriateness and limitations of each of these different skills. Investigative skills and the assessment of fieldwork will always be tested in this unit. You therefore need to take part in personal investigative work in the field to ensure familiarity with these.

Question 1 will be set on one of the two compulsory core sections (physical: rivers, floods and management or human: population change) in Unit 1. It will be based on a variety of resources relating to the topic selected. Question 2 will relate specifically to your own fieldwork and investigative research skills. This fieldwork can be associated with any part of the AS content of Unit 1. The two questions in Unit 2, resource-based and fieldwork, have equal weighting.

Basic skills

There are a number of basic skills with which you should be familiar. These include:

➤ **drawing sketches** — these are important as a descriptive and analytical tool. You should be able to draw sketches in the field to record information and to sketch photographs
➤ **analysing photographs** — you should be able to interpret photographs of different areas. When carrying out investigative work, you should be able to use photographs as descriptive and analytical tools
➤ **labelling and annotation** — you should be able to annotate base maps, sketch maps, Ordnance Survey (OS) maps, diagrams, graphs, sketches and photographs
➤ **use of overlays** — you should be able to use these to identify salient points on photographs and sketches
➤ **literacy skills** — these are particularly important because much information is communicated in writing

Using field sketches and photographs

In your personal investigation, field sketches and photographs are excellent ways to record exactly what you have seen. Field sketches enable you to pick out from the landscape the features that you wish to identify and perhaps comment upon. They are particularly useful in physical geography investigations. Coastal geomor-

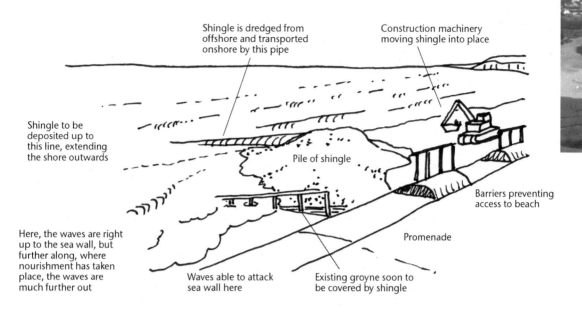

Shingle is dredged from offshore and transported onshore by this pipe

Construction machinery moving shingle into place

Shingle to be deposited up to this line, extending the shore outwards

Pile of shingle

Barriers preventing access to beach

Here, the waves are right up to the sea wall, but further along, where nourishment has taken place, the waves are much further out

Promenade

Waves able to attack sea wall here

Existing groyne soon to be covered by shingle

Figure 9.1
A field sketch made on a coastal survey

phology lends itself to this method — for example, Figure 9.1 shows a field sketch of beach nourishment. However, there is no reason why the technique cannot be used in an urban study. Sketching does not require artistic talent. It is far more important in geographical investigations to produce a clear drawing with good and useful labels.

If you lack the confidence to produce sketches but need to show detail from the area under investigation, then taking photographs is just as valid. However, you must not use them as an attractive 'space-filler' in your report. Any photographs you include must be annotated or labelled. A photograph is only useful when the reader is directed to the information it shows.

Investigative skills

At AS, you are required to develop the following skills:
- identification of geographical questions and issues
- establishment of effective approaches to enquiry
- identification, selection and collection of quantitative and qualitative evidence from primary sources (including fieldwork) and secondary sources
- processing, presentation, analysis and interpretation of evidence
- drawing conclusions and showing an awareness of the validity of such conclusions
- evaluation of a complete enquiry
- risk assessment and identification of strategies for minimising health and safety risks in undertaking fieldwork

Investigative skills *always* form part of the Unit 2 paper. You *must* therefore participate in personal investigative work in the field to ensure you are familiar with such skills.

Your fieldwork investigation

Once you have established the aims and hypotheses of your investigation with the help of your teacher, you should work out what data you need to collect and what methods you will use. Investigations at AS are based on your own observations. This means using such techniques as questionnaires, interviews, river measurements, pedestrian surveys and urban transects. Secondary data from published sources can be added. Two very different ways of collecting primary data are described in detail below: sampling and river surveys.

Sampling

Sampling is used when it is impossible, or simply not necessary, to collect large amounts of data. Collecting small amounts of carefully selected data will enable you to obtain a representative view of the feature as a whole. You cannot, for example, interview all the shoppers in a market town or all the inhabitants of a village, but you can look at a fraction of those populations and from that evidence indicate how the whole is likely to behave.

When you have established the need for a sample survey, you will have to decide on a method that will collect a large enough representative body of evidence. If, for example, you are interviewing the inhabitants of a village, you must ensure that your interviews cover all age ranges in the population.

Types of sampling

The main types of sampling technique you need to consider are random, systematic and stratified (quota).

A **random sampling** is one that shows no bias and in which every member of the population has an equal chance of being selected. The method usually involves the use of random number tables.

In **systematic sampling**, samples are taken at regular fixed intervals, for example every tenth person or house. On a beach you could decide to sample sites at 100 m intervals, and select pebbles at each location using the intersection points on the grid in a quadrat.

Stratified sampling is based on knowing something in advance about the population or area in question. For example, if you are surveying a population with a view to examining the provision of services in the area where they live, and you know its age distribution, your sample must reflect that distribution.

Bias in sampling

It is possible, through poor choice of sampling method or insufficient evidence, to achieve a result that is unrepresentative of the population in question. Taking all samples on the same day of the week or outside the same surgery could lead to a distortion in a healthcare survey, for example.

Sample size

The size of sample usually depends upon the complexity of the survey being used. When using a questionnaire it is necessary to sample sufficient people to take into account the considerable variety introduced by the range of questions. Sample size can be restricted by practical difficulties and this may affect the reliability of results. Your aim should be to keep the sampling error as small as possible. You are not a professional sampler and cannot be expected to conduct hundreds of interviews, but on the other hand, sampling only 20–30 people in an energy conservation survey is not representative of the population as a whole.

Point sampling

Point sampling is carried out in surveys which involve, for example, studies of land use, vegetation coverage and selection of such items as pebbles in longshore-drift studies. Point sampling involves the use of a grid. That produced by Ordnance Survey is ideal, but for field surveys a **quadrat** can be used. A quadrat is a frame enclosing an area of known size (often 1 m²), and may be subdivided by a grid made of wire or string. Both random and systematic sampling can be carried out within this framework.

Collecting data for river surveys

A number of measurements can be made within the channel of a river.

Speed of the river

The best and easiest way to measure the speed of flow in a river is to use a flow meter that either gives a direct reading or allows you to calculate the speed using a conversion chart. Without a flow meter, it is possible to calculate the speed by using a piece of wood or cork as a float (some people swear by dog biscuits). The procedure is as follows:

➤ Measure out a 10 m length of the river.
➤ Measure the time it takes the float to cover the distance.
➤ Repeat several times and at various points across the flow.
➤ Find the average time — this gives the surface speed.
➤ Multiply by 0.8 to find the true speed of the river across the whole channel.

Cross-sectional area and wetted perimeter

Cross-sectional area can be calculated using the following procedure:

➤ Run a tape across the river along the waterline from bank to bank.
➤ Along this tape, calculate the depth of water at 50 cm intervals (this distance can vary according to the width of the river).
➤ Transfer this information to graph paper, making sure that you use the same scale for the vertical and horizontal axes.
➤ Having produced a cross-section diagram, count the squares (the size of which you already know) inside the line and by a simple multiplication you will have the cross-section area of the channel at that point (Figure 9.2).

You can also measure the wetted perimeter from such a diagram.

Figure 9.2 River cross-section and wetted perimeter

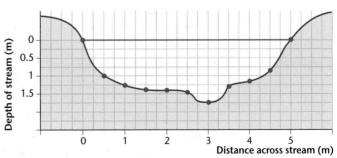

River discharge

To calculate river discharge:

➤ Calculate the speed of flow (m s^{-1}) as described above.
➤ Calculate the cross-sectional area (m^2) as described above.
➤ Multiply the two values to give the discharge in cumecs (m^3 s^{-1}).

Cartographic skills

Cartographic skills fall into two main categories:

➤ the reading and interpretation of maps
➤ the production of maps in order to present information

You should be able to read and interpret:

➤ atlas maps
➤ OS maps at a range of scales, particularly 1:50,000 and 1:25,000
➤ base maps and sketch maps provided by others
➤ detailed town-centre maps and plans

Sketch maps

Sketch maps can be produced to illustrate the location of a case study or an area of personal investigation, and the site or situation of settlements. They should be presented with good and useful labels, including a simple scale and a north point.

Maps with proportional symbols

Figure 9.3 The size of the squatter population in selected world countries

These are maps that include symbols which are proportional in area or volume to the value they represent. Symbols of representative sizes, such as squares or circles, or even small graphs, such as bar graphs or pie graphs, can be placed on a map to show spatial differences (Figure 9.3). It is important that you take great

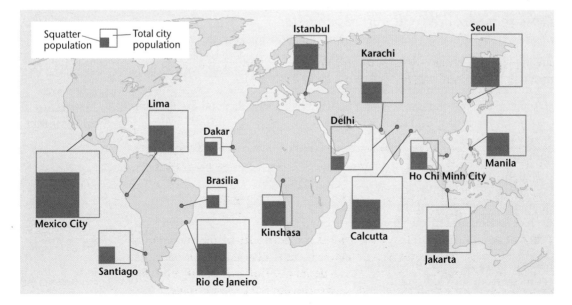

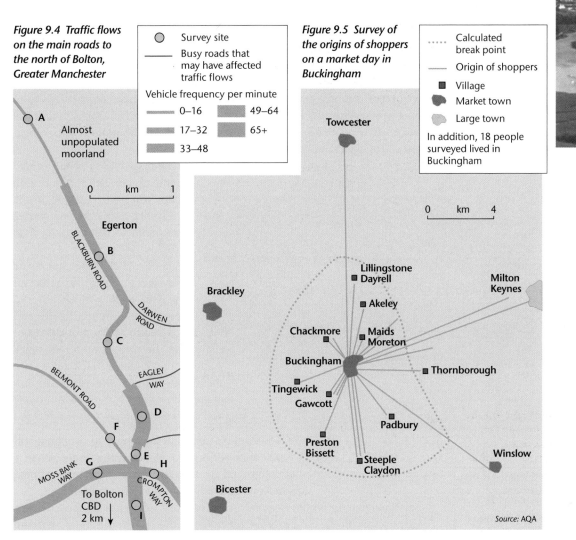

Figure 9.4 Traffic flows on the main roads to the north of Bolton, Greater Manchester

Survey site
Busy roads that may have affected traffic flows

Vehicle frequency per minute
0–16
17–32
33–48
49–64
65+

A
Almost unpopulated moorland

0   km   1

Egerton

BLACKBURN ROAD

B

DARWEN ROAD

Brackley

C

BELMONT ROAD

EAGLEY WAY

D

F

MOSS BANK WAY

G

E   H

CROMPTON WAY

To Bolton CBD 2 km

I

Figure 9.5 Survey of the origins of shoppers on a market day in Buckingham

Calculated break point
Origin of shoppers
Village
Market town
Large town

In addition, 18 people surveyed lived in Buckingham

Towcester

0   km   4

Lillingstone Dayrell

Milton Keynes

Akeley

Chackmore

Maids Moreton

Buckingham

Thornborough

Tingewick

Gawcott

Padbury

Preston Bissett

Winslow

Steeple Claydon

Bicester

Source: AQA

care in placing symbols on a map. It is essential to avoid too much overlap, but it must also be clear which area or place the symbol represents.

Flow lines, desire lines and trip lines

Flow lines and desire lines are similar in that they both represent the volume of movement from place to place. They are useful to show such features as:

➤ traffic movements along particular routes (e.g. roads, railways and waterways)
➤ migration of populations
➤ movement of goods or commodities between different regions
➤ movements of shoppers

In both methods the width of the line is proportional to the quantity of movement. A flow line represents the quantity of movement along an actual route, such as a train or bus route (Figure 9.4). A desire line is drawn directly from the point of origin to the destination and takes no account of a specific route.

Trip lines can be drawn to show regular trips, for example where people shop; lines could be drawn from a town to nearby villages (Figure 9.5).

Choropleth maps

A choropleth is a map on which data values are represented by the density of shading within areas. The data are usually in a form that can be expressed in terms of area, such as population density per square kilometre. To produce such a map certain stages have to be followed:

➤ The material has to be grouped into classes. Before you can do this you have to decide on the number and range of classes required to display your data clearly.

➤ A range of shadings has to be devised to cover the range of the data. Darkest shades should represent the highest figures and vice versa. It is good practice not to use the two extremes of black and white because black suggests a maximum value while white implies that there is nothing in the area. A suitable method of shading is shown in Figure 9.6.

Choropleth maps are fairly easy to construct and are visually effective as they give the reader a chance to see general patterns in an areal distribution. There are, however, a few limitations to the method:

➤ It assumes that the whole area under one form of shading has the same density, with no variations. For example, on maps of the UK the whole of Scotland may be covered by one category, when it is obvious that there could be large variations between the central populated areas and the Highlands.

➤ The method implies abrupt changes at the drawn boundaries which will not be present in reality.

Isoline (isopleth) maps

If you have collected data from different places, they can be represented by points on a map. It is possible to draw a map on which all points of the same value are joined by a line. This allows patterns in a distribution to be seen.

The best-known example of such isolines (also called isopleths) is on Ordnance Survey maps where contour lines join places of the same height. This technique can be applied to a number of other physical factors, such as rainfall (**isohyets**), temperature (**isotherms**) and pressure (**isobars**), as well as human factors, such as travel times (**isochrones**) for commuters and shoppers.

Figure 9.6 Choropleth map showing population density in a metropolitan borough in northern England, 2001

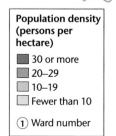

N

0   km   5

Population density (persons per hectare)

- 30 or more
- 20–29
- 10–19
- Fewer than 10

① Ward number

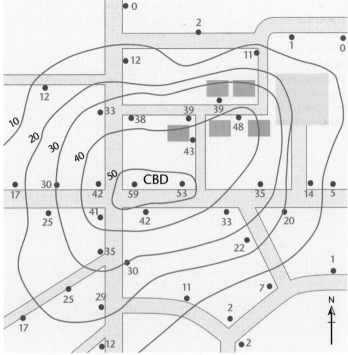

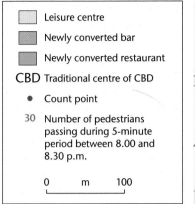

Figure 9.7 is an example of an isoline map showing pedestrian densities in a town centre.

Dot maps

A dot map is a map in which the spatial distribution of a geographical variable is represented by a number of dots of equal size.

Figure 9.7
Isoline map showing pedestrian densities in a town centre

Each dot has the same value and is plotted on a map roughly where that variable occurs. The dot value should be high enough to avoid excessive overcrowding of dots in areas with high concentrations of the variable being mapped and low enough to prevent areas with low concentrations of the variable having no dots at all, so giving a false sense of emptiness.

Dot maps have two limitations:

➤ Large numbers of dots are difficult to count. Therefore, although dot maps are good at giving an impression of distribution, they are less valuable if you need a precise idea of the values they represent.

➤ There must be some accompanying information about the distribution of the variable or the map could be misleading.

Graphical skills

Arithmetic (line) graphs

Arithmetic graphs are appropriate when you want to show absolute changes in data. For example, they are suitable for showing changes in food production through time, population change or stream discharge. When several lines are plotted on the same graph, it is important to recognise whether it is a simple or a compound line graph:

➤ On a simple line graph, the line represents the actual values of whatever is being measured on the vertical axis.

Figure 9.8
A compound line graph showing twentieth-century trends in world use of selected energy sources. Total world population is shown as a simple line

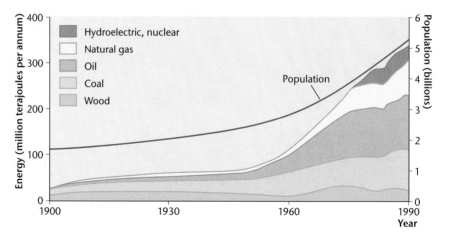

> On a compound line graph, the differences between the points on adjacent lines give the actual values. To show this, the areas between the lines are usually shaded or coloured and there is an accompanying key (Figure 9.8).

It is possible to show two sets of data on the same graph. The left hand vertical axis can be used for one scale and the right hand vertical axis for a different scale, as on Figure 9.8. This can often give a useful visual impression of the connection between two sets of data.

When using arithmetic graphs you should:

> plot the independent variable on the horizontal axis and the dependent variable on the vertical axis. If you are plotting data over time, time should always be plotted on the horizontal axis

> try to avoid awkward scales and remember that the scale you choose should enable you to plot the full range of data for each variable

> clearly label the axes

> use different symbols if you are plotting more than one line

Long sections and cross-sections

These methods are useful for describing and comparing the shape of the land. Long sections are mostly used in river studies; cross-sections can be drawn for a number of landscape features. This method essentially consists of constructing a line graph showing height on the vertical scale against distance on the horizontal scale.

It is usual to take the horizontal scale from the map that you are using, but to use a different vertical scale. If you are working with a standard OS map, the scale would reduce your section, in most cases, to a line showing very little variation. It is therefore necessary to adopt a larger scale on the vertical axis, but care must be taken that it is not massively exaggerated, changing the gentlest of slopes into the north face of the Eiger! The degree of exaggeration can be calculated and presented with your finished work. For example, if you are taking the horizontal scale from a 1:50,000 OS map, 1 cm represents 500 m. If you select a vertical scale of 1 cm to represent 100 m, the vertical exaggeration is 5.

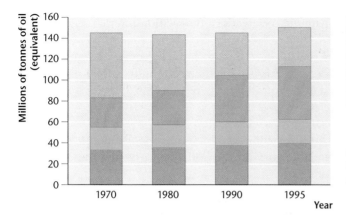

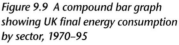

Figure 9.9 A compound bar graph showing UK final energy consumption by sector, 1970–95

Bar graphs

A bar graph (or chart) has vertical columns rising from a horizontal base. The height of each column is proportional to the value that it represents. The vertical scale can represent absolute data or figures as percentages of the whole.

Bar graphs are easy to understand. Values are obtained by reading off the height of the bar on the vertical axis. They show relative magnitudes very effectively (Figure 9.9). Using an appropriate scale, it is also possible to show positive and negative values on the same graph — for example, profit and loss (Figure 9.10).

Scattergraphs

Scattergraphs are used to investigate the relationship between two sets of data (Figure 9.11). They can be used simply to present data, but they are particularly

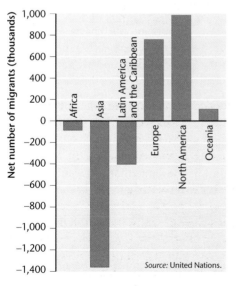

Figure 9.10 A gain–loss bar chart showing annual net migration totals in the world's major areas, 1990–95

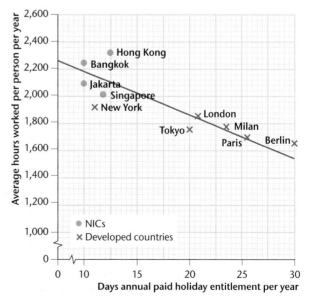

Figure 9.11 A scattergraph showing working patterns in selected cities in developed countries and NICs, 2000

useful in identifying patterns and trends in the relationship that might lead to further inquiry.

A general trend line (**best-fit**) can be added to the graph so that the relationship can be easily observed. This is the red line in Figure 9.11. If it runs from bottom left to top right, it indicates a positive relationship; if it runs from top left to bottom right, the relationship is negative.

Other features of scattergraphs include:

➤ they can be plotted on arithmetic, logarithmic or semi-logarithmic graph paper
➤ the independent variable goes on the horizontal axis and the dependent variable on the vertical axis
➤ it is possible for a correlation to emerge even when a relationship is only coincidental
➤ points lying some distance from the best-fit line are known as **residuals** (anomalies). These can be either positive or negative. Identification of residuals may enable you to make further investigations into other factors that could have influenced the two variables.

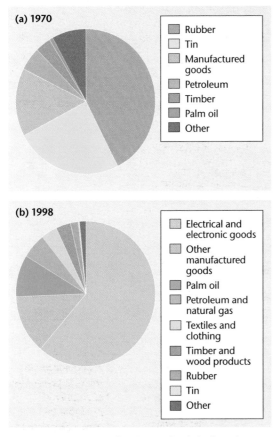

Figure 9.12 Pie charts showing Malaysia's changing pattern of exports

Pie charts (proportional divided circles)

The pie chart is divided into segments according to the share of the total value represented by each segment. This is visually effective — the reader is able to see the relative contribution of each segment to the whole (Figure 9.12). On the other hand, it is difficult to assess percentages or make comparisons between different pie charts if there are lots of small segments.

When a number of pie charts are drawn proportional to the value each represents in total, they are called **proportional divided circles**. The construction of a proportional circle is as follows:

➤ use the formula

$$r = \sqrt{\frac{V}{\pi}}$$

where V is the value that you want the total pie chart to represent and r is the radius of the pie chart. Take the value for π as 3.142
➤ draw a circle of radius r on graph paper

It is important that you are able to state the scale of your proportional circle. The *area* represents the value, so the scale is in the form of:

x units of data = 1 square unit on the graph paper

Triangular graphs

Triangular graphs are plotted on special paper in the form of an equilateral triangle (Figure 9.13). Although this looks, on the surface, to be a method that has widespread application, it is only possible to use it for a whole figure that can be broken down into three components expressed as percentages. The triangular graph cannot therefore be used for absolute data or for any figures that cannot be broken down into three components.

The advantage of using this type of graph is that the varying proportions and their relative importance can be seen. It is also possible to see the dominant variable of the three. After plotting, clusters will sometimes emerge, enabling a classification of the items involved (Figure 9.14).

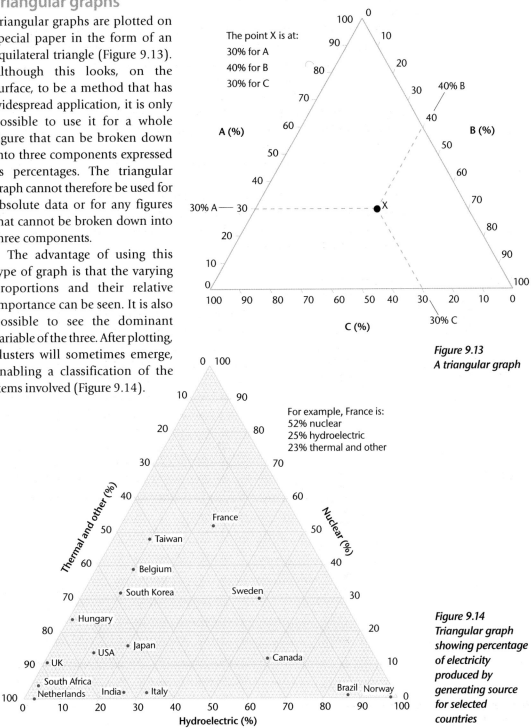

The point X is at:
30% for A
40% for B
30% for C

Figure 9.13
A triangular graph

For example, France is:
52% nuclear
25% hydroelectric
23% thermal and other

Figure 9.14
Triangular graph showing percentage of electricity produced by generating source for selected countries

Kite diagrams

Kite diagrams are a useful way of showing changes over distance, particularly in vegetation (Figure 9.15). One axis is used for distance and the other for individual plant species. The width of the kite, representing a single species, enables a visual comparison to be made of the distribution of vegetation at any point in the section.

Figure 9.15 Kite diagram showing a transect across a dune area in Dorset

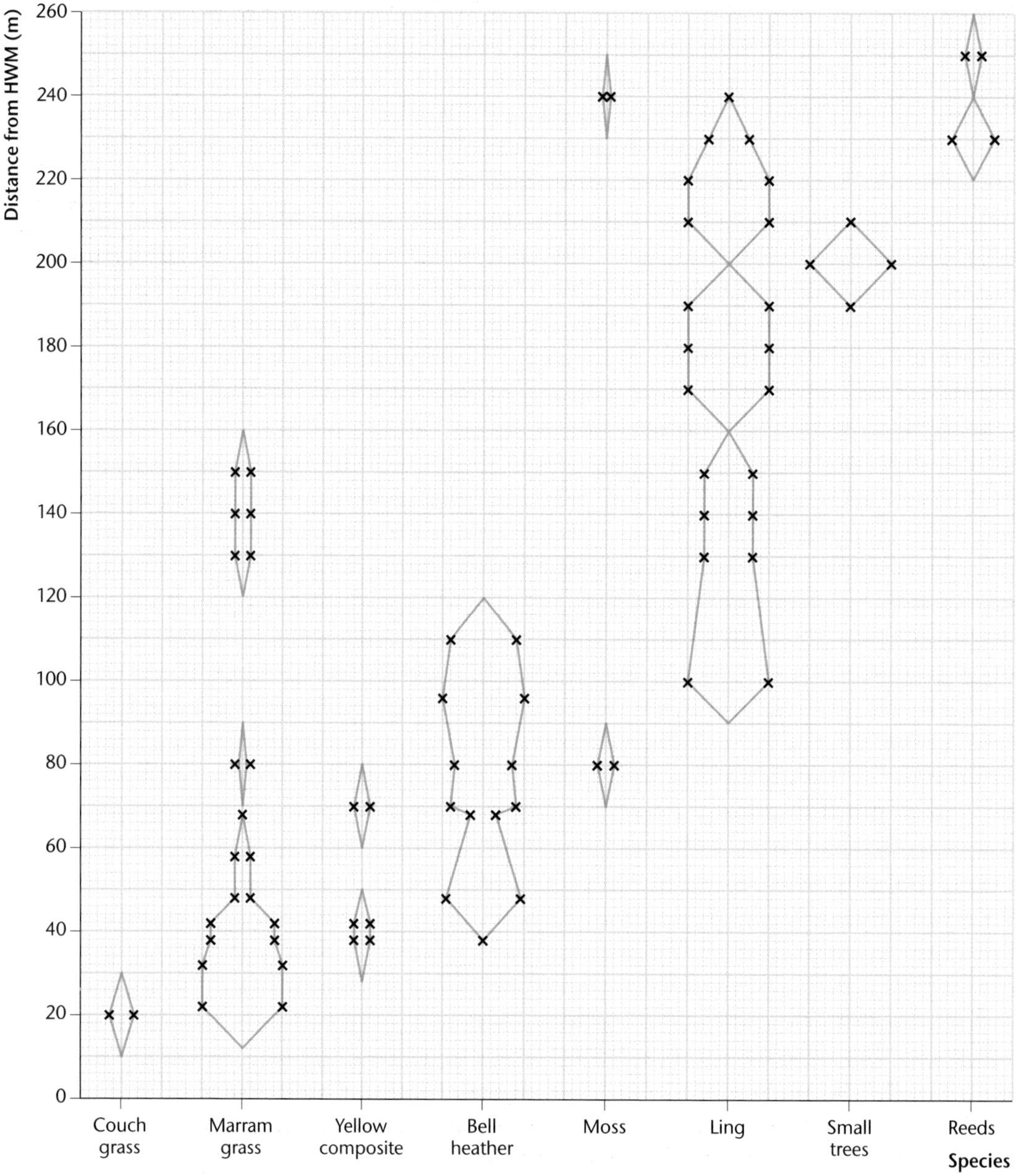

Radial diagrams

Radial diagrams are particularly useful when one variable is a directional feature, for example wind-rose diagrams show both the direction and the frequency of winds. The circumference represents the compass directions and the radius can be scaled to show the percentage of time that winds blow from each direction.

Radial diagrams can also be used when one variable is a recurrent feature, such as a time period of 24 hours or an annual cycle of activity. They can be used to plot traffic flows or pedestrian flows over a period of time during the day, or monthly output figures (Figure 9.16).

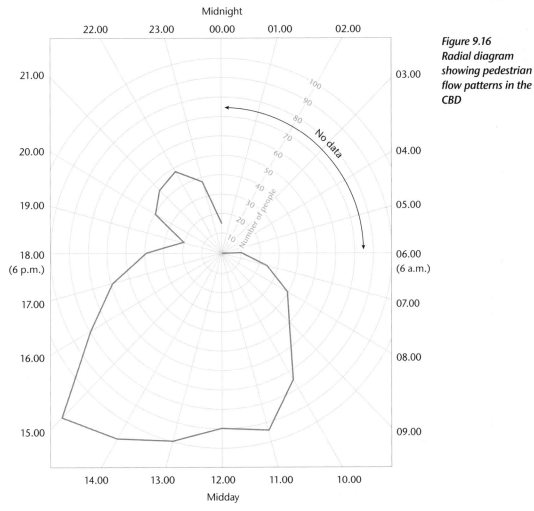

Figure 9.16 Radial diagram showing pedestrian flow patterns in the CBD

Such graphs should only be used for specific types of data. The scale around the circumference can only be used for a variable which is continuous, such as a repeating time sequence or the points of a compass.

Logarithmic graphs

A logarithmic graph is drawn in the same way as an arithmetic line graph except that the scales are divided into a number of cycles, each representing a tenfold increase in the range of values. If the first cycle ranges from 1 to 10, the second will extend from 10 to 100, the third from 100 to 1,000 and so on. You may start the scale at any exponent of 10, from as low as 0.0001 to as high as 1 million. The starting point depends on the range of data to be plotted.

Graph paper can be either fully logarithmic or semi-logarithmic (where one axis is on a log scale and the other is linear or arithmetic). Semi-logarithmic graphs are useful for plotting rates of change through time, where time appears on the linear axis (Figure 9.17). If the rate of change is increasing at a constant proportional rate (e.g. doubling each time period) it will appear as a straight line.

Figure 9.17 Semi-logarithmic graph showing UK production of primary fuels over time

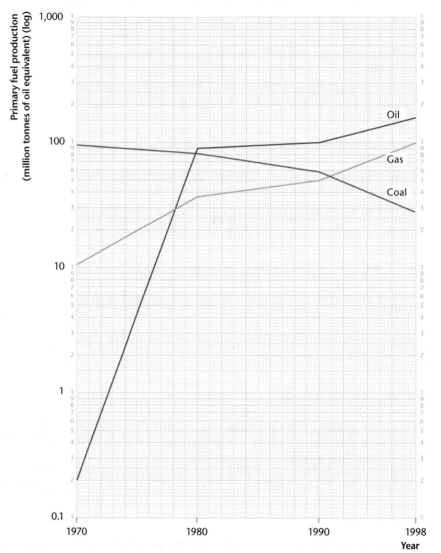

Logarithmic graphs are good for showing rates of change — the steeper the line, the faster the rate. They also allow a wider range of data to be displayed.

Remember that you cannot plot positive and negative values on the same graph and that the base line of the graph is never zero, as this is impossible to plot on such a scale.

Dispersion graphs

Dispersion graphs are used to display the main patterns in the distribution of data (Figure 9.18). The graph shows each value plotted as an individual point against a vertical scale. It shows the range of the data and the distribution of each piece of data within that range. It therefore enables comparison of the degree of bunching of two sets of data.

Statistical skills

Measures of central tendency

There are three such measures.

Arithmetic mean

The mean is calculated by adding up all the values in a data set and dividing the total sum by the number of values in the data set. So,

$$\bar{x} = \frac{\sum x}{n}$$

The arithmetic mean is of little value on its own and should be supported by reference to the standard deviation of the data set.

Mode

This is the value which occurs most frequently in a data set. It can only be identified if all the individual values are known.

Median

This is the middle value in a data set when the figures are arranged in rank order. There should be an equal number of values both above and below the median value. If the number of values in a data set is odd, then the median will be the

$$\frac{n + 1}{2}$$ item in the data set.

So, for example, if the total number of items in a data set is 27, the median will be the fourteenth value in the rank order of the data.

If the number of values in the data set is even, the median value is the mean of the middle two values. Any calculation of the median is best supported by a statement of the inter-quartile range of the data (see page 328).

Distribution of the data set

It is possible that each of these measures of central tendency could give the same

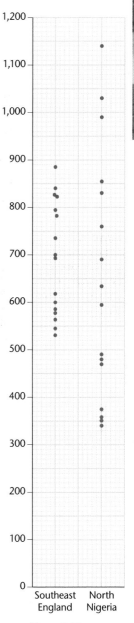

Figure 9.18
Dispersion graph showing rainfall in two selected locations over a 16-year period

result, but they are more likely to give different results. For them each to give the same result the distribution of a data set would have to be perfectly 'normal', and this is extremely unlikely when using real data. It is more likely that the distribution of the data set will be skewed (see Figure 9.20, page 330). The more it is skewed, the greater the variation in the three measures of central tendency.

None of these measures gives a reliable picture of the distribution of the data set. It is possible for two different sets of data to have the same values for mean, mode and median. Measures of the dispersion or variability of the data should therefore also be provided.

Measures of dispersion or variability

There are three measures of dispersion or variability: range, inter-quartile range and standard deviation.

Range

This is the difference between the highest value and the lowest value in a data set. It gives a simple indication of the spread of the data.

Inter-quartile range

The inter-quartile range is calculated by ranking the data in order of size and dividing them into four equal groups or quartiles. The boundary between the first and second quartiles is known as the upper quartile and the boundary between the third and fourth quartiles is the lower quartile. They can be calculated as follows:

➤ the upper quartile (UQ) is the value that occurs at $\dfrac{(n+1)}{4}$ in the data set when arranged in rank order (from highest to lowest)
➤ the lower quartile (LQ) is the value that occurs at $\dfrac{3(n+1)}{4}$ in the data set

The difference between the upper and lower values is the inter-quartile range (IQR):

IQR = UQ − LQ

The IQR indicates the spread of the middle 50% of the data set about the *median* value, and thus gives a better indication of the degree to which the data are spread, or dispersed, on either side of the middle value.

Standard deviation

Standard deviation measures the degree of dispersion about the *mean* value of a data set. It is calculated as follows:

➤ the difference between each value in the data set and the mean value is worked out
➤ each difference is squared, to eliminate negative values
➤ these squared differences are totalled
➤ the total is divided by the number of values in the data set, to provide the variance of the data
➤ the square root of the variance is calculated

$$\text{standard deviation} = \sqrt{\dfrac{\sum(\bar{x} - x)^2}{n}}$$

The standard deviation is statistically important as it links the data set to the normal distribution. In a normal distribution:

➤ 68% of the values in a data set lie within ±1 standard deviation of the mean
➤ 95% of the values in a data set lie within ±2 standard deviations of the mean
➤ 99% of the values in a data set lie within ±3 standard deviations of the mean

A low standard deviation indicates that the data are clustered around the mean value and that dispersion is narrow. A high standard deviation indicates that the data are more widely spread and that dispersion is large. The standard deviation also allows comparison of the distribution of the values in a data set with a theoretical norm and is therefore of greater use than just the measures of central tendency.

Box-and-whisker plots

Box-and-whisker plots provide more detail on the range and spread of data (Figure 9.19). To produce these:

➤ calculate the median and the upper and lower quartiles. Plot these as short bars running parallel to the horizontal axis
➤ draw vertical lines from the upper quartile value to the lower quartile value to box this spread of data. This box represents the inter-quartile range and contains 50% of the data
➤ mark the highest and lowest values by drawing lines parallel to the horizontal axis. Join these to the box

These 'whiskers' show the range of the data.

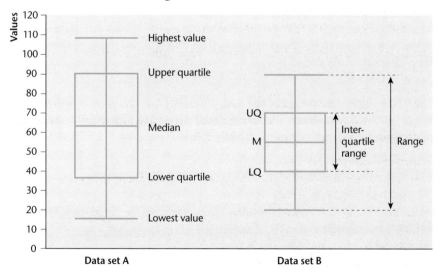

Figure 9.19
A box-and-whisker plot showing two sets of data

Histograms

Histograms are used to show the frequency distribution of data. They use bars to indicate the frequency of each class of data, but do not confuse them with bar graphs. Histograms are used to simplify and clarify data that are easier to analyse when placed into groups, or classes, than when presented as individual data. In this way large amounts of data can be reduced to more manageable proportions which make it possible to see some of the trends present.

Before drawing a histogram you need to group the data, and this can be difficult. You need to illustrate differences between classes while keeping the variation within each class to an absolute minimum. You will need to establish:

➤ the number of classes to be used
➤ the range of values in each class — the class interval

The number of classes you use must depend upon the amount of data you have collected. Choose too many classes and you will have insufficient variation between them and may finish up with too many 'empty' classes; choose too few and you will have difficulty in recognising trends within the data.

One way of deciding on the number of classes is to use the formula:

number of classes = 5 × log of the total number of items in the set

If, for example, you had data about the size of 120 pebbles on a beach, the maximum number of classes would be:

$5 \times \log 120 = 5 \times 2.08 = 10.4$

You would therefore select ten classes.

The range of values is influenced by the number of classes that you have decided to use. This is shown by the formula:

$$\text{class interval} = \frac{\text{range of values (highest to lowest)}}{\text{number of classes}}$$

If, for example, you had data ranging from 96 to 5 and you required four classes, the class interval would be:

$$\frac{96 - 5}{4} = 22.75$$

Figure 9.20 Histograms showing different distributions

It is important that class boundaries are clearly defined so that all individual pieces of data can be assigned without difficulty. Class intervals of 0–25, 25–50, 50–75,

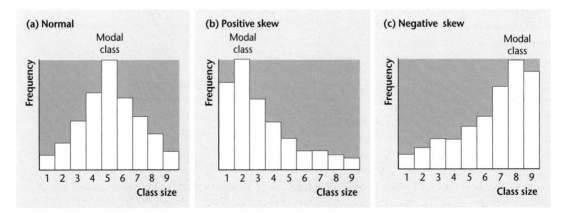

(a) Normal

(b) Positive skew

(c) Negative skew

75–100 should therefore be replaced with 0–24.9, 25–49.9, 50–74.9, 75–100, which do not overlap.

The number of classes and the interval will be influenced by the type of data with which you are dealing and the purpose to which they are being put. You will need to decide exactly what you are trying to illustrate or analyse. The distribution that you finish up with will fit into one of three categories:

➤ If your distribution has a modal class in the middle with progressively smaller bars to each side, then it is similar to the **normal** distribution (Figure 9.20a).
➤ If the modal class lies in the lower classes, then the distribution is said to show **positive skew** (Figure 9.20b).
➤ If the modal class lies to the upper end, the distribution is said to show **negative skew** (Figure 9.20c).

Measuring correlation: the Spearman rank correlation coefficient

Comparisons are made between two sets of data to see whether there is a relationship between them. Note that even if there is a relationship between two variables, this does not prove a causal link. In other words, the relationship does not prove that a change in one variable is responsible for a change in the other. For example, there may be a direct relationship between altitude and the amount of precipitation in a country such as the UK. These two variables (altitude and precipitation) are clearly linked, but a decrease in one does not automatically cause a decrease in the other — they are simply related to each other.

There are two main ways in which relationships can be shown:

➤ using scattergraphs (see page 321)
➤ measuring correlation using the Spearman rank correlation coefficient

The Spearman rank correlation coefficient is used to measure the degree to which there is correlation between two sets of data (or variables). It provides a numerical value which summarises the degree of correlation, so it is an example of an objective indicator. Once it has been calculated, the numerical value has to be tested statistically to see how significant the result is.

The test can be used with any data set consisting of raw figures, percentages or indices which can be ranked. The formula for the calculation of the correlation coefficient is:

$$R_s = 1 - \frac{6 \sum d^2}{n^3 - n}$$

where d is the difference in ranking between the two sets of paired data and n is the number of sets of paired data.

The method of calculation is as follows:

➤ rank one set of data from highest to lowest (highest value ranked 1, second highest 2 and so on)
➤ rank the other set of data in the same way
➤ beware of tied ranks. In order to allocate a rank order for such values, calculate the 'average' rank they occupy. For example, if there are three values which

should all be placed at rank 5, add together the ranks 5, 6 and 7 and divide by three, giving an 'average' rank of 6 for each one. The next value in the sequence will be allocated rank 8

➤ calculate the difference in rank (d) for each set of paired data
➤ square each difference
➤ add the squared differences together and multiply by 6 (A)
➤ calculate the value of $n^3 - n$ (B)
➤ divide A by B, and take the result away from 1

The answer should be a value between +1.0 (perfect positive correlation) and –1.0 (perfect negative correlation).

Some words of warning

➤ You should have at least 10 sets of paired data, as the test is unreliable if n is less than 10.
➤ You should have no more than 30 sets of paired data or the calculations become complex and prone to error.
➤ Too many tied ranks can interfere with the statistical validity of the exercise, although it is appreciated that there is little you can do about the 'real' data collected.
➤ Be careful about choosing the variables to compare — do not choose dubious or spurious sets of data.

Interpreting the results

When interpreting the results of the Spearman rank test, consider the following points.

What is the direction of the relationship? If the calculation produces a positive value, the relationship is positive, or direct. In other words, as one variable increases, so does the other. If the calculation produces a negative value, the relationship is negative, or inverse.

How statistically significant is the result? When comparing two sets of data, there is always a possibility that the relationship shown between them has occurred by chance. The figures in the data sets may just happen to have been the right ones to bring about a correlation. It is therefore necessary to assess the statistical significance of the result. In the case of the Spearman rank test, the critical values for R_s must be consulted. These can be obtained from statistical tables, but Table 9.1 shows some examples.

According to statisticians, if there is a > 5% possibility of the relationship occurring by chance, the relationship is not significant. This is called the rejection level. The relationship could have occurred by chance more than five times in 100, and this is an unacceptable level of chance. If there is a < 5% possibility, the relationship is significant and therefore meaningful.

If there is a < 1% possibility of the relationship occurring by chance, the relationship is very significant. In this case, the result could only have occurred by chance one in 100 times, and this is very unlikely.

Table 9.1
Critical values for R$_s$

n	0.05 (5%) significance level	0.01 (1%) significance level
10	± 0.564	± 0.746
12	0.506	0.712
14	0.456	0.645
16	0.425	0.601
18	0.399	0.564
20	0.377	0.534
22	0.359	0.508
24	0.343	0.485
26	0.329	0.465
28	0.317	0.448
30	0.306	0.432

How does this work? Having calculated a correlation coefficient, examine the critical values given in Table 9.1 (ignore the positive or negative sign). If your coefficient is greater than these values, the correlation is significant at that level. If your coefficient is smaller, the relationship is not significant at that level.

For example, suppose you had calculated an R_s value of 0.50 from 18 sets of paired data. 0.50 is greater than the critical value at the 0.05 (5%) level, but not that at the 0.01 (1%) level. In this case, therefore, the relationship is significant at the 0.05 (5%) level, but not at the 0.01 (1%) level.

Worked example: Spearman rank test

Survey: size of shingle along a storm beach

The beach in question is aligned from southwest to northeast and the dominant approach of the waves is from the southwest. The main ridge appears to increase in height with distance from the southwest. The shingle appears to decrease in size and become more rounded towards the northeast. This may indicate that the direction of longshore drift is from the southwest to the northeast, meaning that the further the shingle is moved, the more it is affected by attrition and, therefore, reduced in size. A scattergraph would show the general trend of the relationship between distance and size. However, there are anomalies, so a correlation test would be useful to decide the strength of that relationship.

The raw data are shown in Table 9.2.

The data required for the calculation of R_s between distance and the mean shingle size are shown in Table 9.3.

$$R_s = 1 - \frac{6\sum d^2}{n^3 - n}$$

$$\sum d^2 = 996.5$$

$$R_s = 1 - \frac{6 \times 996.5}{15^3 - 15}$$

$$= 1 - \frac{5{,}979}{3{,}360}$$

$$= 1 - 1.78$$

$$= -0.78$$

Table 9.2
The characteristics of shingle along a storm beach

Distance from SW end of beach (m)	Height (m)	Mean shingle diameter (cm)	Roundness index
60	5.5	8.4	1.72
180	7.5	8.5	1.77
300	8.0	7.7	1.63
420	11.5	8.1	1.48
540	11.0	6.1	1.58
660	7.5	5.8	1.63
780	10.0	6.2	1.60
900	10.5	7.2	1.41
1,020	10.0	7.5	1.36
1,120	11.0	6.2	1.33
1,220	14.0	6.5	1.35
1,340	12.5	5.8	1.23
1,460	18.0	4.8	1.18
1,580	13.5	5.0	1.17
1,700	15.0	5.8	1.25

Table 9.3 Data for the calculation of R_s

Distance (m)	Rank	Mean shingle diameter (cm)	Rank	Difference in rank (d)	d^2
60	15	8.4	2	13	169
180	14	8.5	1	13	169
300	13	7.7	4	9	81
420	12	8.1	3	9	81
540	11	6.1	10	1	1
660	10	5.8	12	2	4
780	9	6.2	8.5	0.5	0.25
900	8	7.2	6	2	4
1,020	7	7.5	5	2	4
1,120	6	6.2	8.5	2.5	6.25
1,220	5	6.5	7	2	4
1,340	4	5.8	12	8	64
1,460	3	4.8	15	12	144
1,580	2	5.0	14	12	144
1,700	1	5.8	12	11	121
					996.5

The coefficient indicates that there is a negative relationship between the two sets of data — as the distance increases, the mean shingle diameter decreases.

The result is significant at the 0.01 significance level. The R_s value is greater than the critical value when $n = 15$ (0.63). The possibility that such a result occurred by chance is very low — less than 1 in 100.

This statistically reliable result supports the subjective perception of the longitudinal changes with distance from the southwest end of the beach.

ICT skills

You are required to be able to:

➤ use remotely sensed data — photographs and digital images, including those captured by satellite
➤ use databases, e.g. census data, Environment Agency data, Met Office data
➤ use geographical information systems (GIS)
➤ present text and graphical and cartographical images using ICT

Geographical information systems (GIS)

Geographical information systems (GIS) are an integral part of twenty-first century geographical study. They are used extensively by environmental planners, government departments, public utility companies and commercial companies. GIS have the ability to store, retrieve, manipulate and analyse a wide range of spatially related data. They can:

➤ help with questioning and understanding data
➤ enable multiple interrogation of complex data

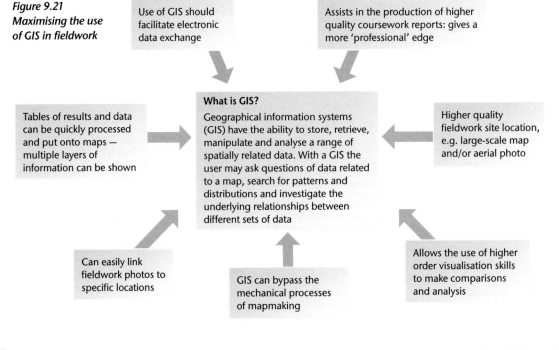

Figure 9.21 Maximising the use of GIS in fieldwork

Use of GIS should facilitate electronic data exchange

Assists in the production of higher quality coursework reports: gives a more 'professional' edge

Tables of results and data can be quickly processed and put onto maps — multiple layers of information can be shown

What is GIS?
Geographical information systems (GIS) have the ability to store, retrieve, manipulate and analyse a range of spatially related data. With a GIS the user may ask questions of data related to a map, search for patterns and distributions and investigate the underlying relationships between different sets of data

Higher quality fieldwork site location, e.g. large-scale map and/or aerial photo

Can easily link fieldwork photos to specific locations

GIS can bypass the mechanical processes of mapmaking

Allows the use of higher order visualisation skills to make comparisons and analysis

> illustrate difficult abstract concepts in a dynamic visual way
> make use of three-dimensional representations
> provide opportunities for modelling and decision-making

GIS are an effective mapping tool and can be major elements in geographical fieldwork. Figure 9.21 summarises the key aspects of GIS and how they can be used in fieldwork.

A number of websites and associated programs have great potential for use in fieldwork. They include Multimap, Aegis, Digital Worlds, Quikmaps and Google Earth. Many allow you to use maps and photos together; others allow annotations to be added (Figure 9.22). Some types of software require a degree of training, whereas others are more straightforward to use. It all depends on your own level of ICT skills.

Global positioning systems (GPS) technology can also be useful in fieldwork. Data can be recorded at points along a transect or other sampling system, and the position of each point can be recorded at the same time. GPS-located data can then be fed into a GIS program, bringing data recording and mapping together.

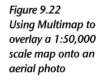

Figure 9.22
Using Multimap to overlay a 1:50,000 scale map onto an aerial photo

Assessment exercises

Unit 2 is assessed by a geographical skills paper. There are two sections, which have equal weighting: a resource-based section and a section that relates specifically to your own fieldwork and investigative research skills. The resource-based question is based on either the core physical topic (Rivers, floods and management) or the core human topic (Population change). Examples of both types are given below.

Core physical section

1 a Figure A shows the number of times per year a river in a city in England rose above flood level between 1885 and 1990. Figure B shows the variation in maximum river level relative to flood level in that city between 1885 and 1990.

Describe and suggest reasons for the trends shown in Figures A and B. (6 marks)

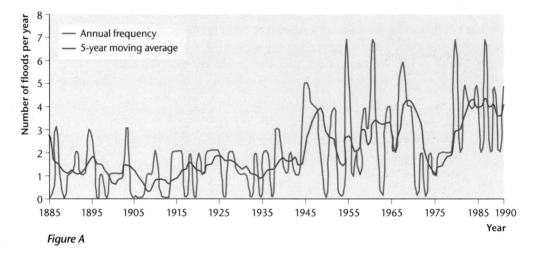

Figure A

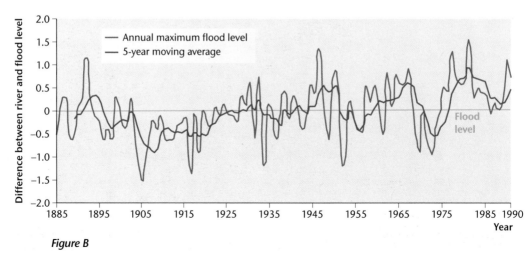

Figure B

b Table A gives a description of the weather and other factors affecting river levels in the catchment area of the above river in 2000. Draw a sketch hydrograph to show the likely effect on the discharge of the river of the weather described in Table A.

(3 marks)

c Explain how the shape of your sketch hydrograph results from the information given in Table A. (4 marks)

Table A

Date	Description
July/August	Summer came close to a washout. Low average temperatures
September	Rain continued to fall steadily. In one night, a month's rain fell in just 6 hours
Mid-October	No let-up from the rain. Water tables on uplands were high again. Relentless rain only made matters worse
End October	Storms produced lowest atmospheric pressure reading on record in England and Wales — 960 mb recorded. Rain and snow lashed the region. 20 cm of precipitation fell in 11 days between end October and early November
Early November	Water was running off the hills at an alarming rate
3 November	River peaked at 3.30 a.m. at highest-ever level since records began
4 November	Further rain predicted

d Study Figure C, the Ordnance Survey extract of Oxford.

(i) Outline the map evidence which suggests ways in which people have increased the risk of flooding.

(5 marks)

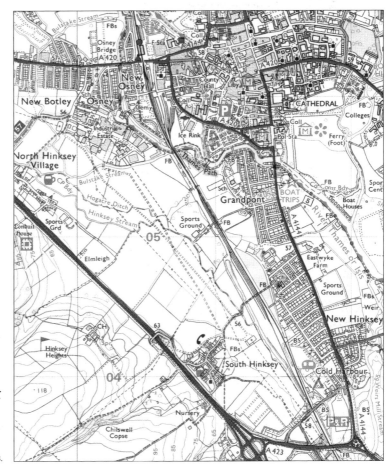

Figure C

Photograph A

Photograph B

(ii) Photograph A is an aerial photograph showing part of Oxford during the summer floods of 2007. Photograph B is a ground-level photo of the same floods. Describe the nature and the effects of the flooding in the area shown.

(7 marks)

(25 marks)

2 You have experience of geography fieldwork as part of your course.

   a For any geography fieldwork study that you have undertaken, briefly outline its aim and state one hypothesis you sought to test. *(3 marks)*

   b For your chosen study, identify one item of primary data which was collected. Briefly state how it was collected, the sampling method used and the reasons for adopting the sampling method described. *(7 marks)*

   c Before visiting an area for fieldwork, a risk assessment must be completed. State one risk associated with carrying out fieldwork in the study area and suggest how you would minimise the risk. *(3 marks)*

   d Stating the results of your investigation, explain how they helped to improve your understanding of the topic or environment investigated. *(7 marks)*

   e Describe one application of ICT skills in carrying out your fieldwork and comment on its usefulness. *(5 marks)*

(25 marks)

Core human section

1 a Figure D shows the city of Cambridge divided into wards. Figure E shows the relationship between the population percentage change in each ward (1981–91) and the percentage of population who migrated into Cambridgeshire within the last year. Complete a copy of Figure E by adding the information given in Table B. *(4 marks)*

   b Using Figure D, describe and suggest reasons for the relationship shown in the completed Figure E. *(6 marks)*

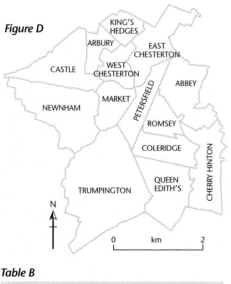

Figure D

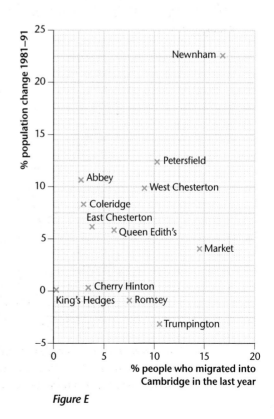

Figure E

Table B

	Population change (%)	Migration into Cambridgeshire (%)
Arbury	–2.3	2.3
Castle	13.4	11.4

c On the Ordnance Survey map extract of Cambridgeshire (Figure F), locate the area north of the A14. Label a sketch of the map to identify the evidence of

(i)   recent growth

(ii) the reasons such locations are attractive to in-migrants.

(7 marks)

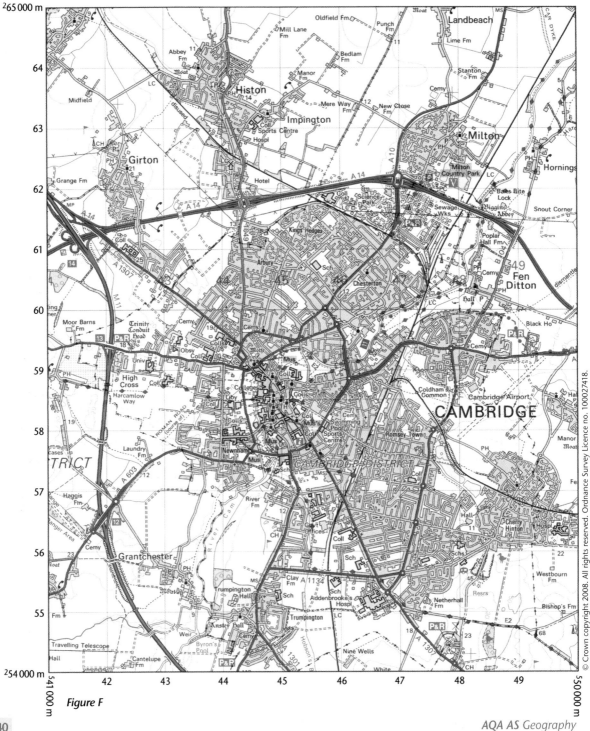

Figure F

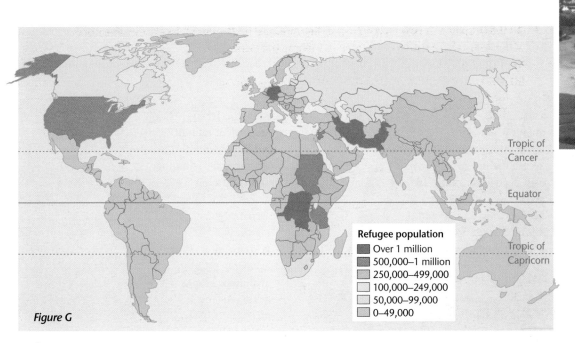

Figure G

d The distribution of refugees by host country is shown on Figure G. Describe and comment
  on the pattern shown by Figure G.   (8 marks)

                                                                                        (25 marks)

2 You have experience of geography fieldwork as part of your course.
  a For any geography fieldwork study that you have undertaken, outline the aim, one objective
    and the theory/concepts that provided the idea for study.   (3 marks)
  b Outline one source of information that you used and assess the extent to which it was 'fit
    for purpose'.   (3 marks)
  c For your chosen study, identify one item of primary data which was collected. Outline the
    method of collection and how one risk related to this collection was minimised.   (5 marks)
  d Describe a method of presentation that you used in your investigation and indicate how
    the chosen method was useful.   (7 marks)
  e Stating the results of your investigation, explain how they helped to improve your
    understanding of the topic or environment investigated.   (7 marks)

                                                                                        (25 marks)

Index

Bold page numbers indicate definitions of key terms